W9-BVI-957

DATE DUE

The Global Etiquette Guide to Asia

Everything You Need to Know for Business and Travel Success

Dean Foster

John Wiley & Sons, Inc.

New York • Chichester • Weinheim • Brisbane • Singapore • Toronto

This book is dedicated to my parents, Joseph and Sylvia,
who first showed me the world

Published by John Wiley & Sons, Inc.
Published simultaneously in Canada

This publication is designed to provide accurate and authoritative information in regard to the subject matter covered. It is sold with the understanding that the publisher is not engaged in rendering professional services. If professional advice or other expert assistance is required, the services of a competent professional person should be sought.

Library of Congress Cataloging-in-Publication Data:

Foster, Dean.
    The global etiquette guide to Asia : everything you need to know for business and travel success / Dean Foster.
      p.   cm.
    Inclues index.
    ISBN 0-471-36949-7 (pbk. : alk. paper)
    1. Etiquette—Cross-cultural studies. 2. Intercultural communication. 3. Business etiquette. I. Title.

  BJ1838.F67   2000
  395'.095—dc21   99-054684

Printed in the United States of America

10 9 8 7 6 5 4 3 2

Contents

Preface

The idea for this series emerged out of the work that my staff and I, and literally thousands of people from around the world that we work with, have been doing for almost two decades: assisting businesspeople and travelers to better understand their colleagues in other cultures. This work has primarily focused on international business and has taken many forms: helping to prepare families of employees adjust to an overseas assignment; assisting individual businesspeople in their negotiations with colleagues abroad; and helping global organizations to build more effective global teams. As business has globalized, the need for cross-cultural information has grown.

But globalization hasn't affected only the businessperson. While most of the work in the cross-cultural field has developed in response to international business needs, the need for cross-cultural information for the nonbusiness international traveler (both actual and of the armchair variety!) has also grown. Unfortunately, the amount of useful, objective, and applicable information, adapted to the needs of the more casual international explorer, has been limited. In most cases, what information was available usually took the form of anecdotal war stories, overgeneralized stereotypes (always interesting, but of dubious veracity), or theoretical statements about culture that were too removed from the day-to-day adventures of the international traveler. As the gap between useful cultural information for international businesspeople and international travelers grew, so did the need to bridge it. Hence, the idea for the Global Etiquette Guides series.

Correction: I embarked on this project at first with the goal of writing one book. But the world, as it turned out, was simply too big, and so was the book. Given my work, I for one should not have been surprised at this development, but at first was concerned about how to handle the dilemma. Nevertheless, under the kind and careful guidance of my editor, publisher, and agent, we expanded the original concept into a series. And I am glad we did. For one thing, it gave me the breathing room to explore all cultures to the degree that was necessary for the reader; for another, it gave me the opportunity to experience just how fine a team I was working with.

My editor, Tom Miller, did double duty, providing patience and insight, through both the serialization of the original book and the actual editorial review of the material. His input, despite my occasional and always incorrect misgivings, gave me focus, pause to rethink when it was important to do so, and perhaps most importantly, impetus and space to keep going in the face of demanding schedules and unpredictable events. A good editor provides the professional expertise to fine-tune the work. A great editor also provides faith. Tom never failed to offer both.

Jane Dystel is everything an author can ask for in an agent. On many levels, this series would not have happened without her. She is always available, always on my side, and equally able to manage scrupulously the details of a particular project while helping me to put the pieces in place for the bigger career; I am very grateful to have her support. This is the second time we have worked together on a project, and I look forward to many more.

Bob Stein is the lawyer behind the scenes. Lawyers are, no doubt, overlooked far too often, and easily forgotten once their job is done. Here I have probably been more neglectful than most, for Bob is also a dear and longtime friend who has never failed to support me, even in my most ridiculous moments, and I fear I have taken advantage of that. Forgive me, Bob, and thank you . . . again.

I also want to thank all the professionals in the cross-cultural field with whom I have had the pleasure to work over the years. They have all contributed in important ways to these books. To my colleagues at Berlitz International and at Windham Interantional, who, around the world, have given me opportunities to play a leading role in the cross-cultural field, I am eternally grateful. To the many professionals in both competing and supporting organizations whom I have learned from, and worked and played with, many, many thanks. Finally, to the diverse thousands of individuals around the globe, of all cultures and backgrounds, who, in their work with me and my staff, have provided us with the joy and opportunity to learn about their unique part of the world, my very heartfelt thanks. Without your perspectives, experiences, and input, my work, and ultimately these books, would never have been possible.

When exploring cultural differences, one quickly observes that there are some cultures that "work to live," and others that "live to work." Balancing these two perspectives is a constant challenge for both cultures and individuals, and my world would surely be quite unbalanced without the love and support of my wife, Sheryl. She has been my constant, both the wind literally beneath my wings and my tether to the shore. I know this has not been easy, as she must also balance her own professional demands with our personal life. That she has done both is a testament to her strength and love. These books, as with so much else in my life, could not have occurred without her.

Leah, my daughter, plays a great role in these books. As I've watched her grow into the intelligent and caring young woman she is today, she serves as a constant reminder that the prize we work so hard for should truly be worth something. It needs to be created in love, based on justice, and worth the struggle. As I hope I have given meaning to her life, she continues to give meaning to mine. We have been growing up together all her life, and although she is now "all grown-up," I have no intention of stopping.

Finally, after crediting all these worthy folks for their kind and important contributions, I must now credit myself: all the shortcomings of these books are mine. If I overstated a culture too broadly, overlooked an important cultural consideration, or in any way misrepresented or misjudged a particular way of life, the error is mine and no one else's. I only ask that the reader please consider the cause as the "anthropologist's dilemma": that is, the impossibility of describing a culture objectively, due to the fact that the "describer" is always viewing the culture being observed in reference to his or her own (in my case, the United States). For some, this unfortunate natural law of the social sciences may be an added bonus (for other Americans, perhaps). For others, this may cause some serious and legitimate misgivings. I hear you both. Please take solace in the fact that every effort has been made to minimize the negative effects of this phenomenon whenever and wherever possible. No doubt I have not succeeded completely.

Why Getting It Right around the World Is So Important

Apparently, the world is getting smaller and smaller every day. We can't make it through a twenty-four hour period without the media informing us of something happening in a distant land, without our local bank accounts being affected by a foreign stock market, without our schools having to make decisions about bilingual education, and without the possibility that our friends, coworkers, neighbors, and possibly family will have come from somewhere else, speak a language we barely understand, and have a perspective on life that may be radically different from our own. As English speakers, isn't it unnecessary that we learn another language . . . or become familiar with another culture? After all, isn't technology spreading the English language and American pop culture so globally that we're all going to understand one another through the medium of Coca-Cola and rock 'n' roll anyway? The answer to all of the above, as anyone who steps off a plane in a foreign land will learn, is a resounding "No."

I like to think that the world is getting bigger, not smaller; that world cultures, perhaps unique among many aspects of life that are indeed being homogenized, will not be; and that cultures more deeply rooted and with far longer histories than that of the American pop culture, along with their languages, will still be with us long after Coca-Cola becomes their favorite soft drink and rock their favorite form of music.

There is no doubt that cultures are in contact with one another to a degree never before experienced in human history. The vastness of human experience, which is the world, is suddenly in our respective faces as never before. Each of us is experiencing not the smallness of the world, but the very bigness of it. For most of us, this is not an easy thing to do. For a variety of reasons, such as the economics of globalization, the development of technology, and the evolution (or devolution, depending upon your point of view) of current political forms, the need to recognize and understand differences in cultures has probably never been more critical than it is today.

Businesspeople traveling the world are learning to appreciate the consequences of the misunderstood gesture, the ill-placed word, the uninformed judgment; workers down the hall are required to communicate effectively with coworkers who may or may not speak their language or understand their ways; world travelers, from tourists to diplomats, evaluate the success of their sojourns more and more according to their ability to understand and appreciate the differences that exist between themselves and their new foreign hosts. Understanding, managing, appreciating, and maximizing the benefits of cultural differences, in fact, have become the most critical factors for the success of the global businessperson, the international diplomat, the manager of a multicultural office, or simply the continent-hopping tourist seeking a vacation of reward and richness. No, the world is not getting smaller—but we *are* being required to act much bigger in order to make sense of it all.

This book can help us to do that. There is no doubt that those forces of economics, politics, and technology that are bringing us in closer contact with one another foster, in some measure, a sense of unity. However, the degree to which understanding is developed simply as a result of cultural contact is questionable. Unfortunately, history provides us with evidence that when cultures collide, through whatever forces and for whatever reasons, the initial results are often disastrous. There is nothing inherent in cultural contact that automatically leads to understanding, homogeneity, peace, love, justice, and universal brotherhood. In fact, the reverse, at least in the short run, has been true. Over time, and only when specific structures such as democratic political forms, legal systems, and economic opportunities are in place, can cultures that once did not understand one another begin to accept one another. All one needs to do to better appreciate this sobering fact is to read the international headlines of any major newspaper any day of the week.

Nevertheless, if we are bound, as we apparently are, to hurtle headlong into one another's cultures, the least we can do is prepare ourselves to understand the other a little better. The forces of globalization carry information that both informs and misinforms one culture about the other. So we cannot depend on what Hollywood tells us about Japan, what Joe Smith relates to us over drinks about his recent trip to China, or what our coworker Jacqueline from Paris tells us about how the French think. Neither the global businessperson nor the casual tourist can afford to make mistakes when abroad, to misunderstand the intent of his or her foreign hosts, or to risk inadvertently offending someone. If we are all now working, living, loving, growing, and having to not only survive but thrive in a universe far larger and more complex than anything we were prepared to handle, it's time, to say the least, to get prepared. And that's the purpose of this book.

What This Book Is . . . and Is Not

This book is one of several in the series of Global Etiquette Guides, each of which focuses on a major world region. Each book follows the same format and structure, so whether you are beginning the series with this book or have already read one of the others, you will recognize a structure that makes the reading fun and provides you with the information you need about the countries in the region quickly and easily.

However, no one book can provide you with everything you've ever wanted to know about any particular culture, let alone the major cultures of even one particular world region. People make lifelong careers out of studying one particular culture, and there are sections in most libraries with many books focused solely on one aspect of one culture. Nor can one book provide you with everything you need to know to do business successfully in those cultures. But this book will look at most major cultures in Asia, those with which most people will have some contact or be influenced by in their lifetimes. It will provide important information about the basic day-to-day behaviors in those countries that enable the inhabitants to pursue what they believe to be the best way to live their lives, achieve their goals, and solve their problems; in short, the day-to-day customs, etiquette, and protocols of these cultures that make them what they are and, perhaps, different, from our own.

The information provided about business issues, practical "do's and don'ts" for all travelers, and the underlying values and belief systems of the various cultures will be useful for global businesspeople, casual international travelers, and cultural researchers. Most important, this information will address the one issue we all have in common in the face of our amazing diversity: our need to create a day-to-day modus operandi for living, for dealing with other people, and for communicating our needs and desires. *The Global Etiquette Guide to Asia* is intended to be a practical and relatively thorough guide to the protocol, etiquette, and customs that are the ways of life in one of the world's most important cultural regions.

What Do We Mean by "Culture"?

Culture is the normative way in which groups of people behave and the belief systems that they develop to justify and explain these behaviors. These behaviors can differ between groups, generally as a result of the unique experiences that disparate groups have had. In turn, these experiences are usually a combination of history, geography, economics, and other factors, which vary from group to group. What makes all cultures similar, however, are the essentially universal problems of life that we all must address, as individuals and as societies. The problems and questions are the same everywhere, but the answers we come up with as societies can be different. This is what defines our individual cultures. Geert Hofstede, one of the seminal researchers in the field of culture, says, "If the mind is the hardware, then culture is the software," meaning that we are all hardwired pretty much the same, but the programs that we run on can be quite dissimilar. Culture is human software, and the challenge is to make the programs compatible.

I also want to emphasize the normative and group aspects of culture. I am constantly amazed at how from person to person we all seem so much alike, and yet from society to society we can be so very different. Culture reveals itself mainly in the group dynamics of the major institutions of society, and not necessarily in the interpersonal behaviors of individuals. In any particular culture, you may run into people, therefore, who behave very differently from the way we describe the culture; in these cases, these individuals are behaving outside the norm. Culture is not a predictor of individual behavior, so when we discuss any cultural protocol, we are talking about general tendencies, expectations, and normative preferences. As someone foreign to a culture, you may be very far from its norm; for that very reason, it is important to know what that norm is, respect it, and adjust to it.

This issue of norms also reminds us that the statements we make about any given culture are generalizations. There are certainly situations, individuals, and conditions that would reveal contradictory behaviors within the same culture. When we make a cultural statement, at least in this book, we are speaking of *primary* tendencies; in no way is this meant to imply that contradictory behaviors will not exist. In fact, it is this delicious complexity of cultures that makes them so fascinating and challenging to work with. In most cases, we are usually also referring to situations between strangers, for once personal relationships are established, many formalities fall by the wayside.

So how important is it really to "go native"? The answer: not very. The goal of this book, and the goal of all cultural understanding, is not to prescribe behaviors for you—behaviors that may be uncomfortable or unnatural to your own culture (many no doubt will be). Rather, the goal of this book is to explain unfamiliar behaviors so that you can come to understand them and why they exist, appreciate the benefits they bring to their culture, and adjust to them to the degree that you are comfortable in order to make someone from that culture equally comfortable with you. No one, however, can be someone he or she is not, and the worst thing you can do is to act inauthentically. There is no greater offense than an awkward and uncomfortable North American, for example, attempting a formal bow when meeting his Japanese colleague in Tokyo for the first time, simply because he read in a book that the Japanese greet each other that way. The greater benefit from such information comes when the American understands the meaning of the Japanese bow, and is prepared to respond to it in a way that is sincere, genuine, and respectful of the intent of his host. Wherever you are, be yourself and be true to your own culture, but be true as an enlightened, informed, and respectful cultural being.

How the Book Is Organized

When you approach a world region, such as Asia, from a cultural perspective, there are first megacultures, and to varying degrees, variations on these megacultural themes, which are usually grouped geographically within the region. For example, there is the megacultural category of Pacific Rim cultures. Within this category are countries such as Japan, Korea, and China in the east Asian subregion, and Thailand, Indonesia, and Singapore in the southeast Asian subregion. These Pacific Rim countries are, in many key ways, more similar to one another than they are to countries within a different megacategory—such as, for example, the cultures of the Levant. Much of what we say about the protocols and etiquette of any one Pacific Rim culture will also be true for most other Pacific Rim cultures; nevertheless, there can also be many differences between them (no two countries, for example, could be more different on some very key measures than Korea and Singapore, yet they share many Pacific Rim cultural similarities). And since the protocol and etiquette *topics* that are discussed for any one country are generally the same for all countries, the Asian cultures are organized according to these main Asian megacultural or regional groups.

Each group begins with a discussion of those cultures that provide the foundations for all the countries within the group, followed by further explorations of the countries within that cultural region and how they differ from one another. This has been done in order to highlight the distinctions that make each country within a cultural region unique and different without having to repeat too much information that is common to all the countries. Nevertheless, many readers will probably want to dip into the book country by country rather than read it as a whole. If that's your style, rest assured that important cultural behaviors and facts are repeated country by country when necessary, so you won't miss too much if you want to read about only one country without referring to others in the same region. To make finding specific countries easy, the contents page lists each country, so you can go straight to the page listed for information on that country's protocol and etiquette if you so desire.

The topics explored for every country are generally the same. Each chapter begins with "Some Introductory Background" on the culture and "Some Historical Context," followed by a quick "Area Briefing," which usually talks about politics and government, schools and education, and religion and demographics. This should give you an appreciation for the forces that have shaped the culture. "Fundamental Cultural Orientations" explores the belief systems that justify the behaviors people reveal to one another on a day-to-day basis, giving you an understanding of why the protocols and etiquette exist as they do. The rest of the chapter takes an in-depth look at the actual customs of the country: greetings and verbal and nonverbal communication styles; protocol in public; dress; dining and drinking; how to be a good guest or host; gift giving; how to celebrate the major holidays; and important aspects of the business culture. For each of these topics, there are subtopics that explore aspects of the culture in relation to men and women, younger and older generations, and both business and social circumstances.

This book does not look at all nations and all cultures within Asia. The world is a dynamic and changing place, and one of the difficulties about writing about culture at this point in world history is the fact that countries and cultures do not necessarily line up. While there is no one country representing the distinct culture of the Kurds, for example, there is most definitely a Kurdish culture in Asia. And while North Korea is an independent Asian country, the degree to which we need to know about and the degree to which there are in fact significant cultural differences between it and South Korea are debatable. For these, and other thorny reasons, the book explores only those countries in the region that are, in the judgment of the author, distinguishably different from one another and of greatest interest to the reader. My apologies if I have not included a country or a culture of interest: it is not out of disrespect or malice, but merely because of space, knowledge, and time limitations.

The Meaning of the Information

In order to understand why the protocol, manners, and etiquette of any particular country are as they are, it is critically important to understand the belief systems and fundamental values that are at the heart of the culture. This is why every country includes a brief discussion of "Fundamental Cultural Orientations." These orientations, of course, change country by country, but the categories themselves remain the same. For example, it is important to arrive at a business meeting in Tokyo at the stated time. It would not be correct to arrive fifteen or twenty minutes late. This protocol is based on a more fundamental cultural orientation in Tokyo around the issue of time. In Jakarta, it might be appropriate to arrive at a meeting five to ten minutes late; this different protocol results from a different fundamental cultural orientation in Indonesia around the same issue, time. Of course, it's important to remember that Japanese *can* be late and Indonesians *can* be on time; it's just that there is, from a cultural point of view, a difference in the concept of what constitutes timeliness. Therefore, let's briefly explore those fundamental orientation issues around which all cultures can differ, because we will be referring to them again and again with each country we visit.

As the example stated earlier illustrated, cultural orientations revolve around some very basic concerns shared by all cultures:

1. What's the Best Way for People to Relate to One Another?

Societies are all about people, and how we organize ourselves in relation to one another is an issue that every culture must sort out for itself. Cultures might insist on honoring a societal hierarchy, structure, and organization, and they do so with all sorts of perks: titles, rank, different signs of respect, different roles for men and women, and so on. Other cultures deemphasize the importance of such things, preferring to treat everyone as equals. So we have cultures that are *hierarchy* and *organization* oriented, and on the opposite end of the spectrum, cultures that are *egality* oriented. Some cultures might reward individuals for standing out, empowering them to make decisions on their own, while other cultures insist that individuals fit into the group, making sure that no one does anything without the consent and support of others. So we have cultures that are *other-independent*, and on the opposite end of the spectrum, cultures that are *other-dependent*. A culture might place a value on devising systems for organizing life, creating interconnected rules and regulations that must apply universally to all, while another culture might place more emphasis on the personal relationships that exist among people as the determinant of how to do things. So we have cultures that are *rule* oriented, and others that are *relationship* oriented. All of these orientations have to do with what a culture believes to be the best ways by which people should relate to one another.

2. What's the Best Way to View Time?

All societies have to handle moving through time, creating a way of understanding and simultaneously managing the flow of things. Cultures might place a great deal of importance on managing and controlling time. For these *monochronic* cultures, clocks, agendas, calendars, and deadlines determine what and when things are done, and time is a limited commodity that must be carefully managed. For other cultures, time exists, but it is not the determinant of people's actions. For these *polychronic* cultures, time stands in the background; there is usually plenty of it, and relationships and immediate needs usually determine what and when things are done. Some cultures might move quickly with a limited amount of information, while other cultures need a great deal of information in order to make even a small decision. Therefore, cultures may be *risk-taking* or *risk-averse*. Finally, do the people put more of their energy into maintaining what they already have, or do they value change for change's sake? A culture may be *past* oriented (and often more fatalistic), while another may be more *future* oriented (and often more controlling).

3. What's the Best Way for Society to Work with the World at Large?

All societies must make decisions about how they fit into, process, and deal with the larger world. Essentially, this means how that culture communicates, thinks, and plans. Some cultures might create, analyze, and communicate information very directly; they depend upon the meaning of the word, and don't embed information in the larger context of the situation. These cultures often place a high value on confrontation and absolute truth: they are *low-context* communicators. However, other cultures value the importance of communicating indirectly—with actions and not only words—and have subtle systems in place for exchanging information appropriate to the situation and the environment through nonverbal behavior. These cultures place a high value on the maintenance of smooth interpersonal relationships; they are *high-context* communicators. One culture might place the greater emphasis on the process by which goals are achieved, while another culture places the greater emphasis on the goal itself, regardless of how it's achieved. Therefore, cultures can be *process* oriented (relying often on deductive logic) or *results* oriented (relying often on inductive logic). In addition, cultures may be more associative in their thought processing; that is, they do things based on the way they know things always have been done, or how they are already being done in a similar situation. Finally, cultures might value the formal, established, reliable, and in some cases almost ritualized way of doing things, while other cultures might value change, informality, and spontaneity. Therefore, cultures may be *formal* or *informal* in their general orientation toward protocol itself.

It's important to remember that very few cultures are either absolutely one way or the other in their orientation. Most fall somewhere in between, and are simply more or less inclined to one way than the other. It's also important to remember that any one culture is a profile made up of all of these orientations, so be careful not to prejudge what one culture's orientation might be in one area just because of its orientation in another: you might be very surprised at the diversity and complexity of the combinations that exist when we tour the Asian region! All world regions, Asia included, provide us with the opportunity to explore an enormous diversity of cultural behaviors; the range, especially in what is considered correct and incorrect, is staggering. Remember, the only constancy is change and the only absolute is complexity. What is correct in one culture may be incorrect in another, and what works in one can be a disaster in the other. As the old saying goes, "When in Rome, do as the Romans," and when in Beijing we must also do as the Chinese, in Delhi as the Indians, in Istanbul as the Turks . . .

PART ONE

The Pacific Rim

It's Not What You Say, but How You Say It

An Introduction to the Region

The ancient Taoist symbol of yin and yang is, among other things, a visual representation of the universe, wherein opposites unite forming one perfect whole: black/white, day/night, female/male, action/passivity, west/east, occident/orient. If there was only one thing that I could say to help Westerners better understand Asia, and to behave more appropriately when there, it might be: do everything opposite to the way you are accustomed. Overly simplistic, yes, but not far from incorrect, for Asia is, indeed, the opposite—geographically, metaphorically, philosophically, and in many other ways—from the West. The reputation of Asian inscrutability, of course, is more a reflection of the inability of Westerners to appreciate this fact than it is an accurate statement of Asian behavior. Asians and their cultures are as understandable as any other peoples, but Westerners need to understand and appreciate the fundamental value differences and resulting behaviors that exist between West and East.

Asia is a vast area, the largest continent in the world, with most of the earth's human population. The cultures, for the most part, are far older than in other parts of the world; the traditions, therefore, run deep and fast, and are agrarian based. The Chinese and the Middle Eastern civilizations go back approximately five thousand years; the Japanese and Korean, thirty-five hundred years; the Indian, three thousand years. Each culture, while sharing certain similarities with its Asian neighbors, nevertheless developed in different ways, resulting in the variety of peoples and customs found in Asian countries today. The best way to approach this complex region is not by ethnic group, religion, or ideology, but rather by geography. Therefore, Part One will look at the Pacific Rim, made up of east Asia, southeast Asia, and Australasia. Part Two will examine south Asia, which is comprised of the subcontinent (India, Pakistan, Bangladesh, Sri Lanka, and the Himalayan kingdoms), central Asia (including five former republics of the Soviet Union), and Eurasia (Turkey and the Caucasus region). Part Three will look at southwest Asia, the Asian Arab world (Gulf Arabia and the Arabian Levant), and Israel. Let's begin with the Pacific Rim.

Getting Oriented

The Pacific Rim for our purposes consists of the following macrocultural groups:

- East Asia: Japan, China (including Hong Kong and Taiwan), and Korea
- Southeast Asia: the Philippines, Malaysia, Singapore, Indonesia, Thailand, Vietnam, Laos, Cambodia, and Myanmar (Burma)
- Australasia: Australia and New Zealand

The East Asian Cultures: Japan

Some Introductory Background on Japan and the Japanese

When the Japanese first visited the Chinese Imperial Court, they introduced themselves as the people who came from the land of the rising sun. The geographical reference is an important one, for even today, in their national motto, the Japanese describe who they are with respect to the Chinese: since the sun rises in the east, the Japanese were stating that they came from a land east of Peking (as the Chinese Imperial City was then known), the "Land of the Rising Sun." There is no doubt that China and Chinese culture are the center of gravity in Asia, yet we will begin our discussion of East Asia with Japan. The reason is simple: although Chinese culture may be more ubiquitous throughout the region, it is the Japanese culture that, by being Asian culture in extremis, provides us with the opportunity to see most strikingly the differences between East and West. In a sense, if we understand Japan, and can master effective behaviors in Nihon (the name the Japanese use to refer to their country) with Nihon-jin (the Japanese), we have already learned, in many ways, the skills required for success in the rest of east Asia.

Some Historical Context

Japan, while perfecting its own indigenous culture and traditions, historically has borrowed heavily from its neighbors (and, as history advanced, from faraway cultures as well—including, most recently, the West), and has integrated, at least on a surface level, many Chinese, central Asian, and southeast Asian cultural attributes. Throughout Japanese history, there has been a swinging back and forth between allowing the gaijin (literally, people from abroad, or foreigners) entry, along with their cultural forms, and barring the outside world from coming in. Throughout all of Asia we see an ambivalence toward outsiders (not only Westerners, but other Asians, as well): a mixture, at different times, of xenophilia and xenophobia—of both admiration and acceptance, and revulsion and rejection—of the outsider's world. In Japan, this has often taken the form of a kind of cultural passive-aggressive personality, mirroring an equally ambivalent sense of superiority-inferiority. While the West often has difficulty reconciling these opposites, such opposites are fundamentally consistent with ancient Asian philosophies (reflected in the concept of yin and yang, for example), as we will see over and over again in regard to many other behavioral patterns. Japanese history (many other Asian cultures mirror this pattern in their own way) is also the history of cycles of struggle between the Shoguns (military governors) and the emperor, the story of the rise and fall and rise again of various powerful feudal families, and the attempts at the consolidation of power (often justified by invoking divine authority) in the face of these feudal struggles by the Imperial Court. While there certainly is a teleology to Asian historical events, there is also a striking repetitiveness to the histories of this part of the world: perhaps this is the nature of history itself, more easily evident in cultures that have had the time to reveal this nature; perhaps it is a unique element of Asian cultural history; most likely, it is a combination of both.

Japan is a very small island nation, with a rugged, mountainous topography that prevents over 70 percent of its land from being used for agriculture—primarily, the growing of the staple rice crop. Always densely concentrated along the coastlines, the people learned to rely on the sea for food (and, in a sense, for economic opportunity in general, which is, at heart, one of the reasons the Japanese were often successful whenever they did swing into their outward expansionist mode). Historically, life in Japan has been difficult and precarious, dependent upon the moods of volcanoes, earthquakes, typhoons, and four very extreme seasons. Early in the development of Japanese culture, it became evident and then self-justified through the ideologies, religions, philosophies, and histories that developed, that there was little room for error in this world, that individual, spontaneous action could prove reckless and irresponsible, and that rules, forms, and rituals were absolutely necessary in order to accomplish what needed to be done—whether it was harvesting the rice, fishing the sea, raising a child, or running a business. It is this aspect of Japanese culture that is its essence: the exquisite ritualization of human life in an effort to create a perfectly harmonious and balanced world. If we understand the nature of these rituals, and perform them well, we will go far in advancing the Japanese ideal; if we fail to recognize, follow, respect, and understand these rituals, we violate, in Japanese eyes, the nature of the world. In part, this rigid discipline is what allows the Japanese to be so focused on the proper placement of a willow branch in a garden, and yet embark on the destruction of a neighboring civilization; of being painfully concerned with the shame that one brings about by saying the wrong thing at the wrong time to the wrong person, and yet exhibit a flagrant disregard for the feelings of whole classes of people. In Asia, one must behave according to certain Asian expectations, and this is particularly true in Japan. With this in mind, let's look at some important aspects of Japanese society, and then move on to the correct ways to practice important traditional Japanese customs.

An Area Briefing

Politics and Government

Today, the government of Japan is modeled on the Western political structure that was imposed on the country after World War II. It must be recognized that the parliamentary system in Japan is essentially a Western concept grafted onto a Japanese base, and that the West, while forcing this system on Japan, also recognized the need to maintain the one aspect of the Japanese political structure that was so critical to the people: the emperor. Therefore, today, Japan has a parliamentary system with a president, a representative prime minister, and a bicameral legislature (the diet), as well as an emperor, who serves as the embodiment of Japan as a cultural entity. Thus, Japan is a constitutional monarchy. The feudal lords and families, the former shoguns, have been transformed today into the modern-day business leaders, rulers of those mighty Japanese industrial conglomerates, an old-boy network that has, in the new millennium, become, in many ways, an enormous albatross around the neck of the Japanese economy and work culture. These people usually represent themselves as guardians of the imperial tradition (the old emperor/shogun feud relived). The old patterns, while challenged, are still at work, and breaking them will require strong leadership from those who can overcome history and put forward a plan for moving the country forward. One waits to see whether Japan can free itself from the grinding paralysis of the modern-day shoguns without rekindling the kind of nationalist aggressiveness that has resulted from similar efforts in the past.

Schools and Education

Japanese schoolchildren work very hard. Throughout elementary school (ages six through twelve), and lower secondary school (ages thirteen through fifteen), right on into upper secondary school (ages sixteen through eighteen), there is little time for independent fun and free play, and the pressure only intensifies as one moves up through the grades. Between the ages of sixteen and eighteen, students with no further academic ambitions may also be attending technical college, or other special schools that train them for administrative or vocational careers. However, most want to go on to university (ages nineteen through twenty-two)—or at least junior college, which will enable them to move on to university—and some will later attend graduate school. Once in university, life suddenly changes, and the rigors of high school lessen dramatically. University and college become, in fact, the first brush with the deeply entrenched old-boy network of the Japanese male work society: colleges and universities become fraternities of future coworkers and funnel students into different levels of responsibility within society. Tokyo University is the top school, and its graduates are the political and business leaders of the nation.

Religion and Demographics

As we will see throughout the rest of eastern Asia, most religions are not institutionalized belief systems as they are in the West. The spiritual influences in Japan are strong, but they are not religions per se. It would be more correct to refer to them as philosophies of life. No one claims to be only a Buddhist, for example, or a Confucian. Elements of both of these philosophies inform the behaviors and beliefs of most individuals, and of society as a whole. There are few preset times of worship (although there are festivals that occur at certain times throughout the year), and priests—if there are any—do not represent the faithful congregation. Eastern Asian religions are really a compilation of the beliefs, writings, teachings, and thoughts of certain spiritual leaders. The three great religious philosophical influences in Japan are Shintoism, Buddhism, and Confucianism.

Shinto is the indigenous religion of Japan, where most of its practitioners are still found today. One of the essential aspects of Shintoism is the belief that all of life—all objects, both animate and inanimate—are inhabited by forces or gods known as *kama.* In Japan today, there is a saying that one is born a Shintoist, but buried a Buddhist (and if married in between, usually in a Christian ceremony!). There are Shinto shrines, prayers, and priests; but philosophically, the impact this religion has on social behavior is its emphasis on harmony in all things, and the need for all of life to be in balance.

Buddhism began in India about 600 B.C. Its founder was Siddhartha Gautama, the Buddha, a privileged Brahmin priest who, in attempting to learn the meaning of life, discovered, among other things, that his privilege brought him no happiness, and that if one were to achieve true happiness, one had to sacrifice in the secular here and now in specific ways in order to achieve a higher level in the next life. In many ways, the theology that evolved was an effort to purify what had become, in the Buddha's mind and others, a debased and corrupt preexisting Hindu religion in India at that time by placing moral responsibility onto the individual, and relying less upon the religious Brahmin hierarchy. This created, as you may imagine, some difficulty for the Buddha and his followers and the existing Brahmin establishment; subsequently, certain Buddhist ideas were both integrated into Hindu theology, while also being exported from India; its principles surviving in China, parts of southeast Asia, and ultimately in Japan. Much of Buddhist tradition emerged in Japan in the form of warrior (or samurai, the "knights" of the shogun) code, the rituals of personal sacrifice and hard work known as the Bushido (or the way of the samurai, represented today in the ethics and behaviors of the modern-day samurai, the "salaryman"), and the idea of *nintai,* or patience (all things, including another shot at life, in time!).

Finally, there is Confucianism, based on the teachings of Confucius, a Chinese sage who lived around 500 B.C. We will have more to say about the influence of Confucius when we look at China specifically, but Japan, borrowing as it did so heavily from China from time to time, could not help but be influenced by Confucian ideas. Confucius lived during a turbulent and chaotic time in China, and established a philosophy of life that attempted to prescribe the correct and proper way for individuals to relate to one another in order to achieve a well-ordered, functioning society. The essence of his ideas involves the importance of observing and maintaining structures, roles, and hierarchy, so that, paraphrasing his words, "the son obeys the father, the wife obeys the husband, the younger brother obeys the older brother, the husband obeys the state," and so on. Society will work when everyone knows his or her place, understands his or her obligations to others in the hierarchy, and, in fact, seeks primarily not to change his or her role, but to perfect it. This provides philosophical support for the Japanese reliance on ritual, structure, hierarchy, obligation, honor, and duty (what is referred to in Japanese as the concepts of *on* and *giri*). *Giri* is the burden one must always carry, the invisible tally sheet that always is there, depending upon one's relationships and the obligations such relationships impose (the rules can be quite arbitrary, and given at birth, last a lifetime). *On* is what one does to discharge these obligations (which, in some cases, depending upon the nature of the *giri,* are never fully discharged: these are literally the burdens that are known as "too great to bear"). As you can see, these ancient traditions play themselves out in modern-day Japan, providing the theoretical framework for a system that requires, among other things, honoring the elderly and one's superiors, humility in front of others, discharging obligations, and always maintaining harmonious relationships.

Japan is demographically an old country; that is, there are many old and rapidly aging people in the country and these people are traditionally venerated. How to continue to provide for them in their old age is part of the pressure that is currently on Japan to reinvent itself. Women in Japan have historically played a minor role in business, although they did run the small family shops (and today, interestingly, do have niche professions, like selling life insurance door to door, for example, or teaching or nursing). And because gender roles, like all behaviors, were ritualized, there was little room for women outside of the nurturing role. At home, women were in complete charge, from shopping (the husband rarely shopped along with the wife) and finances (the salaryman even today usually turns his paycheck over to his wife, and she is fully responsible for it) to childrearing (women were responsible for the education—and academic performance—of the child). Today, it is difficult to find Japanese women at any level of real authority in the large Japanese business organization. Traditionally, if a woman were to work, she would do so until she found a husband, and it was at that point that she was expected to resign, run the house, and raise children. Women who seek business opportunity in corporate Japan today often find it with non-Japanese organizations. (Non-Japanese businesswomen, on the other hand, are not subject to these constraints, and therefore can more easily succeed in the Japanese business environment as long as their authority is clear and maintained, and as long as they, like all businesspeople in Japan, follow the cultural requirements for success in Japan; this is a pattern we will see elsewhere in varying degrees throughout Asia.)

It is important throughout Japan and the rest of Asia not to assume an Asian is of one nationality or another. While most of the people in Japan are Japanese, there is a significant population from other Asian countries in the big urban areas, including a small Korean population. Koreans and the Japanese have been enemies in the past, and confusing a Korean with a Japanese could cause significant problems. The Ainu people, found today mainly in northern Japan (on the island of Hokkaido) were the indigenous people of Japan, residing there before the Chinese and others moved to the islands. Unfortunately, they are treated as indigenous peoples often are everywhere else in the world. Curiously, the Ainu have facial features similar to those of Caucasians.

Fundamental Cultural Orientations

1. What's the Best Way for People to Relate to One Another?

OTHER-INDEPENDENT OR OTHER-DEPENDENT? There was a seminal experiment conducted in Japanese and American nursery schools: the teacher would provide the students with paper, paints, and paintbrushes, and instruct them to make a picture. In Japan, the children would typically wait for further instructions; and then, when none were forthcoming, one child at each table would take a piece of paper and all the children at the table would start to work cooperatively at producing a painting. The same experiment in U.S. nursery schools produced a very different response: before the teacher was finished providing instructions, each child typically would take his or her own piece of paper and begin work on his or her own painting. As they proceeded, the children would periodically look over at the progress being made by their colleagues at the table. Clearly, even at the tender age of four or five, very different fundamental value orientations about the best way for people to work together were already firmly in place. The Japanese continue today to be among the world's highest scorers on the "other-dependent" scale, while Americans continue to score very high on the "other-independent" scale. While the Japanese are taught to subordinate personal agendas for the greater goal of the group (or, if that goal is not known, until the greater goal of the group can be determined), Americans are taught that they are rewarded as individuals if they advance their personal agendas as quickly as possible. The most popular management training program in the United States is team building, precisely because business organizations and society as a whole continue to reward personal achievement: businesses know that they need well-functioning teams, and that as individuals, Americans need to be taught how to do this. The Japanese, on the other hand, are raised to behave as team players; in fact, they have to be taught how to be a little more personally assertive, when needed. The saying in the United States is "Stand up and blow your own horn," while in Japan one maxim says, "The bird that honks gets shot"; in the United States, another proverb says, "The squeaky wheel gets the oil," while in Japan, "The nail that sticks up gets hammered down" is commonly heard. The president of Sony was quoted as having said, "We need a few more nails to stick up from time to time." This tendency on the part of Japanese individuals not to do something until they are confident that it meets with the approval of others does not mean that they do not promote their own ideas, but it does mean that until one's way has won the approval and support of others, it will be very difficult to get things done. Individuals are rarely recognized for their sole achievements or blamed for their personal failings; face is saved, and all are rewarded. In large, traditional Japanese organizations, advancement occurs on "Graduation Day," when all promotions are announced, so that everyone is promoted at once—somewhere within the organization, for better or for worse.

HIERARCHY-ORIENTED OR EGALITY-ORIENTED? Structure and hierarchy are critical at all levels in Japanese society—in the home, at school, in the military, and in business. A formality has developed around what one does and with whom; it is necessary to show the proper respect for individuals, depending on their rank and position, and performing the correct ritual behavior is essential in order to succeed in Japan. Hierarchy is honored through humility; this is done by "lowering" or minimizing oneself. In fact, one makes more of oneself, and raises one's esteem in the eyes of others, by doing so. This is one of the foundations for the self-effacing behavior exhibited by the Japanese when they find themselves to be at the center of attention, for the formal bow upon greeting, for the endless apologies for wrongs committed or not.

RULE-ORIENTED OR RELATIONSHIP-ORIENTED? The requirement for rules, order, and structure, however, does not inevitably lead to rule orientation as a fundamental value. In fact, while some of these rules, structures, and hierarchies need to be made explicit (this is one of the fundamental reasons behind the ritual of the business card, which we will talk about later), many are based on relationships, rules that can only be inferred or learned "off line." In fact, Japan is extremely relationship oriented; that is, what will ultimately determine someone's action or decision is not only the ritual code, but the relationship that exists between the individuals or organizations involved, and the circumstance in which the decision must be made or the action taken. This is one of the reasons for the old-boy network, and the difficulty Japan has in disestablishing its authority.

2. What's the Best Way to View Time?

MONOCHRONIC OR POLYCHRONIC? Because punctuality also reflects other values, such as concern for the other person and humility before someone else's efforts, the Japanese are more or less very punctual; certainly, you should be. Nevertheless, in the big picture, it is difficult to say that the Japanese are monochronic (subordinate to time), because in Japan, as with all traditional Asian cultures, time has historically stood in the background to immediate personal relationships; even in modern-day Japan, this is certainly still the case. Things will take the time they need to take, and the clock is not the ultimate arbiter of what occurs and when. Most Asians have a very big picture of time, and while the day-to-day life of modern Tokyo, for example, certainly requires schedules to be met, and lunches often to be rushed, when investigated a little further, one finds that the clock does not affect the big picture as much as it does in more strictly monochronically defined cultures. Japanese business, for example, usually takes a very big view of things, with business plans that are projected out ten and twenty years or more. The goal often is to obtain market share first and profits later, producing annual or biannual results instead of quarterly results (this is due also to the relative independence of the traditional Japanese business from its shareholders and the paternalistic posture that most traditional Japanese businesses take toward their employees, ultimately founded on these value orientations). Even in the typical Japanese office, where long hours are required of the average salaryman, and much time is spent with one's office buddies, the time spent is not the measure of time worked. It is the style of daily Japanese business to consume much time, but not necessarily to be efficient with it. On balance, we would have to say that Japan is a polychronic culture, as are most of the cultures of Asia.

RISK-TAKING OR RISK-AVERSE? Japan is one of the world's most risk-averse cultures. While the group protects and ensures, comforts and advances, risk aversion seals the effects. Avoiding the unknown, taking all possible precautions, gathering as much information as possible ahead of time, reviewing proposals again and again from all possible angles—all describe Japanese behavior when it comes to risk. When combined with the other aspects of the culture (for example, hierarchy and group orientation), this means that many individuals must act this way, in concert, in order to come up with the most perfect possible solution to the needs of the superior, and must take whatever action is required to protect the supervisor from any problem that might have been avoided had individuals performed more carefully together.

PAST-ORIENTED OR FUTURE-ORIENTED? Nature is not forgiving in Japan: the country is rocked by earthquakes, and typhoons or tidal waves often devastate its shoreline. While mere mortals do what we can, there is no controlling the greater forces of nature; we can appease them perhaps, but only temporarily. This is a common theme throughout ancient Asian cultures, even as they struggle to thrive today, and Japan is no different. The Japanese believe that as they work with all their abilities to make a better world for their children, there are rituals to be observed, traditions to be taken seriously, and ancestors to be listened to in order for the future to work out the way they hope.

3. What's the Best Way for Society to Work with the World at Large?

LOW-CONTEXT DIRECT OR HIGH-CONTEXT INDIRECT COMMUNICATORS? The Japanese rely on high-context communication almost exclusively. Words themselves do not carry the meaning of any given communication; rather, real information is embedded in the context in which the communication occurs. Therefore, nonverbal communication is essential in Japan, and one must learn to "read" the situation in order to assess what is really happening, and to discover the true meaning behind the words. As the context changes, the meaning of the communication changes—for, as is the case throughout Asia, as situations change, the behaviors that are appropriate to those situations also change. What a person says in answer to another's question when the two are one on one may be very different from what the person says when asked the same question in front of his or her supervisor. Forget the words: listen to the situation. This is one of the reasons why Japanese behavior can appear so contradictory. While the Japanese may seem stiff, unapproachable, or unable to make a decision during the workday, they suddenly become warm, friendly, and talkative in the evening over sake, and exchange a great deal of information. High-context behavior in Japan is also related to the group orientation and the need to take care of the other before taking care of oneself; this is reflected in the Japanese concern for face, the need to appear correct, true, and appropriate. (We will see this concern mirrored in many other countries in the region.) In interpersonal communications, the need to help another save face (and by so doing subsequently save your own) means that one does not necessarily say what one feels directly. Outward expression (*tatemae*) is revealed, not inner feelings (*honne*). However, indirect communication, through eye contact and other forms of nonverbal behavior, helps to communicate *honne*. Westerners often see this split as duplicitous: it is not. The intent is to preserve harmony and face, a first priority in Japan (and usually a secondary result in the West), not to deceive.

PROCESS-ORIENTED OR RESULT-ORIENTED? The Japanese, as is the case with all Asian peoples, are fully capable of employing (and do employ) meticulous logic, whether deductively or inductively; however, that is not necessarily the only process used to evaluate things, to make a case for something, or to understand an issue. A connection is made to other similar circumstances, and in that sense, the Japanese also use associative, subjective logic. However, all forms of logic are used in a more holistic way in Asia, so that while process and experience are important steps in arriving at a conclusion, the path may not be linear or progressive. This is related to the polychronic (or not time-bound) nature of the culture: things occur, thought patterns included, not necessarily in a sequential or progressive way, but in a more holistic way. In other words, the elements needed to make decisions are laid out expositionally, when and as the circumstances require it, and add up to a conclusion only when viewed "at once," as if suddenly from forty thousand feet. Do not search for sequence: search for all the facts that must be brought forward, as the situation deems it, and then sit back and evaluate the total result. (This is one reason why it is essential in Asia, Japan included, to take good notes at every meeting! What people mean may not be clear at the table, but may be upon later contemplation.)

FORMAL OR INFORMAL? Japanese culture is one of the world's most formal. From the tea ceremony to the bow, from the way one conducts oneself with a geisha to the way a husband behaves with a wife, a father with a child, and a wife with a mother-in-law, the required behaviors are complex. There is inevitably a prescribed form for most relationships. Spontaneity is difficult to find in Japan: oxymoronically, there must be a time and a place for spontaneity, and it is usually over sake. This makes for the two contradictory elements of the Japanese personality already referred to briefly: the outer person, or *tatemae,* which reflects what one says, and the inner person, or *honne,* which reflects what one truly feels and believes. The two may not be the same at any one time, depending upon the circumstances. *Tatemae* is most often demonstrated in formal situations (in the office, with the boss, on the street), and *honne* is usually demonstrated under more spontaneous circumstances (at the bar at night, or at home in bed).

Greetings and Introductions

Language and Basic Vocabulary

The spoken Japanese language shares little similarity with other Asian languages: if you speak other Asian languages, this will not necessarily help you in Japan. However, the Japanese language has borrowed words heavily from other languages. For example, the word for "thank you," *arigato,* is actually a derivation of the Portuguese word for thank you, *obrigato,* which the Portuguese brought with them in their travels throughout east Asia in the fifteenth century. In more contemporary times, the Japanese have incorporated many English words into their language, as well (*computuh, hambuhguh,* etc.).

The written Japanese language borrows heavily from Chinese written forms, and uses these forms (and variations of these forms) to express both original Japanese words and borrowed words that have become incorporated into Japanese. These written forms, or ideographs, are called kanji, and in Chinese each kanji or two represents a word concept (unlike written European languages, where each letter represents a sound). Kanji may be combined so that several concepts together create a greater concept (this is, in fact, how new words, previously nonexistent, are written). The Japanese use most kanji to represent words. But the Japanese also assign a different sound to each of forty-six special kanji, so that a written "alphabet" of sorts is available, by which one can write out a word using sound-related kanji as if they were letters that spelled out the spoken word. These specially adapted kanji are known as kana. Each kana is really a syllable, not just a one-letter sound by itself (in most cases, a consonant plus a vowel form one kana sound, rarely a vowel or a consonant alone). Therefore, the Japanese kana form, not an alphabet, but a syllabary, which is called the hiragana. Finally, there is a kind of "italic" script form used to write words that are foreign and adapted to Japanese, called katakana (*hambuhguh,* mentioned earlier, would be written in katakana script, for example).

The vowel and consonant sounds in Japanese are similar to those in English, with the exception of *l* and *r*. Those sounds are similar in Japanese because both are made by rolling the tongue when either is spoken; making a clear distinction between the two is therefore difficult for the Japanese. The same is true for the letters *b* and *v*. Given that it is uncommon for a consonant to stand without a vowel, words ending in consonants often have a soft, barely expressed, vowel-like sound following the final consonant (it is represented when written with the letter *u*), as in the common word for *please, onegaishimasu* (the final *u* is barely whispered). There are no articles in Japanese, so it is important to be clear if *the* or *a* is meant. This is usually revealed in the larger context of the text or discussion (this is related to the fact that plurality is also often not expressed directly in Japanese).

The language is not more difficult to learn than most others, but the rules governing its structure and syntax are different from Latin-based languages; this is an especially important issue when it comes to the use of double negatives. In the West, such combinations cancel each other out, thus expressing a positive, but they can cause difficulty in Japan. For example, if you were to ask, "You don't want any of this, do you?", the likely response in Japanese would be "Yes"—meaning, "Yes, I do not want any of this." Because the Westerner would expect a "no," implying agreement, this can cause great confusion for the Japanese. Avoid such constructions. Related to this is the need to avoid asking questions that could result in yes or no answers. In a culture where much emphasis is placed on preserving harmony and face, and where most communication is therefore very high-context and subtle, any answer that could imply difficulty, a rejection of a request, or make the respondent appear uncooperative causes great anxiety for the Japanese. The result is much nonverbal communication and unverifiable verbal responses. *Hai* (Japanese for "yes") more often means "I hear what you are saying, keep talking," not "I agree with what you are saying"; in addition, because it is so difficult directly and openly to say "no" (*ie* in Japanese), you will simply not hear it said. When it needs to be expressed, you will almost always hear *hai* plus a series of nonverbal and verbal cues indirectly indicating the intended "no." Don't complicate the problem, therefore, by asking questions that require yes or no as an answer: the response will give you no reliable information. Instead, ask open-ended questions that require a substantive, informational response.

Many Japanese—especially younger ones, and those in business—speak English today (English is the second language taught to all children in school). However, most English-speaking Japanese are still very self-conscious about their English, and believe it is not good enough to use. Therefore, your excitement at discovering that your Japanese colleagues speak English puts pressure on them. Avoid this response; act pleased that they can communicate with you, apologize for not speaking Japanese better than you can, suggest that an interpreter will be helpful for all of you, and then proceed to work with the interpreters. Moreover, it is important to have your own interpreter if you can, so that the Japanese are aware that someone on your side speaks their language (this will help them communicate to you and minimize the misunderstandings that sometimes emerge when the inevitable caucusing in each other's respective languages occurs in business meetings). If you do know some Japanese, use it; the Japanese will be pleasantly surprised. They will be amazed, and a little suspicious, if you speak it fluently, however, since there is a deep sense among the Japanese that only they can really speak the language (as well that only the Japanese can really understand the subtleties of Japanese culture). Gaijin traditionally have been treated well, but rarely as equals. They are held at a distance, with the rituals making the experience work.

Here are some basic Japanese terms and their English meanings:

ohaiyo gozaimasu	good morning
konichi-wa	good afternoon
konban-wa	good evening
oyasumi nasai	good night
sayonara	good-bye
dozo	please (go ahead)
onegaishimasu (use this often!)	please (please forgive me; this is very humble)
arigato (or more respectfully, *arigato gozaimasu*)	thank you
domo	thank you (in response to *dozo*)
do itashinmashite	you're welcome
sumimasen	excuse me, I'm sorry
Eigo o hanashimasu ka?	Do you speak English?
Nihongo o hanashimasen	I don't speak Japanese
wakarimasen	I don't understand
hai	yes
ie	no
Ogenki desu ka?	How are you?
Hai arigato gozaimasu, anata wa?	Very well, thanks, and you?
hajime mashite	pleased to meet you

Honorifics for Men, Women, and Children

Japanese honorifics mainly display rank and seniority according to Japanese culture, and not gender. Therefore, the word *san,* which is placed after the family name as a suffix, is used for men and women, married or single, and shows respect for them as participating members of society (it is the equivalent of the English "Mr.," "Mrs.," "Ms.," or "Miss"). Other honorifics include *sensai* for a teacher, which is a much higher ranking than *san.* For most travelers and businesspeople, *san* is useful enough. The word is essential when introduced to anyone, and is used virtually forever between business associates. Unless—and only until—your Japanese colleague specifically invites you to use his or her first name, and despite what he or she might use to refer to you, you must always use the family name plus *san.* (In Japan and most Asian cultures, men and women traditionally do not exchange wedding bands or rings; therefore, looking for a wedding band is generally not helpful as an indicator of whether someone is married. Also, in much of Asia, women traditionally do *not* take their husbands' family name when marrying, but retain their own. However, both practices are changing as more and more married couples take on the Western customs.)

Children in Japan are expected to be respectful and not overly conversational when speaking with adults, and must *always* use honorifics when referring to adults. As they probably speak limited English, this makes conversation with Japanese children that much more difficult.

In situations where a title is known, the title plus the word *san* is frequently used, either with or without the name—for example, *kacho-san* (literally, "Mr. Supervisor") or *bucho-san* (literally, "Mr. Senior Manager"). For casual contacts (i.e., with waiters, store help, etc.), just use *sumimasen*. It is very important to greet people at work, in stores, or in restaurants in an appropriate fashion. The Japanese state their family name first, and their given name second, so Tanaka Shunji signifies that the family name is Tanaka and that Shunji is the given name. When addressing him, always call him Tanaka-san. As the relationship develops, he may invite you to use his first name, Shunji, at which point you still use *san* (Shunji-san); even when first names are used, they are rarely employed in business contexts without the *san*. Sometimes the Japanese (as well as other Asians), will Anglicize their names when they know they will be working or meeting with Westerners. (On occasion, they will simply assign a Latin initial as a given first and second name.) Remember that this is done for your convenience, and that the name you are being given is not the real name. (This Anglicized version may also appear on that person's business card.)

The What, When, and How of Introducing People

Always wait to be introduced to strangers; never take that responsibility upon yourself, as doing so is considered inappropriate most of the time. The Japanese are most comfortable with a third-party introduction whenever one is possible, and will go to great lengths to ensure that you are not left alone to decide this for yourself. *Never* presume to seat yourself at a gathering; if possible, wait to be told where to sit. The seating arrangements have usually been carefully worked out in advance, and in most cases reflect the status of the individuals in the group, and the honor that is being accorded the guests. When departing, it is important to say farewell with a quick bow to every individual present: the American group wave is not appreciated. Once you greet someone you will encounter later that day in the same circumstances (e.g., at the office), you will need to acknowledge them with a foreshortened quick bow whenever you see them again. Seniors, or those who are obviously the oldest in a group, are greeted first, seated first, and allowed to enter a room first (usually at the center of the group, however, and preceded in most cases by their younger aides).

Physical Greeting Styles

Like many Asian cultures, but perhaps even more so, Japan is a nontouching culture when it comes to greeting strangers. Only the most intimate of friends (mainly young people) will touch each other in greeting. The handshake is a Western invention, and not native to Japan: over the last century, the Japanese have, of course, become accustomed to it, but because it is done for the Westerner's benefit, it is generally an accommodation added to the more formal Japanese style of greeting, which is the bow and the business card exchange. When the handshake does occur, it is more often than not very soft, almost limp. This does not signify insincerity; rather, it is an indication of humility using a Western convention. Women must always extend their hands first for a handshake, if it is to occur at all; if so, it is inevitably very soft.

The formal Japanese introduction involves the use of business cards, or *meishi*. This is an essential ritual that demonstrates many aspects of Japanese culture—among other things, humility, hierarchy, and face. Always take a large supply of business cards with you to Japan: you must give one to every new person you are introduced to (there is no need to provide another business card when you are meeting someone again unless information about you has changed, such as a new address, contact number, or position). Be sure your *meishi* are in fine shape: the business card is an extension of you as a person, and must look as good as possible. Never hand out a dirty, soiled, bent, or written-on *meishi*. You should, if possible, have your business card translated into Japanese on the reverse side before you go to Japan (many hotels and some airlines, as well as your own business, will do this as a service for you). The traditional Japanese *meishi* is written from top to bottom, and from right to left, with the company name being the first item, the rank and title the second, the name the third, and contact information the last (more modern businesses may organize the information in a more Western format). The group of which you are a member comes first because it is considered the most important piece of information; this is in contrast to the Western idea of putting the individual's name first.

When presenting a *meishi,* you give it to your Japanese associate with the Japanese side up, so that it is readable for him as you hold it (he will, in turn, present his card with the English side up, so it's readable for you); you must hold the card in the upper right- and left-hand corners, requiring the use of two hands, and you also receive your Japanese associate's card with two hands, on the upper right- and left-hand corners. The exchange is done quickly, almost simultaneously. Accompanying the exchange of the cards is the bow. The formal Japanese bow requires men to bow stiffly almost ninety degrees straight down, keeping their hands parallel to the seams of their pants, and women to bow almost as deeply, with their hands either folded in front of them or behind them (stepping back slightly a few steps, as well). This is not done in typical business scenarios today as dramatically as it used to be, nor is it expected of Westerners, considering that such behavior is directly related to the Japanese notion of showing deference for position and seniority, which is typically not natural to most egalitarian Westerners. Instead, it is perfectly appropriate for Westerners simply to bend their waists slightly and drop their heads in a nodlike action as they exchange the cards.

Smiling and other nonverbal forms of communication usually accompany the *meishi* exchange; it is appropriate to appear genuinely pleased to meet the other person. When first introduced to your Japanese colleague, make immediate eye contact, but as soon as the card exchange begins, and definitely when the bow commences, drop your eyes so that they are looking to the ground (this demonstrates respect for the other person). The bow is also a way of indicating your humility: the lower one bows and the longer one stays down, the more respectful one is of the other person's status; this suggests that one is more mindful (this is good) of one's humble position in regard to this status. This is why when two Japanese who do not know each other are first introduced, there can be a kind of double and triple bowing, as each person sizes up the self-perception of the other in regard to himself. Do not overdo this—in fact, for Westerners, it is not necessary—but remember that it will be done by the Japanese.

Information about each other's status is the most important information to be exchanged, and this is provided directly on the business card, as well as indirectly through a number of high-context indicators, such as gray hair (indicating age), gender (mostly male), and the number of people surrounding and assisting the other person (usually the more assistants the more important the individual). Humility for rank can be demonstrated subtly, by placing your card underneath the card of the other person during the exchange. Once you have received the other person's card, it is important to stand upright again, holding the card with two hands, and silently read the card for a few seconds. Then say his name (this is an opportunity for him to correct you if you mispronounce it, and for you to do the same for him) and his title in a way that indicates your respect for him and his position. It is at this point that your eyes may meet again for a moment, as you extend your hand for a soft Western handshake and say, *"Hajime mashite"* ("pleased to meet you"). All this occurs rather quickly, and you will inevitably meet many Japanese at once, so you will have a handful of cards when it is over.

As this ritual usually precedes a sit-down meeting, it is important to arrange the cards you have received in a little seating plan in front of you along the top of the desk or the table at your seat, reflecting the order in which people are seated. This will help you connect the correct names with the correct individuals throughout the meeting. During the meeting, it is important never to play with the business cards (do not write on them—*ever!*); and when the meeting is over, *never* put them in your back pants pockets: pick them up carefully and respectfully, and place them neatly in your *meishi* holder (a nice-looking leather-bound or brass card case would be perfect), then place the *meishi* holder in the left inside jacket pocket of your suit (nearest your heart).

Communication Styles

Okay Topics / Not Okay Topics

This is definitely a context-driven issue: in formal business and social situations (during the day in the office, at meetings, on the street with strangers, at family gatherings with seniors), the *tatemae* face needs to be shown, saving *honne* for informal business and social situations (over sake, in the karaoke bar, at the watercooler, in the lunchroom or the men's room in the office, at home with the family). *Okay:* anything that reflects your personal interests and hobbies, or your curiosity about things Japanese (be sure not to be effusive, however, since it is "over-the-top" and forces your Japanese colleagues, in order to present a humble face, to minimize Japanese culture). *Not okay:* Politics, current events, or any subject that might in any way be controversial needs to be avoided at first. Do *not* inquire about a person's occupation or income in casual conversation. Do *not* inquire about your colleague's family life. Do *not* give your opinions about the role of the emperor, or comment on World War II, or discuss Japan's positions regarding the rest of Asia (or the rest of the world, for that matter). Sticking to general themes of personal interest or business is fine; it is a way of seeking common ground. There will be no need to begin a conversation with the very American "So, what do you do?" since you already know this from the *meishi* exchange; however, further discussions about your company and its work are very much appreciated, as this gives the Japanese a chance to learn more about you and your firm.

Also not okay: money, inquiring about private family matters and spouses (although children are revered in Japan and make for wonderful conversation), or anything that is negative or may cause disharmony. The goal of all conversation is to maintain a harmonious atmosphere, despite the difficult or confrontational nature of the topic being discussed. (This does not mean that Japanese do not demonstrate anger; they do, but when it is shown, it is usually in private, with intimates, or with individuals with whom a relationship no longer matters.) At first, speak about things that you believe you have in common, so that you can build a personal connection, which will go far toward maintaining a harmonious bridge between you. This is appropriate for both individuals and organizations.

Tone, Volume, and Speed

At first, in more formal situations, the tone is quiet and hushed. Speak slowly, for the benefit of those translating, in short phrases, and speak clearly. Try to speak expositionally, without emotion, if possible. Since words for high-context cultures such as Japan are for the most part not the best vehicles for communication, use pictures, graphics, and charts to augment the topic being discussed, whenever possible. Illustrate what you can say, and certainly what you cannot. This is a very symbol-oriented and visual culture.

Use of Silence

Passive silence can be a form of proactive communication in Japan. There may be long pauses between comments, sometimes extending over several minutes. When confronted with silence, for whatever reason, the best response is to remain silent yourself, although this may be difficult and appear unproductive for time-conscious Westerners. (Think of it as an opportunity for a Zen moment: contemplate what is going on. Do as the Japanese often do: close your eyes and meditate briefly on the situation. This is perhaps the most subtle form of communication, yet communication it is.) In Japan, the most effective communication comes from the gut (*hara*), not from the head or mouth. Creating, maintaining, or joining in a harmonious feeling in the room by simply remaining silent may be more important than anything you can say. Feel out the situation: the Japanese are extremely intuitive, and seek out true feelings this way. If your gut tells you that the silence is in response to tension or a possible misunderstanding, it is best to say nothing, or wait a few moments, then make a statement about something you know they will agree with and feel positive about (it can be completely unrelated to what was previously said that created the silence in the first place). For example, you could say, "By the way" (a very common and useful expression in Japan), "Tanaka-san, I meant to tell you earlier how much our team enjoyed the dinner last night; thank you again for your kind hospitality." If your gut tells you that there is no tension or discomfort in the room, but the silence persists anyway, it is probably because your Japanese colleagues are simply thinking about what to say and how to respond. A Japanese friend once told me that Westerners have it easy—we only have to think about what to say; but the Japanese, he explained, because of so many other concerns, also have to think about how to say it. In either case, allow silence (*ma*). Remember, in Asia, given how careful one must be with what one says, "silence is golden"; those who speak too much are considered immature. Because some Westerners find silence disconcerting, they may tend to fill up the space with more talk; resist this impulse, as it may cause you to say more than you might normally be inclined to, and you may unintentionally help the Japanese achieve their goal of gathering as much data and information about you as possible.

Physical Gestures and Facial Expressions

The U.S. "okay" sign, made with the thumb and the forefinger, simply means "money" (i.e., the shape of a coin) in Japan; it does not mean okay (there is no hand signal for that, as the thumbs-up sign is considered a little vulgar). In Japan, there is considerably less physical gesturing of any kind. If you have a tendency to speak with your hands, you will consciously have to try to control it: most of the time, such gesturing is considered far too over the top, and will engender surprise, laughter (embarrassed giggling is more the case), or frozen disbelief. In fact, laughter may or may not be in response to anything humorous in the Western sense (jokes may not be understood); more often, it occurs because the Japanese may find the Westerners' not knowing how to behave so odd that it is funny. Doing things differently from the way tradition would have them be done makes the unknown terribly strange, and therefore, when such behavior is exhibited (more often by unknowing gaijin), it is unexpected, odd, sometimes frightening, and always a threat to the balance of things. Giggling is a way of minimizing the impact of the wrong behavior, and setting things in balance again. Japanese women will often place their hands over their mouths and giggle, as a way of maintaining their distance from men, or as a device to control an uncomfortable situation. Winking, whistling, and similar displays are considered very vulgar. When a Japanese person wants to point to himself, he puts his index finger up to the tip of his nose, not to his heart or chest. A very common nonverbal facial gesture is the sucking of air in through the front teeth, usually done in response to a difficult question. In general, this signals that there is a great displeasure, hesitation, unwillingness, or negativity, despite the *hai* that might accompany the gesture. Public displays of familiarity and affection with the opposite sex are typically expressed only by teenagers.

Waving and Counting

The pinkie represents the number 1, and the thumb represents the number 5, with everything in between ordered from the pinkie down; however, instead of raising the fingers when counting, the whole hand is exposed, and each finger is depressed as the counting is done. It is very insulting to motion to someone with your forefinger; instead, turn your hand with the palm facing down and motion inward with all four fingers at once. If you need to gesture for a waiter, very subtly raise your hand just slightly, or just make eye contact. Waving or beckoning is done with the palm down and the fingers moving forward and backward in a kind of scratching motion. It may seem as if the person making this motion is saying good-bye to you, but in fact you are being summoned over.

Physicality and Physical Space

Most Japanese stand, relative to North Americans, an extra six inches apart from each other; this can create a sense of distance with Westerners, but resist the urge at first to move in closer. Never, upon first greeting a Japanese, touch him beyond the soft handshake: no backslaps, no hugging, no kissing, *ever.* Never speak with your hands in your pockets: always keep them firmly at your side. If men and women must cross their legs when they sit, it must never be ankle over knee; for women, the preferred style is to cross ankle over ankle. Remember, in public, formal is always better than informal: no gum chewing, *ever;* no slouching; no leaning against things. The Japanese are very formal when they sit and stand. Once close relationships are established, and especially in those moments where spontaneity and friendliness are allowed (such as at the karaoke bar), there may be much physicality—touching, for example, or putting arms around other people's shoulders—but generally only between members of the same sex, and not in public between members of the opposite sex. About the only time this general nonphysicality rule is broken is on public transport, where it is very crowded and touching is unavoidable.

Eye Contact

Very indirect eye contact is the Japanese custom. Only upon the first introduction do eyes meet, and respect and humility is demonstrated, whenever necessary, by lowering the eyes. The eyes are used extensively to convey true feelings in formal situations where it is difficult to express *honne* verbally. Tune up your nonverbal antennae.

Emotive Orientation

The cultural code of obligation, *giri,* honor, face, and harmony makes the Japanese extremely intuitive and sensitive, even emotional. At times, emotions must be displayed openly, even publicly, but carefully; for example, crying often accompanies a public admission of shame and wrongdoing, or it can accompany an admission of a long, joyous, and deeply intimate relationship. Most of the time, however, the display of feelings must be done judiciously, and this can make "reading" the Japanese difficult for Westerners. Again, it is important for the Westerner to consciously control emotive impulses for more effective communications.

Protocol in Public

Walking Styles and Waiting in Lines

On the street, in stores, and in most public facilities, people are polite and orderly in lines; however, due to the volume of passengers on public transportation, there can be much pushing. This is not to get into a bus or train ahead of someone else, though; it is merely to get in! In Japan, people—as do drivers—usually stay to the left, and pass on the right.

Behavior in Public Places: Airports, Terminals, and the Market

Customer service is king in Japan, because the "other" (in this case, the customer) is so important. Stores are typically open in the evenings and on weekends, as well as during the day; there is a very good chance you will be bowed to as you enter and leave a store, and by all clerks as they help you. A personal thank-you to store owners, waiters, chefs, and hotel managers for their services is very much appreciated. In food markets, allow the staff to help you select items; in most cases, if you touch the produce, you are expected to buy it. In goods stores, if you buy a product and have problems with it, returning the item is usually no problem, since such a situation causes great loss of face for the store and the manufacturer. Smoking is endemic, and you may have difficulty finding a no-smoking area on public transportation, in restaurants, and in other public places. Bathroom facilities can range from Western-style toilets to Asian-style toilets (holes in the floor, with buckets of water or hoses attached to a water line for cleanup instead of paper); be prepared. Remember that prices in Japan can be shockingly high by Western standards and that there is a high level of comfort in doing things in groups. Consider taking public transportation whenever possible—it is, ultimately, faster and cheaper.

When answering a phone, say, "*Moosh moosh*" (which means "hello" on the phone).

Bus / Metro / Taxi / Car

Driving is on the left, and most drivers are quite considerate and law-abiding. The metros shut down after midnight or 1 A.M. The best way to get a cab is at designated taxi stands (hotels are good places, but sometimes charge more for the same ride: a hotel surcharge is added to the meter fare, in some cases). Most intercity trains have all facilities you will need, as distances are usually not that great (try the high-speed train between Tokyo and Osaka: it is a joy to ride). Hold onto your metro ticket when you buy one, as you may need it when you try to leave the station. When a taxi has been hailed (the red flag in the front window means the taxi is available), the passenger doors will automatically open and close for you: do not open or close the doors yourself when getting in or out of the taxis. Addresses in big cities like Tokyo can be maddeningly illogical (in part due to urban reconstruction after World War II, and in part due to the traditional system of demarcating neighborhoods and intersections, not streets), and even taxi drivers are often mystified: whenever possible, have the address you need to get to written down on a piece of paper (or use the business card of the person you are going to see, if you can) before you hail the cab. A small map outlining the route is great, if you can have one prepared before you go. Don't be surprised if taxi drivers and train conductors wear white gloves!

Tipping

Tipping is usually not done—but if there is a tip, 10 percent is certainly sufficient. This is mainly true for restaurants; taxi drivers do not traditionally expect tips, while porters and hotel help get the equivalent of 5 percent, and theater and bathroom attendants merely fifty or one hundred yen. Restaurants usually do not permit tipping; but if it is typical at an establishment, have the 10 percent tip included already on the bill. If you are unsure if a tip is needed, it's okay to ask if service is included in the bill. There is no need to leave any odd change.

Punctuality

While the culture is essentially polychronic, punctuality is expected in all situations. Do not arrive more than five minutes too soon—or more than five minutes too late, for that matter. The rules are a bit more flexible for social calls outside of the big cities, and it is understood than in places like Tokyo, getting around can sometimes be difficult and involve some delay; however, it is not preferred. You will not be told that your tardiness has caused a problem, of course, but it most likely has.

Dress

People who stand out because of their dress are not thought of very highly. Clothes should be used as a way of fitting in, not standing out. The standard is neither very formal, nor informal, no matter the occasion—business or social, at work, in the restaurant, or on the street, for men and women. Good taste is important, and should be reflected in the clothes one wears. At work, men wear dark suits, white shirts, and subdued ties; shoes must be polished; but beyond a watch, accessories are not often worn. Women can accessorize somewhat, but most often dress simply in a business suit or dress of a conservative length. On the street, informal may mean jeans and sneakers, though that is more common as clothing to wear at the gym or while jogging (some women do wear sneakers to work, but change just before they enter the office, not after going in); and for a social gathering, informal more often than not means tastefully coordinated clothes, sometimes including a jacket and tie for men (it rarely means jeans, sneakers, and T-shirts). "Formal" usually means formal evening wear, but it is rare; most of the time, business clothes are appropriate.

Seasonal Variations

There are four extreme seasons in Japan, and one needs to dress accordingly. Summers can be hot and very humid, with frequent rain, and winters can be damp, snowy, and cold. Spring and autumn can be delightful, however.

Colors

Wear neutral colors whenever possible.

Styles

Modern Japanese are certainly aware of Western styles, and depending upon the industry, age, job, and lifestyle of the individual involved, there can be great attention to style, particularly the most recent Western fad. For the most part, however, most Japanese tend to dress with more of an eye toward conformity than toward making an individual statement. Schools still insist on regulation uniforms, and this is often reflected in the clothes worn at the workplace and in public, as well. Traditional dress, such as the kimono, is rare in modern Japan; it is usually reserved for special occasions, rituals, or entertaining. If wearing a kimono, be sure to wrap it left over right on your body (for funerals, kimonos are wrapped right over left).

Accessories / Jewelry / Makeup

Because there is no Puritan tradition in Japan (or most of Asia), sexual expression is seen as appropriate human behavior, as long as it is done privately; attracting the opposite sex is perfectly acceptable. The right makeup, hairstyle, and accessories, therefore, are important for women but must not be over the top; perfume and cologne are popular.

Personal Hygiene

In Japan, personal hygiene is very important. There is a real concern for cleanliness and smelling good, but sometimes what smells good and bad to the Japanese may be different from Westerners. When Admiral Matthew C. Perry first sailed to Japan in 1853, it is said that some of the Japanese could detect the Westerners coming: they smelled the "milk," because the Western diet relies heavily on dairy products, which are used minimally in Japan (with the exception of ice cream!). Throughout the region, the smell of dairy products on individuals is generally considered offensive, while there is usually no concomitant concern for the smell of other foods, such as garlic or seaweed. The Japanese bathe very frequently; additionally, soaking in a hot bath (traditionally, the thermal springs that are ubiquitous throughout Japan) is a ritual pleasure enjoyed by both men and women. In this situation, the sexes are usually segregated, when possible (if in a thermal spring, this is sometimes not possible, but no sexual activity is implied by any subsequent nudity in this context), and all are expected to wash, bathe, and shower meticulously before entering the hot bath. This is usually done with buckets of hot water and soap, standing outside or beside the bath; occasionally, assistants will help in this task. No one enters the bath without having first cleaned him- or herself: the purpose of the bath is to enjoy the hot, relaxing waters (and the hot soak is often a daily family ritual). This has often caused confusion among Japanese who travel to the West and enter bathrooms with large tubs; soaking in them requires that they clean themselves before entering the tubs—to wash while sitting in one's dirty water is uncommon to them (they typically shower). Do not blow your nose in public: it is considered very rude (if you must blow your nose in public, never use a handkerchief; try disposable tissues). At the end of a meal, it is perfectly acceptable to use a toothpick, but you must cover the "working" hand with the other hand, so that others cannot see your mouth.

Dining and Drinking

Mealtimes and Typical Foods

The typical Japanese diet revolves mainly around seafood, rice, and noodles. Consequently, although there has been increased familiarity with Western foods (you might just as easily have a cappuccino and a croissant for breakfast in Tokyo as rice cereal), most meals are prepared with these ingredients in a variety of ways. We will refer here to the more traditional Japanese meals, not those that have become Westernized.

Breakfast is served from about 7:30 A.M. to 9 A.M., and usually consists of tea and rice; the latter is served either as a porridge-type cereal that can be flavored with any number of ingredients, with eggs in a variety of styles, or with pickled vegetables. Tea in Japan, as is the case elsewhere in the region, is usually drunk without sugar, milk, or lemon.

Lunch was traditionally the main meal of the day, and even today, in busy cities, it can still be an elaborate affair with several courses—or it can be a simple noodle dish bolted down in a matter of minutes. Lunch is served from about noon to 2:30 P.M., often in a bento box (usually a small wooden lacquered box), which consists of several small dishes, each in its own compartment, made of meat, fish, and vegetables (tempura-style or pickled), and some rice and noodles. Lunch can also be a large serving of hot broth or soup, made with a variety of ingredients and noodles. Finally, of course, there are the fine courses of sushi, sashimi, sukiyaki, *shabu-shabu* (a barbecue-style meat sukiyaki), and the like. It should be remembered that these dishes are fairly luxurious and do not constitute the average meal; they are usually reserved for special occasions, quick personal snacks, or entertaining. Typically, the drinks served with lunch and dinner are beer, sake, and/or tea.

Dinner is served from 6:30 P.M. on, with eight to nine o'clock the customary time; salarymen with long commutes usually arrive home late (around 9 P.M. or later) and have their dinner (served to them by the wife) separate from the family. If the main meal of the day was an entertainment lunch, then dinner is lighter—this is often the case with families at home. The dinner menu is often similar to that of the more formal lunch. Dinner drinks may begin with sake, served alone or with appetizers, then move on to beer during the meal, and end with a sweet wine and/or tea. Desserts may or may not be included; when they are, they usually take the form of sweet cakes, fresh fruit, or green tea or ginger ice cream.

Business dinners can last well into the evening, and depending upon the elaborateness of the occasion, may or may not include entertainment (sometimes in the form of geisha). The geisha house itself is not technically a restaurant, and many geisha will work for hire in any restaurant they are called upon to attend. The geisha traditionally make men feel comfortable. They play the roles of mother, girlfriend, sympathizer, supporter, entertainer, and waitress. They should not be judged by Western standards of fidelity and propriety, as they hearken back to a long courtier tradition in Japan. Today, geisha are a very special, and expensive, luxury, and are not a common sight in Japanese restaurants. They will most often work private parties at restaurants, and therefore may never be seen at all unless you are a male guest at one of these functions. Women are never invited to a party being "hosted" by geisha. As a man, try to relax and enjoy the extraordinary hospitality. A geisha will never make you feel uncomfortable. They do not come on to you; they are extraordinarily sensitive to your mood and are there to make the evening meal as relaxing and enjoyable an experience as possible. They follow your cues. But never tip a geisha. At the end of the evening, a simple bow and thank-you is all you need to do.

While we're discussing entertaining, a few words on the ubiquitous karaoke, a unique form of Japanese after-dinner entertainment that has caught on around the world. The karaoke, before it became associated with high-tech sing-along music machines, began as a way to break down whatever barriers between friends that the sake and beer had not already destroyed. The idea is still the same today: be prepared to sing a song, no matter how good or bad your voice or lyric memory; be sincere; be willing to make a fool of yourself in front of others; and be a good sport about it all. Most importantly, be sure to have fun. It's the spirit that counts. The bottom line: don't go to dinner in Japan without having boned-up on the delivery of your favorite song. Women are expected to partake in the evening's business entertainment as long as they are seen as equal business partners (in this case, geisha entertainment will not be part of the evening).

You know restaurants are open when they have little cloth banners (*noren*) strung out over the doorway; they are closed when the *noren* are not visible. And here are some of the different varieties of eateries you may find yourself in:

- *sushi-ya:* Usually informal places, where you sit at counters and order individual dishes of sushi.
- *ryotei:* High-class traditional restaurants, featuring Japanese "haute cuisine"; they absolutely require reservations, and are typically very expensive. A *ryotei* may be difficult to recognize, for it is usually a discreet building placed inside a courtyard set back from the bustle of the street; look for a little mound of salt (*morijio*) placed on the ground to the side of the front entrance. The *morijio* is a welcome sign to customers and symbolizes prosperity, which you must be blessed with in order to pay the prices charged inside!
- *sukiyaki-ya:* Places specializing in sukiyaki and *shabu-shabu;* they are a step up from the noodle shop, and very popular among businessmen.
- *soba-ya:* Strictly *soba* (a popular type of noodle dish, usually served in a broth), strictly simple, and usually family run.
- *tonkatsu-ya:* Tonkatsu is a fried pork cutlet, and that's what you get here mainly.
- *yakitori-ya:* Yakitori is grilled chicken, often served on a skewer. If you see a restaurant with the ubiquitous red paper lantern hanging outside to the side of the front entrance, that's your sign that the restaurant is most likely a *yakitori-ya.* It's a friendly, informal place, where salarymen gather for a bite and some drinks before going home.
- *okonomiyaki-ya:* Okonomiyaki is a kind of pancake, into which all sorts of vegetables are mixed. It's usually cooked right on a griddle at your table. It's very informal and lots of fun, and a specialty of the western region of Japan.
- *oden-ya:* Places serving *oden,* a kind of constantly bubbling stew of vegetables, meat, or fish, which is a favorite in winter.
- department store restaurants: Yes, they are inexpensive and very good family-type places serving all sorts of Japanese food.

A unique feature of many Japanese restaurants is the display of mouth-watering dishes in the front window, tempting passersby with luscious-looking examples of the food to be found inside. It's amazing, really, how the restaurant's chef turns out these display dishes every single day. Well, really, they just dust them off. The fact is, they are plastic models, and if you don't speak Japanese, just bring the waiter outside for a moment and point to the dish in the window that you want. And if you don't know what it is, say, "*Are o kudasai*" ("What is this one, please?"). You'll get a smile and, most likely, a high-school-English-as-a-second-language attempt at an explanation.

Regional Differences

While different cities in Japan will certainly have their local specialties, the food is remarkably similar throughout the country. There are some notable delicacies though, such as Kobe beef (rare and expensive because the cattle are grazed on specially manicured grass and treated exquisitely, including being given hand massages and meals of beer; this is all the more extraordinary when one considers how valuable real estate is in Japan—precisely the reason why cattle are not typically raised in the first place), chicken sushi (yes, raw and marinated chicken), and fugu (the specially prepared meat from the occasionally poisonous blowfish). But for the most part, the food is uniquely Japanese, everywhere.

Typical Drinks and Toasting

The most common liquor is sake (pronounced "sa-kay"), which is a fermented rice wine. It is best drunk at room temperature, neither warmed (although cheaper sakes are in winter) nor chilled (although the same sakes are in summer), in small ceramic sake cups. Each person is usually given a sake cup and a small flask filled with sake. Because you must *never* pour your own drink (be it sake, beer, or tea), you must always be alert throughout the meal as to whether your neighbor's sake cup, teacup, or beer glass needs refilling. If it is less than half full, it needs refilling; alternately, if yours is less than half full, your neighbor is obliged to refill it. If he or she does not, do *not* refill it yourself, for this will cause your neighbor to lose face; instead, diplomatically indicate your need by pouring a little more drink into your neighbor's glass, even if it doesn't really need it. Sake is sometimes drunk in shots, beer usually is not.

The toast in Japan is *kampai,* which means "bottoms up" or "drain the glass." Sake can be strong, so go slow. If you are the honored guest, you will be expected to make a toast, usually soon after the host does (but before the main course is served) or at the end of the meal before everyone departs. An appropriate toast is to the health of the host and all those present, and to the prosperity of the business that brought you together.

Table Manners and the Use of Utensils

Let's start with perhaps the most formal Japanese dining event, the tea ceremony, and work our way down from there. The tea ceremony is a classic Zen event, requiring strict adherence to rules designed to promote tranquillity through the discovery of much in what is little (remember, the Japanese excel at perfecting the miniature, as evidenced in the art of bonsai). You will be served special green tea (*o-cha*), unsweetened, which has a slightly bitter taste. But remember, rice and tea are sacred in Japan. If you are invited to a tea ceremony, ask about the formality of the occasion: in most cases, unless you are instructed otherwise, men should wear dark suits and ties, and women should wear skirts and blouses. You will remove your shoes upon entering, as you would in a Japanese home, and you will probably be seated on a tatami flooring or a *zabuton* (a cushion or pillow), so be sure your socks aren't worn-out and that you don't wear tight-fitting clothes. As when entering a home, there is an area just inside the front door known as the *genkan*: this is where you remove your shoes and put on slippers, if they are made available. Once your shoes are removed, it is imperative never to step down on the *genkan* in your stockinged or slippered feet, but instantly step up onto the tatami. This way, you avoid bringing whatever dirt there may be in the *genkan* area into the house.

Once you have entered the tatami room, greet the guests who are already there with a slight bow, and sit down in the place indicated. No talking, please. And no handshaking or exchanging of business cards (*meishi*). Stay in your place, bow, and then be seated silently.

First, you will be served a small cake (*o-kashi*) on a small plate. Pick up the plate with one hand and hold it at chest level so that crumbs fall on the plate. Crumbs *must not* fall anywhere on you or the tatami. Eat the cake in several small bites, then put the plate back down in the place from which you originally picked it up.

After you have eaten the *o-kashi,* the tea will be served to you. Before you pick up your cup, bow to those guests who have not yet been served tea (they will be served, as you are served, individually, and in order of status, after each individual has performed this ceremony), pick up the cup (actually a small bowl—there will be no handle) with your right hand, bring it to chest level, and hold it there with both hands for a moment. Now turn the bowl clockwise two quarter turns (this keeps you from having to drink from the front of the bowl), and drink the tea completely in several sips. When you are finished drinking, turn the bowl *counterclockwise* in two similar quarter turns back to the original position and place the bowl down in front of you on the tatami just inside the seam. Make a formal bow to the hostess when you are finished drinking and have set the bowl down. Keep in mind that tea bowls and utensils are ceremonial objects, often worthy of the status of high art, and therefore must be handled with great care. If there are other guests waiting to be served, look admiringly at your tea bowl while they are being served. If there are many others to be served, polite conversation with those either waiting or finished drinking is acceptable. Take special care not to be loud, too talkative, or disruptive of anything that could break the peace and harmony of the event. Once everyone has been served, everyone makes a bow of gratitude to the hostess and then departs.

At this event, and at other formal traditional Japanese dinners, you may be sitting in a *seiza* position (on one's heels with the legs tucked underneath the buttocks), which can be uncomfortable for many Westerners. Your hostess will probably notice your discomfort and suggest that you "get comfortable"; when she does, you may sit cross-legged (if male), or with your legs tucked to one side (if female). Never spread your legs directly out in front of you.

How many American businessmen have endured excruciating leg cramps while attempting to enjoy a Japanese meal, sitting cross-legged in a business suit on the floor? How many Western women have had to endure the discomfort of sitting legs sideways on the floor while dining with men at the same meal? Yes, traditional Japanese meals are taken sitting on the floor—well, really the tatami, which is a reedlike mat inset into the top part of the floor, so that the top of the mat surface is level with the surface of the floor surrounding it. Most Westerners can't do this for more than five minutes without experiencing hospitalization-level pain. How to get around this? Practice and wear loose fitting clothes. However, most Japanese restaurants have dining areas in which the table is built around a "dugout," so that once you settle in you can dangle your legs to your heart's content under the table.

There is a far more informal event that you may be invited to, and that is tea at a Japanese home or office. This is not the tea ceremony described above; this is a friendly, casual event, at which a tray will be brought out with a cup of tea, a small plate with a cake, and a hot, wet cloth (an *o-shibori*). Why the custom of *o-shibori* has not caught on in all restaurants around the world, I do not understand, for it is a wonderfully refreshing, and sanitary, way to start off any meal. You wipe your hands with the towel, not your face, and you do so before you touch any of the food, not after the meal.

As far as chopsticks (*o-hashi*) are concerned, let's start by setting the record straight: not every country in Asia uses them. In fact, the "chopstick cultures" were originally only China, Japan, and Korea. In most of southeast Asia, you simply do not use chopsticks: in Thailand, for example, you eat with spoons and forks, but no knives, and no chopsticks. (Next time you're in your favorite Thai restaurant, don't ask for chopsticks: eat your sticky rice with a spoon and fork.) Chopsticks can be fancy (made of silver or ivory, inlaid or carved with drawings and sayings) or simple (just two sticks of wood), but no matter how basic or aristocratic, they are held and operated exactly the same way. I personally find the simple wooden kind the best: food sticks to them better, the friction makes picking up food easier, and the wood absorbs all the wonderful flavors. I find fancy ivory and lacquered jobs far too slippery: the food keeps sliding off them, and they don't absorb any flavors. There are lots of ways to teach someone how to use chopsticks, but I like the "pencil" approach:

• Hold the first chopstick horizontally in your hand as you would a pencil, the bottom of the chopstick resting on the top side of your thumb, and the top of the chopstick being controlled by your index and/or middle finger lightly pressing down on it. Notice the little loophole created by your thumb and forefinger.

• Holding the second chopstick with your other hand, slip the second chopstick through the loophole starting from the inside of your palm, until it is parallel to the first chopstick. Always hold both chopsticks so that the pointy end is the end you'll use to pick up the food with, and the blunt end is pointing back at you. If you were to let go of the second chopstick with your other hand at this point, it would wobble and fall out of the loophole, so you've got to hold it down somehow. Well, you've got several other fingers left, so use either your middle or third finger (or both) to hold down that second chopstick against the inside of your thumb. You've done it! The "pencil" chopstick moves up and down, while the second chopstick remains stationary. The latter is the one against which the food is scooped, picked up, and eaten.

Having said all this, remember that learning to actually use chopsticks is like learning to drive: I can tell you what to do, but the only way you'll really do it is to, well, just do it. Practice, practice, practice.

Chopsticks should always rest together parallel to each other, most preferably in a north-south line along the right side of the plate on a chopstick rest or on the plate itself. In Japan, and throughout all chopstick cultures, never cross your chopsticks like an *X*, never rest them on separate sides of the plate, and never ever use them to point at things. No matter how pointy, they must never be used to spear your food. And the biggest no-no of all: *never* stick your chopsticks into your rice so that they stand upright. It may seem to the Japanese that you are mocking the Japanese requirement to use them well. Moreover, when someone dies, a bowl of rice with upright chopsticks is often used as a funeral offering.

Chopsticks with soup? In Japan and elsewhere in the chopstick region, you use the chopsticks to lift the solid foods out of the soup bowl and into your mouth. When you are finished with all the food pieces, you drink the broth straight from the bowl. Since soup is wet, of course, you hold the bowl close to your mouth, scooping the food pieces with your chopsticks directly into your mouth with as little empty space between the bowl and you as possible. When nothing but the broth is left, you rest your chopsticks, hold the bowl *with two hands* (important!) at your lips, and drink the broth like a cup of tea.

The same procedure is used with rice, minus the drinking part (unless it's sake, or "liquid rice" as it is sometimes referred to). Rice is the main grain of Asia, and in Japan it holds a sacred place. It is most often served in individual small rice bowls, to be eaten all at once after the main dish has been eaten (the preferred way), or you can

A. pick up some food with your chopsticks in your chopstick hand;

B. then, with your other hand, pick up your little rice bowl and hold it up to your chin;

C. then, holding the food in your chopstick over the rice bowl, put it in your mouth, and quickly scoop in some rice from the bowl as a follow-up.

It is important to eat every grain of rice in your rice bowl: rice is sacred, and leaving any over is considered bad breeding. Additionally, rice is never mixed with food or sauce: it is always eaten plain.

Remember that in Japanese culture every action is functional precisely because it is also done gracefully and efficiently. This concept is a manifestation of Zen ideals, so much at the heart of Japanese traditions. Japanese chopsticks differ slightly from Chinese chopsticks (Japanese chopsticks are typically slightly shorter, with squared-off edges; Chinese chopsticks are typically longer and rounder) and need to be more formally handled: no waving chopsticks around aimlessly over different dishes trying to select what you want (*mayoi*), no sticking the chopstick ends into the food like a spear (*sashi*), and no drawing the bowl or plate nearer to you with your chopsticks (*yosi*). You might also note that pickled vegetables (*tsukemono*), a common accompaniment to the main dish, usually served in a small dish or bowl on the side, will often come with their own pair of serving chopsticks. Use them to transfer the *tsukemono* onto your plate: this way, the strong flavor of the pickles does not affect the other food you might pick up with your chopsticks, especially the subtle and mild flavors of fish.

Japanese chopsticks are usually simple, raw wooden sticks, connected at the blunt end, and rounded slightly at the other, and are typically presented in a paper wrapper. Everything in Japan has a meaning, so don't just slip the chopsticks out of their paper wrapping and discard it. Slide the chopsticks out, and lay them carefully on the right side of your plate, north-south, blunt connected end facing north. Now get to work on the paper wrapper: fold it horizontally in half, so that you have a long, thin, rectangular ribbon of paper. Holding both ends of the ribbon, tie it into a knot. Place the knotted paper to the right side of your plate (near the two o'clock position), and rest the mouth end (the rounded end) of your chopsticks on the paper knot. Voilà! You have made a rest for your Japanese chopsticks. Now the food-stained ends of your chopsticks never have to touch the table while you dine. The Japanese do this all the time (unless, of course, they are provided with chopstick rests, which usually happens only at the classier restaurants and events). An important point about using Japanese chopsticks: they first need to be separated at the connected blunt end. So once you've created your little paper chopstick rest, pick up your chopsticks and, *holding them over your lap* (this is important, because little splinters of wood may break away, and you don't want them to land on your plate and eventually in your food), snap them apart like a wishbone. Then gently rub the separated ends a few times together (again, holding them over your lap), as if sharpening a knife, the idea being to whittle any wooden splinters away. Now they're ready to use, and you can place the food ends down against your paper rest (food ends facing north, blunt ends facing south).

If you really want to score points with your Japanese hosts, don't just reach over and grab your chopsticks. If you've made your little paper chopstick rest, you've already started down the correct path; complete the journey by learning how to pick up your chopsticks *bushido*—the right way. With your right hand held hovering over your chopsticks, push your elbow out to the right and rotate your hand counterclockwise so that the fingers you will use to pick up your chopsticks land with your thumb on the right side of the right chopstick, and your index and middle fingers on the left side of the left chopstick. Pick up the chopsticks from the blunt base end this way, and as you lift them off their rest, bring your elbow back in toward your body, rotating your hand clockwise and upward, so that you can see the tips of your fingers. The chopsticks swing elegantly in an arc, and are perfectly ready to be used. This is a single, beautiful, and graceful motion that, again with practice, avoids the clumsy two-handed setup that chopstick novices usually suffer with.

If you use chopsticks with soup, you must also use them for grains of rice, little bitty peanuts, and practically every item on your plate, no matter how small, round, or difficult. Never use your fingers; *always* use your chopsticks. Really. Sushi is the only exception to this rule, based on the fact that if you pick up sushi with chopsticks, it is physically impossible to dip it into the soy sauce fish-side down; this forces you to soak the rice on the bottom of the sushi with soy sauce, and not the fish, so by the time the soya-soaked rice gets to your mouth, it has fallen apart all over your plate. Your best bet is to pick up the sushi with your hand and dip it, fish-side down, quickly (for just a taste) into the soya sauce. If you simply cannot master chopsticks, it's perfectly all right in modern-day Japan to ask for Western cutlery: you will get a spoon and a fork (rarely a knife).

Use your chopsticks to cut up pieces of food, if necessary; remember, the meat or fish is marinated before cooking, so it will be easy to break up the flesh with the chopsticks: there will be no need for knives. Certain foods, like soups, are served in bowls with lids on them: it is important at the end of the meal to place the lid back on top of the bowl when you are finally finished. Unlike in some rural parts of Asia, bones, gristle, and other remains of your meal do not get scattered on the floor or on the table; in Japan, these are placed neatly on the side of your plate. If you are using soya sauce, be sure to pour out only the amount you think you will actually use, and make sure you pour it into the shallow, empty little bowl that is usually brought out to you with your meal. That's what it's there for. Most Westerners use far too much soy sauce, and drench their sushi and sashimi in it: just a quick little dip, please. A well-bred diner in Japan usually has just a trace of soya sauce left in their bowl.

When eating sushi, mix a little wasabi—a pungent green herb that tastes like horseradish—into your soya sauce bowl with your chopsticks, and stir a bit, slowly so it does not splash. No soya sauce should stain the tray, the tablecloth, or the mat, and wasabi should never be eaten by itself, or spread directly onto the fish.

When seated at the Japanese table, be sure to sit upright, not slouched over your food, with your legs flat down against the floor, not cross-legged (if seated Western style). There is an exception to this rule, and it is the same situation that allows for an exception to the no-noise rule: the eating of noodles. Day-to-day dining in Japan revolves around vegetables, noodles, fish, and soups; the salaryman's typical lunch consists of a bowl of ramen (Chinese-style yellow-colored noodles) in a steaming broth filled with vegetables, egg, and chicken. When eating any kind of noodles (many of which can be served either hot or cold), it is perfectly acceptable to slurp. Slurping hot noodles cools them off, and, hot or cold, it is believed that slurping air into the mouth along with the noodles enhances the flavor. How vigorous a slurp? Listen to those around you. And, of course, slurping such wet food also requires that you bend over your bowl a bit so that the slurp doesn't splash. Slurping is also okay when it comes to miso soup or bowls of noodle broth. Splashing is not okay. (However, *never* slurp your tea: sip it quietly.)

The two main kinds of non-soup noodle dishes are *soba* (brownish buckwheat-and-wheat noodles) and *udon* (whiter, wheat-only noodles). Cold noodles will be served to you on a bamboo rack in a lacquer box, with a small bowl of broth on the side and a small bowl of condiments to mix into the broth. You take some noodles with your chopsticks and dip them directly into the broth bowl. Do *not* pour the broth over the noodles. You may also be served a *yuto,* a small, square container with a ladle-like handle and a spout, into which was poured some of the broth that the noodles were cooked in the kitchen.

If the *yuto* is brought out to your table, pour a little of the broth from it into your broth bowl: it supposedly adds to the flavor of your dipping broth. It is considered an honor if the chef selects you to receive the *yuto*. Both *soba* and *udon* are served in limitless varieties, either plain, or in soups and broths, sometimes with a raw egg on top, sometimes with strips of nori (dried seaweed) or tempura (batter-fried vegetables or shrimp). One interesting tradition in Japan is to eat *soba* while listening to the temple bells ringing at midnight on New Year's Eve. *Soba* eaten this way is called *toshikoshi-soba,* with the long, thin noodles representing a long life and many years to come. Additional varieties of noodles are *somen* (wheat-based noodles, the thinnest of all), and *hiyamugi* (wheat-based noodles, and not as thin as *somen,* but thinner than *udon*). All noodle dishes in Japan are served with condiments, to add more flavor to the very subtle *soba* and *udon*. The following condiments also appear on the Japanese table, in general, so it's good to become familiar with them. Sprinkle them (carefully) on whatever you like; feel free to experiment with them.

- *negi:* diced spring onions or scallions
- *schichimi:* a combination blend of seven tastes—*mikan* (mandarin orange peel), *sansho* (pepper), *kurogama* (sesame), *asanomi* (hempseeds), *keshi* (poppy seeds),

togarashi (cayenne), and *hoshinori* (ground dried seaweed)—served in a shaker on the table

- wasabi: a green, ground, pastelike herb that tastes like horseradish (*very* strong!)
- *mitsuba:* ground, greenish-yellow coriander-type fresh vegetable leaves
- *yuzu:* ground Chinese lemon peel, with a unique citruslike taste
- shoyu: soy sauce
- *su:* rice vinegar
- *mirin:* heavily sweetened sake (or rice liquor); used only as a food dressing
- fish sauce: made from vinegar and fish paste, imparting a dark, fishy taste

When you are served a lunch in Japan, it will either be on a place mat, the tablecloth, the tatami, or in a bento box. The bento box was designed as an easy, simple way for salarymen and workmen to get all the ingredients and dishes in a transportable meal quickly and easily. It is a mastery of design, efficiency, and presentation. Foods served to you will come in a variety of containers, the most common being the following:

- *chawan* (the rice bowl)
- *shiru-wan* (the soup bowl)
- *yakimono-zara* (the ceramic dish on which the food is placed)
- *nimono-wan* (a wide-mouthed bowl for boiled foods).

Additionally, there are three small bowls for side dishes:

- *chuzara* (medium sized to small)
- *kozara* (very small)
- *kobachi* (a tiny bowl for little delicacies)

Soba or *udon* is served in lidded china bowls known as *domburi-bachi.* Finally, the tall handleless cups in which tea is served are called *yunomi-jawan.*

Any dish served in a container with a lid on it probably contains liquid, so be careful removing the lid. When you remove it, place it upside down on the table or tray, so that it doesn't roll and so that the condensation that has probably formed on the inside does not drip onto the table or tablecloth.

Seating Plans

The most honored position is at the middle of the table, with the second most important person seated next. This means that the host will sit at the middle of the table on one side, and the honored guest in the middle on the other side, opposite the host. (Spouses are usually not invited to business meals, and most formal meals in restaurants are business meals: do not ask if your spouse can join you; it will embarrass your Japanese colleague into doing something that is uncomfortable for him.) The honored guest sits on the side of the table farthest from the door. (This is the same at business meetings, with the key people sitting in the middle, flanked on either side in descending order by their aides, with the least important people sitting at the ends of the table farthest from the middle, and closest to the door; the arrangement is mirrored on the other side, because the rules of hierarchy demand that everyone must be able to speak with their opposite peers and those who rank below them, but those below should not speak with those above.) If women are present, they will probably be given the honored positions first, although practically speaking there will be far fewer women. In Japan, women typically rise when men enter the room, hold doors open for men, and escort men into a room first.

Refills and Seconds

Japanese food is typically served, depending on the dishes, either individually or as a communal dish. If it's a communal dish, or if you are dining at someone's home, you will always be offered more food. Leave a bit on your plate (but never any rice in your rice bowl) if you do not want more food. You will be implored to take more two or three times, in the form of a little ritual. The game is as follows: first you refuse, then the host insists, then you refuse again, then the host insists again, and then you finally give in and take a little more. Usually the host will be apologizing to you for the terrible food and begging you to take it anyway to make them feel better. If you really don't want more, take very little and leave it on your plate. You may always have additional beverages; drink enough to cause your cup or glass to be less than half full, and it will generally be refilled. A reminder: never refill your own glass; always refill your neighbor's glass, and he or she will refill yours. Portions are generally smaller than in the United States, but there are generally more courses, for both lunch and dinner. It is not about quantity, but quality, and exquisitely prepared dishes that look as good as they taste.

At Home, in a Restaurant, or at Work

In Japan, it is expected before you begin eating or drinking anything that you say "*itidakimasu*" (basically "*bon appétit*"), and that after the meal you say "*gochisosama deshita*" (basically, "thanks for a great meal") to the host or hostess.

At the table in Japan, try to relax and see the meal as an opportunity to enjoy peacefully the company of other people in an atmosphere whose sole purpose really is to create a harmonious and Zen-like feeling of satisfaction—with the food, with one another, and with life. Try mirroring both your Japanese colleagues' actions and words. To begin, it's best not to drink or eat until your Japanese host does and, throughout the meal, try to follow the cues of your colleagues in terms of when they drink, eat, and toast. Match the relaxation levels they are striving for as the meal progresses. It might begin rather quietly and formally, but the Japanese meal can get quite convivial and lively once the sake starts flowing and the wasabi is mixed.

In informal restaurants, you may be required to share a table. If so, do not force conversation: act as if you are seated at a private table. Waitstaff may be summoned by making eye contact; waving or calling their names is very impolite. The business breakfast is a fact of life, but not as ubiquitous as in the West. The business lunch (more common than dinner) and dinner are quite common; but, depending upon how well developed your relationship may be, it is generally not the time to make business decisions. Take your cue from your Japanese associates: if they bring up business, then it's okay to discuss it, but wait to take your lead from their conversation. If you're in a restaurant and being hosted by your Japanese colleagues, it is perfectly all right to ask your host to order for you, if you are unsure of the food.

When invited to a Japanese colleague's home for a formal meal, you will be told where to sit, and there you should remain. It is a great honor to be invited into a Japanese home, because the Japanese feel that many Westerners will find their homes too small and crowded; also, older family members might be living there, and your presence will probably make things uncomfortable for you and them (no mutually intelligible language!). When you approach a Japanese house (not an apartment), you generally announce who you are at the front door, without ringing a bell or knocking. Once invited in, you will need to remove your shoes (wear good socks): this is still a custom in many restaurants as well. Remove your shoes in the *genkan,* and never put your stockinged feet down on the *genkan* once you have removed your shoes: step directly into the house onto the tatami. Both men and women should remove their shoes before stepping onto the tatami.

In typical Japanese fashion, one doesn't simply remove one's shoes: there is a prescribed "way" of doing it. As soon as you approach the tatami, turn around and face the direction from which you came, and slide your feet out of your shoes. Your shoes should automatically be facing outward and away from the dining area. Place the shoes side by side next to the other shoes that are lined up in front of the tatami, or in the "shoe area" (it will be made obvious to you). Whatever you do, *never ever* put your shoes on the tatami. Now, turn around and step onto the tatami. (In some homes, you may be offered slippers after you remove your shoes. It is perfectly appropriate to put them on; however, if you need to use the bathroom at any point you must take the slippers off before entering the bathroom, and place them back on when leaving the bathroom.)

The ritual of removing shoes ensures that your shoes are "ready for you"; that is, when the meal is over, all you need to do is step up to your shoes and slide right into them and keep on walking! No klutzy fumbling around. Grace and efficiency. That's Japanese. This all presupposes that you realized beforehand that in Japan it's best to wear shoes that slip on and off, as opposed to shoes that buckle or lace. A very high-profile U.S. businessman was being coached on just this point prior to his first, and very important, trip to Japan. "Hell, I never wear those loafery shoes," he scorned, and took his very British lace-ups with him to Tokyo. He fumbled the shoes. He fumbled the meals. And he fumbled the deal.

Once inside the home, do not wander from room to room: much of the house is really off-limits to guests. If you move from room to room in a Japanese home, be sure to always allow the more senior members of your party to enter the room ahead of you. Once at the table or tatami, be sure to look for place cards or wait until the host indicates your seat: do not presume to seat yourself.

Being a Good Guest or Host

Paying the Bill

Usually the one who does the inviting pays the bill, although the guest is expected to make an effort to pay. Sometimes other circumstances determine the payee (such as rank). Making payment arrangements ahead of time so that no exchange occurs at the table is a very classy way to host, and is very common. When men are present at the table, women will not really be able to pay the bill at a restaurant: if you want to, make arrangements ahead of time, and don't wait for the check to arrive at the table. The only time it is considered appropriate for a woman to pay the bill is if she is a businesswoman from abroad.

Transportation

It's a very nice idea, when acting as the host, to inquire ahead of time whether your guests will require transportation. If necessary, you should arrange for taxi service at the end of the meal. When seeing your guests off, you must remain at the entrance of the house or the restaurant, or at the site where you deposited your guests into the car, until the car is out of sight: it is very important not to leave until your guests can no longer see you, should they look back. Guests are seated in cars (and taxis) by rank, with the honored guest being placed in the back directly behind the front passenger seat; the next honored position is in the back behind the driver, and the least honored position is up front with the driver.

When to Arrive / Chores to Do

If invited to dinner at a private home, offer to help with the chores, but do not expect to be taken up on your offer. Nor should you expect to visit the kitchen. Do not leave the table unless invited to do so. Spouses might be invited to dinners at a private home, because another person's spouse will probably be there. Be on time.

Gift Giving

In general, gift giving in Japan is a way of maintaining the obligations that exist between people, and of honoring the role that others play in your life. In business settings, it usually takes the form of personal gifts that symbolically say the correct thing about the nature of the relationship. When going to Japan on business, you must bring gifts for everyone you will see. The general rule is pastries for the office staff, good-quality corporate logo items (all the same) for business associates, and an especially thoughtful, somewhat personalized gift for the key man you will be working with. You give your gifts at the end of the first or second meeting in Japan, as a sign of your sincerity and best wishes (it is too distracting if you give it at the beginning of the meeting, and the first meeting may not be an appropriate time). You will receive a farewell gift at your last meeting in Japan before you leave to go home. When the Japanese visit your country, they will also bring you a gift, and before they leave, you should give them gifts. Holiday cards are appropriate for less formal relationships, particularly as a thank-you for their business during the previous year, and should be mailed in time to be received at least one week before New Year's Day. The Japanese postal system will usually hold them and deliver them precisely on New Year's, an old tradition.

The most appropriate gift for a personal visit to a home, or as a thank-you for dinner, would be a box of fruits, pastries, cakes, cookies, or other sweets. If you know the family, however, any small item that would be appreciated is okay; and if there are children, it is important to bring along a little something for them as well. Flowers are generally not appropriate (however, a growing plant is appreciated, as long as it does not carry negative symbolism associated with death, such as lilies and carnations: a pine tree or a small bonsai or bamboo is very well received). In addition to the gift (and certainly necessary if you did not send or bring one), be sure to send a handwritten thank-you note on a card the very next day after the dinner party; it is best if it is messengered and not mailed. If you are staying with a family, an appropriate thank-you gift would be a high-quality item that represents your country and is difficult to get in Japan; this is also a good idea for a key business associate. Acceptable gifts may include coffee-table books about the United States, or anything that reflects your host's personal tastes (the cap of a famous American team for the football-playing son of the family, for example). For other business associates, fancy fruit baskets or gourmet foods make fine gifts (they can be shared around, as well); well-framed and well-mounted photographs of the group, including you, are also much appreciated. Do not give money as a gift under any circumstances (there are certain occasions where money is given in Japan, such as at funerals, or to children with whom one has a close family relationship, but these are best reserved for Japanese).

The more you can personalize your "key man" gift, the more it is appreciated. Sometimes the best gift you can give is a fine bottle of whiskey or cognac (more cognac is drunk in Japan than in France each year). The gifts exchanged must be equal to or slightly finer—and perhaps more expensive—than gifts previously exchanged. A fine gift for an elderly man is a statuette of a crane: this is a symbol of long life and wisdom.

If your gift consists of several items, be sure that the total number is not an even number (bad luck), never four (*very* bad luck), not nine (also bad luck), and preferably three or seven (*very* good luck). For both giving and receiving gifts, two hands are always used. Gifts are typically not opened by the receiver in front of the giver; they are usually received, graciously acknowledged, and placed aside to be opened once the giver is no longer present.

Gifts must be wrapped well. When purchasing any of the previously mentioned items in Japan, it will be wrapped beautifully for you—especially if you make it known that it is a gift. Gift giving in Japan is an art, and, in fact, has been institutionalized into two gift-giving seasons during the year: the month of June, or summer gift giving, called *ochugen;* and the month of December, or winter gift giving, called *oseibo,* coinciding with Christmas and New Year's. There are special gifts and special gift-giving rules for these situations (the best gifts in either case are fine whiskies, fancy dried foods, condiments, and nori, or seaweed). However, no matter what the occasion—whether a thank-you for a meal or a thank-you for a special favor—the gift-giving protocols typically are not that much different. If you are unsure, ask an intermediate Japanese colleague or the recipient's secretary for help: they both will be willing to assist you and make the correct selection for you (the secretary will probably insist on buying the gift for you: she will know the most appropriate gift, being familiar with her supervisor, and in which store to get it and get it wrapped).

Most gifts are wrapped in ordinary paper first, and then wrapped again in a sheet of white paper. Red is a fine color for gifts or cards, unless the occasion is an illness, since red signifies blood. Although the color white is associated in

Asia with funerals, in this case its meaning will be offset by the ribbons (*mizu-hiki*) and other details of the wrapping. To be absolutely safe, use red or yellow paper; in that case, no special *mizuhiki* are required. If using white paper, you must also use *mizuhiki*. Typically, the *mizuhiki* are red and white, and they can be tied in either of two ways:

- the *cho-misubi* style: it looks like a stylized butterfly's wings, and is used for gifts exchanged as a thank-you, a wish for happiness or prosperity, birthdays, and the like
- the *musubikiri* style: the ends of the ribbon are cut short, indicating that the sad event for which you are giving the gift (illness, sympathy, etc.) should end quickly

Clearly, the *cho-misubi* style is the one used for gifts given by most visitors to Japan as a thank-you. Don't worry about how to tie these bows, because your gift will be tied and packaged the appropriate way when you buy it, and you can always specify the occasion to the clerk; he or she will know exactly which ribbon to give you. Typically, directly above the knot of the *mizuhiki,* the giver of the gift would write in an inscription celebrating the event, and directly below the knot of the bow, they would also write his or her name. A very traditional additional touch is to add the "seal," or a decoration known as the *noshi,* directly to the right of the inscription, in the upper right-hand corner of the gift. The *noshi* today is usually merely an illustrative symbol of what it originally once was: a thin strip of dried abalone wrapped in red and white paper folded in a very special way. It represents a wish for prosperity and long life.

Special Holidays and Celebrations

Major Holidays

August (the *obon* holiday) is a top vacation time, although most Japanese take only a week or so of vacation; other popular vacation times are from the end of December through January 10 (*oshogatsu*), and Golden Week, which usually falls at the end of April or in early May.

January 1–3	New Year's holiday
January 15	Adult's Day
February 11	National Foundation Day
March 21 or 22	Vernal Equinox Day
April 29	Green Day
End of April/Early May	Golden Week, including Constitution Day, Citizen's Day, and Children's Day
September 15	Respect for the Aged Day
September 23 or 24	Autumnal Equinox Day
October 10	Health and Sports Day
November 3	Culture Day
November 23	Labor Day/Thanksgiving Day
December 23	Emperor's Birthday

Business Culture

Daily Office Protocols

The traditional Japanese office has an open design; there are few doors, with the exception of the offices of those holding higher positions, and people work mainly at long, large tables or in individual or shared cubicles. Doors, if they exist, are usually open. The large tables are usually shared by sections, consisting of workers of the same rank dedicated to a particular project. Each section is usually headed by a manager (*kacho*), with a submanager (*kakaricho*) dedicated to each table. The director, or *bucho,* to whom the *kacho* reports, is commonly in charge of the entire worker floor. In the traditional Japanese office, "office ladies," or OLs (also known as the "flowers of the office"), usually hold the simple clerical positions, or do menial tasks such as pouring tea. (By the way, when providing refreshments in the office, be sure they are served in porcelain tea sets or sake cups: the use of paper or Styrofoam shows disrespect and is very bad form.) Executives are usually on other floors. You probably will not be invited onto the section floors until the proposed project has been set in motion. This is the back office. (By the way, "window people," or the *madogiwazoku,* are not highly respected: they are seated by the window because they are the least important or the most expendable, and are probably preretirement; the key positions, and offices, are physically in the middle of the office layout— with the exception of the executives, who do have larger windowed offices!).

Work beings at 9 A.M. and ends officially at 6 P.M.; but dinners and entertaining are clearly a part of the workday for most. Many businesses have Saturday half-day hours.

Management Styles

The Japanese organizational scheme is rigid and almost militaristic; the levels are as follows:

kaicho	chairman
shacho	president
fuku-shacho	vice president
senmu-torishimariaku	senior executive vice president
jomu-torishimariaku	executive managing director
torishimariaku	director
bucho	division manager
bucho dairi	deputy division manager
kacho	section manager (section chief)
kacho dairi	deputy section manager
kakaricho	section submanager
hira-shain	office workers; section members
office ladies (OLs)	administrative support

Because of this rigid hierarchy, titles are very important. The highest ones (e.g., vice president) are usually reserved for very senior, executive-level positions, and should not be used as casually as they are in the United States.

Compliments and rewards for work done well are usually not given publicly. Deference is shown by subordinates to their seniors; paternalistic concern is often shown by executives to their subordinates (in fact, in more traditional organizations, the company was expected to take care of its workers before it took care of its stockholders, meaning that layoffs due to downturns were not done, and efficiencies designed to produce more with less expense were secondary to making sure that the highest quality and constant perfection processes—*kaizen*—were in place with dependable, well-taken-care-of workers).

Boss-Subordinate Relations

The decision-making system in Japan has been referred to as a "bottom-up" process. It is more formally known as the *ringi seido* system (literally, "reverential inquiry from below of my supervisor's intentions"). Through formal meetings and (most importantly) informal networking, dialoguing, and consensus-building, supervisors inform their subordinates about their goals, feelings, and plans; then, amongst themselves, as a group, the responsible teams set about coming up with solutions to the problem or goal they have been set with. These teams will not risk their supervisor's disapproval, so they perfect their plans before sending the final version upward for their supervisor's acceptance. In most cases, this will mean that all risks will be minimized, and much information needs to be gathered so that everyone involved fully understands the project and can proceed. Once the team produces its results, they are passed upward to its supervisor. The supervisor of a well-functioning team trusts the team's work, and generally approves its recommendations. In this case, the supervisor literally puts his stamp of approval on the team's work (the stamp is placed in a square on a document called a *ringi,* which is then passed on to the next level for approval after the supervisor's staff has had time to review and add their piece to the project). This process is repeated until all appropriate teams have been involved. It can take a long time, but everyone, when it is completed, has intimate knowledge of the project and knows exactly what to do. Decision making is slow, but implementation can be rapid. (For many Westerners, this is a frustrating experience, in that as individualists, they often have made decisions more rapidly on far less information, are more willing to take risks and fix mistakes later, and are not as concerned about full and total consensus; for Westerners, decision making is often rapid, but implementation can be slow.)

Rank most definitely has its privileges, and there is a rigid chain of command that must be respected. No matter what field you are in, there is a hierarchy you must respect—a proper way for communicating with particular individuals, and an expected procedure to follow. Deviating from the proper or expected way will generally make more problems, even if the intent is to bypass what appear to be difficulties or obstacles. Bosses are expected to provide guidance, information, and make decisions; subordinates are expected to provide detailed information and follow the lead of their superiors. While the group protects individual team workers, the supervisor must individually take responsibility for the results, and will publicly take the shame if things turn out badly, but publicly pass the success back down to the group when things turn out well. Traditionally, subordinates usually stay in the office till quite late, certainly later than their boss, to indicate their diligence and hard work.

Conducting a Meeting or Presentation

At your first meeting in Japan, you will probably be received in a very comfortable waiting area, which may or may not be where most of the meeting is conducted between yourself and your colleague. If this is the case, you are merely being sized up, and your colleague is a gatekeeper. At meetings of peers, there can be open communication and sharing of ideas: however, most meetings are formalities at which information is exchanged, or decisions that have already been made are confirmed. Meetings are too risky for open problem solving and decision making, given the group and hierarchy orientation in Japan. If this is just the beginning of a business relationship, expect to spend most of the time sharing information about your organization with different individuals; you may need to repeat the same things to different people. This is okay; it usually means your plans are advancing to the right people in the organization, and that those you have previously met with have approved of you and moved you on. Patience and third-party connections are key.

Negotiation Styles

The first meeting is usually very formal, with the Japanese sizing up you and your organization. Expect no decisions at the table, and be willing to provide copious amounts of information, to the degree that you can, in response to their questions and in anticipation of their needs. Presentations should be well prepared and simply propounded. Details are best left to questions and backup material, which should be translated into Japanese and left behind. Ideally, you should present your material to the Japanese for study, along with a proposed agenda, prior to the meeting. Have extra copies available, as you will meet more people than you expect. You should come with a well-organized team, and the roles of your team should be well thought out. Never disagree with one another in front of the Japanese, or appear uncertain or unsure.

The Japanese dislike bargaining: if the terms are good and the price is reasonable, that is enough. Changing terms at the last minute to make something more attractive implies unreliability and untrustworthiness. If they like you and your product, the price is often secondary as long as it is fair. Although the contract must be legal down to the dotted i's, it is often just a seal of something they have already decided they will do as discussed.

Plan your meetings as carefully and as well in advance as you can, and avoid surprises and any unexpected changes: this makes the Japanese uncomfortable and suspicious. Keep communications, especially when at a distance, open: share more information than you normally would, not less; information overkill does not exist in Japan.

Written Correspondence

Your business letters should be very formal and respectful of rank and hierarchy. Last names are usually written in uppercase; dates are given in the year/month/day format (with periods in between, not slashes), and an honorific plus the title is as common as an honorific plus the last name. You should write your e-mails, letters, and faxes in a precise way: use a brief introduction, then quickly get down to business. Keep it simple, however, and outline all important matters. In Japan, and throughout most of the region, the address is usually given as follows:

Line one: country and postal code
Line two: city (and prefecture)
Line three: street address
Line four: company and/or personal name

The East Asian Cultures: China, Hong Kong, and Taiwan

CHINA

Some Introductory Background on China and the Chinese

First, some sobering facts: there are more people in China learning English today than there are Americans; it is the world's oldest continuous civilization; the statistical variation used when calculating the population of China is greater than the entire population of the United States. Napoléon once said that China is a sleeping giant, and the world had better watch out when it awakens. It has awakened. In true Asian form, somehow the Chinese have managed to reconcile two opposites, Communist political ideology with wild-west capitalist economics, to create what they currently euphemistically call a "socialist market" society. In reality, it is an authoritarian government using ancient Chinese cultural traditions to justify its power and carefully control the free-market forces that are driving their society today. And this society is much larger than China, per se. When we speak of China, we are referring to what was previously thought of as "the mainland," which now currently includes Hong Kong and Tibet. Chinese culture, of course, goes far beyond the mainland; it includes Taiwan and the expatriate Chinese communities that drive the economies of many countries (such as Singapore); in fact, expatriate Chinese are often the economic dynamos of many cities and states, and need to be considered when working in places like Bangkok, Jakarta, and Kuala Lumpur. It is simply impossible to understand these places and behave effectively there without understanding Chinese culture, as it is very likely that interactions in these locations will be with Chinese. We will first look at China, and then at Hong Kong and Taiwan (the former, though newly reunited with the mainland, is still a different culture).

On the mainland itself, we find many Chinese cultures operating more or less in harmony with each other (China's history is, in many ways, the story of the consolidation and maintenance of these various cultures in one nation, and even today, some of the more outlying regions—those of greatest cultural distance from Beijing—pose a challenge of secession and independence) at a time when one of the world's great mass migrations is under way: the movement of millions of people from the traditional agricultural farms of China to discover the new opportunities of the nation's expanding cities. In this sense, while 90 percent of the people today in China are Han Chinese, the Chinese in Shanghai are different from the Chinese in Xingdu. Yet we can find many overarching similarities that unite most Chinese into one single culture, and we will explore those similarities here.

Some Historical Context

Winston Churchill said that China is a civilization in search of a nation. A Chinese colleague of mine, upon hearing this, said, "Yes, and the United States is a nation in search of a civilization." China is an ancient agrarian culture that is struggling to define itself in modern political and economic terms. It is in many ways still a developing nation, yet one which is going through both the industrial and information revolutions practically simultaneously. An ancient symbol that most Chinese are very fond of, the crane, today can be found everywhere, most particularly on the skylines of the cities that are exploding along the coast and throughout the country; however, these cranes are not graceful birds, but the construction devices that seem to put high-rises up overnight. The interplay between ancient Chinese culture and modern China is found everywhere: the lack of infrastructure, but the ubiquitous cellular phone; the modern skyscrapers that are designed according to ancient *feng shui* principles (allowing fortuitous spirits in, keeping menacing spirits out); the new risk-taking capitalist entrepreneur and the old gambling shopkeeper; the predictions from I Ching sticks in a Buddhist temple; and the efforts to control the development of the largest country in the world by a few old men in Beijing. But this is Asia, and opposites, like yin and yang, always go together. Today, Beijing, the administrative center, the agricultural delta along the coast where the great rivers empty (as well as the cities along those rivers), Shanghai, traditionally the commercial and business center of China, and the Guangzhou/Hong Kong region in the south playing the role of ports of entry for the world into China, all fit together into the complexity that is China today.

An Area Briefing

Politics and Government

The old dynastic system that ruled China for most of its history came to an official end in 1911, with the overthrow of the last emperor. For thousands of years, the "government" was a vast bureaucracy of administrators and tax collectors fanning out across the country, all responsible ultimately to the Imperial Court in Beijing. If centralization and bureaucracy were made an art in Europe by the French, its cause was no less advanced in Asia by the Chinese. For thousands of years, dynasties and emperors came and went, with little effect on the country or the people; Chinese history, in this simplistic sense, is the repetitive story of one dynasty replacing another, with no real change occurring. The system was unresponsive to and unrepresentative of the people, and was mainly a self-justifying bureaucracy in ultimate control of daily life, yet out of touch with the people over whom it ruled.

In a sense, since the last official dynasty ended in 1911, with the exception of the brief period of republican government headed by Sun Yat-sen and Chiang Kai-shek, the same system has been put in place, but with a different face. The effort to reform China and create a modern republic ultimately failed under the pressures of corruption, two world wars, invading Japanese, intransigent European colonialists, a worldwide depression, a population with no experience with representative government, and the final challenge by Mao Tse-tung and his Communist followers.

In 1949, the Nationalists (or the Kuomintang, the republican Chinese led by Chiang Kai-shek) retreated from the mainland onto the small island of Taiwan, where today they officially still cling to the idea that they represent all the Chinese people, strenuously object to Beijing's rule, and resist both the ideas of independence and reunification under the Communists. And while Taiwan has been successful as a capitalist economy, in the 1980s, China, too, made a very bold decision to take the same route, while keeping socialist ideology. When the Communists took over in Beijing, they established a bureaucracy similar to the dynastic model, which reached into the lives of all Chinese. Philosophically and culturally, the Chinese were already prepared for a socialist ideology based on communal effort and rigid hierarchy, so replacing older Confucian-driven dynastic hierarchical structures with totalitarian Communist ones was not revolutionary (despite Mao's rhetoric). Even today, in many ways, by allowing free capitalism alongside ideological socialism, the government stays at just enough distance from the people to allow them their day-to-day activities, remains essentially unrepresentative and unresponsive, and intervenes essentially only when necessary to preserve its authority. The government structure today requires that members of the National People's Congress, the unicameral legislature, also be high-ranking members of the Communist Party; since the congress also appoints the Standing Committee, which is made up of the prime minister, the president, and his cabinet, and because one of these positions is also usually held by the secretary-general of the Communist Party, it can be said that the dynastic system, albeit in new robes, is still in place and functioning well in China today.

Schools and Education

Schooling is free and mandatory for all elementary-grade children. The Chinese equivalent of high school follows after grade school, and state-run universities are available to those who qualify academically after high school. Schools do not necessarily, even at the university level, provide the skills or the connections needed for advanced placement in society; that is guaranteed by family affiliation with the Communist Party, and the role that the family has historically played in the politics of its region or China as a whole. Education has always been an essential Confucian ideal, and parents place great hope on the advancement of their children through education. More and more, this also includes girls, although only boys were traditionally privileged to receive an education. Many Chinese students seek to advance their university studies by going abroad to the West; such programs often require that after their studies, these students return to China to bring their knowledge and skills back home. Many do not.

Religion and Demographics

As we will see throughout the rest of eastern Asia, religions are not institution-alized belief systems as they are in the West. The religious influences in China are strong, but they are not religions per se. It would be more correct to refer to them as philosophies of life. No one claims to be only a Buddhist, for example, or a Confucian. Elements of both of these philosophies inform the behaviors and beliefs of most individuals, and of society as a whole. There are no preset times of worship (although there are festivals that occur on certain days through-out the year), and priests—if there are any—do not represent the faithful. East-ern Asian religions are really a compilation of the beliefs, writings, teachings, and thoughts of certain spiritual leaders. The three great religious philosophical influences in China are Taoism, Buddhism, and Confucianism.

Buddhism began in India around 600 B.C. Its founder was Siddhartha Gau-tama, the Buddha, a privileged Hindu priest who, in attempting to learn the meaning of life, discovered, among other things, that his privilege brought him no happiness, and that if one was to achieve true happiness, one had to sacrifice in the secular here and now in specific ways in order to achieve a higher level in the next life. In many ways, the theology that evolved was an effort to purify what had become, in the Buddha's mind and others, a debased and corrupt Hindu religion in India at that time by placing moral responsibility onto the individual, and relying less upon the religious hierarchy. This created, as you may imagine, some difficulty for the Buddha and his followers and the existing Hindu establishment; subsequently, Buddhist beliefs were ultimately integrated into Hinduism and simultaneously officially banished from India. Its principles survived, however, rooting in China, parts of Southeast Asia, and ultimately in Japan. Buddhist traditions in China still reveal themselves in the form of the Chinese dependence on greater forces, whether these forces be fate, ancestors, or the gods that control climate, floods, and the weather. There is a sense that life and the universe is well beyond the understanding and control of mere mor-tals, certainly in the here and now. The form of Buddhism that spread through-out China was mainly Mahayana Buddhism, which emphasized that individuals can, through sacrifice and hard work, attain nirvana and break through the end-less cycles of life and its suffering. By placing the responsibility of achieving nirvana on the individual, Mahayana Buddhism mitigated against other Chinese group-orientation forces, such as those resulting from Confucianism, making Chinese group-orientation less powerful than, say, the small island Japanese group-orientation culture.

Confucianism, based on the teachings of Confucius, a Chinese sage who lived around 500 B.C., has had a powerful impact on Chinese thought. Confucius lived during a turbulent and chaotic time in China, and established a philosophy of life that attempted to prescribe the correct and proper way for individuals to relate to one another in order to achieve a well-ordered, functioning society. The essence of his ideas involves the importance of observing and maintaining structures, roles, and hierarchy, so that, paraphrasing his words, "the son obeys the father, the wife obeys the husband, the younger brother obeys the older brother, the husband obeys the state," and so on. Society will work when every-one knows his or her place, understands his or her obligations to others in the hierarchy, and, in fact, seeks primarily not to change his or her role, but to per-fect it. This provides philosophical support for the rigid hierarchies that have politically and socially existed in China, for the static nature of the society, for the orientation against change for change's sake, for the lack of pressure from a vast population for a representative government, and for the importance of face, honor, and humility. Equally important, it is one of the central reasons for the Chinese dependence on informal networks of relationships and obligations between people (what the Chinese refer to as *guanxi*) instead of legitimate, dependable, and universally rationalized and codified legal systems.

Finally, Taoism, the third philosophical influence, supports many of the fundamental principles of Buddhism and Confucianism. Founded by Lao-tzu around the same time as Confucius, Lao-tzu developed a more spiritually oriented explanation for the nature of the universe, using theories of opposites to explain the reasons for the difficulties of life (remember, the yin-yang symbol is a Taoist symbol). Essentially, all secular activity is a representation of an imperfect existence, and when perfection is achieved, action ceases. This results in, among other things, a belief in the power of passivity (as evidenced in many areas of Chinese life, including the martial arts, for example, where the strength of the opponent is used against him or her, as opposed to a proactive contest of greater individual strength) and a justification for the static nature of the world.

Children are revered in China, and despite a prohibition against couples having more than one child, there is a great desire for more children in families. Boys have traditionally been more valued than girls (a not uncommon phenomenon in agricultural societies where a son working in the field is more useful to a struggling farming family than arranging the wedding of a daughter at a price) but this is changing slowly in China today. Women in China have traditionally played a role in family businesses, and have, under the Communists, been at least nominally made equal to men (in fact, women do hold high positions in government ministries, and in the health and education fields); nevertheless, men do have more opportunities than women. (Non-Chinese businesswomen, on the other hand, are not subject to these constraints, and therefore can succeed or fail in the Chinese business environment as long as their authority is clear and maintained, and as long as they, like all businesspeople in China, follow the cultural requirements for success in China.)

It is important throughout China (and throughout all of Asia) not to assume an Asian is of one nationality or another: while most of the people in China are Han Chinese, many are Mongol, Tibetan, central Asian, Korean, or from other groups. It is best not to assume.

Fundamental Cultural Orientations

1. What's the Best Way for People to Relate to One Another?

OTHER-INDEPENDENT OR OTHER-DEPENDENT? As we saw, while being essentially a group-oriented culture, China also has a powerful tradition of individual responsibility: the peasant farmer and shopkeeper were often alone in the world, having to eke out an existence without the support of the government. There is a powerful sense of self-reliance among individuals, which is often in conflict with greater uncontrollable realities (and a belief in such), including an overarching communal ethic that today is represented in the state. (The state is, in a sense, as were the dynasties, the final and ultimate "group," which is why group orientation in China has often been xenophobic: out-groups stay out, and members within the group are drawn in closer. The great Middle Kingdom of China, seeing itself as the center of the world, is an example of this. Only recently has the leadership of China left the country to go out into the rest of the world; traditionally, if you wanted to do business with the Chinese, you went, as Marco Polo and millions of Westerners after him did, to China.) Dependency upon others often takes the form of communal goals being achieved by many individuals repeating the same task over and over again (think about how the Great Wall was built or how a communal rice field is harvested; there is a saying in Chinese: "Endurance can turn an iron bar into a needle"). This is one of the reasons for the reticence of the Chinese to deal with Western notions of individual rights, and for the West's difficulty understanding Chinese concepts of group rights (as in the duplication of proprietary material for dissemination and profit).

HIERARCHY-ORIENTED OR EGALITY-ORIENTED? Structure and hierarchy are critical at all levels in Chinese society—in the home, at school, in the military, and in business. A Confucian formality has developed around what one does and with whom; it is essential to show the proper respect for individuals, depending on their rank and position, in order to succeed in China. Hierarchy is honored through humility and saving face; this is done by "lowering," or minimizing, oneself. In fact, one makes more of oneself, and raises one's esteem in the eyes of others, by doing so. This emphasis on hierarchy also normalizes unequal relationships: it is, after all, natural (at least according to Confucian ideas) that some be in charge and others not, that some have power and others not, that some dictate and others follow.

RULE-ORIENTED OR RELATIONSHIP-ORIENTED? While there are many rules imposed by the hierarchy from above, the control factor in Chinese society is the relationship between individuals. These important connections, and the obligations that arise from them, is known as *guanxi*. There has historically been little else that one could depend upon in China. There is, even today, no really dependable legal system for redress (civil, business, or otherwise); only recently is there a financial system; there is no representative political system. The one dependable thing in the Chinese world is the spiderlike network of relationships and obligations that one builds with others, usually friends and family. This will determine future action. The Westerner usually accomplishes a task, and is freed by the discharging of his or her responsibility; the Chinese, by taking care of a task, are obligating themselves further with the other person, so that in the future, new action and claims for action can be made. There is little distinction in this universe between professional and personal, and how one behaves professionally is a statement of his or her value to the other personally.

2. What's the Best Way to View Time?

MONOCHRONIC OR POLYCHRONIC? Because punctuality also reflects other values, such as concern for the other person and humility before someone else's efforts, the Chinese are more or less punctual; certainly, you should be. Nevertheless, in the big picture, as with all traditional Asian cultures, time has historically stood in the background to immediate personal relationships; even in modern-day Chinese cities, this is certainly still the case. Things will take the time they need to take, and the clock is not the ultimate arbiter of what occurs and when. Mao Tse-tung was once asked what he thought of the French Revolution; his answer was, "It's too soon to tell." The Chinese will move very quickly to seize an advantage if one presents itself; they certainly want to succeed as quickly as possible, but they will not do anything that is not in their best interest simply because of time. Unless it is on their terms, they have time to wait it out.

Daily life in China has historically been arranged according to vast, agriculturally based blocks of time, over which no individual or government had control: seasons, days and nights. Even today, the workday in China begins fairly early (around 7 or 8 A.M.), and ends early (around 4 or 5 P.M.). Most workers take an hour break and a midafternoon nap after lunch. On balance, China is a polychronic culture, as are most of the cultures of Asia; the clock is not the ultimate reason for action.

RISK-TAKING OR RISK-AVERSE? China is essentially a risk-taking culture. Perhaps this is a result of the need to seize the few fortuitous opportunities that might come one's way from time to time, perhaps it comes from the fact that when one is not in control, one has little to lose, or perhaps it is the result of a removed, distant bureaucracy that enabled the average peasant of the past and businessperson of today to try some things out on their own. Whatever the reason, Chinese society is composed of numerous small entrepreneurs who will generally gamble and take risks when given the chance. This is probably one of the cultural reasons for the resounding success and startling numbers of Chinese immigrant communities around the world.

PAST-ORIENTED OR FUTURE-ORIENTED? Fatalism has always held China back, and the country's history has always seemed to justify the fatalism. Despite the age of the culture, today the average Chinese struggles against the fates, and puts much energy into appeasing those forces over which he or she believe they have little control. The pro-democracy movement and the events of Tiananmen Square on June 3–4, 1989, were, for this reason, both remarkable and predictable. Great stock is placed in fortuitous moments, omens, superstitious practices, and guidance from ancestors, the stars, and sages.

3. What's the Best Way for Society to Work with the World at Large?

LOW-CONTEXT DIRECT OR HIGH-CONTEXT INDIRECT COMMUNICATORS? Context does drive communication in China, but it often allows for direct and confrontational speech. The Chinese can be blunt, and can and do say "no," unlike the Japanese. Nevertheless, the requirements of the essential fundamentals of the culture, such as Confucian hierarchy, humility, respect, and face, require a sensitivity to the context in which the communication occurs. There is a great reliance on symbolic expression, whether verbally or pictorially (after all, the written language is built on this). Speaking symbolically allows one to say more easily what cannot be said directly ("A picture is worth a thousand words" is a Chinese saying). The Chinese also say that "He who says the least says the most."

In this high-context culture, the situation determines the action, in most cases, and not the rules or regulations: this is related to both the polychronic nature of Chinese culture and their reliance on personal relationships. This means that as situations (and the individuals involved in the situations) change, flexibility is required. The terms of a contract signed in January may no longer be applicable in July, if the situation in July is different from the way it was in January; therefore, in July, the Chinese will seek to renegotiate with the trusted business partners what they established in January, often only to be disappointed in the Westerners' resistance to altering the terms of the agreement. As a result, the Chinese often lose trust in Western contracts, and Westerners often believe the Chinese have little regard for contract law. This is part of the reason why the Chinese much prefer short statements of intent, called memorandums of understanding, as opposed to the complex and heavy legal documents of the West, which attempt to control all future aspects of how the business partners will work together in an unpredictable and always changing world.

PROCESS-ORIENTED OR RESULT-ORIENTED? The Chinese, as is the case with all Asian peoples, are fully capable of employing (and do employ) meticulous logic, whether deductively or inductively; however, that is not necessarily the only process used to think things through, to make a case for something, or to understand people or events. A connection is made to the way similar situations have turned out, and in that sense, the Chinese also use associative, subjective logic. However, all forms of logic are used in a more holistic way in Asia, so that while process and experience are important steps in arriving at a conclusion, the path may not be linear or progressive. This is related to the polychronic nature of the culture: things occur, thought patterns included, not necessarily in a sequential or progressive way, but in a holistic way. In other words, the elements needed to make decisions are laid out expositionally, when and as the circumstances require it, and add up to a conclusion only when viewed "at once," as if suddenly from forty thousand feet. Do not search for sequence: search for all the facts that must be brought forward, as the situation deems it, and then sit back and evaluate the total result. (This is one reason why it is essential in China to take good notes at every meeting! What people mean may not be clear at the table, but only upon later contemplation.)

FORMAL OR INFORMAL? Until one is brought into the inside, the Chinese culture is formal and keeps the outsider out; when one has earned respect and trust, and built enough good *guanxi* with important enough people, then one is on the inside, and action can be more spontaneous and informal. The Chinese can move easily and quickly between formal and informal; it is important to begin with an understanding of the culture's formal customs, but be prepared to adjust to informality as the opportunity presents itself.

Greetings and Introductions

Language and Basic Vocabulary

While English is certainly the second language being taught in China, it is for many Chinese not the second language spoken. Most Chinese speak a regional language, called a dialect (it is, in fact, a separate language, in many cases), and have also learned the official spoken language, Mandarin. Mandarin is spoken in Beijing and throughout the north and central regions, but there are over forty different languages spoken in China, including Shanghainese (in the Shanghai central coast region), Hunanese, Yunanese (in the central region), and Cantonese (in the south coastal region) among others.

All spoken forms of Chinese are tonal languages, so the same word spoken with a different tonality may have a different meaning (there are four tones, for example, in Mandarin, and nine tones in Cantonese). Cantonese speakers in Guangzhou cannot converse with Mandarin speakers in Beijing. However, they can read the same text, and this is one of the reasons why the Chinese written language never advanced from an ideograph system to an alphabet. As China was consolidating itself into one cultural entity, communicating across many language barriers was a great obstacle. However, ideographs convey concepts and ideas, not sounds, so that the newspaper that is read in Guangzhou is also understood when read in Beijing. It takes a working knowledge of between two and four thousand ideographs to be effectively literate in Chinese. The learning method is mainly rote memorization. The role of the student is to learn and practice the information provided to him or her by the teacher. Confucian principles further require that the student place the teacher above all else and not question or challenge the teacher. Compare this to Western pedagogy: the challenge for the reader of English is to decipher the sounds the twenty-six letters of the alphabet make to discover the words within, thus emphasizing creativity and problem solving, not rote memorization.

There are no articles in the Chinese language, so it is important to be clear if *the* or *a* is meant, in keeping with the context of the discussion. This is also the case with tenses; there are no past or future tenses, only present, so one conveys when something happens by the context or the use of additional words to further define the tense.

The language is not more difficult to learn than most others, but the rules governing the formation of words and concepts are different from Latin-based languages; this is an especially important issue when it comes to the use of double negatives and the need to avoid asking questions that could result in yes or no answers. In a culture where emphasis is placed on preserving harmony and face, and where much communication is therefore very high-context and subtle, any answer that could imply difficulty, a rejection of a request, or make the respondent appear uncooperative is often evaded. This evasion is expressed in a number of ways nonverbally, but often results in unreliable verbal responses. "Yes" more often means "I hear what you are saying, keep talking," not "I agree with what you are saying." Don't complicate the problem, therefore, by asking questions that require yes or no as an answer: the response will give you no reliable information. Instead, ask open-ended questions that require a substantive, informational response.

Most older Chinese speak little or no English; many of the younger ones do, and do not want to speak Chinese with you in order to practice their English. In business meetings, because the English competency of your Chinese colleagues may be low, it is important to have interpreters—preferably your own—throughout. If you know some Chinese, use it: the Chinese will be grateful and impressed that you have respected them (this is especially true in a toast).

Here are some basic Mandarin terms and their English meanings:

Nee hao ma?	Hello, how are you?
Hen hao!	Fine, thank you.
ni hao	hi
mafan ni	excuse me
zaoshang hao	good morning
wanshang hao	good evening
xie xie	thank you
zaijan	good-bye

In an effort to transliterate the sounds made when Chinese is spoken into a written form that is usable by Westerners, the Chinese devised in the mid-twentieth century the pinyin system of pronunciation, which assigns a Chinese sound to a roman letter. Most of the roman letters retain their original sound, but some are different, representing, in some cases, unique Chinese sounds. Here are the pinyin roman letters with special sounds:

c is pronounced like the *ts* in *its*

e is pronounced like the *er* in *her*

ei is pronounced like the *a* in *way*

i is pronounced like the *e* in *feet,* unless preceded by the letters *r, c, ch, s, sh, z,* and *zh,* in which case the sound is like the *ir* in *sir*

ie is pronounced like the *e* in *yes*

q is pronounced like the *ch* in *check*

u is pronounced like the *oo* in *loop*

x is pronounced like the *sh* in *sheep,* but with the air being sent across more teeth, not just the front

zh is pronounced like the *z* in *azure*

Honorifics for Men, Women, and Children

Chinese honorifics display rank and seniority mainly according to age and not gender. All honorifics appear after the family name. Family names always are placed first, followed by a given generational name, and then finally a given name (placed last). There is often a hyphen between the generational and the given names, making the two given names more often than not a two- (or more) syllable name. Most of the time, the Chinese family name is a single syllable (there are in fact only several hundred family or clan names, so most Chinese have similar family names, with the generational and the given names primarily distinguishing one individual from the other). If Haiying Yang has introduced himself as such, he has reversed the Chinese name format to accommodate the Westerner, putting his given name first and his family name last, Western style (you know this because the two-syllable name, usually the combination of the generational and the given names, is being presented first). You would refer to this person with the correct honorific after Yang, no matter where it appears.

For travelers and businesspeople, the following guide is sufficient:

- *Laoshi:* an honorific for a teacher or mentor (the highest honorific); for example, Li Min-wen becomes Li Laoshi (literally, "Li, the professor")

- Xiansheng: Mr.; for example, Haiying Yang becomes Yang Xiansheng
- Xiaojie: Miss; for example, Zhang Hong-bo becomes Zhang Xiaojie

There are two forms for addressing a married woman. Traditionally, Chinese women did not lose their own family name, nor take their husband's family name. Therefore, traditional (mostly mainland) Chinese married women identify themselves as being married with the honorific *nushi* placed after their own family name. For example, Hong-bo Li would be referred to as Li Nushi (literally, Mrs. Li) when she marries.

Many expatriate and more modernized mainland Chinese women, however, take their husband's name when marrying; this is indicated by the honorific *taitai* placed after the husband's family name. For example, Li Hong-bo could be called Yang Taitai (literally, Madame Yang) after she marries Yang Haiying.

Never use the term *tongzhi* (comrade); it is reserved solely for Communists, and is very out of fashion these days.

Older people with whom one has a close relationship may be referred to with the honorific *lao,* which in this case is placed before the family name. This gives respect and honor to the older person (for example, Lao Tzu, or literally, "Sage Tzu"). Similarly, younger people with whom you have a close relationship may be referred to with the prefix *xiao* placed before the family name; this shows paternalistic care and concern (for example, Xiao Li, or literally, "little Li").

Unless and until your Chinese colleague specifically invites you to use his or her "first" name, and despite how he or she might refer to you, you must always use the family name (it is acceptable not to use the honorific once you have established a personal relationship). Children in China are expected to be respectful and not overly conversational when speaking with adults, and must always use honorifics when referring to adults. As they probably speak limited English, this makes conversation with children that much more difficult.

In situations where a title is known, the title plus the honorific is frequently used, either with or without the name (e.g., Mr. Engineer, or Engineer Li). For casual contacts (e.g., with waiters, store help, etc.), just use *xiansheng* or, more likely, *xiaojie.* It is very important to greet people at work, in stores, or in restaurants in an appropriate fashion for the time of day. Sometimes the Chinese (as well as other Asians) will Anglicize their names when they know they will be working or meeting with Westerners (for example, "Eddie Li"). On occasion they will simply assign a Latin initial as a given first and second name; recognize that this is done for your benefit, and that the name you are being given is not the real name. (This Anglicized version may also appear on that person's business card.)

The What, When, and How of Introducing People

In addition to the introductory vocabulary words above, the following are two very common informal greetings in Chinese. They merely mean "hi," and do not require any substantive response:

Nar qu ya? Where are you going? (Response: "Just down here" or "Just this way.")
Chi le ma? Have you eaten yet? (Response: "Yes, thanks, and you?" or
    "I'll be eating soon.")

Moreover, sometimes upon greeting you, the Chinese will simply call you by your family name, or make a comment about the task you are performing: this also does not require a substantive response.

Always wait to be introduced to strangers; never take that responsibility upon yourself, as doing so is considered inappropriate most of the time. The Chinese are most comfortable with a third-party introduction whenever one is possible, and will go to great lengths to ensure that you are not left alone to decide this for yourself. Never presume to seat yourself at a gathering; if possible, wait to be told where to sit. The seating arrangements have usually been carefully worked out in advance, and in most cases reflect the status of the individuals in the group, and the honor that is being accorded the guests. When departing, it is important to say farewell with a quick bow to every individual present: the American group wave is not appreciated. Once you greet someone you will encounter later that day in the same circumstances (e.g., at the office), you will need to acknowledge them with a quick, foreshortened bow whenever you see them again. Seniors, or those who are obviously the oldest in a group, are greeted first, seated first, and allowed to enter a room first (usually at the center of the group, however, and preceded in most cases by their younger aides).

Physical Greeting Styles

Like many Asian cultures, China is a nontouching culture. Only the most intimate of friends (mainly young people) will touch each other in greeting. The handshake is a Western invention, and not native to China: the Chinese have, of course, become accustomed to it, but because it is done for the Westerner's benefit, it is generally an accommodation added to the Chinese bow and the business card exchange. When the handshake does occur it is more often than not very soft, almost limp. This does not signify insincerity; rather, it is an indication of humility using a Western convention. Western women must always extend their hands first for a handshake, if one is to occur at all; if so, it is inevitably very soft.

The traditional Chinese introduction involves the use of business cards and a bow, though neither is done with the same formality or complexity as the Japanese greeting. Always take a large supply of business cards with you to China: you must give one to every new person you are introduced to (there is no need to provide another business card when you are meeting someone again unless information about you has changed, such as a new address, contact number, or position). Be sure your business cards are in fine shape: they are extensions of you as a person, and must look as good as possible. Never hand out a dirty, soiled, bent, or written-on card. You should, if possible, have your business card translated into Chinese on the reverse side before you go to China (some finer hotels and some airlines, as well as your own business, will do this as a service for you). The traditional card is written in Chinese from top to bottom, and from right to left, with the company name being the first item, the rank and title the second, the name the third, and contact information the last (more modern businesses may organize the information in a more Western format); if you use gold ink in the printing on the Chinese side, it will indicate respect for them. When presenting a business card, you give it to your Chinese associate with the Chinese side up so that it is readable for him as you hold it (he will, in turn, present his card with the English side up, so it's readable for you); you must hold the card in the upper right- and left-hand corners, requiring the use of two hands, and you also receive your Chinese associate's card with two hands, on the upper right- and left-hand corners. The exchange is done quickly, almost simultaneously. Accompanying the exchange of the cards is a small bow. The traditional Chinese bow requires both men and women to place the right fist in the palm of the left hand, and hold both hands at stomach level, while bowing deeply. This is not done as dramatically as it used to be, nor is it expected of Westerners. It is perfectly appropriate for Westerners simply to bend their waists slightly and drop their heads in a nodlike action as they exchange the cards.

Smiling and other nonverbal forms of communication usually accompany the card exchange; it is appropriate to appear genuinely pleased to meet the other person. When first introduced to your Chinese colleague, make immediate eye contact, but as soon as the card exchange begins, and definitely when the bow commences, drop your eyes so that they are looking to the ground (this demonstrates respect for the other person).

Information about each other's status is the most important information to be exchanged, and this is provided directly on the business card, as well as indirectly through a number of high-context indicators, such as gray hair (usually indicating age), gender (usually male), and the number of people surrounding and assisting the other person (important people are usually surrounded by assistants). Humility before rank can be demonstrated subtly, by placing your business card underneath the card of the other person during the exchange. Once you have received the other person's card, it is important to stand upright again, holding the card with two hands, and silently read the card for a few seconds. Then say his name (this is an opportunity for him to correct you if you mispronounce it, and for you to do the same for him) and his title in a way that indicates your respect for him and his position. It is at this point that your eyes may meet again for a moment, as you extend your hand for a soft Western handshake. All this occurs rather quickly, and you will inevitably meet many Chinese at once, so you will have a handful of cards when it is over.

As this ritual usually precedes a sit-down meeting, it is important to arrange the cards you have received in a little seating plan in front of you along the top of the desk or the table at your seat, reflecting the order in which people are seated. This will help you connect the correct names with the correct individuals throughout the meeting. During the meeting, it is important never to play with the business cards (do not write on them—ever!); and when the meeting is over, never put them in your back pants pockets: pick them up carefully and respectfully, and place them neatly in your business card holder (a nice-looking leatherbound or brass case would be perfect), then place the card holder in the left inside jacket pocket of your suit (nearest your heart). By the way, if you are applauded while making a presentation in China, it is customary for you to applaud back to the audience.

Communication Styles

Okay Topics / Not Okay Topics

Okay: anything that reflects your personal interests and hobbies, or your curiosity about things Chinese, especially food! The Chinese regard food as "the first pleasure," and Chinese cuisine is rightly ranked as one of the world's greatest.

The Chinese love to talk about children (not their own, however; and do not comment about the country's one-child-per-family policy). Sticking to general themes of personal interest or business is fine; it is a way of seeking common ground. There will be no need to begin a conversation with the very American "So, what do you do?" since you already know this from the business card exchange; however, further discussions about your company and its work are very much appreciated, as this gives the Chinese a chance to learn more about you and your firm. The goal of all conversation, at least at the beginning, is to create and maintain a harmonious atmosphere, despite the difficult or confrontational nature of the topic being discussed. At first, speak about things that you believe you have in common, so that you can build a personal connection, which will go far toward maintaining a harmonious bridge between you. This is appropriate for both individuals and organizations. ***Not okay:*** Politics, current events, or any subject that might in any way be controversial needs to be avoided at first. Do not inquire about a person's occupation or income in casual conversation, although it may be inquired of you (if so, this is just a way of getting to know more about your country, and not a personal investigation: answer specifically, and fully, with an explanation as to what things cost at home, why you do what you do, etc.). Do not inquire about your colleague's family life. Do not give your opinions about the Communist Party, or comment on World War II, or discuss China's goals for the region. Avoid current Chinese difficulties with your home country (e.g., proprietary rights issues for Westerners). Conversations about sex are absolutely taboo (although China is not a Puritanical society, sex is a very private matter and embarrassing to discuss openly): do not discuss religion, either, as this Western concept may not actually be understood.

Tone, Volume, and Speed

At first, in more formal situations, the tone is quiet and hushed. Speak slowly, for the benefit of those translating, in short phrases, and speak clearly. Try to speak expositionally, without emotion, if possible. As words are for the most part not the best vehicles for communication when different languages are spoken, use pictures, graphics, and charts to augment the topic being discussed, whenever possible. Illustrate what you can say, and certainly what you cannot. This is a very symbol-oriented culture.

However, as you get deeper into your discussions, and as relationships are built, the Chinese will become direct and animated. On the street and in restaurants, the noise level can be exceptionally high: remember, the Chinese love firecrackers on New Year's!

Use of Silence

Passive silence—allowing time to pass simply, without words—can be a form of proactive communication in China, but not as profoundly so as in Japan. There may be long pauses between comments, but rarely extending over several minutes. When confronted with silence, for whatever reason, the best response is to remain silent yourself, although this may be difficult and appear unproductive for time-conscious Westerners. This is perhaps the most subtle form of communication, yet communication it is. If you must say something, bring up something positive, even if it is unrelated to the previous statement. Remember, in Asia, "silence is golden"; those who speak too much are considered imma-ture, given how careful one must be with what one says. Because some West-erners find silence disconcerting, they may tend to fill up the space with more talk; resist this impulse, as it only enhances the effectiveness of the silence, by forcing the Westerner to say more than he or she might normally be inclined to, and goes a long way toward achieving the Chinese goals of the meeting, which in many cases, in the early stages, is simply to gather as much data and infor-mation as possible.

Physical Gestures and Facial Expressions

In China, there is considerably less physical gesturing of any kind. If you have a tendency to speak with your hands, you will consciously have to try to control it: most of the time, such gesturing is considered excessive, and will engender surprise, laughter, and sometimes anger. In fact, laughter may or may not be in response to anything humorous in the Western sense (jokes may not be under-stood). Winking, whistling, and similar displays are considered very vulgar. Pub-lic displays of familiarity and affection with the opposite sex are expressed only by teenagers. When physically coming between or passing people, it is appro-priate to bow slightly as you go by.

Waving and Counting

The pinkie represents the number 1, and the thumb represents the number 5, with everything in between ordered from the pinkie down; however, instead of raising the fingers when counting, the whole hand is exposed, and each finger is depressed as the counting is done. It is very insulting to motion to someone with the forefinger; instead, turn your hand with the palm facing down and motion inward with all four fingers at once. If you need to gesture for a waiter, very subtly raise your hand. Waving or beckoning is done with the palm down and the fingers moving forward and backward in a kind of scratching motion. It may seem as if the person making this motion is saying good-bye to you, when in fact you are being summoned over.

Physicality and Physical Space

Most Chinese stand, relative to North Americans, just a little farther apart; resist the urge at first to move in closer. Never, upon first greeting a Chinese, touch him beyond the soft handshake: no backslaps, no hugging, no kissing, *ever.* Never speak with your hands in your pockets: always keep them firmly at your side. If men and women must cross their legs when they sit, it must never be ankle over knee; for women, the preferred style is to cross ankle over ankle. Remember, in public, formal is always better than informal: no gum chewing, *ever;* don't slouch; and don't lean against things. The Chinese are very formal when they sit and stand in business settings. Once close relationships are estab-lished, and especially in those moments when spontaneity and friendliness are allowed (such as at a bar or walking down the street after an evening meal), there may be much physicality—touching, for example, or putting arms around other people's shoulders, or holding hands—but generally only between members of the same sex, and not in public between members of the opposite sex. About the only time this nonphysicality rule between strangers is broken is on public transport, where it is very crowded and touching is unavoidable, or on crowded streets, where you are very likely to be poked and prodded as people jostle by.

Eye Contact

Eye contact is generally indirect. Only upon the first introduction do eyes meet, and respect and humility is demonstrated, whenever necessary, by lowering the eyes. The eyes are used extensively to convey true feelings in formal situations where it may be difficult to express certain ideas verbally. Tune up your nonverbal antennae.

Emotive Orientation

Emotional exchanges can be subtle, or they can be direct and profound. The Chinese can be quiet and sedate, but if they feel offended, or that they are being used, they can very loudly censure you, and can become very emotive. Westerners should not act the same in kind; it is important for the Westerner to consciously control emotive impulses, and keep them in check.

Protocol in Public

Walking Styles and Waiting in Lines

On the street, in stores, and in most public facilities, people pay little attention to maintaining orderly lines. Due to the volume of passengers on public transportation, there can be much pushing and jostling. This is generally not to get into a train or bus ahead of someone else; it is merely to get in!

Behavior in Public Places: Airports, Terminals, and the Market

Customer service is catching on in China, because the "other" (in this case, the customer) is so important, and because providing service involves showing deference to the customer. Stores in the cities are open in the evenings and on weekends, as well as during the day. A personal thank-you to store owners, waiters, chefs, and hotel managers for their services is very much appreciated. In food markets, don't worry about touching the produce, since everybody does, and it doesn't obligate you to buy it; but in goods stores, if you buy a product and have problems with it, returning the item is usually difficult. Smoking is endemic, and you may have difficulty finding a no-smoking area on public transportation, in restaurants, and in other public places. Bathroom facilities can range from Western-style toilets to Asian-style toilets (holes in the floor, with buckets of water or hoses attached to a water line for cleanup instead of paper); be prepared. Westerners may want to think twice about using public transportation when private transportation is typically inexpensive and plentiful.

When answering a phone, say *"Nee hao"* ("hello") or just your family name. Cell phones are ubiquitous, as the wire networks are unreliable or nonexistent.

Bus / Metro / Taxi / Car

Driving is on the right, and whether in the country or city, being in a car can be hazardous to your health. The roads are not necessarily in good repair, marked, or where maps say they are. Government roadblocks are frequent, and obtaining fuel when and where you need it can be a problem.

The metros shut down after 11 P.M. or midnight. The best way to catch a cab is at designated taxi stands (hotels are good places, but often charge more for the same ride: a hotel surcharge is added to the meter fare, in some cases). When a taxi has been hailed, negotiate the price, as the meter may or may not be working (even if it is, it doesn't always matter). Addresses in big cities like Shanghai can be maddeningly illogical (in part due to the massive amount of construction going on, and the traditional system of demarcating neighborhoods and intersections as well as streets), and even taxi drivers are often mystified: whenever possible, have the address you need to get to written down on a piece of paper (or use the business card of the person you are going to see, if you can) before you hail the cab. A small map outlining the route is great, if you can have one prepared before you go.

Tipping

Tipping is still technically illegal in China: don't worry about tipping. It is not done. Period. There is no need to leave any odd change.

Punctuality

While China is essentially polychronic, punctuality is expected in most situations. Do not arrive more than five minutes early—or more than five minutes late, for that matter. (Your Chinese associates may arrive sooner, however; this is due to the fact that they are eager to meet with you. Moreover, getting around in China today can take some time, and is usually filled with unexpected delays.) You will not be told if your tardiness has caused a problem, of course, but in most cases, it will not help your image. When a meeting is over in a Chinese office, it is best to leave the room before the Chinese do, as they may need to discuss your proposal for quite some time after you leave. Do not expect them to always see you out.

Dress

People who stand out because of their dress are not thought of highly. Clothes should be used as a way of fitting in, not standing out. The standard is neither very formal, nor informal, no matter the occasion—business or social, at work—in the restaurant, or on the street, for men and women. Style is not that important; until recently, all workers had standard issued uniforms. At work, male managers wear dark suits, white shirts, and subdued ties, and the shoes should be polished; but accessories are not often worn, beyond a watch. Women can accessorize somewhat, but most often dress simply in a business suit or dress of a conservative length and low heels. On the street, informal may mean jeans and sneakers, though that is more common as clothing to wear at the gym or while jogging (some women do wear sneakers to work, but change just before they enter the office, not after going in); for a social gathering, informal more often than not means tastefully coordinated clothes, sometimes including a jacket and tie for men (it rarely means jeans, sneakers, and T-shirts). "Formal" usually means dressy business suits.

Seasonal Variations

There are four extreme seasons in China, as well as several distinct regions—a warmer south, a colder north, and a dry west. Geographically and climatically, China is similar to the United States——it is almost the same size in miles—and one needs to dress accordingly. The summers can be hot and very humid, with frequent rain; the winters can be damp, snowy, and cold; spring and autumn can be delightful, however.

Colors

Wear neutral colors whenever possible.

Styles

For the most part, the Chinese tend to dress with more of an eye toward conformity than toward making an individual statement. Schools still insist on regulation uniforms, and the desire to conform in appearance is reflected at the workplace, as well. Regional traditional dress is rare in modern China today, and is usually reserved for special occasions, rituals, or entertaining.

Accessories / Jewelry / Makeup

Public attempts to attract the opposite sex, call attention to oneself, or make oneself particularly noticeable in a way that clearly calls attention to oneself are definitely not acceptable in China. The right makeup, hairstyle, and accessories, therefore, are important for women, but must not be excessive. Perfume and cologne are not very popular.

Personal Hygiene

In China, personal hygiene is very important. There is a real concern for cleanliness and smelling good, but what smells good and bad to the Chinese may be different from Westerners. The Western diet relies heavily on dairy products, which are used minimally in China (except for yogurt in the north and the west). Throughout the region, the smell of dairy products on individuals is considered offensive, while there is usually no concomitant concern for the smell of other foods, such as garlic or seafood, etc. Do not blow your nose in public: it is considered very rude (if you must blow your nose in public, never use a handkerchief; try disposable tissues). Many Chinese do, however, spit on the street. At the end of a meal, it is perfectly acceptable to use a toothpick, but you must cover the "working" hand with the other hand, so that others cannot see your mouth.

Dining and Drinking

Mealtimes and Typical Foods

The typical Chinese diet revolves mainly around the local foods, mostly rice and noodles. The north is more of a noodle culture, since wheat is grown there, and the south is more of a rice culture, since that is where rice grows. Chinese cuisine reflects these regional differences, and can be as varied as any other major cuisine in the world. Due to the history of recurring famines and droughts, food is a major concern in the daily life of average Chinese, and they have learned to make the most out of the least, including ingredients that may be quite challenging to those unfamiliar with the local produce. It seems as if the Chinese are, in fact, always eating. This is not the case, of course, but there is a great love for good food in China, and as a foreigner, you will be served their best. Although the Chinese are becoming increasingly familiar with Western food, they love their cuisine the best, and most enjoy a fine Chinese meal (if you are hosting them in your country, unless they directly express an interest in trying a local cuisine, take them to the best local Chinese restaurant you can find, and tell the restaurant manager that you are hosting some important Chinese national guests: they will go out of their way to make the meal very fine for you). Avoid Western food, especially cheese: the taste is unpleasant to most Chinese.

Breakfast is served from about 7:30 to 9 A.M., and usually consists of tea and rice; the latter is served either as a porridge-type cereal (congee) that can be flavored with any number of ingredients, with eggs in a variety of styles, or with seafood, chicken, or pickled vegetables. Tea in China, as elsewhere in the region, is usually drunk without sugar, milk, or lemon.

Lunch was traditionally the main meal of the day, and even today, in busy cities, it can still be an elaborate affair with several courses—or it can be a simple noodle dish bolted down in a matter of minutes. Lunch is served from about noon to 1 P.M., and consists of meat, fish, and/or vegetables, with rice and/or noodles. Lunch can also be a large serving of hot broth or soup, made with a variety of ingredients. Many dishes can be steamed, stir-fried, or boiled in a variety of different ways, either simply or more elaborately. Typically, the drinks served with lunch and dinner are water, beer, and/or tea.

Dinner is served from 6 P.M. on, with 7 P.M. the customary late time. Even if the main meal of the day was lunch, dinner is only slightly lighter—this is often the case with families at home. The formal dinner menu is often similar to that of the more formal lunch. Dinner drinks may begin with *mao tai* (a very potent clear rice liquor), served alone or with appetizers, then move on to beer or wine during the meal, and end with a sweet wine and/or tea.

The business dinner mainly takes the form of the Chinese banquet; this is an important aspect of doing business in China, and one which needs to be taken very seriously. Women are expected to partake in the evening's business entertainment as long as they are seen by the Chinese as equal business partners.

THE CHINESE BANQUET. The cuisine will be mainly representative of the region in which you are staying, but will also often include dishes from other regions, particularly famous Chinese dishes such as Peking duck or winter melon soup. It usually begins rather early, at around 6 or 6:30 P.M., and lasts for two hours or so. It begins when the host invites everyone to eat, and ends rather quickly with the host announcing after the last course that it was his pleasure to have had everyone there with him tonight. You are then expected to leave. There may be very little conversation during the meal, as the Chinese really are there, first and foremost, to enjoy the food. Be sure to take just a little on your plate, as there can be anywhere from six to fifteen different courses; often the best dish is served later on or last in the meal. You will, in most cases, have a setting of small plates, plus a separate rice bowl, preventing you from loading too much onto the plate at any one time. Traditionally, the banquet begins with little sweet treats and ends with a special dessert soup (just the reverse from the West!). There is an order to the banquet; the dishes usually proceed as follows, each one being a prelude to the grander dish that follows:

- appetizer morsels (sweet dumplings, etc.)
- vegetables (of all sorts—steamed, braised, but rarely raw)
- seafood (not fish; usually shrimps, lobsters, sea cucumber, snails, etc.)
- meats (chicken, duck, pork; usually a variety, starring a regional favorite of each—e.g., Peking duck)
- fish (usually the highlight of the meal, especially a grand *garoupa* (usually grouper), prepared with wonderful herbs and sauces. Fish are usually served whole; that is, with the head, skins, and fins. Eat the fish as one would in the West; that is, remove the skin on one side, and debone the skeleton, but never remove the head or tail. (Also taboo: never flip the fish over to get to the meat on the other side. It is considered bad luck; if you deboned the skeleton properly, you should not have to flip the fish over to get to the remaining meat.)
- soup (a grand finale, usually of winter melon, with delectably subtle flavors)
- dessert (sometimes served as a nod to Western habits: it is usually not very sweet and can be a disappointment, from the Western perspective; but it can sometimes be a remarkable adventure of soy custards, fried frog's fat, and other exotic delectables. At best, it is a simple and wonderful assortment of fresh fruits, like litchi, oranges, and mangosteens, and perhaps the odiferous but tasty king of Asian fruits, the durian.)

Compliments are expected. Praise the food throughout, as well as the wisdom and taste of your host. Leave controversial topics and business matters for later. Be diplomatic. Be pleasant. Be humble, and appreciative of the bounty prepared in your honor, and don't hesitate to say so. This is probably one of the few times the Chinese will accept your compliments without denying them.

Regional Differences

As a quick overview:

• Northern Chinese cuisine (Beijing): The foods from the north are usually rich and the cuisine is very haute, as in Peking duck. These are sophisticated Mandarin dishes, with a tendency to oily sauces.

• Shanghai cuisine (central): The foods typically found midway down the belly of China, and on the coast, emphasize seafood and fish, fried and home-style preparation, and generally are accompanied by sauces on the slightly sweet side.

• Cantonese cuisine (Guangzhou/Hong Kong): In the tropical south, along the coast, the emphasis is on fresh, fresh, fresh: seafood, fish, and vegetables are served in sauces that are very subtle and usually mild, in order to let the freshness stand out.

• Szechuan/Hunan cuisine (central region): The emphasis in foods from the south-central region is on preserving the harvests and meats through the tough winters. This means salted and spicy foods, with bold flavors.

Typical Drinks and Toasting

The most common liquor is *mao tai,* made from fermented rice. It is best drunk at room temperature, neither warmed nor chilled, in individual small glasses. Because you must never pour your own drink (be it *mao tai,* beer, or tea), you must always be alert throughout the meal as to whether your neighbor's cup or glass needs refilling. If it is less than half full, it needs refilling; alternately, if yours is less than half full, your neighbor is obliged to refill it. If he or she does not, do *not* refill it yourself, for this will cause your neighbor to lose face; instead, diplomatically indicate your need by pouring a little more drink into your neighbor's glass, even if it doesn't really need it. *Mao tai* is drunk in shots.

The toast in China is *gambai,* which means "bottoms up" or "drain the glass." *Mao tai* can be strong, so go slow. So what to do if you don't drink? It really isn't an insult to refuse one, as long as you have a reasonable explanation. I've heard people say, "My doctor doesn't advise me to drink just now," or "It's my ulcer" (Asians, particularly the Japanese and Chinese, are keenly aware of stomach problems since such ailments are quite common there, and are receptive to such explanations; however, once such information is shared, be prepared to be offered all sorts of remedies that they absolutely insist will work, and that you might want your own doctor to check out before using), and any number of other little white lies. Many liquors are made in China for medicinal purposes, some from the most amazing plants and creatures (and their selected parts!), all with specific curative powers, so it's no wonder that the Chinese will insist that drinking *mao tais* with them is a healthy experience. You can decide that the next morning.

If you are the honored guest, you will be expected to make a toast, usually soon after the host does or at the end of the meal, just before everyone departs. An appropriate toast is to the health of the host and all those present, and to the prosperity of the business that brought you together.

Avoid drinking tap water anywhere in China (this means you should brush your teeth with bottled water and not take ice in any of your drinks; drink only bottled water, or brewed tea or coffee or soft drinks, and avoid getting water from the morning shower into your mouth; and never eat fresh fruits or vegetables that cannot be peeled first, and ideally cooked later before eating). This is a serious matter: there are some very nasty bugs going around in developing countries.

Table Manners and the Use of Utensils

China is one of the traditional chopstick cultures, along with Japan and Korea. Please see the information about proper chopstick use in the chapter on Japan; it is appropriate in China as well. There is one major difference, though; Chinese chopsticks are usually round, as opposed to the more square-sided Japanese kind, and do not come attached (they do not require snapping apart).

Proper chopstick etiquette means no waving chopsticks around aimlessly over different dishes trying to select what you want, no sticking the chopstick ends into the food like a spear, and no drawing the bowl or plate nearer to you with your chopsticks. Chinese chopsticks are rarely presented in paper wrappers, so unless you have little ceramic chopstick rests, you need to rest the "mouth" end of your chopsticks alongside the plate, the idea also being that the food end of the chopsticks should never touch the table. Use chopsticks to eat soup (see the chapter on Japan for the proper technique), rice, peanuts, and practically every item on your plate, no matter how small, round, or difficult. Never use your fingers; *always* use your chopsticks. Really. Also use your chopsticks to cut up pieces of food, if necessary; remember, the meat or fish is cooked or marinated, so it will be easy to break up the flesh with the chopsticks: there will be no need for knives. If you simply cannot master chopsticks, it's perfectly all right in the major cities in China to ask for Western cutlery: you will get a spoon and a fork (rarely a knife); just keep in mind that Western cutlery may not be available in the smaller towns.

While rice is a staple, it is not necessary to eat every grain of rice in your bowl; leaving some is fine. Also, sauce may be mixed with the rice, and the main dish may be eaten with the rice, unlike the practice in Japan. You are expected to hold the rice bowl by your mouth, take a bit of food and sauce from the plate below, hold it over the rice bowl, and shovel it all in together. If you're eating noodles or broth, it is not appropriate to slurp the food; however, hot tea may be slurped quietly to cool it off as it enters the mouth.

So there you are, being served "everything" at the Chinese banquet: thousand-year-old eggs, duck feet marinated in blood, fried frog's fat (a tasty dessert), the works, and trying it all. Good for you. And then, after putting a morsel of sea cucumber into your mouth, you suddenly realize that it is not a vegetable, nor does it chew like a fish. What to do? Same problem with that gristle and bone from the chicken that's been hacked, bones and all, into bite-size pieces. Same problem with the claws from the chicken feet you've been nibbling—now they're caught in your teeth. In rural restaurants, and in people's modest country homes, throughout Asia, the traditional response has been to spit the bones or gristle out, sometimes onto the floor; sometimes, onto the table. To be fair, in modern Chinese cities, this custom is strongly frowned upon, but it exists to a greater extent than many Western sensibilities can tolerate. If napkins are available (at modern Chinese banquets they indeed are, but they may not be in all restaurants throughout the country), simply place the napkin to your mouth and remove the unsavory item. Keep it in the napkin until you can dispose of it discreetly.

Because the banquet is a communal affair, with enormous numbers of dishes set out for everyone to enjoy, each dish usually comes with its own set of serving chopsticks, which are to be used by everyone, one person at a time, to serve themselves or their neighbor by picking out the food from the main service and placing it on their plate. You must never keep the serving chopsticks after using them; put them back on the main dish after you're done. But sometimes the dishes are presented without serving chopsticks at all. This means that you have to serve yourself with your own chopsticks. This further means that everybody at the table will be sticking their already used chopsticks into the communal dish. For germ-obsessed Westerners, this can sometimes be a problem. If you're considered part of the family, and if you're at someone's home, it will simply be expected that you stick your chopsticks into the main dish like everybody else. As China has modernized, however, a trend has developed of "reversing" the ends of your chopsticks to take food from the serving plate if serving chopsticks are unavailable. It's tricky, but considerate. It goes like this: Hold your chopsticks by the pointy end and pick up food from the main service with the "blunt" end, then place the food on your plate. After that, place the chopsticks down on their rests. When you're ready to eat from your own plate, pick up the chopsticks so that the "food" end is ready, and eat as you normally would. It's sometimes a little tricky holding chopsticks that have been used on both ends, but it's a lot trickier surviving someone else's gastrointestinal infection, or facing down the stares from your table guests who are worried about catching yours.

In this same vein, all throughout China and most parts of Asia you will see people more or less discreetly using toothpicks at the end of the meal. The best way to handle a toothpick is to work away at your teeth with one hand, while keeping the other hand in front of it over the mouth, as a sort of mask. If you cover the working hand this way, you can join in the toothpick session in public at the end of the meal with the best of them! Just never do it walking down the street: that's simply not done.

A word about smoking: it is ubiquitous all throughout Asia. At the banquet, smoking is usually done only at the end (not in between courses).

Seating Plans

The most honored position is at the middle of the table, with the second most important person seated next. This means that the host will sit at the middle of the table on one side, and the honored guest in the middle on the other side, opposite the host. (Spouses are usually not invited to business meals, and most formal meals in restaurants are business meals: do not ask if your spouse can join you; it will embarrass your Chinese colleague into doing something that is uncomfortable for him.) The honored guest sits on the side of the table farthest from the door. (This is the same at business meetings, with the key people sitting in the middle, flanked on either side in descending order by their aides, with the least important people sitting at the ends of the table farthest from the middle, and closest to the door; the arrangement is mirrored on the other side, because the rules of hierarchy demand that everyone must be able to speak with their opposite peers and those who rank below, but those below cannot speak with those above.) Because many banquet tables are round, a curious situation often develops: the least important person from one side ends up sitting next to the host or the most important person on the other side. (This is usually not an issue at business meetings, where tables are more often rectangular.) If women are present, they will probably be given the honored positions first, although practically speaking there will be far fewer women. In China, women typically rise when men enter the room, hold doors open for men, and escort men into a room first.

Refills and Seconds

You will always be offered more food. Leave a bit on your plate if you do not want more food. If you want more at a banquet, merely move the lazy Susan around slowly (after making sure that no one else is preparing to do the same at the same time!). You will be implored to take more two or three times, in the form of a little ritual. The game is as follows: first you refuse, then the host insists, then you refuse again, then the host insists again, and then you finally give in and take a little more. Usually the host will be apologizing to you for the terrible food and begging you to take it anyway to make him feel better. If you really don't want more, take very little and leave it on your plate. You may always have additional beverages; drink enough to cause your cup or glass to be less than half full, and it will generally be refilled. A reminder: never refill your own glass; always refill your neighbor's glass, and he or she will refill yours.

There is a curious custom associated with tea, unique mainly to the south of China (the Hong Kong/Guangdong area) that needs to be explained. I was first introduced to it at a dinner on a floating restaurant in Hong Kong: mysteriously, my Chinese friend across the table seemed to get his tea refilled almost automatically while I sometimes had to wait. Then I noticed that each time the waiter came round to fill his cup, my friend would tap the table slightly with his index and middle finger, and make a subtle forward rolling motion with those fingers. He noticed that I was watching this and offered a most wonderful story for a very common custom. Tapping the first two fingers on the tabletop in southern China is a way of saying "thanks," and then rolling the same two fingers forward is a way of adding a special humility to the gesture. A long time ago, so he explained, the emperor was traveling through this area of China, a long way from the Forbidden City. Now, emperors, when traveling, needed to do so incognito, else they would have been recognized. So the emperor disguised himself and went into a restaurant for a meal. However, he was traveling with his entourage, who still felt the need to demonstrate subservience and humility to him, even though he was disguised and in public. One of his ministers, therefore, devised a clever system of demonstrating obeisance in public without giving away the charade: whenever he felt the need to demonstrate deference to the mighty emperor, he would tap his fingers on the table and roll them forward, imitating the bow and kowtow (literally, "bending toward the earth"). This quickly became a way of showing appreciation, humility, and, at least today in southern China, thanking the waiter for bringing a little more *cha* (tea) for the cup.

At Home, in a Restaurant, or at Work

In China, it is expected before you begin eating or drinking anything that you say "*youyi*" (basically, "here's to friendship"), and after the meal that you thank the host. Remember, it's best not to drink or eat until your Chinese host does; in fact, throughout the meal, try to follow the colleagues's lead in when to drink, eat, or make a toast.

In informal restaurants, you may be required to share a table. If so, do not force conversation; act as if you are seated at a private table. Waitstaff may be summoned by making eye contact; waving or calling their names is very impolite. The business breakfast is really unknown in China. The business lunch is catching on somewhat, but dinner or a banquet is the proper venue for business hosting. It is generally not the time to discuss business or make business decisions, however. Take your cue from your Chinese associates: if they bring up business, then it's okay to discuss it, but wait to take your lead from their conversation.

When invited to a Chinese colleague's home for a formal meal, you will be told where to sit, and there you should remain. It is a great honor to be invited into a Chinese home, because many Chinese feel that Westerners will find their homes too small and crowded; also, older family members might be living there, and your presence will probably make things uncomfortable for you and them (no mutually intelligible language!). Once invited to enter a Chinese home, you will need to remove your shoes (this is not the custom in Chinese restaurants, however). Once inside the home, do not wander from room to room: much of the house is really off-limits to guests. If you move from room to room in a Chinese home, be sure to always allow the more senior members of your party to enter the room ahead of you. Be judicious about touching things and moving them about: many items have probably been placed where they are because it is auspicious to do so according to *feng shui,* a common tradition in the south of China. Objects are placed, and buildings and rooms designed, so that bad spirits are kept out and good spirits are invited in. The judicious placement of mirrors, which reflect bad spirits, and water, which attracts good spirits, as well as sculptures and other items, is important in *feng shui.* Even the most sophisticated people take this quite seriously.

Being a Good Guest or Host

Paying the Bill

Usually the one who does the inviting pays the bill, although the guest is expected to make an effort to pay. Sometimes other circumstances determine the payee (such as rank). Making payment arrangements ahead of time so that no exchange occurs at the table is a very classy way to host, and is very common. When men are present at the table, women will not really be able to pay the bill at a restaurant: if you want to, make arrangements ahead of time, and don't wait for the check to arrive at the table. The only time it is considered appropriate for a woman to pay the bill is if she is a businesswoman from abroad.

Transportation

It's a very nice idea, when acting as the host, to inquire ahead of time as to whether your guests will require transportation. If necessary, you should arrange for taxi service at the end of the meal. When seeing your guests off, you must remain at the entrance of the house or the restaurant, or at the site where you deposited your guests into the car, until the car is out of sight: it is very important not to leave until your guests can no longer see you, should they look back. Guests are seated in cars (and taxis) by rank, with the honored guest being placed in the back directly behind the front passenger seat; the next honored position is in the back behind the driver, and the least honored position is up front with the driver.

When to Arrive / Chores to Do

If invited to dinner at a private home, offer to help with the chores, but do not expect to be taken up on your offer. Nor should you expect to visit the kitchen. Do not leave the table unless invited to do so. Spouses might be invited to dinners at a private home, because another person's spouse will probably be there. Be on time. When in someone's home, be careful not to admire things too effusively: the Chinese may feel obligated to give it to you, and you in turn will then be required to present them with a gift of equal value. Instead of saying things like "I love that vase," say something like "Vases that beautiful in my country are only found in museums." Your compliments will always be dismissed ("*Bu hao, bu hao*"—not good, not good) because of the humble nature of the Chinese: if you compliment a child, you will be told that he does not do well enough in school; if you say the house is lovely, you will be told it is too small; if you say the food is delicious, you will be told that it didn't turn out quite as well as it should have, but that it is hoped you will try it, for the host's sake, just the same.

Gift Giving

In general, gift giving in China is not as formal as it is in Japan, but it is still common. In business settings, it usually takes the form of personal gifts that symbolically say the correct thing about the nature of the relationship. When going to China on business, you must bring gifts for everyone you will see. The general rule is pastries for the office staff, high-quality corporate logo items (all the same) for business associates, and an especially thoughtful, somewhat personalized gift for the key man you will be working with. Your gifts do not have to be elaborate or expensive; in fact, practical housewares (small kitchen items) or stationery are most appreciated as thank-yous for being served dinner at someone's home. You present your gifts at the beginning of your first meeting in China, as a sign of your sincerity and best wishes. You will receive a farewell gift at your last meeting in China before you leave to go home, or when you present your gifts. When the Chinese visit your country, they will bring you a gift, and before they leave, you should give them gifts. Holiday cards are appropriate for less formal relationships, particularly as a thank-you for their business during the previous year.

The most appropriate gift for a personal visit to a home, or as a thank-you for dinner, would be a box of fruits, pastries, cakes, cookies, calendars, English-language books, items for the children (games, toys), maps, prints, stamps, tapes and CDs, or T-shirts. Flowers are generally not appropriate. There is no need to send a handwritten thank-you note the day after the dinner party. If you are staying with a family, an appropriate thank-you gift would be a high-quality item that represents your country and is difficult to get in China; this is also a good idea for a key business associate. Acceptable gifts include coffee-table books about the United States or anything that reflects your host's personal tastes (the cap of a famous American team for the football-playing son of the family, for example). Native handicrafts or well-framed and well-mounted photographs of you and your Chinese associates are also appreciated. Be sure the gift you give does not have a tag or sticker on it that says it was made in China,

Taiwan, Hong Kong, or anywhere else in Asia. Do not give money as a gift under any circumstances (although there are certain specific occasions when money is given in China, especially in the Hong Kong area, but this is related to bonuses at work).

The more you can personalize your "key man" gift, the more it is appreciated. In more westernized Chinese communities, the best gift you can give to business associates is often a bottle of fine whiskey or cognac, or some other luxury item.

If your gift consists of several items, be sure that they do not total up to an even number (generally bad luck), never to four (very bad luck) or nine (also bad luck), and preferably to three or eight (very good luck). Eight is an extremely lucky number for the Chinese; many wealthy Chinese, particularly in the south, will pay thousands of dollars for a phone number with several eights in it. Do not give clocks as a gift, as the word for clock is similar to the word for death. Also avoid handkerchiefs, as they symbolize sadness, and cutlery, which symbolizes the severing of a relationship. For both giving and receiving gifts, two hands are always used. Gifts are typically not opened by the receiver in front of the giver; they are usually received, graciously acknowledged, and placed aside to be opened once the giver is no longer present.

Gifts must be wrapped well. When you purchase any of the previously mentioned items in China, it will be wrapped beautifully for you, especially if you make it known that it is a gift. Most gifts are wrapped in ordinary paper first and then wrapped again in either red or gold (royal colors) or yellow or pink (happy colors) paper. Several colors are not used for wrapping: green; white and black, because they are funereal colors; and blue, a color of mourning.

Special Holidays and Celebrations

Major Holidays

The most popular vacation time in China is during Chinese New Year (it is a lunar holiday, so the date changes every year, as is the case with all lunar holidays). The celebration lasts at least a week, if not longer, in some areas, and everybody simply stops work and goes home to family and friends. This is a very slow time of year for business.

January 1 (solar)	*yuan dan* (New Year's Day)
January/February (lunar)	*chun jie* (Chinese New Year)
March 8 (solar)	*funu jie* (Woman's Day)
March 15 (lunar)	*qing ming* (Feast of the Ancestors)
May 1 (solar)	*loadong jie,* or *wuyi* (Labor Day)
May 4 (solar)	*zhongguo qing nian jie* (Youth Day)
May 15 (lunar)	*duan wu* (Dragon Boat Festival)
June 1 (solar)	*ertong jie* (Children's Day)
August 1 (solar)	*zhongguo renmin jiefang jun jian jun jie* (National Liberation Army Day)
August 15 (lunar)	*zhong qiu jie* (Mid-Autumn Festival)
October 1 (solar)	*guo qing jie* (National Day)

Business Culture

Daily Office Protocols

The traditional Chinese office has an open design; there are few doors, with the exception of the offices of those holding higher positions, and people work mainly in individual or shared cubicles. Doors, when they exist, are usually open.

In the Chinese organization, there are strictly business titles and also government titles, since most managers and higher-level executives are also officials in the Communist Party and hold some responsibility in the government bureaucracy (usually in the appropriate minister's office). Business titles and rank are:

changzhang	factory manager or director
chejian zhuren	plant foreman
gonchenshi	engineer
zhuren	director
jingli	manager
zong	chief (as in *zong jingli,* or general manager)

Government ministry titles and rank are:

zhuxi	chairman of a committee
buzhang	minister
chuzhang	director
fu	deputy, or vice (as in *fu buzhang,* or vice minister)
fu zongli	cadre (pronounced "cahd-er"; a party official)
kezhang	section head
shengzhang	governor
shizhang	mayor
zongli	premier

When providing refreshments in the office, be sure they are served in porcelain tea sets or cups: the use of paper or Styrofoam shows disrespect and is very bad form. Executives usually have offices on different floors than those occupied by the rank and file. You probably will not be invited onto the workers' floors until the proposed project has been set in motion.

Work begins early at 8 A.M. and ends officially at 4 P.M., but dinners and other entertainments are part of the workday for most. Many businesses have Saturday half-day hours. The rules about numbers stated earlier in the section on gift giving apply to business dealings as well: Schedule business appointments at eight o'clock on the eighth day of the month; do not schedule the meetings for four o'clock with four people on the fourth day of the month, and so on.

Management Styles

Because of the rigid rank and hierarchy orientation in Chinese businesses, titles are very important; the highest ones (e.g., vice president) are usually reserved for very senior, executive-level positions and should not be used as casually as they are in the United States.

Complimenting and rewarding employees publicly is usually not done. Deference is shown by subordinates to their seniors; paternalistic concern is often shown by executives to their juniors. As you go higher up in a large Chinese business organization, you are also simultaneously going higher up in the government bureaucracy, which means that politics will increasingly play a significant role in the ability of your Chinese associate (and subsequently you) to do what you expect to be able to do, and you may or may not know what he has to deal with in his chain of command. As is the case with many bureaucracies, the primary goal is to protect oneself and one's position vis-à-vis one's superiors (as well as to protect one's superiors) rather than to get immediate goals accomplished. This usually means negotiations or projects can move very slowly at some times, and rapidly at others.

Boss-Subordinate Relations

The decision-making system usually works from the top on down, with key decisions often coming from individuals in high positions of authority. There are formal and informal networking opportunities, but generally, access to power is what determines action.

Conducting a Meeting or Presentation

At your first meeting in China, you will probably be received in a very comfortable waiting area, which may or may not be where most of the meeting is conducted between yourself and your Chinese colleague. If this is the case, you are merely being sized up, and your colleague is a gatekeeper. At meetings of peers, there can be open communication and sharing of ideas: however, most meetings are formalities at which information is exchanged, or decisions that have already been made are confirmed. Meetings are too risky for open problem solving and decision making, given the group and hierarchy orientation in China. If this is just the beginning of a business relationship, expect to spend most of the time sharing information about your organization with different individuals; you may need to repeat the same things to different people. This is okay; it means your plans are advancing to the right people in the organization, and that those you have previously met with have approved of you and moved you on. Patience and third-party connections are key.

Negotiation Styles

The first meeting is usually very formal, with the Chinese sizing up you and your organization. Expect no decisions at the table, and be willing to provide copious amounts of information, to the degree that you can, in response to their questions and in anticipation of their needs. Presentations should be well prepared and simply propounded. Details are best left to questions and backup material, which should be translated into Chinese and left behind. Ideally, you should present your material to the Chinese for study, along with a proposed agenda, prior to the meeting. Have extra copies available, as you will meet more people than you will expect. You should come with a well-organized team, whose roles have been clearly thought out and defined. No one on your team should ever disagree with one another in front of the Chinese, or appear uncertain or unsure.

The Chinese are wonderful bargainers, and they expect to get the best possible deal out of you: they approach negotiating as a win/lose scenario, and most of the time play their cards as if they are the poor and needy Chinese and that you are the powerful and resource-rich Westerner. This may feel great at first (especially during that first night's banquet), but you may then be asked to provide much more than you are getting in return: after all, the teacher is expected to totally provide to the student, and unequal relationships in this Confucian society are appropriate. They may make overblown demands, offer to give up something that in fact may be meaningless in the hope that you will give them something valuable in turn; stall and delay until you have one foot on the plane back home, and use all sorts of negotiating tricks. Enjoy the show, play your part, and stick to win/win negotiating strategies based on an equal relationship. Although the contract must be legal down to the dotted i's, remember that to the Chinese it is a piece of paper that merely signifies the beginning of the negotiation; things can change over time, and good partners must take care of each other by being flexible.

Plan your meetings as carefully and as well in advance as you can, and avoid surprises and any unexpected changes (but expect them in this fluid world). Remember, finalizing a deal requires a celebratory meal or drink and the signing should be scheduled at an auspicious or lucky time (this may require you to put things off a bit). Keep communications, especially when at a distance, open and stay in touch with your Chinese colleagues often: share more information than you normally would expect, not less; and have a contact on the ground in China who can always keep you informed of what is really going on.

Written Correspondence

Your business letters should be very formal and respectful of rank and hierarchy. Last names are usually written in uppercase; dates are given in the year/month/day format (with periods in between, not slashes); and an honorific plus the title is as common as an honorific plus the last name. You should write your e-mails, letters, and faxes in a precise way: use a brief introduction, then quickly get down to business. Keep it simple, however, and outline all important matters. In China, and throughout most of the region, the address is usually given as follows:

Line one: country and postal code
Line two: city (and prefecture)
Line three: street address
Line four: company and/or personal name

HONG KONG

Note: The special status territory of Hong Kong and the nation of Taiwan share essentially the same cultural traditions as mainland China. The information that follows discusses additional cultural patterns that are specific to Hong Kong and Taiwan.

Hong Kong is now a busy, modern, fast-paced S.A.R. (Special Administrative Region) city of China, enjoying a special status due to its remarkable background, but superimposed, in many ways, onto the ancient Chinese culture that is at its heart. In this city, you can go from a gleaming, air-conditioned skyscraper to an ancient Chinese alley in a matter of minutes. In order to succeed in Hong Kong, you need to be as fast on your feet as any Western entrepreneur, ready to seize opportunities as they come, yet understand the fundamental Asian values that are at its heart and that were discussed in the previous section on China.

Modern Hong Kong began as the prize in the world's biggest drug deal: simply put, when the British were winning the Opium War in the nineteenth century with China, they agreed to stop the hostilities (and to stop importing opium into China) in exchange for Hong Kong. The Chinese acquiesced. At the time, Hong Kong was a sleepy fishing village in the tropical belly of China (not unlike Singapore was to Malaya). As an economically free port imbued with the spirit of laissez-faire capitalism (though it was not politically free . . . ever; the gnashing of Western teeth over Hong Kong's losing its freedom when it was returned to China was somewhat hypocritical in the sense that it was not free as a British Crown colony, either: the governor was appointed by the British Crown, not elected by a popular vote, and the legislature became representative only in the last year of Hong Kong's colonial status), Hong Kong exploded in size, wealth, and influence as trade in the region grew. Today, the magnificent harbor and the new airport attest to Hong Kong's achievements as the port of world entry into and out of China, but there is a cloud—Beijing's support of the reemergence of Shanghai as the commercial (and in some ways, cultural, as the Communist Party had its beginnings in Shanghai) center of China—and whether Hong Kong can continue to play its special role as the business center of China remains to be seen. Hong Kong also played a powerful role and grew rich as the broker between offshore Chinese money (investment money from Chinese communities around the world outside of China) and the reinvestment of this money into the mainland, when it was illegal in China to do so directly. Much of this money came from Taiwan. If the Taiwan question is settled, and if the movement toward an open system continues, the need for such a brokering role will lessen as direct investment grows. This, too, casts a cloud over Hong Kong's future.

Women play more of a role in business in Hong Kong than they do on the mainland, and, in fact, adopt many Western customs and habits. Hong Kong Chinese move fast and are comfortable with uncertainty. Different from mainlanders, they look to the future, but with their feet rooted deeply in Chinese cultural ways. Many are Western educated and employ modern Western modes of thinking more often than intuitive, associative, or holistic modes of thought.

The language spoken is Cantonese, which has nine tones and is substantively different from Mandarin, although many businesspeople also speak Mandarin or are learning it quickly now that Hong Kong is responsible to Beijing. English is the lingua franca, but it is important to remember that the form spoken there is mainly British English (please see the chapter on England in *The Global Etiquette Guide to Europe* for further information about the British form of the English language). Hong Kong Chinese tend to use Anglicized names, and married women often take the honorific *taitai*.

In addition to the concerns listed in the section on China, topics to avoid are politically loaded subjects like Taiwan and Macao or human rights. Hong Kong Chinese tend to speak very fast and loud, both English and Cantonese. There is little use of or time for silence. The "V for Victory" sign must be done with the palm side out, or else it is considered obscene, as it is in the United Kingdom. Customer service is quick and thorough; shopping is a way of life in Hong Kong. Driving is on the left, and the city is one of the most densely populated places on earth: cars, traffic, and congestion are everywhere and people will always be elbowing nearby. As opposed to the mainland customs, clothing in Hong Kong can be very high fashion, like in any western European city. The cuisine in this part of China relies mainly on fresh seafood: the flavors are subtle and clean. Gift-giving rules in Hong Kong are similar to the mainland, but the gifts tend to be more valuable Western luxury-type items. At the Chinese New Year's, a red envelope filled with cash, the *hong bao,* is the traditional gift; it is given by parents and good friends to children; it is given by businesspeople to associates who provided assistance during the previous year (never to government employees or clients or customers), and it is given by employers to employees. The cash amount varies (for employees, it is usually the annual bonus, equivalent to about one month's wages), but the cash must always be in fresh, new bills, with each bill being an even—not odd—denomination, totaling a rounded-up even number. (It is bad luck to do it any other way, and sends a very bad sign.) The Dragon Boat Festival is one of the most popular holidays in Hong Kong.

TAIWAN

Before the Kuomintang came to the island the Portuguese had previously named Formosa (meaning "beautiful island" in their language), the native people were indigenous Taiwanese, a blend of traditional Pacific island and Chinese peoples living a basically rural and agrarian life. Several million Nationalists descended on the island in 1949, however, usurping the Taiwanese in their own homeland, and changing their lives forever. This event is not necessarily appreciated by the ethnic Taiwanese. Yet it was not the first conquest to occur in Taiwan. Over a hundred years ago, the Chinese and the Japanese fought a bitter war won by Japan; it ended in the Treaty of Shimonuseki, which gave Taiwan to the Japanese. Taiwan remained Japanese ruled until the end of World War II. As a result, many older Taiwanese speak Japanese (in fact, they may have been educated in

Japanese schools), as well as their native Taiwanese (a version of Fujianese, the language spoken just across the channel on the mainland in the province of Fujian, the wealthy coastal corridor between Shanghai and Hong Kong). English is the second language taught in schools, and many businesspeople, especially the younger ones, understand and speak English well enough to communicate in the language.

Once the Kuomintang set up the Nationalist regime in Taipei, it proclaimed itself the true legitimate government of all the Chinese people, and vowed to fight on to reclaim one day the mainland and free the people from the authoritarian Communist regime of Mao Tse-tung. Beijing, on the other hand, saw Taiwan as a renegade province of China, needing to be brought back into the fold, and became committed to bringing Taiwan under the control of the mainland. Now, after fifty years of this undefined condition, an entirely new generation of Taiwanese have been brought up on the success of high-tech capitalism, which has transformed this island into one of the wealthiest nations in Asia, if not the world. Taiwan's development into an economic power was incremental: first it served as a source of cheap piece-goods labor (cheaper than Japan and, later, South Korea); then it moved on to electronics component production and assembly; and now it is a leading supplier of chips and information systems. These new Taiwanese want no part of mainland China, for the most part, either as conqueror or conquered, and most would just as soon become independent and keep their own finely tuned success to themselves. Neither Taipei nor Beijing will permit this. This is the current state of affairs.

The Taiwanese have a reputation for being low key, rarely displaying emotions like anger or open frustration, and emphasizing indirect patterns of speech in order to avoid open conflict, perhaps to a greater degree than their mainland cousins. There is a strong rural and agricultural ethos that informs much of the behavior even in modern-day Taipei (in fact, the greatest collection of traditional Chinese art can be found, not in Beijing, but in the Chinese museum in Taipei—it was taken from the mainland during the revolution). Business entertaining in Taiwan is serious work, and banquets often are just the start of a long evening of drinking and other revelries: while the mainland Chinese might tuck in by 9 P.M., the Taiwanese entertain over drinks and singing long into the night. Because of the climate, Taiwanese take their vacations at the beginning of the year, incorporating Chinese New Year's: therefore, business is best accomplished after March or April. Taiwan does not celebrate the official government holidays of Beijing, but does celebrate its own Nationalist Day. Remember, the economic system is capitalist, and the government is modeled on representative democracy; the Taiwanese pride themselves on knowing both East and West and the balance that they maintain between the two.

CHAPTER THREE

The East Asian Cultures: South Korea

Some Introductory Background on South Korea and the South Koreans

If you are traveling to East Asia for the first time, one of the worst things you can do is assume that South Korea is similar to the other countries in the region. There are, of course, some similarities. But there may be as many differences between South Korea and Japan, say, than there are similarities.

For one thing, the Korean people are central Asian in root, emerging from the same group that went west to Finland and Hungary; the Korean branch went east, and intermarried with other peoples of the region. An examination of the Korean language reveals striking similarities to Finnish and Hungarian, and the physiognomies of the three peoples are related. The Korean language is nothing like the languages spoken by its neighbors, China and Japan; it has the only original written alphabet (Hangul) of all three. Though Korea has been periodically vanquished by Mongols, Chinese, and Japanese over the centuries, in some cases several times over, it has never stayed vanquished for long. And though the conquerors in almost all cases isolated Korea from the rest of the world when they took it over (not a difficult thing to do, given that it is a peninsula nation surrounded on three sides by water, and bordered on the fourth by a rugged mountain range), giving it the sobriquet of "Hermit Kingdom," Koreans are very quick to remind foreigners that while the Chinese civilization was falling apart and the Japanese civilization just emerging, Korea had a supremely advanced civilization in the region, in which the arts and sciences flourished, and a written language was created that the others have yet to match. Koreans will also remind you that they have never been the aggressors in the region, but have been victimized more than once by aggressor neighbors. An American businessperson once said that "South Koreans are the Avis of Asia," meaning that they make a strong show of being the best although they are currently the underdog, while one British fellow once quipped that "South Koreans are the Irish of Asia"—conquered, pugnacious, risk taking, emotional, with a unique indigenous culture but living in a difficult environment where nothing goes quite as planned. Go to South Korea, and you quickly realize that the South Koreans are eager to show you a good time, do business with you, take some risks, and be open and direct, warm and good-natured.

Some Historical Context

The topography formed much of the Korean culture, and history has done the rest, from the beginning of the formative Korean kingdoms of the region of Chosen (the original name of the country in Korean, meaning "land of the morning calm") to the current split and resulting tensions between north and south. The peninsula is rugged, mountainous, in a difficult climate; in an earlier agrarian time, the tortured landscape kept people apart, and was instrumental in creating the three groups of Koreans that exist today, and who lived then in what was known as the Three Kingdoms. In the north (roughly paralleling the contemporary division between North and South Korea) was the original Koguryo kingdom, agricultural, very central Asian in its roots, aggressive, and dominant; the Silla kingdom in the southeast; and the Paekche kingdom in the southwest. The Silla kings finally consolidated the three warring kingdoms in the seventh century A.D., but even today, there is clannish mistrust between the groups. The Sillas see themselves as aristocratic, urbane, sophisticated businesspeople and merchants; the Paekche are viewed as rural folk by Silla Koreans, while the Paekche see themselves as the salt of the Korean earth and culture, with the refined Sillas as self-deluding and corrupt; and both the Sillas and the Paekche are suspicious of the less familiar north. It is ironic that the current state of Korean politics so profoundly mirrors perspectives born of these ancient differences. Once the country was consolidated by the Silla kings, Confucian values of hierarchy and organization replaced earlier Buddhist traditions in an effort to develop Korean society, which ultimately reached its zenith in the thirteenth century.

Two Japanese invasions, the most recent in the twentieth century, have left Koreans suspicious and untrusting of their Japanese neighbors. These invasions have also left the people defensive, feisty, and defiant, out to prove their worth to others. After World War II, the country was divided into two zones of occupation along the thirty-eighth parallel: the Soviet Union controlled the north; the United States controlled the south. In 1950, the Communists in the north precipitated the Korean conflict; the bloody war permanently divided the nation between the north and the south, which were separated by a demilitarized zone (DMZ). It also left over half the population living in the Seoul area within the Republic of Korea (known as South Korea), less than thirty minutes from the DMZ, and within minutes of a rocket attack. Nevertheless, the South Koreans went about building a remarkably successful economy in an environment that was still technically at war (the armistice that ended the fighting between North and South Korea has never been signed by either side, and the two remain in a technical state of war), with a nominally democratic government that could (and still does, periodically) impose martial law at any time. The support given to Korea by the United States in these circumstances, while appreciated, is also a source of discontent, especially among the young, who view the constant state of war, and the U.S. support of the status quo, as an excuse for the government to exercise totalitarianism powers that are increasingly seen as abusive and intolerable.

An Area Briefing

Politics and Government

For our purposes, this chapter only concerns itself with South Korea. Although many South Korean cultural attributes no doubt will also apply to North Koreans, a full generational cycle has passed since the end of World War II, with both North and South Koreans developing as separate peoples in very different societies. The north is especially closed, and there is little opportunity to understand the current state of affairs there. If unification were to occur, there would no doubt be a great cultural challenge, similar to and perhaps greater than the one experienced in Germany after German east-west unification. Nominally democratic but pragmatically authoritarian when and where it needs to be, the South Korean government has been blamed for trampling human rights and for not advancing the democratization of the society faster; for its part, the government claims that it must retain the right to its extraordinary powers, given the current state of affairs.

Schools and Education

Schooling is free and mandatory for all students through high school. There is mandatory military service for two and a half years for all men immediately after high school at age nineteen or after they graduate from college, if they attend one. After middle school, students enter the equivalent of a high school, and get on either a humanities track, which will lead them to a university, or a vocational/technical track, which can lead them to a vocational/technical college. Education has always been an essential Confucian ideal, and parents place great hope on the advancement of their children through education. More and more, this also includes girls, although only boys were traditionally privileged to receive an education. Seoul University is *the* prestigious college in Korea. Many Korean students seek to advance their university studies by going abroad to the West; such programs often require that after their studies, these students return to South Korea to bring their knowledge and skills back home. Many do, but some do not.

Religion and Demographics

As we have seen throughout the rest of eastern Asia, religions in Korea are not institutionalized belief systems as they are in the West, with the exception of the Christian churches, whose members comprise almost 50 percent of the population. Protestantism came to Korea around the turn of the twentieth century by missionaries, and was eagerly adopted by the Koreans, who, in the past, also were eager to adopt Buddhism and Confucianism. (There is also an indigenous shamanistic religion that is popular in the rural areas.)

These other non-Christian religious influences in Korea are strong, but they are not religions per se. It would be more correct to refer to them as philosophies of life. Elements of both of these philosophies inform the behaviors and beliefs of most individuals, and of society as a whole. There are no preset times of worship (although there are festivals that occur at certain times throughout the year), and priests—if there are any—do not directly represent the faithful. Eastern Asian religions are really a compilation of the beliefs, writings, teachings, and thoughts of certain spiritual thinkers. (For a more detailed look at the Confucian and Buddhist belief systems, please see the chapters on China and Japan.)

Buddhist traditions in Korea reveal themselves in the form of dependence on greater forces, whether these forces be fate, ancestors, or the gods that control climate, floods, and the weather. There is a sense that life and the universe are well beyond the understanding and control of mere mortals, certainly in the here and now, although we must always, of course, try. The form of Buddhism that spread throughout Korea was mainly Mahayana Buddhism, which emphasized that individuals can, through sacrifice and hard work, attain nirvana and break through the endless cycles of life and its suffering; this lays some of the foundation for the more individualistic behavior found in South Korea. Confucianism provides philosophical support for the rigid hierarchies that dominate daily life in the country, and for the importance that is placed on seniority, rank, face, honor, and humility.

Children are revered in South Korea, but not as much as the elderly (and ancestors), who hold the highest positions in society. Boys have traditionally been more valued than girls (a not uncommon phenomenon in agricultural societies where working in the field is more useful than being wedded off at a price to a struggling farming family), but this is changing slowly in South Korea today. Women in South Korea have traditionally played a role in family businesses, but have few opportunities in large South Korean businesses today. Non–South Korean businesswomen, while not directly subject to these constraints, will still find it difficult to be taken seriously by South Korean businessmen, especially older ones. This is changing, slowly.

It is important throughout South Korea (and throughout all of Asia) not to assume an Asian is of one nationality or another: while most of the people in Korea are Korean, what Korean group they belong to can be an important determinant of how others treat them. There are populations of Chinese, Japanese, and Mongol in Korea, as well.

Fundamental Cultural Orientations

1. What's the Best Way for People to Relate to One Another?

OTHER-INDEPENDENT OR OTHER-DEPENDENT? As we saw, while being essentially a group-oriented culture, Korean Buddhism and Korean history have provided Koreans with a powerful tradition of individual responsibility: the peasant farmer and shopkeeper were often alone in the world, having to eke out an existence without the support of the government or other people. There is a strong sense of self-reliance among individuals, which is often in conflict with greater uncontrollable realities (and a belief in such), including an overarching obligation to the family (sometimes this "family" ethic includes the workers and salaried people in the family business). This makes for strong individual decision making at the top, based on advice and information from below. This is also one reason why many meetings in South Korea are not with groups, but with only a single individual (or a few people); and while this person at the beginning may only be a gatekeeper, he might also be the decision maker (especially if he has gray hair, meaning he is older or more senior).

HIERARCHY-ORIENTED OR EGALITY-ORIENTED? Structure and hierarchy are critical at all levels in South Korean society—in the home, at school, in the military, and in business. A Confucian formality has developed around what one does and with whom; it is essential to show the proper respect for individuals, depending on their rank and position, in order to succeed in South Korea. Hierarchy is honored through humility and making face; this is done by "lowering," or minimizing, oneself. In fact, one makes more of oneself, and raises one's esteem in the eyes of others, by doing so. This emphasis on hierarchy also normalizes unequal relationships: it is, after all, natural that some be in charge and some not, that some have power and some not, that some dictate and some follow, that older be deferred to by younger.

RULE-ORIENTED OR RELATIONSHIP-ORIENTED? While there are many rules imposed by the hierarchy from above, the control factor in South Korean society is the relationship between individuals. These important connections, and the obligations that arise from them, are the grease that moves the wheels in South Korea. It is absolutely essential that a good *kibbun,* or feeling, emerge between individuals and organizations. This is an indefinable element that has nothing to do with rational effectiveness, but everything to do with trust and intuitive logic. The one dependable thing in an unpredictable world is the spiderlike network of relationships and obligations that one builds with others, usually friends and family. This will determine future action. In the especially fluid South Korean environment, where businesses and government work arm in arm, one's relationship with and obligations to the right people can determine success or failure: if these individuals suddenly are out of favor or power, business prospects can change dramatically.

2. What's the Best Way to View Time?

MONOCHRONIC OR POLYCHRONIC? Because punctuality also reflects other values, such as concern for the other person and humility before someone else's efforts, South Koreans are more or less punctual; certainly, you should be. Nevertheless, in the big picture, as with all traditional Asian cultures, time has historically stood in the background to immediate personal relationships; this is certainly still the case in South Korea today. Things will take the time they need to take, and the clock is not the ultimate arbiter of what occurs and when. South Koreans will move very quickly to seize an advantage if one presents itself; they certainly want to succeed as quickly as possible, but they will not do anything that is not in their best interest simply because of time. Unless it is on their terms, they have time to wait it out.

The workday in South Korea begins around 9 A.M. and ends officially at 5 P.M., but can begin earlier and last longer. Most workers take an hour break and a midafternoon nap after lunch. On balance, South Korea is a polychronic culture, as are most of the cultures of Asia, precisely because the clock is not the ultimate reason for action.

RISK-TAKING OR RISK-AVERSE? South Korea has essentially a risk-taking culture, making it very different from its Japanese neighbor. The combination of history and topography have provided the South Korean people with a win-ner-take-all attitude toward business, and in some sense, toward life. Since life is so uncertain, it must be lived to the fullest right now, and one cannot dwell on sadness and uncertainty. This sense of immediacy, of course, allows for rational risk taking and an emotional approach to life. However, South Koreans are not foolish, and need information, as well as good *kibbun,* in order to make a deal. They may, however, be very quick to tell you that they will be able to do whatever needs to be done to make something happen, when in fact, this might not be the case. You need informants on the ground who understand South Korea to get the full picture.

PAST-ORIENTED OR FUTURE-ORIENTED? South Koreans are fatalistic when things do not work out, and are always half expecting them not to; but there is enough of a sense of control that enables them to believe that ultimately they have the better way, and that ultimately they will not only survive, but succeed.

3. What's the Best Way for Society to Work with the World at Large?

LOW-CONTEXT DIRECT OR HIGH-CONTEXT INDIRECT COMMUNICATORS? Context does drive communication in South Korea, but it often allows for direct and confrontational speech. While South Koreans are direct, they are rarely blunt; while they say what they feel (feeling is especially important), they are careful not to cause loss of face or be disrespectful of the Confucian-based order of things. South Koreans make decisions and communicate intuitively: they evaluate people and things with mind reading, or *pummi* (when your South Korean associate sits quietly and looks at you very intently, he or she is using *pummi* to get a feeling about you; relax). There is less of a reliance on symbolic verbal expression; nevertheless, to overcome language barriers, using pictures, graphs, charts, and numbers is very effective.

In this high-context culture, the situation determines the action, in most cases, and not the rules or regulations: this is related to both the polychronic nature of South Korean culture and the reliance on personal relationships. This means that as situations (and the individuals involved in the situations) change, flexibility is required. The terms of a contract signed in January may no longer be applicable in July, if the situation in July is different from the way it was in January; therefore, in July, the South Koreans may seek to renegotiate with the trusted business partners they established in January, often only to be disappointed in the Westerners' resistance to altering the terms of the agreement. As a result, the South Koreans, like the Chinese, often lose trust in Western contracts, and Westerners often believe the South Koreans have no regard for contract law. This is part of the reason why South Koreans much prefer short statements of intent, called memorandums of understanding, as opposed to the complex and heavy legal documents of the West, which attempt to control all future aspects of how the business partners will work together in an unpredictable and always changing world.

PROCESS-ORIENTED OR RESULT-ORIENTED? South Koreans, as is the case with all Asian peoples, are fully capable of employing (and do employ) meticulous logic, whether deductively or inductively; however, that is not necessarily the only process used to think things through, to make a case for something, or to understand people or events. A connection is made to other similar situations, and in that sense, South Koreans rely heavily on associative, subjective logic. However, all forms of logic are used in a more holistic way in Asia, so that while process and experience are important steps in arriving at a conclusion, the path may not be linear or progressive. This is related to the polychronic nature of the culture: things occur, thought patterns included, not necessarily in a sequential or progressive way, but in a holistic way. In other words, the elements needed to make decisions are laid out expositionally, when and as the circumstances require it, and add up to a conclusion only when viewed "at once," as if suddenly from forty thousand feet. Do not search for sequence (although the process is clearer with South Koreans than with the Chinese in this regard): search for all facts to be brought forward, as situations deem it, and then sit back and evaluate the total result.

FORMAL OR INFORMAL? The South Koreans can be spontaneous, once trust is established (which can be quick); but one should remain obedient to formal Confucian role requirements at all times. South Koreans can move easily and very quickly between formal and informal; it is important to begin with an understanding of the culture's formal customs, but be prepared to adapt to informality as the opportunity presents itself.

Greetings and Introductions

Language and Basic Vocabulary

Most South Koreans do not speak English, including senior businesspeople, although younger people, because it is taught in school, do speak it. Do not use Japanese, if you speak it, unless you are sure that you are not misunderstood as also working for a Japanese organization, even if you are with an older Korean (who might have been forced to learn that language). Hangul, the written Korean language, is a unique Asian alphabet, which assigns sounds to symbols to create written Korean words, as we do in the West.

Here are some basic Korean terms and their English meanings:

Annyong haseo?	How are you? (literally, "Are you at peace?")
annyong	hi (usually between children or people who know each other well)
annyong hashimnikka	hello (a general greeting at any time of day appropriate to demonstrate humility to the people being greeted)
kamsa hamnida	thank you

kamsa hashimnikka	good-bye
kulsee yo	fine, let's just see what happens
	(this is also used to avoid conflict)

In Korean, there is no distinction made between the *L* and the *R* sounds.

Honorifics for Men, Women, and Children

Korean honorifics display rank and seniority mainly according to age and not gender. All honorifics appear after the family name. Family names always are placed first, followed by a given generational name, and then finally a given name (placed last). There is often a hyphen between the generational and given names, making the two given names more often than not a two- (or more) syllable name. Most of the time, the Korean family name is a single syllable (there are in fact only a limited number of family or clan names, such as Lee, Park, Kim, and so on, so most Koreans have similar family names, with the generational and given names primarily distinguishing one from the other). If Dae-jung Kim has introduced himself as such, he has reversed the Korean name format to accommodate the Westerner, putting his given and generational names first and his family name last, Western style (you know this because the two-syllable name, usually the combination of the generational and given names, is being presented first). You would refer to this person with the correct honorific after Kim, no matter where it appears. For travelers and businesspeople, the following guide is sufficient:

- *sonsaengnim:* an honorific for a teacher or mentor (the highest honorific), added as a suffix at the end of the family name; for example, Dae-jung Kim becomes Kim-sonsaengnim (literally, "Kim, the teacher")
- *ssi:* Mr., Mrs., Ms., or Miss (added as a suffix at the end of the family name); for example, Kim Dae-jung becomes Kim-ssi (literally, "Mr. Kim")

There are two forms for addressing a married woman. Traditionally, Korean women did not lose their own family name, nor take their husband's family name. However, if you do not know a Korean woman's name, it is appropriate to refer to her by her husband's family name and the honorific "madame" (for example, Li-ssi might be a woman's maiden name, but if you do not know for sure, you may refer to her as "Madame Kim," if you know that she is married to Kim-ssi).

Unless and until your Korean colleague specifically invites you to use his or her "first" name, and despite how he or she might refer to you, you must always use the family name (it is acceptable not to use the honorific once you have a relationship). Children in Korea are expected to be respectful and not overly conversational when speaking with adults, and must always use honorifics when referring to adults. As they probably speak limited English, this makes conversation with children that much more difficult.

In situations where a title is known, the title plus the honorific is frequently used, either with or without the name (e.g., "Mr. Engineer" or Engineer Lee). For casual contacts (e.g., waiters, store help, etc.), use no honorifics; just make eye contact. It is very important to greet people at work, in stores, or in restaurants in an appropriate fashion. Sometimes South Koreans (as well as other Asians) will Anglicize their names when they know they will be working or meeting with Westerners. (On occasion, they will simply assign a Latin initial as a given first and second name.) Recognize that this is done for your benefit, and that the name you are being given is not their real name. (This Anglicized version may also appear on that person's business card.)

The What, When, and How of Introducing People

Sometimes upon greeting you, Koreans will simply call you by your family name, or make a comment about the task you are performing: this does not require a substantive response.

Always wait to be introduced to strangers; never take that responsibility upon yourself, as doing so is considered inappropriate most of the time. Koreans are most comfortable with a third-party introduction whenever one is possible, and will go to great lengths to ensure that you are not left alone to decide this for yourself. Never presume to seat yourself at a gathering; if possible, wait to be told where to sit. The seating arrangements have usually been carefully worked out in advance, and in most cases reflect the status of the individuals in the group, and the honor that is being accorded the guests. When departing, it is important to say farewell with a quick bow to every individual present: the American group wave is not appreciated. Once you greet someone you will encounter later that day in the same circumstances (e.g., at the office), you will need to acknowledge them with a quick, foreshortened bow whenever you see them again.

Physical Greeting Styles

Like many Asian cultures, South Korea is a nontouching culture (at least at first). Only the most intimate of friends (mainly young people) will touch each other in greeting. The handshake is a Western invention, and not native to Korea: the South Koreans have, of course, become accustomed to it, but because it is done for the Westerner's benefit, it is generally an accommodation added to the Korean bow and the business card exchange. When the handshake does occur it is more often than not very soft, almost limp. This does not signify insincerity; rather, it is an indication of humility using a Western convention. In addition, when the right hand is extended for the handshake, the left hand reaches over and touches the same lower right forearm just in front of the elbow, indicating extra sincerity. This is a uniquely Korean gesture of hospitality and welcome, and gifts, drinks, documents, and meals are also given and received this way, with "elbow support." Women must always extend their hands first for a handshake, if it is to occur at all; if so, it is inevitably very soft.

The traditional South Korean introduction involves the use of business cards and a bow, though neither is done with the same formality or complexity as the Japanese greeting. Always take a large supply of business cards with you to South Korea: you must give one to every new person you are introduced to (there is no need to provide another business card when you are meeting someone again unless information about you has changed, such as a new address, contact number, or position). Be sure your business cards are in fine shape: they are extensions of you as a person, and must look as good as possible. Never hand out a dirty, soiled, bent, or written-on card. You should, if possible, have your business card translated into Korean on the reverse side before you go to South Korea (some finer hotels and some airlines, as well as your own business, will do this as a service for you). The traditional card is written in Korean from left to right, with the company name being the first item, the rank and title the second, the name third, and contact information the last (more modern businesses may organize the information in a more Western format). When presenting a business card, you give it to your South Korean associate with the Korean side up, so that it is readable for him as you hold it (he will, in turn, present his card with the English side up, so it's readable for you); you must hold the card in the upper right- and left-hand corners, requiring the use of two hands, and you also receive your Korean associate's card with two hands, on the upper right- and left-hand corners. The exchange is done quickly, almost simultaneously. Accompanying the exchange of the cards is a small bow. This is not as dramatic, deep, or long-lasting as the Japanese version: a quick, slight bow is all that is required, certainly of the Westerner (perhaps slightly deeper if one is greeting an obviously older person).

Smiling and other nonverbal forms of communication usually accompany the card exchange; it is appropriate to appear genuinely pleased to meet the other person. When first introduced to your Korean colleague, make immediate eye contact, but as soon as the card exchange begins, and definitely when the bow commences, drop your eyes so that they are looking to the ground (this demonstrates respect for the other person).

Information about each other's status is the most important information to be exchanged, and this is provided directly on the business card, as well as indirectly through a number of high-context indicators, such as gray hair (usually an indication of age), gender (usually male), and the number of people surrounding and assisting the other person (indicating an important person). Humility before rank can be demonstrated subtly, by placing your business card underneath the card of the other person during the exchange. Once you have received the other person's card, it is important to stand upright again, holding the card with two hands, and silently read the card for a few seconds. Then make eye contact and say his name (this is an opportunity for him to correct you if you mispronounce it, and for you to do the same for him) and his title in a way that indicates your respect for him and his position; then extend your hand for a soft Western handshake, with accompanying elbow support. All this occurs rather quickly, whether you are meeting one or many Koreans.

As this ritual usually precedes a sit-down meeting, it is important if you have been introduced to several Koreans that you arrange the cards you have received in a little seating plan in front of you along the top of the desk or table at your seat, reflecting the order in which people are seated. This will help you connect the correct names with the correct individuals throughout the meeting. Even if you have only one card and are meeting only one person, keep the card out and in the proper position throughout the entire meeting. During the meeting, it is important never to play with the business cards (do not write on them—ever!), and when the meeting is over, never put them in your back pants pockets: pick them up carefully and respectfully, and place them neatly in your business card holder (a nice-looking leatherbound or brass case would be perfect); then place the card holder in the left inside jacket pocket of your suit (nearest your heart).

Communication Styles

Okay Topics / Not Okay Topics

Okay: anything that reflects your personal interests and hobbies, or your curiosity about things Korean, including food, the Silla kings and Korean history, the Olympics, and kite flying or tae kwon do (both are national pastimes). *Not okay:* Politics, current events, or any subject that might in any way be controversial needs to be avoided at first. Do not inquire about a person's occupation or income in casual conversation, although it may be inquired of you (if so, this is just a way of getting to know more about your country, and not a personal investigation: answer specifically, but fully, with an explanation as to what things cost at home, why you do what you do, etc.). Do not inquire about your colleague's family life. Do not give your opinions about the North Koreans, the Communists, the Japanese, or American troops. Sex is not necessarily a taboo subject, but until you get to know each other, there is no real reason to bring it up (there are lots of jokes about sex that Koreans will love to share with you over drinks!). Sticking to general themes of personal interest or business is fine; it is a way of seeking common ground. There will be no need to begin a conversation with the very American "So, what do you do?" since you already know this from the card exchange; however, further discussions about your company and its work are very much appreciated, as this gives the South Koreans a chance to learn more about you and your firm. The goal of all conversation, at least at the beginning, is to create and maintain a harmonious atmosphere, despite the difficult or confrontational nature of the topic being discussed. At first, speak about things that you believe you have in common so that you can build a personal connection, which will go far toward maintaining a harmonious bridge between you. This is appropriate for both individuals and organizations.

Tone, Volume, and Speed

At first, in more formal situations, the tone is quiet and hushed. Speak slowly, for the benefit of those translating, in short phrases, and speak clearly. Try to speak expositionally, without emotion, if possible. Since words are for the most part not the best vehicles for communication when different languages are being spoken, use pictures, graphics, and charts to augment the topic being discussed whenever possible. Illustrate what you can say, and certainly what you cannot. This is a very symbol-oriented culture.

However, as you get deeper into your discussions, and as relationships are built, South Koreans will open up quickly and become very emotive, although not necessarily animated. On the street and in some restaurants, the noise level can be exceptionally high.

Use of Silence

Passive silence—allowing time to pass simply, without words—can be a form of proactive communication in Korea, but not as profoundly as in Japan. More often than not, it expresses the fact that either your South Korean associate did not understand you (your idea, your language, etc.), or is practicing *pummi* to get a feeling about you. There may be pauses between comments, but rarely extending over several minutes. When confronted with silence, for whatever reason, the best response is to remain silent yourself, although this may be difficult and appear unproductive for time-conscious Westerners. This is perhaps the most subtle form of communication, yet communication it is. If you must say something, bring up something positive, even if it is unrelated to the previous statement. Remember, in Asia, "silence is golden"; those who speak too much are considered immature, given how careful one must be with what one says. Because some Westerners find silence disconcerting, they may tend to fill up the space with more talk; resist this impulse, as it only enhances the effectiveness of the silence, by forcing the Westerner to say more than he or she might normally be inclined to, and goes a long way toward achieving the South Korean goal of the meeting, which in most cases, in the early stages, is simply to gather as much data and information as possible.

Physical Gestures and Facial Expressions

In South Korea, there is considerably less physical gesturing of any kind. If you have a tendency to speak with your hands, you will have to consciously be aware of reducing it: most of the time, such gesturing is considered over-the-top and will engender surprise, laughter, and sometimes anger. In fact, laughter may or may not be in response to anything humorous in the Western sense (jokes may not be understood). Winking and whistling are very vulgar. Public displays of familiarity and affection with the opposite sex are expressed only by teenagers. When having to come between people or pass others, it is appropriate to bow slightly as you go by.

Waving and Counting

The pinkie represents the number 1, the thumb represents the number 5, with everything in between ordered from the pinkie down; however, instead of raising the fingers when counting, the whole hand is exposed, and each finger is depressed down as the counting is done. It is very insulting to call someone with the forefinger (instead, turn the hand palm facing down and motion inward with all four fingers at once). If you need to gesture for a waiter, very subtly raise your hand. Waving or beckoning is done with the palm down and the fingers moving forward and backward in a kind of scratching motion. It may seem as if the person is saying good-bye to you when, in fact, you are being summoned over.

Physicality and Physical Space

Most South Koreans stand, relative to North Americans, just a little farther apart; resist the urge at first to move in closer. Never, upon first greeting a South Korean, touch him beyond the soft handshake: no backslaps, no hugging, no kissing, *ever.* Never speak with your hands in your pockets: always keep them firmly at your side when standing. If men and women must cross their legs when they sit, it must never be ankle over knee; for women, the preferred style is to cross ankle over ankle. Remember, in public, formal is always better than informal: no gum chewing, *ever;* don't slouch; and don't lean against things. South Koreans are *very* formal when they sit and stand in business settings.

Do not remove your jacket at a meeting unless and until the senior South Korean man has already done so. Once close relationships are established, and especially in those moments when spontaneity and friendliness are allowed (such as at a bar or walking down the street after an evening meal), there may be much physicality—touching, for example, or putting arms around other people's shoulders, or holding hands—but generally only between members of the same sex, and not in public between members of the opposite sex. About the only time this nonphysicality rule is broken is on public transport, where it is very crowded and touching is unavoidable, or on crowded streets, where you are very likely to be poked and prodded as people jostle by. It is usually considered bad luck to walk behind someone, so if someone is nearby while you are speaking with a third party, that person might walk between the two of you rather than behind your back: step aside and allow this to happen.

Eye Contact

Eye contact can be very direct in South Korea. Except at the beginning greeting, where bowing and humility is demonstrated (and where eyes are lowered to the ground during the bow), eye contact is generally maintained throughout discussions. If you are being "stared at," look at your South Korean associate's chin until he moves on to another topic. Tune up your nonverbal antennae.

Emotive Orientation

South Koreans can become emotional and expressive very quickly, but generally it will be over pleasant things; if there is a confrontation, South Koreans will generally be evasive with their emotions. Westerners should not act in kind; it is important for the Westerner to consciously control emotive impulses but be sincere and outgoing in their feelings and thoughts.

Protocol in Public

Walking Styles and Waiting in Lines

On the street, in stores, and in most public facilities, people pay little attention to maintaining orderly lines. Due to the volume of passengers on public transportation, there can be much pushing and jostling. This is not to get into a train or bus ahead of someone else, though; it is merely to get in!

Behavior in Public Places: Airports, Terminals, and the Market

Customer service is a finely tuned art in South Korea, because the "other" (in this case, the customer) is so important, and because demonstrating customer service involves showing deference to the customer. Stores in the cities are open in the evenings and on weekends, as well as during the day; there is a very good chance you will be bowed to as you enter and leave a store, and by all clerks as they help you. A personal thank-you to store owners, waiters, chefs, and hotel managers for their services is very much appreciated. In food markets, don't worry about touching the produce, since everybody does, and it doesn't obligate you to buy it; in goods stores, if you buy a product and have problems with it, returning the item will not be difficult. Smoking is endemic, and you may have difficulty finding a no-smoking area on public transportation, in restaurants, and in other public places. Bathroom facilities can range from Western-style toilets to Asian-style toilets (holes in the floor, with buckets of water or hoses attached to a water line for cleanup instead of paper); be prepared. Westerners may want to think twice about using public transportation when private transportation is usually inexpensive and plentiful.

When answering a telephone, just state your family name. Cell phones are ubiquitous.

Bus / Metro / Taxi / Car

Driving is on the right, and whether in the country or city, being in a car can be hazardous to your health. With the exception of the major highways (which are in fine shape, although usually crowded), the roads are not necessarily in good repair, marked, or where maps say they are.

The best way to catch a cab is at designated taxi stands (hotels are good places, but often charge more for the same ride: a hotel surcharge is added to the meter fare, in some cases). When a taxi has been hailed, get an estimate on the price to be sure the meter price is fair when you get to your destination. Addresses in big cities like Seoul can be maddeningly difficult to find (in part due to the massive amount of construction going on, and the traditional system of demarcating neighborhoods and intersections, not streets), and even taxi drivers are often mystified: whenever possible, have the address you need to get to written down on a piece of paper (or use the business card of the person you are going to see, if you can) before you hail the cab. A small map outlining the route is great, if you can have one prepared before you go.

Tipping

Tipping is not common in South Korea, but waiters, cab drivers, and porters do appreciate the equivalent of 5 percent or so in won for their services.

Punctuality

While the culture is essentially polychronic, punctuality is expected in all situations. Do not arrive more than five minutes too soon—or more than five minutes late, for that matter. (Your South Korean associates may arrive sooner, however; this is due to the fact that they are eager to meet with you; moreover, getting around in Seoul and in South Korea today can take some time, and is usually filled with unexpected delays.) You will not be told if your tardiness has caused a problem, of course, but in most cases, it will not help your image. When a meeting is over in a South Korean office, it is best to leave the room before the Koreans do, as they may need to discuss your proposal for quite some time after you leave.

Dress

South Koreans dress more or less conservatively, and individuals who stand out because of their clothing are not taken seriously. The standard is neither very formal, nor informal, no matter the occasion—at work or on the street—for men and women. Style is not important at work, but in social situations, particularly among the young, there is great eagerness for Western styles. At work, male managers wear dark suits, white shirts, and subdued ties, and the shoes should be polished; but accessories are not often worn beyond a watch. Women can accessorize somewhat, but most often dress simply in a business suit or dress of a conservative length and low heels. On the street, informal may mean jeans and sneakers, though that is more common as clothing to wear at the gym or while jogging (some women do wear sneakers to work, but change just before they enter the office, not after going in); for a social gathering, informal more often than not means tastefully coordinated clothes, sometimes including a jacket and tie for men (it rarely means jeans, sneakers, and T-shirts). "Formal" usually means dressy business suits.

Seasonal Variations

There are four extreme seasons in South Korea, and one needs to dress accordingly. The summers can be hot and very humid, with frequent rain; the winters can be damp, snowy, and cold. Spring and autumn can be delightful, however.

Colors

Wear neutral colors whenever possible (do not wear blue, as it is considered the color of mourning).

Styles

For the most part, South Koreans tend to dress with more of an eye toward conformity than toward making an individual statement. Traditional dress (the beautiful *hanbok,* worn by both men and women) is common on holidays and during special events.

Accessories / Jewelry / Makeup

Makeup, hairstyles, and accessories are important for women, but must not be excessive. Perfume and cologne are popular.

Personal Hygiene

In South Korea, personal hygiene is important. There is a real concern for cleanliness and smelling good, but what smells good and bad to the Koreans may be different from Westerners. South Koreans love garlic, and their favorite foods are often heavily laden with it; the smell can come through the skin. However, remember that *they* are particularly sensitive to the smell of dairy products and red meat on Westerners. Do not blow your nose in public: it is considered very rude (if you must blow your nose in public, never use a handkerchief; try disposable tissues). Some South Koreans do, however, spit on the street. At the end of a meal, it is perfectly acceptable to use a toothpick, but you must cover the "working" hand with the other hand, so that others cannot see your mouth.

Dining and Drinking

Mealtimes and Typical Foods

The typical Korean diet revolves mainly around the local vegetables, seafood, meat, and rice. Due to the extremes of climate, much food is heavily spiced in order to preserve it during the long winter. The spices used can be hot chilies and strong garlic. Although the South Koreans are becoming increasingly familiar with Western food, they love their cuisine, and most enjoy a fine Korean or Chinese meal (if you are hosting them in your country, unless they directly express an interest in trying a local cuisine, take them to the best local Korean or Chinese—not Japanese—restaurant you can find, and tell the restaurant manager that you are hosting some visiting Korean nationals: they will go out of their way to make the meal very fine for you). Avoid Western food, especially hamburgers and cheese: the taste is generally unpleasant to most Koreans.

Breakfast is served from about 7:30 to 9 A.M., and usually consists of tea and rice; the latter is served either as a porridge-type cereal that can be flavored with any number of ingredients, with eggs in a variety of styles, or with pickled vegetables. Tea in Korea, as elsewhere in the region, is usually drunk without sugar, milk, or lemon. The ubiquitous kimchi, or garlic pickle, is served at almost every meal. Originally, kimchi was a way of preserving the vegetables and fruits of summer: they would be put up in jars with hot spices and garlic, and placed in the cold ground for the winter. Every family has its own special kimchi recipes.

Lunch is traditionally the main meal of the day, and even today, in busy cities, it can still be an elaborate affair with several courses—or it can be a simple rice dish bolted down in a matter of minutes. Lunch is served from about noon to 1 P.M., and consists of meat, fish, and/or vegetables, with rice and/or noodles. Lunch can also be a large serving of hot broth or soup, made with a variety of ingredients, or a *pulkogi,* a barbecue of thinly sliced meats and grilled vegetables (often grilled at your table). Many dishes can be steamed, stir-fried, or boiled in a variety of different ways, either simply or more elaborately. Typically, the drinks served with lunch and dinner are beer, liquor, and/or tea.

The Korean barbecue, which is as close to the Chinese banquet as one finds in Korea, usually involves a hot pot and a grill brought right out to the table. The hot pot is set to bubbling, and all sorts of ingredients keep coming to the table that you either grill or drop into the bubbling brew to cook. It can be a very communal event, even though individuals sometimes get their own hot pots instead of sharing a large communal one. The large communal hot pot, of course, absorbs the flavors of just about everything that has been cooked in it throughout the meal, so it's really a wonderful stew by the time the evening comes to an end. Certain items are, however, never prepared in a communal hot pot; for example, there are usually separate hot pots for fish and meat, and sometimes for vegetables, for those preferring to keep vegetarian. If you're not sure, ask, but please don't dunk your fish or meat into just any bubbling kettle.

Dinner is served from 6 P.M. on, with seven o'clock the customary late time. Even if the main meal of the day was lunch, dinner is only slightly lighter—this is often the case with families at home. The dinner menu is often similar to that of the more formal lunch. Dinner drinks may begin with *sujol* (a very potent clear rice liquor) served alone or with appetizers, then move on to beer during the meal, and end with a sweet wine and/or tea. The business dinner mainly takes the form of an elaborate smorgasbord of Korean dishes.

There may be very little conversation during the meal, as the Koreans really are there to enjoy the food, first and foremost. Be sure to take just a little on your plate, as you can often go back for more, especially if the dishes are served "smorgasbord" style. Compliments are expected. Praise the food throughout, as well as the wisdom and taste of your host. Leave controversial topics and business matters for later. Be diplomatic. Be pleasant. Be humble, and appreciative of the bounty prepared in your honor, and don't hesitate to say so.

Regional Differences

Because South Korea is a small country, the regional differences that exist are based more on the availability of different foods—for example, seafood along the coast and fresh vegetables in the summer.

Typical Drinks and Toasting

The most common liquor is *sujol,* made from fermented rice. It is best drunk at room temperature, neither warmed nor chilled, in individual shot glasses. Because you must never pour your own drink (be it *sujol,* beer, or tea), you must always be alert throughout the meal as to whether your neighbor's cup or glass needs refilling. If it is less than half full, it needs refilling; alternately, if yours is less than half full, your neighbor is obliged to refill it. If he or she does not, do not refill it yourself, for this will cause them to lose face; instead, diplomatically indicate your need by pouring a little more drink into your neighbor's glass, even if it doesn't really need it. When you pour for your neighbor or pass plates of food to him or her, you should use the "elbow support" gesture.

In South Korea, there is a traditional twist on the pouring rule that is quite charming, if a bit unsanitary. At traditional and family feasts, after the first glass is filled by your neighbor and then drained by you, South Koreans often refill their own glass, but pass it to the person sitting on their right. Of course, your neighbor on the left has done the same with their glass and given it to you. Then, after you drink, you refill the glass, and pass it again to the neighbor on your right, with everyone at the table doing the same thing. This is usually done during a series of toasts. As you can imagine, with everyone drinking out of everyone else's glass, there can be some risk, but the liquor is usually strong, and the number of drinks enough, that after the first few rounds, nobody really cares very much; moreover, the charm of this tradition leaves everyone with a chummy glow.

Sujol can be strong, so go slow. Sujol is drunk in shots. So what to do if you don't drink? It really isn't an insult to refuse one, as long as you have a reasonable explanation. I've heard people say, "My doctor doesn't advise me to drink just now," or "It's my ulcer" (Asians are keenly aware of stomach problems since such ailments are quite common there, and are receptive to such explanations; however, once such information is shared, be prepared to be offered all sorts of remedies that they absolutely insist will work, and that you might want your own doctor to check out before using), and any number of other little white lies.

The toast in Korea is *cangai,* which means "bottoms up" or "drain the glass." If you are the honored guest, you will be expected to make a toast, usually soon after the host does or at the end of the meal, just before everyone departs. An appropriate toast is to the health of the host and all those present, and to the prosperity of the business under discussion.

Avoid drinking tap water anywhere in South Korea (this means you should brush your teeth with bottled water and not take ice in any of your drinks; drink only bottled water, or brewed tea or coffee or soft drinks, and avoid getting water from the morning shower into your mouth; and never eat fresh fruits or vegetables that cannot be peeled first, and ideally cooked later before eating). This is a serious matter: there are some very nasty bugs going around in developing countries.

Table Manners and the Use of Utensils

South Korea is one of the traditional chopstick cultures, along with China and Japan. Please see the information about proper chopstick use in the chapter on Japan; it is appropriate in South Korea as well. There is one major difference, though; Korean chopsticks are more like the rounded Chinese kind, as opposed to the square-sided Japanese chopsticks, and do not come attached (they do not require snapping apart).

Proper chopstick etiquette requires that you not wave chopsticks around aimlessly over different dishes trying to select what you want, not stick the chopstick ends into the food like a spear, and not draw the bowl or plate nearer to you with your chopsticks. Korean chopsticks are rarely presented in paper wrappers, so unless you have little ceramic chopstick rests, you need to rest the "mouth" end of your chopsticks alongside the plate, the idea also being that the food end of the chopsticks should never touch the table. Never place your chopsticks parallel to each other across the top of a rice bowl (this is considered to be very rude), and never place bits of unwanted food in a used rice bowl (also considered very rude). Use chopsticks to eat soup (see the chapter on Japan for the proper technique), rice, peanuts, and practically every item on your plate, no matter how small, round, or difficult. Never use your fingers; *always* use your chopsticks. Really. Also use your chopsticks to cut up pieces of food, if necessary; remember, the meat or fish is marinated before cooking, so it will be easy to break up the flesh with the chopsticks: there will be no need for knives. If you simply cannot master chopsticks, it's perfectly all right in the major cities to ask for Western cutlery: you will get a spoon and a fork (rarely a knife); just keep in mind that Western cutlery may not be available in the smaller towns.

While rice is a staple, it is not necessary to eat every grain of rice in your bowl (and there are some Korean dishes where rice is served on the plate with the food); leaving some is fine. Also, a sauce may be mixed with the rice, and the main dish may be eaten with the rice, unlike the practice in Japan. In South Korea, it is not appropriate to hold the rice bowl up to your lips: you should keep the bowl down on the tabletop, if possible, which requires you to do some serious bending over in order to eat it (that's okay; raising the rice bowl is not).

If you're eating noodles or broth, it is not appropriate to slurp the food; however, hot tea may be slurped quietly to cool it off as it enters the mouth. It is appropriate to make a little burp at the end of the meal, indicating satisfaction and fullness.

If there is an unappetizing bit of something in your mouth, and napkins are available (they are at modern restaurants, but may not be in all restaurants throughout the country), simply place the napkin to your mouth and remove the unsavory item from your mouth. Keep it in the napkin until you can dispose of it discreetly.

Dishes may come with their own set of serving chopsticks, which are to be used by everyone, one person at a time, to serve themselves or their neighbor by picking out the food from the main service and placing it on their plate. You must never keep the serving chopsticks after using them; put them back on the main dish after you're done. But sometimes the dishes are presented without serving chopsticks at all. This means that you have to serve yourself with your own chopsticks. This further means that everybody at the table will be sticking their already used chopsticks into the communal dish. For germ-obsessed Westerners, this can sometimes be a problem. If you're considered part of the family, and if you're at someone's home, it will simply be expected that you stick your chopsticks into the main dish like everybody else. As South Korea has modernized, however, a trend has developed of "reversing" the ends of your chopsticks to take food from the serving plate if serving chopsticks are unavailable. It's tricky, but considerate. It goes like this: Hold your chopsticks by the pointy end and pick up food from the main service with the "blunt" end, then place the food on your plate. After that, place the chopsticks down on their rests. When you're ready to eat from your own plate, pick up the chopsticks so that the "food" end is ready, and eat as you normally would. It's sometimes a little tricky holding chopsticks that have been used on both ends, but it's a lot trickier surviving someone else's gastrointestinal infection, or facing down the stares from your table guests who are worried about catching yours.

A word about smoking: it is ubiquitous all throughout Asia. Smoking is usually done after the meal (not in between courses).

Seating Plans

The most honored position is at the middle of the table, with the second most important person seated next. This means that the host will sit at the middle of the table on one side, and the honored guest in the middle on the other side, opposite the host. (Spouses are usually not invited to business meals, and most formal meals in restaurants are business meals: do not ask if your spouse can join you; it will embarrass your Korean colleague into doing something that is uncomfortable for him.) The honored guest sits on the side of the table farthest from the door. (This is the same at business meetings, with the key people sitting in the middle, flanked on either side in descending order by their aides, with the least important people sitting at the ends of the table farthest from the middle, and closest to the door; the arrangement is mirrored on the other side, because the rules of hierarchy demand that everyone must be able to speak with their opposite peers and those who rank below, but those below cannot speak with those above.) Because many banquet tables are round, a curious situation often develops: the least important person from one side ends up sitting next to the host or the most important person on the other side. (This is usually not an issue at business meetings, where tables are more often rectangular.) If women are present, they will probably be given the honored positions first, although practically speaking there will be far fewer women. In South Korea, women typically rise when men enter the room, hold doors open for men, and escort men into a room first.

Refills and Seconds

You will always be offered more food. Leave a bit on your plate if you do not want more food. If you want more at a banquet, merely move the lazy Susan around slowly (after making sure that no one else is preparing to do the same at the same time!). You will be implored to take more two or three times, in the form of a little ritual. The game is as follows: first you refuse, then the host insists, then you refuse again, then the host insists again, and then you finally give in and take a little more. Usually the host will be apologizing to you for the terrible food and begging you to take it anyway to make him feel better. If you really don't want more, take very little and leave it on your plate. You may always have additional beverages; drink enough to cause your cup or glass to be less than half full, and it will generally be refilled. A reminder: never refill your own glass; always refill your neighbor's glass, and he or she will refill yours.

At Home, in a Restaurant, or at Work

In South Korea, it is expected that you wait until the senior person is served and begins to eat before you begin eating or drinking. Try to follow your colleagues' lead in when to drink, eat, or make a toast.

In informal restaurants, you may be required to share a table. If so, do not force conversation; act as if you are seated at a private table. Waitstaff may be summoned by making eye contact; waving or calling their names is very impolite. The business breakfast is really unknown in South Korea. The business lunch is catching on somewhat, but a dinner is the proper venue for business hosting. It is generally not the time to discuss business or make business decisions, however. Take your cue from your Korean associates: if they bring up business, then it's okay to discuss it, but wait to take your lead from their conversation. When the meal is over, the fun usually really begins: drinks get poured, and there can be much singing and joke telling; the key here is to join in the fun. Have a song or two prepared; it doesn't matter how bad you sound or whether they understand the English words, just that you participate and have fun and that everybody enjoys themselves with you.

When invited to a Korean colleague's home for a formal meal, you will be told where to sit, and there you should remain. It is a great honor to be invited into a South Korean home, because many South Koreans feel that Westerners will find their homes too small and crowded; also, older family members might be living there, and your presence will probably make things uncomfortable for you and them (no mutually intelligible language!). Once invited to enter a South Korean home, you will need to remove your shoes (this is not the custom in South Korean restaurants, however). You will probably sit at a table or, more traditionally, on the floor in the middle of the room. Traditional Korean homes are heated with an interesting system known as the *ondol;* hot rocks placed under the house make the floors quite comfortable. Once inside the home, do not wander from room to room: much of the house is really off-limits to guests.

If you move from room to room in a Korean home, be sure to always allow the more senior members of your party to enter the room ahead of you. Be judicious about touching things and moving them about: many items have probably been placed where they are because it is auspicious to do so according to traditional beliefs.

Being a Good Guest or Host

Paying the Bill

Usually the one who does the inviting pays the bill, although the guest is expected to make an effort to pay. Sometimes other circumstances determine the payee (such as rank). Making payment arrangements ahead of time so that no exchange occurs at the table is a very classy way to host, and is very common. When men are at the table, women will not really be able to pay the bill at a restaurant: if you want to, make arrangements ahead of time, and don't wait for the check to arrive at the table. The only time it is considered appropriate for a woman to pay the bill is if she is a businesswoman from abroad.

Transportation

It's a very nice idea, when acting as the host, to inquire ahead of time as to whether your guests will require transportation. If necessary, you should arrange for taxi service at the end of the meal. When seeing your guests off, you must remain at the entrance of the house or the restaurant, or at the site where you deposited your guests into the car, until the car is out of sight: it is very important not to leave until your guests can no longer see you, should they look back. Guests are seated in cars (and taxis) by rank, with the honored guest being placed in the back directly behind the front passenger seat; the next honored position is in the back behind the driver, and the least honored position is up front with the driver.

When to Arrive / Chores to Do

If invited to dinner at a private home, offer to help with the chores, but do not expect to be taken up on your offer. Nor should you expect to visit the kitchen. Do not leave the table unless invited to do so. Spouses might be invited to dinners at a private home, because another person's spouse will probably be there. Be on time. When in someone's home, be careful not to admire things too effusively: Koreans may feel obligated to give it to you, and you in turn will be required to present them with a gift of equal value. Instead of saying things like "I love that vase," say something like "Vases that beautiful in my country are only found in museums." Your compliments will always be dismissed.

Gift Giving

In general, gift giving in South Korea is not as formal as it is in Japan, but it is still very common. In business settings, it usually takes the form of personal gifts that symbolically say the correct thing about the nature of the relationship.

When going to South Korea on business, you must bring gifts for everyone you will see. The general rule is pastries for the office staff, high-quality corporate logo items (all the same) for business associates, and an especially thoughtful, somewhat personalized gift for the key man you will be working with. You present your gifts at the end of your first meeting in South Korea, as a sign of your sincerity and best wishes. You will receive a farewell gift at your last meeting in South Korea before you leave to go home, or when you present your gifts. When South Koreans visit your country, they will bring you a gift, and before they leave, you should give them gifts. Holiday cards are appropriate for less formal relationships, particularly as a thank-you for their business during the previous year.

The most appropriate gift for a personal visit to a home, or as a thank-you for dinner, would be a box of fruits, pastries, cakes, cookies, or ginseng from the United States (where Koreans believe the finest ginseng is grown). Flowers are generally not appropriate. Never sign a card or note in red ink; it is believed to bring bad luck. There is no need to send a handwritten thank-you note the day after the dinner party. If you are staying with a family, an appropriate thank-you gift would be a high-quality item that represents your country and is difficult to get in South Korea; this is also a good idea for a key business associate. Acceptable gifts include coffee-table books about the United States, or anything that reflects your host's personal tastes (the cap of a famous American team for the football-playing son of the family, for example). Native handicrafts or well-framed and well-mounted photographs of you and your Korean associates are also appreciated. Be sure the gift you give does not have a tag or sticker on it that says it was made in Korea, Japan, China, or anywhere else in Asia.

The more you can personalize your "key man" gift, the more it is appreciated. For a high-ranking key male, the best gift you can give is often a bottle of fine whiskey or cognac, or some other luxury item.

If your gift consists of several items, be sure that they do not total up to an even number (bad luck), never to four (very bad luck) or nine (also bad luck), and preferably to three or seven (very good luck). Avoid handkerchiefs, as they symbolize sadness, and cutlery as a gift, which symbolizes the severing of a relationship.

For both giving and receiving gifts, two hands are always used (with the "elbow support" gesture). Gifts are typically not opened by the receiver in front of the giver; they are usually received, graciously acknowledged, and placed aside to be opened once the giver is no longer present.

Gifts must be wrapped well. When purchasing any of the previously mentioned items in South Korea, it will be wrapped beautifully for you, especially if you make it known that it is a gift. Most gifts are wrapped in ordinary paper first, and then wrapped again in either red or gold (royal colors) or yellow or pink (happy colors) paper. Several colors are not used for wrapping: green; white and black, because they are funereal colors; and blue, the color of mourning.

Special Holidays and Celebrations

Major Holidays

The most popular vacation time in South Korea is during the Korean New Year (it is a lunar holiday, so the date changes every year, as is the case with all lunar holidays). The celebration lasts at least a week, if not longer, in some areas, and everybody simply stops work and goes home to family and friends. This is a very slow time of year for business.

January 1–3 (solar)	New Year
January/February (lunar)	Lunar (Korean) New Year
March 1 (solar)	Independence Movement Day
April 5 (solar)	Arbor Day (unofficial)
May (lunar)	Buddha's Birthday
May 5 (solar)	Children's Day
July 17 (solar)	Constitution Day
August 15 (solar)	Independence Day
September (lunar)	*Ch'usok* (Thanksgiving Day)
October 1 (solar)	Armed Forces Day
October 3 (solar)	National Foundation Day
October 9 (solar)	Korean Language Day (unofficial)
December 25 (solar)	Christmas

In addition, in South Korea, birthdays are not traditionally celebrated on a yearly basis; however, special year-marker birthdays are, usually with a feast with the family. When a child reaches his or her third birthday, there is a celebration, and when a man reaches his sixtieth birthday, there is a special celebration (*hwan'gap*).

Business Culture

Daily Office Protocols

The traditional Korean office has an open design; there are few doors, with the exception of the offices of those holding higher positions, and people work mainly at long large tables or in individual or shared cubicles. Doors, if they do exist, are usually open. The open scheme is similar to the office arrangement described in the chapter on Japan.

In the Korean business organization, decision making usually occurs at the highest levels. Executives have their offices on different floors than those occupied by the rank and file. You probably will not be invited onto the section floors until the proposed project has been set in motion.

Work begins at around 9 A.M. and ends officially at 5 P.M., but dinners and other entertainments are part of the workday for most. Many businesses have Saturday half-day hours.

Management Styles

Because of the rigid rank and hierarchy orientation in Korean businesses, titles are very important; the highest ones (e.g., vice president) are usually reserved for very senior, executive-level positions, and should not be used as casually as they are in the United States. Complimenting and rewarding employees publicly is usually not done. Deference is shown by subordinates to their seniors; paternalistic concern is often shown by executives to their juniors. In South Korea, your ability to get things done is directly proportionate to who you know, and major business contacts also usually work hand in hand with the government or with the blessings of a cabinet minister or official. It is important, therefore, to always be apprised of the standing of your counterparts vis-à-vis the government ministers that they work with. This will affect your business success.

Boss-Subordinate Relations

The decision-making system usually works from the top on down, with key decisions often coming from individuals in high positions of authority. There are formal and informal networking opportunities, but generally, access to power is what determines action.

Conducting a Meeting or Presentation

At your first meeting in South Korea, you will probably be received in a very comfortable waiting area, which may or may not be where most of the meeting is conducted between yourself and your South Korean colleague. If this is the case, you are merely being sized up, and your colleague is a gatekeeper. When serving any refreshments in the office, be sure they are served in porcelain tea sets or sake cups: the use of paper or Styrofoam shows disrespect and is very bad form. At meetings of peers, there can be open communication and sharing of ideas: however, most meetings are formalities at which information is exchanged, or decisions that have already been made are confirmed. In most cases, you will be meeting with an individual; if he is high ranking, and if the meeting is not in the introductory stage, this individual may well be the decision maker. Remember, most traditional South Korean businesses are also members of larger conglomerates, or *chaebols;* this means there may be others that even your key South Korean contact may have to involve in order for things to move forward, and this may take some time. If this is just the beginning of a business relationship, expect to spend most of the time sharing information about your organization; you may need to repeat the same things to different people. This is okay, for it means your plans are advancing to the right people in the organization, and that those you have previously met with have approved of you and moved you on. Patience and third-party connections with the most senior people from the beginning are key.

Negotiation Styles

The first meeting is usually very formal, with your South Korean counterpart(s) sizing up you and your organization. Expect no decisions at the table, and be willing to provide copious amounts of information, to the degree that you can, in response to their questions and in anticipation of their needs. Presentations should be well prepared and simply propounded. Details are best left to questions and backup material, which should be translated into Korean and left behind. Ideally, you should present your material to the South Koreans for study, along with a proposed agenda, prior to the meeting. Have extra copies available, as you will meet more people than you will expect. You should come with a small, well-organized team, whose roles have been clearly thought out and defined. Never disagree with one another in front of the South Korean team, or appear uncertain or unsure.

The South Koreans will bargain, although if they have a good feeling about you, price usually will not be an issue, if it is fair. Although the contract must be legal down to the dotted i's, remember that to the South Koreans it is a piece of paper that merely signifies the beginning of the negotiation; things can change over time, and good partners must take care of each other by being flexible.

Plan your meetings as carefully and as well in advance as you can, and avoid surprises and any unexpected changes (but expect them in this fluid world). Keep your communications, especially when at a distance, open and stay in touch often with your South Korean colleagues: share more information than you normally would, not less; and have a contact on the ground in South Korea who can always keep you informed of what is really going on.

Written Correspondence

Your business letter should be very formal and respectful of rank and hierarchy. Always begin with the opening, "To my dear respected . . . [name plus title]." Last names are usually written in uppercase; dates are given in the year/month/day format (with periods in between, not slashes); and an honorific plus the title is as common as the honorific plus the last name. You should write your e-mails, letters, and faxes in a precise way; use a brief introduction, then quickly get down to business. Keep it simple, however, and outline all important matters. In South Korea, and throughout most of the region, the address is usually given as follows:

Line one: country and postal code
Line two: city (and prefecture)
Line three: street address
Line four: company and/or personal name

The Southeast Asian Cultures: Thailand

Some Introductory Background on Thailand and the Thais

Formerly known as Siam, this kingdom (yes, it is still a kingdom) is an anomaly in Southeast Asia in several ways; most significantly, it is the only country in the region never to have been colonized by an outside power or captured by one of its neighbors. This is a powerful example of the Thai value for independence; in fact, Thais and Americans have a lot in common, based primarily on this fact. There is much, however, that is very different between the two peoples (particularly the Thai emphasis on hierarchy and Confucian values). Nevertheless, the Thai people do have a remarkably iconoclastic sense of independence and individualism, relative to the rest of the region; in fact, the word *Thai* means "free people." They do not appreciate being confused with their Southeast Asian neighbors.

Some Historical Context

As with most of the countries in Southeast Asia, Thailand has had to struggle against both its larger neighbors to the north (China and Japan, particularly: it is ironic, for the Thais, as a people, had their origins in southern China, and the Chinese culture still heavily influences Thai culture; in fact, much of the dynamic city of Bangkok is controlled by the Chinese immigrant community there) and European colonial powers. In the nineteenth century, King Mongkut steered his country on a treacherous course between the French on one side and the British on the other. Admittedly, he had to deal, negotiate, compromise, and fight, but he managed to keep Thailand free; subsequently, his son, King Chulalongkorn, continued along the delicate path of maintaining freedom and independence from the West while adapting some of its ways to help his country modernize (he banished slavery in Thailand, for example). For most of its history, Thailand was, in an almost classic sense, a paradise; when discovered by the West, it was romanticized. Its people were mostly agrarian, tending to crops that would almost pick themselves. They were surrounded by plenty, both on land and in the sea, in an environment that was easy and for the most part unchallenging. The land provided a tranquil way of life; it certainly did not promote struggle, or support the development of concepts like delayed gratification, reward for effort, original sin, or other notions brought later by Westerners. Today, Thailand is a complex mixture of both the original culture and Western influences. Bangkok is a fast-paced, chaotic jumble of Western business practices and Thai cultural beliefs, and a train ride out of Bangkok to the up-country region near the city of Chiang Mai is a quick return to the paradisiacal Thailand of the past.

An Area Briefing

Politics and Government

Thailand is a constitutional monarchy, with the king as supreme head of state. The king and the royal family are beloved by the Thais: make no comment about them that is disparaging in any way. (Even commenting on the film *The King and I,* or *Anna and the King of Siam,* the story on which it is based, is not appreciated: Thais find the film and the book very offensive, as they romanticize Thailand through Western values, and use the royal family as entertainment for Westerners, against whom Thais often had to struggle to maintain their freedom. There is a representative government (the National Assembly), headed by the prime minister, who is in charge of the government. It is the king, however, who is seen as the leader of the country.

Schools and Education

Schooling is free and mandatory for all elementary-grade children. The Thai equivalent of high school follows after grade school, and state-run universities are available to those who qualify academically after high school. Chulalongkorn University in Bangkok is the premier college, and students there typically are funneled into the top government and business positions. Education has always been an essential Confucian ideal, and parents place great hope on the advancement of their children through education. More and more, this also includes girls, although only boys were traditionally privileged to receive an education. Many Thai students seek to advance their university studies by going abroad to the West; such programs often require that after their studies, these students return to Thailand to bring their knowledge and skills back home. Many do, some do not.

Religion and Demographics

As we will see throughout the rest of eastern Asia, religions are not institutionalized belief systems as they are in the West. The religious influences in Thailand are strong, but they are not religions per se. It would be more correct to refer to them as philosophies of life. Most Thais (over 90 percent) are Buddhists. Elements of Confucianism and even Islam also influence the behaviors and beliefs of the society as a whole.

Theravada Buddhism is the primary influence in Thailand. Buddhism began in India around 600 B.C. Its founder was Siddhartha Gautama, the Buddha, a privileged Hindu priest who, in attempting to learn the meaning of life, discovered, among other things, that his privilege brought him no happiness, and that if one was to achieve true happiness, one had to sacrifice in the secular here and now in specific ways in order to achieve a higher level in the next life. In many ways, the theology that evolved was an effort to purify what had become, in the Buddha's mind and others, a debased and corrupt Hindu religion in India at that time by placing moral responsibility onto the individual, and relying less upon the religious hierarchy. This created, as you may imagine, some difficulty for the Buddha and his followers and the existing Hindu establishment; subsequently, Buddhism was both integrated into existing Hindu belief, and banished from India. Its principles survived, however, rooting in China, parts of Southeast Asia, and ultimately in Japan. As Buddhism spread eastward, it developed two branches: Mahayana Buddhism (mainly in the north), which makes the individual responsible for attaining nirvana directly, and Theravada Buddhism (mainly in the south), in which a much more rigid hierarchy exists, and in which individuals are dependent on ordained monks, for it is only monks (and nuns) who can achieve nirvana. Theravada Buddhism, coupled with strong hierarchical Confucian values from China, combine to give the Thais a very strong preference for hierarchy.

Confucianism, based on the teachings of Confucius, a Chinese sage who lived around 500 B.C., has had a powerful impact on Asian culture. Confucius lived during a turbulent and chaotic time in China, and established a philosophy of life that attempted to prescribe the correct and proper way for individuals to relate to one another in order to achieve a well-ordered, functioning society. The essence of his ideas involves the importance of observing and maintaining structures, roles, and hierarchy, so that, paraphrasing his words, "the son obeys the father, the wife obeys the husband, the younger brother obeys the older brother, the husband obeys the state," and so on. Society will work when everyone knows his or her place, understands his or her obligations to others in the hierarchy, and, in fact, seeks primarily not to change his or her role but to perfect it. This provides much philosophical support for the rigid hierarchies that exist in Thailand and elsewhere in Asia.

Children are revered in Thailand, girls as well as boys. There is no real discrimination against girls. Women in Thailand have traditionally played a role in the family businesses, but are not equal to men in the business hierarchy. Non-Thai businesswomen, though still difficult for many Thai businessmen to understand and work with, are not subject to these constraints, and may succeed in the Thai business environment as long as their authority is clear and maintained, though they must be nonaggressive and respectful.

It is important throughout Thailand (and throughout all of Asia) not to assume an Asian is of one nationality or another: while most of the people in Thailand are Thai, there is a sizable Chinese minority, especially in Bangkok.

Fundamental Cultural Orientations

1. What's the Best Way for People to Relate to One Another?

OTHER-INDEPENDENT OR OTHER-DEPENDENT? Independence and freedom are such a central part of Thai culture that it would be easy to see Thais as strong individualists; in many ways they are, and each individual is responsible for his or her actions. But overlaid on top of this strong spirit of independence is an awareness that one acts individually in order to benefit one's group first, and only then oneself, as a secondary consequence. One's group usually consists of one's family, beginning with the nuclear family, but quickly spreading out to include a vast array of uncles and aunts, and most extended (by Western standards) family members—both living and dead! One's group may also include the people with whom one works; however, unless and until a Thai feels an association with one group or another, their actions must always first be true to themselves. In short, they are independent thinkers.

HIERARCHY-ORIENTED OR EGALITY-ORIENTED? Structure and hierarchy are critical at all levels in Thai society—in the home, at school, in the military, and in business. A Confucian formality has developed around what one does and with whom; it is essential to show the proper respect for individuals, depending on their rank and position, in order to succeed in Thailand. There is even a more formal Thai language that must be used when speaking with people at the highest levels of government and with Thai royalty. Hierarchy is honored through humility and making face; this is done by "lowering," or minimizing, oneself. In fact, one makes more of oneself, and raises one's esteem in the eyes of others, by doing so. Women and men, young and old, royal and commoner, all have separate roles in society. This emphasis on hierarchy also normalizes unequal relationships: it is, after all, natural that some be in charge and others not, that some have power and others not, that some dictate and others follow. This is of critical importance to Thais.

RULE-ORIENTED OR RELATIONSHIP-ORIENTED? Rules are universal within the constraints of both the hierarchy and the demands of the situation. There is a tension in Thai society between the obligations that one faces based on one's relationships with individuals of different ranks, and the need for individuals to take care of themselves, as well as those for whom they are responsible. This is revealed in a "here-and-now" attitude: what is best for all involved in the immediate given situation, after considering all factors, is usually what determines the chosen action.

2. What's the Best Way to View Time?

MONOCHRONIC OR POLYCHRONIC? Because punctuality also reflects other values, such as concern for the other person and humility before someone else's efforts, the Thais are more or less punctual; certainly, you should be. Nevertheless, in the big picture, as is the case with most traditional Asian cultures, time has historically stood in the background to immediate personal relationships; and this is still very much the case in Thailand today. Things will take the time they need to take, and the clock is not the ultimate arbiter of what occurs and when. Thais will move very quickly to seize an advantage if one presents itself; they certainly want to succeed as quickly as possible, but they will not do anything that is not in their best interest simply because of time. Unless it is on their terms, they have time to wait it out.

Daily life in Thailand has historically been arranged according to vast, agriculturally based blocks of time, over which no individual or government had control: seasons, day and night. Even today, schedules tend to be loose and flexible; the workday begins around 8 A.M. and ends around 5 P.M. Most workers take an hour break and a midafternoon nap after lunch. But time moves more slowly in general than in the modern West, and there is no advantage to rushing about.

RISK-TAKING OR RISK-AVERSE? Essentially, individual Thais are comfortable with uncertainty, although groups tend to have a higher need for certainty, probably as a result of their obligation to protect higher-ups in the chain of command in the hierarchy.

PAST-ORIENTED OR FUTURE-ORIENTED? Buddhism is essentially fatalistic, and in that sense, there is an acceptance of events that occur unexpectedly and outside of one's control. However, the prevailing ethic of individualism, coupled with the country's paradisiacal traditions (live and work for and in the here and now), give Thais a strong orientation to the present: neither the past (it has already happened, so why bother dwelling on it?), nor the future (it is not in their control) are of great concern to the people. Thais are focused on the here and now, on what they can do to enjoy themselves today. This attitude differs from other Asians in the region, who have a strong orientation to the past, and from Americans, who have a strong orientation to the future. Action for Thais is for now, not for tomorrow, and not because of yesterday (although the Buddhist traditions of honoring and respecting one's ancestry are very strong).

3. What's the Best Way for Society to Work with the World at Large?

LOW-CONTEXT DIRECT OR HIGH-CONTEXT INDIRECT COMMUNICATORS? The Thais are a very high-context people. They avoid confrontation, and will speak in terms that maintain harmony at all costs, even if this results in speech that is indirect and evasive. Because circumstances rather than universal laws mainly determine the action to be taken, sensitivity to the context is critical if you want accurate information on what is really being meant or done. However, Thais are aware of the importance of contracts and will be bound by them; it's just that they will perform according to the terms of the agreement because they want to, not because it is on a piece of paper. Making them want to means being sure that it is in their best interest, and that trust and good relations exist between you.

PROCESS-ORIENTED OR RESULT-ORIENTED? Thais, as is the case with all Asian peoples, are fully capable of employing (and do employ) meticulous logic, whether deductively or inductively; however, that is not necessarily the only process used to think things through, to make a case for something, or to understand people or events. A connection is made to similar situations; in fact, the Thais rely primarily on this associative, subjective logic. This is often applied in a holistic, nonsequential way: process and experience are important steps in arriving at a conclusion, but the path may not be linear or progressive. This is related to the polychronic nature of the culture: things occur, thought patterns included, not necessarily in a sequential or progressive way, but in a holistic way. In other words, the elements needed to make decisions are laid out expositionally, when and as the circumstances require it, and add up to a conclusion only when viewed "at once," as if suddenly from forty thousand feet.

FORMAL OR INFORMAL? In Thailand, rigid hierarchies and fluid situations require flexible forms of behavior: people can be formal at one moment, and informal the next. The "here-and-now" orientation of the people is also supported by the importance that Thais place on doing things that are fulfilling and fun: the concept is called *senuke*. If things aren't *senuke*, then they simply are not worth doing. *Senuke* is the pleasure one gets out of life, either because one is doing something one finds fulfilling, or doing it with people one enjoys, or relaxing with family and friends. *Senuke* can also come from following the rules, but it is associated more with doing things in daily life in a way that brings harmony and joy. It is a result of the paradisiacal traditions of southeast Asia, and is often the reason why Thais may sometimes be resistant to long-term planning and delayed gratification. Life is to be lived.

Greetings and Introductions

Language and Basic Vocabulary

The Thai language can be difficult for Westerners to master, pronunciation being one of the hurdles. There are no articles in Thai, so it is important to be clear if *the* or *a* is meant, in keeping with the meaning of the context of the discussion. This is also the case with tenses; there are no past or future tenses, only present, so one conveys when something happens by the context or the use of additional words to further define the tense.

Because it is so important for Thais to avoid disharmony, do not use double negatives, and do not ask questions that could result in yes or no answers. In a culture where the emphasis is placed on preserving harmony and face, and where much communication is therefore very high-context and subtle, any answer that could imply difficulty, a rejection of a request, or make the respondent appear uncooperative is evaded. This evasion is expressed in a number of ways nonverbally, but often results in unreliable verbal responses. "Yes" more often means "I hear what you are saying, keep talking," not "I agree with what you are saying." To avoid this problem, ask open-ended questions that require a substantive, informational response.

Most Thais speak little or no English (younger ones are learning English in school, however); well-educated Thai businesspeople probably do speak some English. In business meetings, because the English competency of your Thai colleagues may be low, it is important to have interpreters—preferably your own—throughout. If you know some Thai, use it: your Thai colleagues will be amazed and charmed!

Here are the necessary starters in Thai:

sawadee-krup	hello, thank you (for a male speaker)
sawadee-kah	hello, thank you (for a female speaker)
gahroonah	thank you
choo-ay	please

Honorifics for Men, Women, and Children

Until recently, most Southeast Asian cultures did not use surnames: people were referred to by their given names (their membership in a particular clan was understood). However, Thais and other peoples in modernizing Southeast Asian cultures have gradually incorporated the family name into the full name, and the order of both the given and the family names are generally as in the West: first name first, family name second. Because the given name has traditionally been the more important one, any use of honorifics is more common with the given name, and not the lately adopted family name. In addition, many Chinese Thais use their Chinese names, or use Anglicized initials in place of their Thai or Chinese name, as an accommodation to Westerners (this Anglicized version may also appear on their business cards). Recognize that ethnic Thais usually take the positions in government, while Chinese Thais often have premier positions in business: relations are not always easy between the two groups.

If Chinese Thais are using their Chinese names, they will usually order their names, in most cases, the Chinese way: family names first, followed by a given generational name, and then finally a given name (last). There is often a hyphen between the generational and the given names, making the two given names more often than not a two- (or more) syllable name. Most of the time, the Chinese family name is a single syllable (there are in fact only several hundred family or clan names, so most Chinese have similar family names, with the generational and the given names primarily distinguishing one from the other). If Hong-bo Tan has introduced herself as such, she has reversed the Chinese name format to accommodate the Westerner, putting her given name first and her family name last, Western style (you know this because the two-syllabled name, usually the combination of the generational and the given names, is being presented first). You would refer to this person with the correct Chinese honorific after the family name, because it is a Chinese name. If Thais are using their Thai names, they may abbreviate the first and/or last name(s) (again, an accommodation to the Westerner), as Thai names often are complicated for Westerners. In this case, you would use the Thai honorific with the first name.

Khun is the honorific used most often for Mr./Mrs./Ms. or Miss (there are longer forms for different levels, but for most Western travelers and businesspeople, *khun* suffices). This is placed, as in the West, before the name; but the name used, more often than not, will be the given (or first) name. For example, Churamart (given name) Bamrungsook (family name) becomes Khun Churamart; or Zhang (Chinese family name) Kai-chek (generational name + given name) becomes Khun Zhang.

A Thai married woman would be properly addressed as *khun* plus the name she uses. However, there are two forms for addressing a married Chinese Thai woman. Traditionally, Chinese women did not lose their own family name, nor take their husband's family name. Therefore, for married Chinese women, use the honorific "madame" plus her family name. For example, if Li Hong-bo marries Chang Kai-chek, she would be correctly referred to as Madame Li, *not* Mrs. Chang.

Do not worry about moving from the last name to the first name, or formal to informal, when using Thai names. In Thailand, "first" names is already the formal way. Children in Thailand are expected to be respectful and not overly conversational when speaking with adults, and must always use honorifics when referring to adults. As they probably speak limited English, this makes conversation with children that much more difficult.

In situations where a title is known, the title plus the honorific is frequently used, either with or without the name (e.g., Mr. Engineer or Engineer Surachart for an ethnic Thai, and Engineer Li for a Chinese Thai). For casual contacts (e.g., with waiters, store help, etc.), just use *khun*. It is very important to greet people at work, in stores, or in restaurants in an appropriate fashion for the time of day.

The What, When, and How of Introducing People

Sometimes upon greeting you, Thais will simply call you by your first or last name, or make a comment about the task you are performing: this does not require a substantive response.

Always wait to be introduced to strangers; never take that responsibility upon yourself, as doing so is considered inappropriate most of the time. Thais are most comfortable with a third-party introduction whenever one is possible, and will go to great lengths to ensure that you are not left alone to decide this for yourself. Never presume to seat yourself at a gathering; if possible, wait to be told where to sit. The seating arrangements have usually been carefully worked out in advance, and in most cases reflect the status of the individuals in the group, and the honor that is being accorded the guests. When departing, it is important to say farewell with a quick bow to every individual present: the American group wave is not appreciated. Once you greet someone you will encounter later that day in the same circumstances (e.g., at the office), you will need to acknowledge them with a quick, foreshortened bow, or *wai* (see later in this chapter), whenever you see them again. Seniors, or those who are obviously the oldest in a group, are greeted first, seated first, and allowed to enter a room first (usually at the center of the group, however, and preceded in most cases by their younger aides).

Physical Greeting Styles

Like many Asian cultures, Thailand is a nontouching culture—at least at first. Only the most intimate of friends (mainly young people) will touch each other in greeting. The handshake is a Western invention, and not native to Thailand: the Thais have, of course, become accustomed to it, but because it is done for the Westerner's benefit, it is generally an accommodation added to the traditional greeting, called the *wai*. To do this, put your hands together in a prayer position and hold them in front of your chest so that when you bend your head down enough for your eyes to see the floor the tips of your fingers just barely touch your forehead. Should there be a follow-up handshake, it is usually very soft, almost limp. This does not signify insincerity; rather, it is an indication of humility using a Western convention. Western women must always extend their hands first for a handshake, if one is to occur at all; if so, it is inevitably very soft. If you are introduced to a monk or nun, never extend your hand; monks must never be touched by anyone (especially women; in fact, women cannot even touch something that will then be passed on to a monk).

The traditional Thai business introduction also includes the exchange of business cards. Always take a large supply of business cards with you to Thailand: you must give one to every new person you are introduced to (there is no need to provide another business card when you are meeting someone again unless information about you has changed, such as a new address, contact number, or position). Be sure your business cards are in fine shape: they are extensions of you as a person, and must look as good as possible. Never hand out a dirty, soiled, bent, or written-on card. You should, if possible, have your business card translated into Thai on the reverse side before you go to Thailand (some finer hotels and some airlines, as well as your own business, will do this as a service for you). When presenting a business card, you give it to your Thai associate with the Thai side up, so that it is readable for him as you hold it (he will, in turn, present his card English side up, so it's readable for you); you must hold the card in the upper right- and left-hand corners, requiring the use of two hands, and you also receive your Thai associate's card with two hands, on the upper right- and left-hand corners. The exchange is done quickly, almost simultaneously. Remember, the *wai* comes first, the exchange of business cards later. When you *wai,* be sure that the position of the person you are recognizing is demonstrated by the depth of the accompanying bow: deeper and longer for more senior and older people and less so for less senior and younger people (for example, the *wai* is used to greet people on the street, but you wouldn't *wai* to waiters—they serve you; you would *wai* to acquaintances, most definitely to senior family members, and more deeply to supervisors and clients).

Smiling and other nonverbal forms of communication usually accompany the card exchange; it is appropriate to appear genuinely pleased to meet the other person. When first introduced to your Thai colleague, drop your eyes as you *wai.*

Information about each other's status is the most important information to be exchanged, and this is provided directly on the business card, as well as indirectly through a number of high-context indicators, such as gray hair (indicating age), gender (male), and the number of people surrounding and assisting the other person (important people have many assistants). Humility before rank can be demonstrated subtly, by placing your business card underneath the card of the other person during the exchange. Once you have received the other person's card, it is important to stand upright again, holding the card with two hands, and silently read the card for a few seconds. Do not try to say his name, as this may be embarrassingly difficult for you. It is at this point that the soft and limp handshake should occur, if at all. All this happens rather quickly, and should you meet more than one Thai, you will have a handful of cards when it is over.

As this ritual usually precedes a sit-down meeting, it is important to arrange the cards you have received in a little seating plan in front of you along the top of the desk or the table at your seat, reflecting the order in which people are seated. This will help you connect the correct names with the correct individuals throughout the meeting. Do this even if you are just meeting one person; it is expected. During the meeting, it is important never to play with the business cards (do not write on them—ever!); and when the meeting is over, never put them in your back pants pockets: pick them up carefully and respectfully, and place them neatly in your business card holder (a nice-looking leatherbound or brass case would be perfect), then place the card holder in the left inside jacket pocket of your suit (nearest your heart). By the way, if you are applauded while making a presentation in Thailand, or anywhere in Southeast Asia, it is customary to applaud back.

Communication Styles

Okay Topics / Not Okay Topics

Okay: anything that reflects your personal interests and hobbies, or your curiosity about things Thai. *Not okay:* Politics, current events, or any subject that might in any way be controversial needs to be avoided at first. Do not inquire about a person's occupation or income in casual conversation, although it may be inquired of you (if so, this is just a way of getting to know more about your country, and not a personal investigation: answer specifically, but fully, with an explanation as to what things cost at home, why you do what you do, etc.). Do not inquire about your colleague's family life. Do not give your opinions about the role of the king or the royal family in *any* way (if images such as photographs or paintings of the royal family or the king appear, you must stand up). Do not discuss negatively the spiciness of Thai food (it can be incredibly hot), or the economic difficulties in the region. Avoid conversations about sex. Do not discuss religion, either, as this Western concept may not actually be understood. Do not complain: things that are annoying are best left ignored, and while Thais will probably dismiss any words of admiration, like everyone, they love to be flattered. Sticking to general themes of personal interest or business is fine; it is a way of seeking common ground. There will be no need to begin a conversation with the very American "So, what do you do?" since you already know this from the business card exchange; however, further discussions about your company and its work are very much appreciated, as this gives the Thais a chance to learn more about you and your firm. The goal of all conversation, at least at the beginning, is to create and maintain a harmonious atmosphere, despite the difficult or confrontational nature of the topic being discussed. At first, speak about things that you believe you have in common so that you can build a personal connection, which will go far toward maintaining a harmonious bridge between you. This is appropriate for both individuals and organizations.

Tone, Volume, and Speed

Thais generally speak in soft, hushed tones. Speak slowly, for the benefit of those translating, in short phrases, and speak clearly. Try to speak expositionally, without emotion, if possible. As words are for the most part not the best vehicles for communication when attempting to overcome language differences, use pictures, graphics, and charts to augment the topic being discussed, whenever possible. Illustrate what you can say, and certainly what you cannot. This is a very symbol-oriented culture. As an American once said to me, "No matter how I act in Thailand, I always feel like a bull in a china closet." Tone your reactions way down.

Use of Silence

Passive silence—allowing time to pass simply, without words—can be a form of proactive communication in Thailand. There may be long pauses between comments, but rarely extending over several minutes. When confronted with silence, for whatever reason, the best response is to remain silent yourself, although this may be difficult and appear unproductive for time-conscious Westerners. This is perhaps the most subtle form of communication, yet communication it is. If you must say something, bring up something positive, even if it is unrelated to the previous statement. Remember, in Asia, "silence is golden"; those who speak too much are considered immature, given how careful one must be with what one says. Because some Westerners find silence disconcerting, they may tend to fill up the space with more talk; resist this impulse, as it only enhances the effectiveness of the silence, by forcing the Westerner to say more than he or she might normally be inclined to.

Physical Gestures and Facial Expressions

In Thailand, there is little physical gesturing of any kind. If you have a tendency to speak with your hands, you will consciously have to try to control it: most of the time, such gesturing is considered excessive, and will engender surprise, laughter, and sometimes frozen disbelief (always with a smile, though, which makes for a very odd expression on the face!). In fact, laughter may or may not be in response to anything humorous in the Western sense (jokes may not be understood); more often, laughter, in the form of giggling, is an expression of embarrassment when the Thais do not understand something. The eternal Thai smile, however, is a general way of getting through the day, of keeping things pleasant and soft. Practice it. Winking, whistling, and similar displays are considered very vulgar. Public displays of familiarity and affection with the opposite sex are expressed only by teenagers. When physically coming between or passing people, it is appropriate to bow slightly as you go by. Never touch anyone, including small children, on his or her head: this is considered to be the holiest part of the body. Equally, do not point with or intentionally show the sole of your shoe to anyone: this is considered vulgar, as the bottom of the shoe touches the ground, and is therefore the dirtiest part of the body. Always give a small donation to monks and the indigent when you pass them on the street.

Waving and Counting

The pinkie represents the number 1, the thumb represents the number 5, with everything in between ordered from the pinkie down; however, instead of raising the fingers when counting, the whole hand is exposed, and each finger is depressed as the counting is done. It is very insulting to motion to someone with the forefinger; instead, turn your hand with the palm facing down and motion inward with all four fingers at once. If you need to gesture for a waiter, very subtly raise your hand. Waving or beckoning is done with the palm down and the fingers moving forward and backward in a kind of scratching motion. It may seem as if the person making this motion is saying good-bye to you, when in fact you are being summoned over.

Physicality and Physical Space

Most Thais stand, relative to North Americans, just a little farther apart; resist the urge at first to move in closer. Never, upon first greeting a Thai, touch him beyond the soft handshake: no backslaps, no hugging, no kissing, *ever*. Never speak with your hands in your pockets: always keep them firmly at your side when standing. If men and women must cross their legs when they sit, it must never be ankle over knee (for women, the preferred style is to cross ankle over ankle). Remember, in public, formal is always better than informal: no gum chewing, *ever;* don't slouch; and don't lean against things. The Thais can be very formal at first when they sit and stand in business settings, but they can relax quickly: take your cues from them. Once close relationships are established, and especially in those moments when spontaneity and friendliness are allowed (such as at a bar or walking down the street after an evening meal), there may be much physicality—touching, for example, or putting arms around other people's shoulders, or holding hands—but generally only between members of the same sex, and not in public between members of the opposite sex. About the only time this nonphysicality rule is broken is on public transport, where it is very crowded and touching is unavoidable, or on crowded streets, where you are very likely to be poked and prodded—but with a smile—as people jostle by.

Eye Contact

In Thailand, eye contact is very indirect. Only upon the first introduction do eyes meet, and respect and humility are demonstrated, whenever necessary, by lowering the eyes. Interest in what one's supervisor is saying is shown by averting the eyes, not by making eye contact. The eyes are used extensively to convey true feelings in formal situations where it may be difficult to express one's thoughts verbally. Tune up your nonverbal antennae.

Emotive Orientation

Thais can be very restrained emotionally, but not stony. Keep the smile, but turn down the volume. It is important for the Westerner to consciously control emotive impulses.

Protocol in Public

Walking Styles and Waiting in Lines

On the street, in stores, and in most public facilities, people pay little attention to maintaining orderly lines. Due to the volume of passengers on public transportation, there can be much pushing and jostling. This is not to get into a train or bus ahead of someone else, though; it is merely to get in!

Behavior in Public Places: Airports, Terminals, and the Market

Customer service is a well-developed practice in Thailand, because the "other" (in this case, the customer) is so important, and because demonstrating good customer service involves showing deference to the customer. Stores in the cities are open in the evenings and on weekends, as well as during the day; there is a very good chance you will be bowed to as you enter and leave a store, and by all clerks as they help you. A personal thank-you to store owners, waiters, chefs, and hotel managers for their services is very much appreciated. In food markets, don't worry about touching the produce, since everybody does, and it doesn't obligate you to buy it; but in goods stores, if you buy a product and have problems with it, returning the item may be difficult. Smoking is endemic, and you may have difficulty finding a no-smoking area on public transportation, in restaurants, and in other public places. Bathroom facilities can range from Western-style toilets to Asian-style toilets (holes in the floor, with buckets of water or hoses attached to a water line for cleanup instead of paper); be prepared.

When answering a telephone, say "*sawadee-krup*" or "*sawadee-kah,*" or just your given name. Cell phones are ubiquitous.

Bus / Metro / Taxi / Car

Driving is on the right, and whether in the country or city, being in a car can be hazardous to your health. The roads are not necessarily in good repair, marked, or where maps say they are; and obtaining fuel when and where you need it can be a problem. Bangkok traffic is a maddening and chaotic nightmare, and construction sites are everywhere.

The best way to catch a cab is at designated taxi stands (hotels are good places, but often charge more for the same ride: a hotel surcharge is added to the meter fare, in some cases). When a taxi has been hailed, negotiate the price, as the meter may or may not be working (even if it is, you must negotiate the price ahead of time). Whenever possible, have the address you need to get to written down on a piece of paper (or use the business card of the person you are going to see, if you can) before you hail the cab. A small map outlining the route is great, if you can have one prepared before you go. Taking a *tuk-tuk*—a one- or two-person, open-air seat on the back of a motorbike—is a good idea; they can whiz right through stalled traffic. You might get soaked, however, in one of the endless tropical downpours sitting in one.

Tipping

Tipping is not really part of the scene in Thailand, but if you leave approximately 5 percent for restaurant, taxi, or porter service, it will be appreciated.

Punctuality

While the culture is essentially polychronic, punctuality is expected in all situations. Do not arrive more than five minutes too soon—or more than five minutes late, for that matter. Your Thai associates, however, may be late: wait patiently. You will not be told if your tardiness has caused a problem, of course, but in most cases, it will not help your image. When a meeting is over in a Thai office, it is best to leave the room before the Thais do, as they may need to discuss your proposal for quite some time after you leave. Do not expect them to always see you out.

Dress

The Thai standard is more or less fashionable and western. It is neither very formal, but certainly not informal, at work; and socially, dressing up instead of down is preferred. Thais like to see people looking as successful as they want others to think they are. At work, male managers wear dark suits, white shirts, and snappy ties, and the shoes should be polished; accessories such as tie clips and bracelets are not uncommon. Women can accessorize, and often come to work fully made up. A stylish business dress is appropriate for women at work, and it need not be conservative. Heels are fine. On the street, informal may mean jeans and sneakers, though that is more common as clothing to wear at the gym or while jogging (some women do wear sneakers to work, but change just before they enter the office, not after going in); because of the heat, shorts are okay on the street with T-shirts (but not at temples), and business suits and jackets should be very lightweight. For social gatherings, informal more often than not means tastefully coordinated clothes, sometimes including nicely pressed jeans and a dress shirt. Short-sleeved dress shirts are acceptable, due to the heat. "Formal" can mean, as it does in Europe, tuxedo and evening clothes.

Do not remove your jacket at a business meeting until the senior person in the room does the same, and do not ask to if he or she does not. It is inappropriate to wear rubber sandals on the street (although for casual touring about, leather sandals are okay). Remember, if you visit temples, you will need to remove your shoes, leave them inside the entrance, and walk barefoot while inside.

Seasonal Variations

There are two extreme seasons in Thailand—wet and hot, cool and dry—and one needs to dress accordingly. The summers are hot and very humid, with frequent rain; winters can be cooler and dryer (but still very warm, except high in the up-country mountains).

Colors

Wear neutral colors whenever possible. Do not wear blue, as it is the color used for mourning; also, black dresses and suits are usually worn only at funerals.

Styles

For the most part, Thais have a keen sense of Western clothing and style. No particular traditional Thai dress is worn in day-to-day life.

Accessories / Jewelry / Makeup

Makeup, hairstyle, and accessories are important for women. Perfume and cologne are popular.

Personal Hygiene

In Thailand, personal hygiene is very important. There is a real concern for cleanliness and smelling good, but what smells good and bad to the Thais may be different from Westerners. Throughout the region, the smell of dairy products on individuals is considered offensive, while there is usually no concomitant concern for the smell of other foods, such as garlic or seafood. Do not blow your nose in public: it is considered very rude (if you must blow your nose in public, never use a handkerchief; try disposable tissues). Some Thais do spit on the street, however. Men do not sport facial hair. At the end of a meal, it is perfectly acceptable to use a toothpick, but you must cover the "working" hand with the other hand, so that others cannot see your mouth.

Dining and Drinking

Mealtimes and Typical Foods

The typical Thai diet revolves mainly around the local foods, especially vegetables and seafood, rice and noodles. Although the Thais are becoming increasingly familiar with Western food, they love their own cuisine, and most enjoy a fine Thai or Chinese meal (if you are hosting them in your country, unless they directly express an interest in trying a local cuisine, take them to the best local Thai or Chinese restaurant you can find, and tell the restaurant manager that you are hosting some visiting Thai nationals: they will go out of their way to make the meal very fine for you). Avoid Western food, especially cheese: the taste is unpleasant to most Thais.

Breakfast is served from about 7:30 to 9 A.M. and usually consists of tea and rice; the latter is served either as a porridge-type cereal that can be flavored with any number of ingredients, with eggs in a variety of styles, or with pickled vegetables. Tea in Thailand, as elsewhere in the region, is usually drunk without sugar, milk, or lemon.

Lunch was traditionally the main meal of the day, and even today, in busy cities, it can still be an elaborate affair with several courses—or it can be a simple noodle dish bolted down in a matter of minutes. Lunch is served from about noon to 1 P.M., and consists of meat, fish, and/or vegetables, with rice and/or noodles. Lunch can also be a large serving of hot broth or soup, made with a variety of ingredients. Many dishes can be steamed, stir-fried, or boiled in a variety of different ways, either simply or more elaborately. Typically, the drinks served with lunch and dinner are beer, soft drinks, and/or tea.

Dinner is served from 6 P.M. on, with seven o'clock the customary late time. Even if the main meal of the day was lunch, dinner is only slightly lighter—this is often the case with families at home. The dinner menu is often similar to that of the more formal lunch. Dinner drinks may begin with a beer or rice wine, then move on to beer during the meal, and end with a sweet wine and/or tea.

Regional Differences

Most Thai food is very hot and spicy to Westerners, although the degrees of spice and heat do vary, based on the regions and the foods. It is generally milder in the south, and hotter in the north. You can ask for the heat to be moderated when you order your foods, if you like, but remember that the spice and heat are not just gratuitous. In Thai cooking, there is a belief that the heat helps to express the complexity of the flavors that are used in the dishes; while it may seem blazingly intense, it is the backdrop for the flavors. Thai cuisine incorporates and blends hot and bland, sweet and salty, sweet and sour, sometimes all in one dish: the heat helps hold it all together, so that nothing is canceled out, but everything is made that much more intense. Heat tip: don't douse the heat with water, beer, or juice. Liquid only spreads the heat throughout your mouth. Eat rice instead: it absorbs the capsaicin, the chemical in chilies and peppers that gives them their bite. And keep a napkin or towel nearby to wipe your brow. Seafood is very common along the coast and in Bangkok, while preserved vegetables and rice dishes, often mixed with coconut and, when available, chicken, in a variety of ways, predominate in the up-country. Most food can be spiced up even more with a salty fish sauce (*nam plah*) that is always on every table.

Typical Drinks and Toasting

The most common alcoholic drink is beer, and Thai beer is usually very good and generally served cold. Because you must never pour your own drink (be it beer or tea), you must always be alert throughout the meal as to whether your neighbor's cup or glass needs refilling. If it is less than half full, it needs refilling; alternately, if yours is less than half full, your neighbor is obliged to refill it. If he or she does not, do not refill it yourself, for this will cause your neighbor to lose face; instead, diplomatically indicate your need by pouring a little more drink into your neighbor's glass, even if it doesn't really need it.

What to do if you don't drink? It really isn't an insult to refuse one, as long as you have a reasonable explanation. I've heard people say, "My doctor doesn't advise me to drink just now," or "It's my ulcer" (Asians are keenly aware of stomach problems since such ailments are quite common there, and they are receptive to such explanations; however, once such information is shared, be prepared to be offered all sorts of remedies that they absolutely insist will work, and that you probably would want your own doctor to check out before using) and any number of other little white lies.

If you are the honored guest, you will be expected to make a toast, usually soon after the host does or at the end of the meal, just before everyone departs. An appropriate toast is to the health of the host and all those present, and to the prosperity of the business under discussion.

Avoid drinking tap water anywhere in Thailand (this means you should brush your teeth with bottled water and not take ice in any of your drinks; drink only bottled water, or brewed tea or coffee or soft drinks, and avoid getting water from the morning shower into your mouth; and never eat fresh fruits or vegetables that cannot be peeled first, and ideally cooked later before eating). This is a serious matter: there are some very nasty bugs going around in developing countries.

Table Manners and the Use of Utensils

The traditional chopstick cultures are China, Japan, and Korea. Chopsticks are not traditionally used in Thailand, except when eating Chinese dishes in a Chinese restaurant. In Thailand, spoons and forks are used (never knives). If you need to cut things, use the side of your spoon first, then move on to the fork, if necessary (most foods come already cut). Since the spoon is more important than the fork, if you are right-handed, keep the spoon in your right hand and the fork in your left. Unlike in some rural parts of Asia, bones, gristle, and other remains of your meal do not get scattered on the floor or on the table; these are placed neatly on the side of your plate.

Rice is generally served in separate bowls, not on the same plate with your food. While rice is a staple, it is not necessary to eat every grain in your bowl; leaving some over is fine. In fact, if you eat everything in your rice bowl or on your plate, it means you want more. Do not take the last bit of food from a central serving plate; that means there will be none left in case someone else wants some. Also, a sauce may be mixed with the rice, and the main dish may be eaten with the rice, unlike the practice in Japan. You are expected to hold the rice bowl by your mouth, take a bit of food and sauce from the plate below, hold it over the rice bowl, and shovel it all in together. If you're eating noodles or broth, it is not appropriate to slurp the food; however, hot tea may be slurped quietly to cool it off as it enters the mouth.

Toothpicks are generally used at the end of the meal. The best way to handle a toothpick is to work away with one hand, while keeping the other hand in front of it over the mouth, as a sort of mask. If you cover the working hand this way, you can join in the toothpick session in public at the end of the meal with the best of them! Just never do it walking down the street: that's simply not done.

A word about smoking: it is ubiquitous all throughout Asia. The smoking in Thailand can be overwhelming; but it is usually not done at the table until the meal is finished.

Seating Plans

The most honored position is at the middle of the table, with the second most important person seated next. This means that the host will sit at the middle of the table on one side, and the honored guest in the middle on the other side, opposite the host. (Spouses are usually not invited to business meals, and most formal meals in restaurants are business meals: do not ask if your spouse can join you; it will embarrass your Thai colleague into doing something that is uncomfortable for him.) The honored guest sits on the side of the table farthest from the door. (This is the same at business meetings, with the key people sitting in the middle, flanked on either side in descending order by their aides, with the least important people sitting at the ends of the table farthest from the middle, and closest to the door; the arrangement is mirrored on the other side, because the rules of hierarchy demand that everyone must be able to speak with their opposite peers and those who rank below, but those below cannot speak with those above.) Because many banquet tables are round, a curious situation often develops: the least important person from one side ends up sitting next to the host or the most important person on the other side. (This is usually not an issue at business meetings, where tables are more often rectangular.) If women are present, they will probably be given the honored positions first, although practically speaking there will be far fewer women. In Thailand, women typically rise when men enter the room, hold doors open for men, and escort men into a room first.

Refills and Seconds

You will always be offered more food. Leave a bit on your plate if you do not want more food. You will be implored to take more two or three times, in the form of a little ritual. The game is as follows: first you refuse, then the host insists, then you refuse again, then the host insists again, and then you finally give in and take a little more. If you really don't want more, take very little and leave it on your plate. You may always have additional beverages; drink enough to cause your cup or glass to be less than half full, and it will generally be refilled. A reminder: never refill your own glass; always refill your neighbor's glass, and they will refill yours.

At Home, in a Restaurant, or at Work

Do not begin to eat or drink until the oldest man at the table has been served and has begun. It is appropriate to thank the host at the end of the meal for the fine food.

In informal restaurants, you may be required to share a table. If so, do not force conversation: act as if you are seated at a private table. Waitstaff may be summoned by making eye contact; waving or calling their names is very impolite. The business breakfast is unknown in Thailand. The business lunch is catching on somewhat, but dinner is the proper venue for business hosting. It is generally not the time to discuss business or make business decisions, however. Take your cue from your Thai associates: if they bring up business, then it's okay to discuss it, but wait to take your lead from their conversation.

When invited to a Thai colleague's home for a formal meal, you will be told where to sit, and there you should remain. It is a great honor to be invited into a Thai home, because many Thais feel that Westerners will find their homes too small and crowded; also, older family members might be living there, and your presence will probably make things uncomfortable for you and them (no mutually intelligible language!). Once invited to enter a Thai home, you will need to remove your shoes (this is not the custom in Thai restaurants, however). Once inside the home, do not wander around: much of the house is really off-limits to guests. If you move from room to room in a Thai home, be sure to always allow the more senior members of your party to enter the room ahead of you. Be judicious about touching things and moving them about: many items have probably been placed where they are because it is auspicious to do so according to *feng shui,* a common tradition brought to Thailand from the south of China. Objects are placed, and buildings and rooms designed, so that bad spirits are kept out and good spirits are invited in. The judicious placement of mirrors, which reflect bad spirits, and water, which attracts good spirits, as well as sculptures and other items, is important in *feng shui.* Even the most sophisticated people take this quite seriously.

Being a Good Guest or Host

Paying the Bill

Usually the one who does the inviting pays the bill, although the guest is expected to make an effort to pay. Sometimes other circumstances determine the payee (such as rank). Making payment arrangements ahead of time so that no exchange occurs at the table is a very classy way to host, and is very common. When men are at the table, women will not really be able to pay the bill at a restaurant: if you want to, make arrangements ahead of time, and don't wait for the check to arrive at the table. The only time it is considered appropriate for a woman to pay the bill is if she is a businesswoman from abroad.

Transportation

It's a very nice idea, when acting as the host, to inquire ahead of time as to whether your guests will require transportation. If necessary, you should arrange for taxi service at the end of the meal. When seeing your guests off, you must remain at the entrance of the house or the restaurant, or at the site where you deposited your guests into the car, until the car is out of sight: it is very important not to leave until your guests can no longer see you, should they look back. Guests are seated in cars (and taxis) by rank, with the honored guest being placed in the back directly behind the front passenger seat; the next honored position is in the back behind the driver, and the least honored position is up front with the driver.

When to Arrive / Chores to Do

If invited to dinner at a private home, offer to help with the chores, but do not expect to be taken up on your offer. Nor should you expect to visit the kitchen. Do not leave the table unless invited to do so. Spouses might be invited to dinners at a private home, because another person's spouse will probably be there. Be on time. When in someone's home, be careful not to admire things too effusively: Thais may feel obligated to give it to you, and you in turn will be required to present them with a gift of equal value. Instead of saying things like "I love that vase," say something like "Vases that beautiful in my country are only found in museums." Your compliments will most likely be dismissed.

Gift Giving

In general, gift giving in Thailand is not as formal as it is in Japan, for example, but it is still an important custom. In business settings, it usually takes the form of personal gifts that symbolically say the correct thing about the nature of the relationship. When going to Thailand on business, you must bring gifts for everyone you will see. The general rule is pastries for the office staff, high-quality corporate logo items (all the same) for business associates, and an especially thoughtful, somewhat personalized gift for the key man you will be working with. Your gifts do not have to be elaborate or expensive; in fact, giving something too overtly costly obligates your Thai associates to do the same, something they may not be able to do. You present your gifts at the end of your first meeting in Thailand, as a sign of your sincerity and best wishes. You will receive a farewell gift at your last meeting in Thailand before you leave to go home, or when you present your gifts. When Thais visit your country, they will bring you a gift, and before they leave, you should give them gifts. Holiday cards are appropriate for less formal relationships, particularly as a thank-you for their business during the previous year.

The most appropriate gift for a personal visit to a home, or as a thank-you for dinner, would be a box of fruits, pastries, cakes, cookies, calendars, English-language books, items for the children (games, toys), maps, prints, stamps, tapes and CDs, T-shirts, stationery, and practical housewares (small kitchen items). Flowers are fine dinner gifts, especially as they are used in garlands and fancy decorations throughout Thailand; but if you choose flowers, be sure you do not bring marigolds or carnations—they are used primarily for funerals (orchids are best, and plentiful in this part of the world). There is no need to send a hand-written thank-you note the day after the dinner party. If you are staying with a family, an appropriate thank-you gift would be a high-quality item that represents your country and is difficult or expensive to get in Thailand; this is also a good idea for a key business associate. Acceptable gifts include coffee-table books about the United States, or anything that reflects your host's personal tastes (the cap of a famous American team for the football-playing son of the family, for example). Native handicrafts or well-framed and well-mounted photographs of you and your Thai associates are also appreciated. Be sure the gift you give does not have a tag or sticker on it that says it was made in Thailand, China, Taiwan, Hong Kong, or anywhere else in Asia.

If your gift consists of several items, and especially if it's for a Chinese Thai, be sure that they do not total up to an even number (bad luck except for eight), never to four (very bad luck) or nine (also bad luck); three or eight (very good luck) is preferable. For Chinese Thai colleagues, do not give clocks as a gift, as the word for clock is similar to the word for death. Also avoid handkerchiefs, as they symbolize sadness, and cutlery as a gift, which symbolizes the severing of a relationship. For both giving and receiving gifts, two hands are always used. Gifts are typically not opened by the receiver in front of the giver; they are usually received, graciously acknowledged, and placed aside to be opened once the giver is no longer present.

Gifts should be wrapped well. When purchasing any of the previously mentioned items in Thailand, it will be wrapped beautifully for you, especially if you make it known that it is a gift. Most gifts are wrapped in ordinary paper first, and then wrapped again in gold or yellow (royal colors) or pastels and pink (happy colors): avoid red, unless you are giving a gift to a Chinese Thai (native Thais associate the color with Chinese Thais). Several other colors are never used: green; black, because it is a funeral color (in Thailand, white is not a funeral color); and blue, the color of mourning.

Special Holidays and Celebrations

Major Holidays

The most popular vacation time in Thailand is during the Thai New Year's celebrations; therefore, try to avoid making a business trip there during that season (it is a lunar holiday, so the date changes every year, as is the case with all lunar holidays). The celebration lasts at least a week, if not longer, in some areas, and everybody simply stops work and goes home to family and friends. During this holiday, Thais throw buckets of colored water on one another in the streets: it is a lot of fun, and is not meant in a malicious way—join in!

January 1 (solar)	New Year's Day
February (lunar)	Maka Puja Day

April (lunar)	*Songkran* (Thai New Year) Water Festival
April 6 (solar)	King Rama I Memorial (Chakra) Day
May (lunar)	Ploughing Ceremony
May 1 (solar)	Labor Day
May 3 (lunar)	Visakha Puja Day
May 5 (solar)	Coronation Day
June/July (lunar)	*Khao Phansa* (first day of Buddhist "Lent")
July (lunar)	Plains Retreat (most Thai males go off for two weeks each year to live as Buddhist monks)
August 12 (solar)	Her Majesty the Queen's Birthday
October (lunar)	*Ok Pansa*
October 23 (solar)	Chulalongkorn (or Ramses V, his official royal title) Day
December 5 (solar)	His Majesty the King's Birthday/National Day
December 10 (solar)	Constitution Day
December 31 (solar)	New Year's Eve

Business Culture

Daily Office Protocols

The traditional Thai office has generally an open design; there are few doors, with the exception of the offices of those holding higher positions, and people work mainly at long, large tables or in individual or shared cubicles. Doors, if they exist, are usually open. The open scheme is similar to the office arrangement described in the chapter on Japan.

In the Thai business organization, executives are usually located on different floors than those occupied by the rank and file. You probably will not be invited onto the section floors until the proposed project has been set in motion.

Management Styles

Because of the rigid rank and hierarchy orientation in Thai businesses, titles are very important; the highest ones (e.g., vice president) are usually reserved for very senior, executive-level positions, and should not be used as casually as they are in the United States. Complimenting and rewarding employees publicly is fine; criticizing them publicly is not (criticism must be done very carefully). Deference is shown by subordinates to their seniors; paternalistic concern is often shown by executives to their juniors. As is the case with many bureaucracies, the primary goal may be to protect oneself and one's position vis-à-vis one's superiors (as well as to protect one's superiors), rather than to get immediate goals accomplished. This usually means negotiations or projects can move very slowly at some times, and rapidly at others. It is important to recognize the role of *senuke:* because things must be pleasant and enjoyable, establishing tasks that are hardships will act as a disincentive; office environments must be soft and easy. While Thais certainly like to feel a sense of accomplishment, hard sacrifice is not traditionally part of their experience.

Boss-Subordinate Relations

The decision-making system usually works from the top on down, with key decisions often coming from individuals in high positions of authority. There are formal and informal networking opportunities, but generally, access to power is what determines action.

Conducting a Meeting or Presentation

At your first meeting in Thailand, you will probably be received in a very comfortable waiting area, which may or may not be where most of the meeting is conducted between yourself and your Thai colleague. If this is the case, you are merely being sized up, and your colleague is a gatekeeper. When serving refreshments in the office, be sure they are served in porcelain tea sets: the use of paper or Styrofoam shows disrespect and is very bad form. At meetings of peers, there can be open communication and sharing of ideas: however, most meetings are formalities at which information is exchanged, or decisions that have already been made are confirmed. Meetings are generally too risky for open problem solving and decision making, given the group and hierarchy orientation in Thailand. If this is just the beginning of a business relationship, expect to spend most of the time sharing information about your organization with different individuals; you may need to repeat the same things to different people. This is okay; it means your plans are advancing to the right people in the organization, and that those you have previously met with have approved of you and moved you on. Patience and third-party connections are key.

Negotiation Styles

Expect no decisions from the Thais at the table, and be willing to provide copious amounts of information, to the degree that you can, in response to their questions and in anticipation of their needs. Presentations should be well prepared and simply propounded. Details are best left to questions and backup material, which should be translated into Thai and left behind. Ideally, you should present your material to the Thais for study, along with a proposed agenda, prior to the meeting. Have extra copies available, as you will meet more people than you will expect. You should come with a well-organized team, whose roles have been clearly thought out and defined. Never disagree with one another in front of the Thais, or appear uncertain, unsure, not authorized to make a decision, or out of control in any way.

Thais generally do not like to bargain, but when they do, they approach it as a win/win possibility (something should be in it for both sides). Although the contract must be legal down to the dotted i's, remember that to the Thais it is a piece of paper that merely signifies that an agreement has been reached and which will be followed because of the trust and commitment that has been built between you. Keep communications, especially when at a distance, open and stay in touch often with your Thai associates: share more information than you normally would, not less; and have a contact on the ground in Thailand who can always keep you informed of what is really going on, if you can.

Written Correspondence

Your business letters should be very formal and respectful of rank and hierarchy. First names are usually written in uppercase; dates are given using the year/month/day format (with periods in between, not slashes); and an honorific plus the title is as common as an honorific plus the last name. You should write your e-mails, letters, and faxes in a formal, precise way: use a brief, warm introduction, then quickly get down to business. Keep it simple, however, and outline all important matters. In Thailand, and throughout most of the region, the address is usually given as follows:

Line one: country and postal code
Line two: city (and prefecture)
Line three: street address
Line four: company and/or personal name

The Southeast Asian Cultures: Indonesia

Some Introductory Background on Indonesia and the Indonesians

Indonesia is the world's largest Muslim nation. It is an archipelago nation comprised of over thirteen thousand islands. The world's fourth most populous nation, it covers an area equal in size to the United States. Today, Indonesia is a unified nation that struggles with threats of secession and divisiveness among its more than one hundred cultural groupings. There are over thirty different indigenous languages spoken and four major religions. The style of life reels from Western cosmopolitan urbanity through developing world poverty to Stone Age tribalism. It is, in short, a vast, complex world within a world that most of the rest of the world knows little about.

Indonesia has made remarkable progress in moving from an agrarian, hunting, and fishing society to a developing nation, but has done so with great pain, to itself and to its people. The future of Indonesia, while uncertain, will surely be significant, as a land this large, diverse, and important cannot be overlooked. As a Southeast Asian country, its traditions and cultural life have evolved from the same issues that formed many of the cultures in the region: a paradisiacal agrarian past, coupled with waves of invasions from neighbors and colonial exploitation from the West, culminating in revolutionary and unstable independence.

Some Historical Context

Indonesia's early development was as a Southeast Asian Pacific island culture, where nature provided all essentials in an easy and "soft" environment, and where indigenous systems of belief provided the required explanations for life. This state of things began to change with a series of invasions, beginning as early as the third century B.C.: the Chinese were the first to bring trade to the region and settled in various parts of the archipelago. The Indians (Tamils, or southern Indians, primarily) brought Hinduism to the islands around the seventh century A.D., which challenged the existing Sailendra and Sri Vijaya Buddhist empires.

These Hindu and Buddhist kingdoms finally gave way to the Majapahit empire, which began on Java in the late thirteenth century; the influence of Buddhism eventually spread throughout the islands, and lasted up until the sixteenth century. This was an important time in Indonesian history, and the Majapahit kings are respected even today, for this empire attempted to unite the Buddhist and Hindu cultures, then at war with each other, into an economic, political, and cultural union. But in the fourteenth and fifteenth centuries, Islam slowly encroached into the region, and by the late 1500s had replaced the Hindus and the Buddhists in power (with the exception of Bali, which remains primarily Hindu today). This weakened the union, softening it up for the Europeans as they began their exploration of the region in the sixteenth century, beginning with the Portuguese (who extended their influence into Indonesia from their bases in Malacca on the Malay Peninsula and Macao in China). By the mid 1600s, the Dutch had taken over, pushing the Portuguese into a small encampment on the island of Timor, and renamed the archipelago Batavia. The main concern of the Dutch was primarily trade in Java. They retained control until the Japanese invasion of the islands during World War II. After the war, Indonesia finally received its independence. However, independence from foreign domination did not prevent internal political upheaval. The independent country's first leader, Sukarno, who was also its founder, eventually instituted authoritarian rule. His replacement, General Suharto, stepped in to quell a major Communist coup attempt in the mid 1960s, when Sukarno's power began to erode. Suharto's reign ended in charges of widespread corruption and a severe economic crisis.

An Area Briefing

Politics and Government

Today, Indonesia is nominally a democracy, with a representative unicameral legislature, a prime minister, and a president. However, all candidates for public office and all ministers have been handpicked by the leader of the ruling party. There is no monarchy or royalty. As political and economic turmoil again swept Indonesia in the late 1990s, it is difficult to see what the political future holds, as no real democratic traditions have been established in the nation.

Schools and Education

Schooling is free and mandatory for all elementary-grade children. The Indonesian equivalent of high school follows after grade school, and state-run universities are available to those who qualify academically after high school. Education, however, is very difficult for most families to provide, as poverty and daily life make it imperative that children assist in supporting the family. Distance, resources, and cultural and linguistic differences also contribute to reducing the effectiveness of public education. Moreover, where functioning schools exist, education is first made available mainly to boys. Wealthy Indonesians usually advance their education abroad.

Religion and Demographics

The religious traditions in Indonesia are primarily Islam, Buddhism, and Hinduism, and are associated with the three major groups in the country, as well: Buddhism with the Chinese minority, who play a major role in the economics and business of the country; Hinduism with the Indians, who play a service role in the country (shopkeepers and service workers); and Islam with ethnic Indonesians (and non-Hindu Indians), who make up the bulk of the population and fill the government posts. (Ethnic Indonesians refer to themselves as Bumiputras, or Bumis for short, meaning natives of the soil.) In addition, many people practice Christianity, although the Western traditions of Christianity have not been translated into the cultural values of Indonesia. Most of the indigenous Indonesians are Javanese (about 50 percent), and the people on each major island in the archipelago were originally of their own group, with their own language and systems of belief. The form of Islam that established itself in Indonesia is not the fundamentalist Islam found today in the Gulf Arab world: it has been adapted to fit the Hindu/Buddhist/animist traditions of Indonesia: it is "softer," less ideological, less "by the book," having lost its "Western" prescriptive moral nature to the Southeast Asian need for a more pragmatic and flexible approach for day-to-day existence. Muslim Indonesians follow the basic tenets of Islam, but their daily customs are often less restrictive than those of Middle Eastern Muslims.

Islam is a codified institutionalized religion, while Buddhism and Hinduism are more philosophies of life. Hinduism emerged in India as a compilation of essential indigenous beliefs that developed over time to become the unifying religion of the subcontinent. It emphasizes dharma, or right conduct, the four stages of human existence, reincarnation, and a pantheon of gods organized in an eternal hierarchy. The *varnas,* or caste system, merely reflects in the secular world the stages different souls are at in their cycles of reincarnation. Reincarnation is a central aspect of Hinduism, and faith in the cycles, and the abandonment of secular reality, should be the orientation of individuals if they want to achieve ultimate freedom from the repetition of these cycles, and move onward toward knowing the truth (or the "godhead") and attaining nirvana. The *Mahabharata* and the *Ramayana* are two Hindu epics that teach Hindu ideals, and are revered everywhere by Hindus: whenever they are read or performed, they gather large audiences. Many of the original Hindu writings have been compiled into the Upanishads, a compilation of Hindu theological writings (or Vedic texts), which is the body of Hindu law and belief that defines the religion.

Buddhism began in India around 600 B.C. Its founder was Siddhartha Gautama, the Buddha, a privileged Hindu priest who, in attempting to learn the meaning of life, discovered, among other things, that his privilege brought him no happiness, and that if one were to achieve true happiness, one had to sacrifice in the secular here and now in specific ways in order to achieve a higher level in the next life. In many ways, the theology that evolved was an effort to purify what had become, in the Buddha's mind and others, a debased and corrupt Hindu religion in India at that time by placing moral responsibility onto the individual, and relying less upon the religious hierarchy. This created, as you may imagine, some difficulty for the Buddha and his followers and the existing Hindu establishment; subsequently, Buddhism was both integrated into the existing higher culture and simultaneously banished from India. Its principles survived, however, rooting in China, parts of Southeast Asia, and ultimately in

Japan. As Buddhism spread eastward, it branched into Mahayana Buddhism (mainly in the north), which makes the individual responsible for attaining nirvana directly, and Theravada Buddhism (mainly in the south), in which a much more rigid hierarchy exists, and in which individuals are dependent on ordained monks, for it is only monks (and nuns) who can achieve nirvana. While there is a strong influence of Southeast Asian Theravada Buddhism in Indonesia, the Indonesian Buddhists are mainly ethnic Chinese who brought with them the softer Mahayana Buddhism, which was also seriously influenced by Confucianism. The Chinese, armed with Buddhism and Confucianism, brought strong hierarchical traditions with them, which did not essentially conflict with the already rigid hierarchies brought to Indonesia by the Indian Hindus.

Confucianism, based on the teachings of Confucius, a Chinese sage who lived around 500 B.C., has had a powerful impact on Chinese thought. Confucius lived during a turbulent and chaotic time in China, and established a philosophy of life that attempted to prescribe the correct and proper way for individuals to relate to one another in order to have a well-ordered, functioning society. The essence of his ideas involves the importance of observing and maintaining structures, roles, and hierarchy, so that, paraphrasing his words, "the son obeys the father, the wife obeys the husband, the younger brother obeys the older brother, the husband obeys the state," and so on. Society will work when everyone knows his or her place, understands his or her obligations to others in the hierarchy, and, in fact, seeks primarily not to change his or her role, but to perfect it.

Islam is the youngest of the West's three great religious traditions, which began with Judaism and Christianity. As a Western religion, it is linked to the Judeo-Christian belief system and rejects many of the paradigms of the Eastern Asian "philosophies" of Buddhism, Confucianism, and Hinduism. Incorporating both Judaism and Christianity into its system of beliefs, Islam claims that it is the final revelation of a monotheistic God, as revealed to the world through the prophet Muhammad in the early seventh century, and that previous "messiahs," such as Jesus and Moses, are merely prophets, along with Muhammad, proclaiming the word of God. Muslims do not follow Muhammad (therefore, they are not Muhammadans, a derogatory term); they believe in Allah, the Arabic term for the same God worshiped by Christians and Jews. Muhammad and his followers wrote down the law of God as revealed to them in the Koran (or Qu'ran), the Islamic holy book. It does not negate the Old or New Testaments: it merely provides, in the eyes of the Muslim faithful, the final required text. Islam spread rapidly throughout the Middle East, into Europe, and eastward across Asia, reaching Southeast Asia and Indonesia by the late fourteenth century. While it underwent a serious split almost immediately following Muhammad's death (two major camps emerged, the Shia and the Sunni, in an effort to decide how to continue the faith), it nevertheless rapidly gathered huge followings. Sunni Muslims believe that only the genealogical descendants of Muhammad should lead the faith, and that the word of the original caliphs (or Islamic church leaders) is absolute; Shiite Muslims believe that only the most holy, as determined by external criteria and not genealogical relationship to Muhammad, should lead the faithful, and that the original caliphs were, in fact, usurpers (needless to say, politics play a strong role in such debates; when we explore the Arab world and Southwest Asia, we will see how this split has influenced the emerging cultures of those regions), but this dispute has not played a serious role in the unique Indonesian version of Islam as practiced on the archipelago.

Muslims must abide by five basic tenets, or Pillars of Faith:

- Proclaim the supremacy of the one true God, Allah, above all others
- Pray to Allah five times daily
- Observe Ramadan, the holy month, the ninth month of the Islamic calendar, which is essentially a celebration of the first time God revealed his word to Muhammad
- Give alms to the poor and needy
- Perform the hajj, or spiritual (and physical) journey to Mecca, at least once in their lifetime if they are capable of doing so

As practiced in Indonesia, these requirements have significant implications for day-to-day life, as we will see. Devout Muslims in Indonesia are referred to as Santri.

Women in Indonesia have an equal role with men, not only legally, but culturally; their traditional role as homemaker and nurturer for the home is not seen as subordinate to the male provider role, and, in fact, Indonesian women do have opportunities in business and work (although perhaps not as great as men, in general). Outside of the home and the traditionally female professions such as medicine and teaching, there are many women holding high-level positions in the ministries and government in Indonesia. It should not be difficult, therefore, for non-Indonesian businesswomen, as long as their authority is established, clear, and maintained, and as long as they follow the necessary cultural customs described in this chapter, to be successful in Indonesia. Indonesia is also demographically a very young country, with the bulk of its population under the age of thirty.

Fundamental Cultural Orientations

1. What's the Best Way for People to Relate to One Another?

OTHER-INDEPENDENT OR OTHER-DEPENDENT? There is a strong need for all involved in or affected by an action or decision to be consulted. The group orientation is very strong; individuals typically will not do things, say things, or make decisions until they are sure that those who are affected by a program or proposal have already bought into it. Family, clan, and other membership groups that define an individual (such as work and religion) are primary considerations for all action. Individual initiative, while important, must be justified as producing results that will benefit others, and must ultimately involve others if it is to succeed.

HIERARCHY-ORIENTED OR EGALITY-ORIENTED? Structure and hierarchy are critical at all levels in Indonesian society—in the home, at school, in the military, and in business. Indonesians must know where you, they, and anyone else they come in contact with fit in the hierarchy of the society. Therefore, a strong formality has developed in which people are treated according to their rank and status. Hierarchy is honored through humility and making face; this is done by "lowering," or minimizing, oneself. In fact, one makes more of oneself, and raises one's esteem in the eyes of others, by not causing others to lose face or be embarrassed (*malu* is loss of face and pride; people will go to great lengths to avoid this happening to them or be the cause of it for others). Women and men, young and old, all have separate roles in society. This emphasis on hierarchy also normalizes unequal relationships: it is, after all, natural that some be in charge and some not, that some have power and some not, that some dictate and some follow. The higher-ups make the decisions.

RULE-ORIENTED OR RELATIONSHIP-ORIENTED? There is much less concern for abstract moralizing, and more concern for doing what is best given the situation and the people involved. Systems and processes are questioned, and generally not seen as benefiting only those who create them. Subjective relationships and whom you know determine the outcome of things (along with forces that are beyond your control). This is revealed in a "here-and-now" attitude: what is best for all involved in the immediate given situation, after considering all factors, is usually what determines the chosen action.

2. What's the Best Way to View Time?

MONOCHRONIC OR POLYCHRONIC? Indonesia is an extremely polychronic culture. There is a concept throughout the country known as "rubber time," in which the clock stretches to fit human needs, not the other (Western) way around. Things will take the time they need to take, and the clock is not the ultimate arbiter of what occurs and when. Events can move very slowly, or very quickly, but only if it makes sense according to the individuals and the situations they are in each and every day. Indonesians will move very quickly to seize an advantage if one presents itself; they certainly want to succeed as quickly as possible, but they will not do anything that is not in their best interest simply because of time. Unless it is on their terms, they have time to wait it out.

Daily life in Indonesia has historically been arranged according to vast, agriculturally based blocks of time, over which no individual or government had control—for example, the seasons, day, and night. Even today, schedules tend to be loose and flexible; the workday begins around 8 A.M., and ends around 4 P.M. Most workers take an hour break and a midafternoon nap after lunch. But time moves much more slowly in general, and there is no advantage to rushing about. This changes by group, with ethnic Indonesians being least time conscious, and Chinese being most time conscious.

RISK-TAKING OR RISK-AVERSE? Indonesia is essentially a risk-avoiding culture, because the social and business hierarchies and individual people's positions must be carefully considered within the larger group context. There may be much information that will need to be exchanged before decisions are made, and many people brought into the process in order to develop trust (with outsiders, such as the foreign businessperson) and consensus. There is a high need for certainty and much energy will be spent looking to minimize danger and risk. Immigrants, in general, may be more prone to taking risks than natives, with Chinese Indonesians (who have a more individualistic background) perhaps more willing to take risks than Hindu Indian immigrants (who have a caste-bound tradition).

PAST-ORIENTED OR FUTURE-ORIENTED? All three religious traditions (Hindu, Buddhist, and Islam) emphasize the fatalistic nature of the universe; Indonesians certainly want to do things that will bring success to themselves and their families, but action is not taken with the belief that it builds a better tomorrow, or that it is even being done with tomorrow in mind. Rather, things are done because it is appropriate to do so now in response to the current opportunities and risks, with a knowledge that the outcome may not ultimately be in our control. Muslims say that "such and such will happen, Inshallah"—meaning "if God wills"—thus diminishing human responsibility for the ultimate success or failure of an event (in fact, it may be difficult to make long-term plans in such an environment, for it is sometimes seen as foolish, even slightly heretical, to presume the ability to control things so far into the future). Hindus see both the future and the past as essentially the same (a repeating cycle), and Chinese Buddhists are very sensitive to the power of forces beyond their control (*feng shui,* ancestors, auspicious and inauspicious moments, etc.).

3. What's the Best Way for Society to Work with the World at Large?

LOW-CONTEXT DIRECT OR HIGH-CONTEXT INDIRECT COMMUNICATORS? Indonesians are very high-context communicators. They avoid confrontation, and will speak in terms that maintain harmony at all costs, even if this results in speech that is indirect, evasive, or contradictory. Because circumstances rather than universal truths or laws determine action, sensitivity to the context is critical if you want accurate information on what is really being meant or done. The use of the word *yes*, even though *no* is meant; the avoidance of explanations and statements that even gently criticize or make someone look bad; the eternal smile, even when things are not going well; the failure to provide bad news or important negative information: all of these are common characteristics in Indonesia, which can be ultimately understood and precluded if one develops the ability to read between the lines. Read the context, not the words.

PROCESS-ORIENTED OR RESULT-ORIENTED? Indonesians, as is the case with all Asian peoples, are fully capable of employing (and do employ) meticulous logic, whether deductively or inductively; however, that is not necessarily the only process used to think things through, to make a case for something, or to understand people or events. A connection is made with similar situations, and Indonesians rely primarily on this associative, subjective logic. Chinese Indonesians often apply this in a holistic, nonsequential way: process and experience are important steps in arriving at a conclusion, but the path may not be linear or progressive. This is related to the polychronic nature of the culture: things occur, thought patterns included, not necessarily in a sequential or progressive way, but in a holistic way. In other words, the elements needed to make decisions are laid out expositionally, when and as the circumstances require it, and add up to a conclusion only when viewed "at once," as if suddenly from forty thousand feet. Muslim Indonesians will also do this, but more because it is an effective way to avoid conflict if you don't want to talk about certain things at a certain time. Well-educated Indonesians employ all of these methods, with well-honed sophistication.

FORMAL OR INFORMAL? Indonesian society is formal and ritualized; and each group has its own way of honoring the hierarchies, establishing respect and deference, making face, treating different groups and different levels, and dealing with different situations. It is even more formal, when one is on the outside, or beginning to establish relationships with the in-group. Once inside, it is very personal, but rarely informal.

Greetings and Introductions

Language and Basic Vocabulary

The language that unifies the country is Bahasa Indonesian (one of the reasons it was made the official language of the country was because it was not affiliated with any one religious group). It is related to the Bahasa Malay language spoken in Malaysia (in fact, Malaysians and Indonesians can often understand each other while speaking in their own languages), except that Malaysians were influenced by the British and their language, and Indonesians were influenced by the Dutch and their language. It is not a difficult language for Westerners to learn or use, as it developed, in part, as a way for the many peoples of the region to communicate with each other over issues of trade, as the area became a major intersection for the Chinese, Indonesians, Indians, and Europeans. It is even written in Roman letters, from left to right. Because of the importance placed on avoiding disharmony, do not use double negatives, and do not ask questions that could result in yes or no answers (although when Chinese speakers use English, they have a habit of asking questions with both yes and no presented as options: this sounds very demanding to the Western ear, but isn't meant to be; it is the result of the translation from Chinese to English). In a culture where the emphasis is placed on preserving harmony and face, and where much communication is therefore very high-context and subtle, any answer that could imply difficulty, a rejection of a request, or make the respondent appear uncooperative is evaded. This evasion is expressed in a number of ways nonverbally, but often results in unreliable verbal responses. Sometimes Indonesians use the phrase *belum:* it means, more or less, "we'll see." It really means that there's a problem and I don't want to deal with it right now with you in front of me. In other contexts, "yes" more often means "I hear what you are saying, keep talking," not "I agree with what you are saying." If there is any expression of negativity, even in the slightest, it usually signals rejection. Don't complicate the problem, therefore, by asking questions that require yes or no as an answer: the response will give you no reliable information. Instead, ask open-ended questions that require a substantive, informational response.

In Jakarta and the major business centers, many businesspeople speak English as well as a native language. Your Indonesian associate may, in fact, speak Indonesian, English, Chinese, and Javanese. If you know some Bahasa Indonesian, use it: your Indonesian colleagues will be thrilled!

Here are the basic terms in Bahasa Indonesian, and their English meanings:

halo	hello
Apa kabar?	How are you?
Baik, terima kasih.	Fine, thank you.
terima kasih	thank you
Siapa nama anda?	What is your name?
Nama saya . . .	My name is . . .

Selamat datang!   Welcome!
selamat jalan   good-bye
terima kasih   please

Honorifics for Men, Women, and Children

ETHNIC INDONESIANS (MUSLIMS). Until recently, most Southeast Asian cultures did not use surnames: people were referred to by their given names (their membership in a particular clan was understood). However, Indonesians and other peoples in modernizing Southeast Asian cultures have gradually incorporated the use of the family name into the full name, and in this case, the order of both the given and the family name is as in the West: first name first, family name second. Because the given name has traditionally been the more important one, any use of honorifics is more common with either the given name, and not the lately adopted family name, or both. Generally, more well-educated Indonesians will use two or more names—one given, one family—and because many Indonesian names can be quite long, they may reduce one or more names to merely an initial.

The most common honorifics for Muslim Indonesians are:

- *bapak:* Mr. (literally, "father")
- *ibu:* Mrs./Ms./Miss/Madame (literally, "mother")
- *hajji:* For a Muslim man who has completed the hajj (replaces *bapak*)
- *hajja:* For a Muslim woman who has completed the hajj (replaces *ibu*)

Titles and positions are very important in Indonesia, so if an individual has one (e.g., lawyer), it needs to come immediately after the honorific, followed by the full or first name. Sometimes, on a business card, you might see the following initials after a name (they are derived from the Dutch equivalents):

DRS: doctor (male) / DRA: doctor (female)
IR: engineering degree
SH: lawyer

Some Muslim Indonesians may Arabicize their names, if they are devout, because in Islam the Koran was written in Arabic, making it the language of God.

For men, use the first (given) name plus *bin* (meaning "son of") plus the father's given (first) name (e.g.: Ali bin Muhammad). The proper form of address is Mr. Ali.

For women, use the first (given) name plus *binti* or *binte* (meaning "daughter of") plus the father's given (first) name (e.g.: Asmah binti Naguib). The proper form of address is Mrs./Miss/Ms. Asmah. If Asmah and Ali were married, she might also be referred to by her husband's name after hers: thus the proper form of address is Mrs. Asmah Ali.

If Muslim names are Arabicized, and if titles are known, all titles come before the entire name (e.g.: Bapak Doctor Ali bin Muhammad).

CHINESE INDONESIANS. Many Chinese Indonesians use their Chinese names, or use Anglicized initials in place of their Indonesian or Chinese names, as an accommodation to Westerners (this Anglicized version may also appear on their business cards). Recognize that Bumis usually take the positions in government, while Chinese Indonesians often have premier positions in business: relations are not always easy between the two groups.

If they are using Chinese names, they will order their names, in most cases, the Chinese way: family names first, followed by a given generational name, and then finally a given name. There is often a hyphen between the generational and the given names, making the two given names more often than not a two- (or more) syllable name. Most of the time, the Chinese family name is a single syllable (there are in fact only several hundred family or clan names, so most Chinese have similar family names, with the generational and the given names primarily distinguishing them one from the other). If Min-wen Zhang has introduced himself as such, he has reversed the Chinese name format to accommodate the Westerner, putting his given name first and his family name last, Western style (you know this because the two-syllable name, usually the combination of the generational and the given names, is being presented first). You would refer to this person with the correct Bahasa honorific after the family name, because it is a Chinese name.

A married Muslim Indonesian woman would use the correct honorific plus the name she uses. However, there are two forms for addressing a married Chinese Indonesian woman. Traditionally, Chinese women did not lose their own family name, nor take their husband's family name. Therefore, for married Chinese women, use the honorific "madame" plus her family name. For example, if Li Min-wen marries Zhang Liu-tse, she would be correctly referred to as Madame Li, not Mrs. Zhang.

Do not worry about moving from the last name to the first name, or formal to informal, when using Indonesian names. In Indonesia, first names are already the formal way; however, the correct honorific plus all titles must always be used. Children in Indonesia are expected to be respectful and not overly conversational when speaking with adults, and must always use honorifics when referring to adults. As they probably speak limited English, this makes conversation with children that much more difficult.

In situations where a title is known, the title plus the honorific and the name must be used together (e.g., "Mr. Engineer" or "Mr. Engineer Sukarno" for an ethnic Indonesian, and "Engineer Li" for a Chinese Indonesian). For casual contacts (e.g., with waiters, store help, etc.), just use bapak or ibu. It is very important to greet people at work, in stores, or in restaurants in an appropriate fashion.

INDIAN INDONESIANS (HINDUS). Indians will sometimes refer to themselves using the traditional Indian form, which means there is no family name (surname) used. Both men and women simply put the first initial of the father's first (given) name before their own given (first) name. For example, in the name R. Sarinda, Sarinda is the person's first (given) name, and R. is the initial of his father's first name (Ravi); the proper form of address is Mr. Sarinda. If a woman named K. Sardar marries M. Sarinda, she would properly be addressed as Mrs. Sardar Sarinda.

The What, When, and How of Introducing People

Sometimes upon greeting you, Indonesians will simply call you by your first or last name plus your title, or make a comment about the task you are performing: this requires no substantitive response.

Always wait to be introduced to strangers; never take that responsibility upon yourself, as doing so is considered inappropriate most of the time. Indonesians are most comfortable with a third-party introduction whenever one is possible, and will go to great lengths to ensure that you are not left alone to decide this for yourself. Never presume to seat yourself at a gathering; if possible, wait to be told where to sit. The seating arrangements have usually been carefully worked out in advance, and in most cases reflect the status of the individuals in the group, and the honor that is being accorded the guests. When departing, it is important to say farewell with a quick bow to every individual present: the American group wave is not appreciated. Once you greet someone you will encounter later that day in the same circumstances (e.g., at the office), you will need to acknowledge them with a quick, foreshortened bow without a hand-shake whenever you see them again. Seniors, or those who are obviously the oldest in a group, are greeted first, seated first, and allowed to enter a room first (usually at the center of a group, however, and preceded in most cases by their younger aides. Names can indicate much about the people you are with: they may be Dutch, Portuguese (probably from Macao), Malaysian, Chinese, Thai, Filipino, English, and so on.

Physical Greeting Styles

Like many Asian cultures, Indonesia is essentially a nontouching culture—at least at first. Only the most intimate of friends (mainly young people) will touch each other casually. The handshake is a Western custom, and not native to the region, but because of the significant Western influences in Indonesia, it is used as the typical greeting, along with a slight bow. The handshake is usually very soft, almost limp. This does not signify insincerity; rather, it is an indica-tion of humility using a Western convention. Western women must always extend their hands first for a handshake, if one is to occur at all; if so, it is inevi-tably very soft. (Muslim women and men rarely touch; men, therefore, should not extend their hands to a Muslim woman, unless she extends her hand first; if she does, she is no doubt Westernized.) The handshake lasts for several seconds (usually slightly longer than in the West), often with the other hand clasping the grasped hand. To show extra sincerity, when you release your grasp, draw your right hand back to your heart and touch it.

The traditional Indonesian business introduction also includes the exchange of business cards. Always take a large supply of business cards with you: you must give one to every new person you are introduced to (there is no need to provide another business card when you are meeting someone again unless in-formation about you has changed, such as a new address, contact number, or position). Be sure your business cards are in fine shape: they are extensions of you as a person, and must look as good as possible. Never hand out a dirty, soiled, bent, or written-on card. You should, if possible, have your business card translated into Bahasa Indonesian on the reverse side before you go to Indone-sia (some finer hotels and some airlines, as well as your own business, will do this as a service for you). If you know you will be visiting Chinese Indonesians, it is extra nice to have your card translated into Chinese on the back, in gold let-tering. When presenting your business card, you give it to your Indonesian associate with the Indonesian side up, so that it is readable for him as you hold it (he will, in turn, present his card English side up, so that it's readable for you); you must hold the card in the upper right- and left-hand corners, requiring the use of two hands, and you also receive the other person's card with two hands on the upper right- and left-hand corners. The exchange is done quickly, *almost* simultaneously. Bow slightly first, then exchange your business cards.

Smiling and other nonverbal forms of communication usually accompany the card exchange; it is appropriate to appear genuinely pleased to meet the other person. When first introduced to your Indonesian colleague, drop your eyes as you bow. More traditional Hindu Indonesians (Indians) might greet you with the *namaste,* which requires that the hands be held in a prayer position at chest level while bowing slightly. Information about each other's status is the most important information to be exchanged, and this is provided directly on the business card, as well as indirectly through a number of high-context indicators, such as gray hair (a sign of age), gender (usually male), and the number of people surrounding and assisting the other person (important people generally have assistants). Humility before rank can be demonstrated subtly, by placing your business card underneath the card of the other person during the exchange. Once you have received the other person's card, it is important to stand upright again, holding the card with two hands, and silently read the card for a few seconds. It is appropriate to say his name, as he will say yours; this is the time to correct each other if there is any mispronunciation. But remember, never laugh at the other person's name, although it may sound odd to you. All this occurs rather quickly, and should you meet more than one Indonesian, you will have a handful of cards when it is over.

As this ritual usually precedes a sit-down meeting, it is important to arrange the cards you have received in a little seating plan in front of you along the top of the desk or the table at your seat, reflecting the order in which people are seated. This will help you connect the correct names with the correct individuals throughout the meeting. Do this even if you are just meeting one person; it is expected. During the meeting, it is important never to play with the business cards (do not write on them—ever!); and when the meeting is over, never put them in your back pants pockets: pick them up carefully and respectfully, and place them neatly in your business card holder (a nice-looking leatherbound or brass case would be perfect), then place the cardholder in the left inside jacket pocket of your suit (nearest your heart). By the way, if you are applauded while making a presentation in Indonesia, or anywhere in Southeast Asia, it is customary to applaud back.

Communication Styles

Okay Topics / Not Okay Topics

Okay: anything that reflects your personal interests and hobbies, or your curiosity about things Indonesian, like food, Indonesian puppet theater (*wayang*), and so on. Sticking to general themes of personal interest or business is fine; it is a way of seeking common ground. There will be no need to begin a conversation with the very American "So, what do you do?" since you already know this from the business card exchange; however, further discussions about your company and its work are very much appreciated, as this gives the Indonesians a chance to learn more about you and your firm. The goal of all conversation, at least at the beginning, is to create and maintain a harmonious atmosphere, despite the difficult or confrontational nature of the topic being discussed. At first, speak about things that you believe you have in common so that you can build a personal connection, which will go far toward maintaining a harmonious bridge between you. This is appropriate for both individuals and organizations. *Not okay:* Politics, current events, or any subject that might in any way be controversial needs to be avoided at first. Do not inquire about a person's occupation or income in casual conversation, although it may be inquired of you (if so, this is just a way of getting to know more about your country, and not a personal investigation: answer specifically, but fully, with an explanation as to what things cost at home, why you do what you do, etc.). Do not inquire about your colleague's family life. Do not give your opinions about the role of the Suharto family in politics, the Communist Party, immigrant Chinese, and the like. Do *not* talk about sex or tell dirty jokes (they are not understood and it's in very bad taste). Do not discuss religion, either, as in this part of the world such conversations can be offensive to some (Muslims, depending on what you say) and mystifying to others (Buddhists, for example). Do not complain: things that are annoying are best left ignored, as only immature people complain openly about things.

Tone, Volume, and Speed

Indonesians generally speak in soft, hushed tones. Speak slowly, for the benefit of those translating, in short phrases, and speak clearly. Try to speak expositionally, without emotion, if possible. As words are for the most part not the best vehicles for communication when language differences are present, use pictures, graphics, and charts to augment the topic being discussed, whenever possible. Illustrate what you can say, and certainly what you cannot. This is a very symbol-oriented culture. Tone emotional opinion way down.

Use of Silence

Passive silence—allowing time to pass simply, without words—can be a form of proactive communication in Indonesia. There may be long pauses between comments, but rarely extending over several minutes. When confronted with silence, for whatever reason, the best response is to remain silent yourself, although this may be difficult and appear unproductive for time-conscious Westerners. This is perhaps the most subtle form of communication, yet communication it is. If you must say something, bring up something positive, even if it is unrelated to the previous statement. Remember, in Asia, "silence is golden"; those who speak too much are considered immature, given how careful one must be with what one says. Because some Westerners find silence disconcerting, they may tend to fill up the space with more talk; resist this impulse, as it only enhances the effectiveness of the silence, by forcing the Westerner to say more than he or she might normally be inclined to.

Physical Gestures and Facial Expressions

In Indonesia, there is considerably less physical gesturing of any kind. If you have a tendency to speak with your hands, you will consciously have to try to control it: most of the time, such gesturing is considered excessive and will engender surprise, laughter, and sometimes frozen disbelief (always with a smile, though, which makes for a very odd expression on the face!). In fact, laughter may or may not be in response to anything humorous in the Western sense (jokes may not be understood); more often, laughter, in the form of giggling, is an expression of embarrassment when Indonesians do not understand something. The oft-offered smile, however, is a general way of getting through the day, of keeping things pleasant and soft. Practice it. Winking, whistling, and similar displays are considered very vulgar. Public displays of familiarity and affection with the opposite sex are expressed only by teenagers. When physically coming between or passing people, it is appropriate to bow slightly as you go by. Never touch anyone, including small children, on his or her head: this is considered the holiest part of the body. Do not point with or intentionally show the sole of your shoe to anyone: this is considered vulgar, as the bottom of the shoe touches the ground, and is therefore the dirtiest part of the body. Standing with your arms on your hips is considered very aggressive and should always be avoided. Always give a small donation to the indigent when you pass them on the street if you can.

For any action or gesture that would naturally be done with only one hand, do not use your left hand, especially in the presence of Muslims, as this is considered the unclean hand (the hand traditionally used for personal hygiene). Pass all documents, food, and money *only* with your right hand (if you're a southpaw, you will have to practice this).

Waving and Counting

The pinkie represents the number 1, the thumb represents the number 5, with everything in between ordered from the pinkie down; however, instead of raising the fingers when counting, the whole hand is exposed, and each finger is depressed as the counting is done. It is very insulting to motion to someone with the forefinger; instead, turn your hand so that the palm faces down and motion inward with all four fingers at once. If you need to gesture for a waiter, very subtly raise your hand. Waving or beckoning is done with the palm down and the fingers moving forward and backward in a kind of scratching motion. It may seem as if the person making this gesture is saying good-bye to you, when in fact you are being summoned over. If you need to point to something or someone, use a full palm motion, or clench your fist as if you were hitchhiking and use the thumb as if it were the index finger to point.

Physicality and Physical Space

Most Indonesians stand, relative to North Americans, just a little farther apart; resist the urge at first to move in closer. Never, upon first greeting an Indonesian, touch him beyond the soft handshake: no backslaps, no hugging, no kissing, *ever.* Never speak with your hands in your pockets: always keep them firmly to your side when standing. If men and women must cross their legs when they sit, it must never be ankle over knee (for women, the preferred style is to cross ankle over ankle). Remember, in public, formal is always better than informal: no gum chewing, *ever;* don't slouch; and don't lean against things. Indonesians can be very formal at first when they sit and stand in business settings, but they can relax quickly: take your cues from them. Once close relationships are established, and especially in those moments when spontaneity and friendliness are allowed (such as at a bar or walking down the street after an evening meal), there may be much physicality—touching, for example, or putting arms around other people's shoulders, or holding hands—but generally only between members of the same sex, and not in public between members of the opposite sex. About the only time this nonphysicality rule is broken is on public transport, where it is very crowded and touching is unavoidable, or on crowded streets, where you are very likely to be poked and prodded as people jostle by.

Eye Contact

In Indonesia, eye contact is very indirect. Only upon the first introduction do eyes meet, and respect and humility is demonstrated, whenever necessary, by lowering the eyes. Interest in what one's supervisor is saying is shown by averting the eyes, not by making eye contact. The eyes are used extensively to convey true feelings in formal situations where it may be difficult to express your thoughts verbally. Tune up your nonverbal antennae.

Emotive Orientation

Indonesians can be very restrained emotionally, but not stony. Keep the smile, but tone down the emotional expression. It is important for the Westerner to consciously control emotive impulses.

Protocol in Public

Walking Styles and Waiting in Lines

On the street, in stores, and in most public facilities, people pay little attention to maintaining orderly lines. Due to the volume of passengers on public transportation, there can be much pushing and jostling. This is not to get into a train or a bus ahead of someone else, though; it is merely to get in!

Behavior in Public Places: Airports, Terminals, and the Market

Customer service is a well-developed practice in most stores, because the "other" (in this case, the customer) is so important, and because demonstrating good customer service involves showing deference to the customer. Stores in the cities are open in the evenings and on weekends, as well as during the day; there is a very good chance you will be bowed to as you enter and leave a store, and by all clerks as they help you. A personal thank-you to store owners, waiters, chefs, and hotel managers for their services is very much appreciated. In food markets, don't worry about touching the produce, since everybody does, and it doesn't obligate you to buy it; in goods stores, if you buy a product and you have problems with it, returning the item is usually difficult. Smoking is endemic, and you may have difficulty finding a no-smoking area on public transportation, in restaurants, and in other public places (be sure not to smoke in front of Muslims during Ramadan, when they abstain). Bathroom facilities can range from Western-style toilets to Asian-style toilets (holes in the floor, with buckets of water or hoses attached to a water line for cleanup instead of paper); be prepared.

When answering a telephone, say "Allo" or just your given name. Cell phones are ubiquitous, as the wire networks may be unreliable or nonexistent.

Bus / Metro / Taxi / Car

Driving is on the right, and whether in the country or city, being in a car can be hazardous to your health. The roads are not necessarily in good repair, marked, or where maps say they are; and obtaining fuel when and where you need it can be a problem. The traffic in Jakarta and other major cities is maddening and chaotic, and construction sites are everywhere.

The best way to catch a cab is at designated taxi stands (hotels are good places, but often charge more for the same ride: a hotel surcharge is added to the meter fare, in some cases). When a taxi has been hailed, negotiate the price, as the meter may or may not be working (even if it is, the price needs to be negotiated). Whenever possible, have the address you need to get to written down on a piece of paper (or use the business card of the person you are going to see, if you can) before you hail the cab. A small map outlining the route is great, if you can have one prepared before you go.

Taking open motorbikes is a good idea: these are usually one- or two-person, open-air seats on the backs of motorbikes, which can whiz right through stalled traffic. You might get soaked, however, in one of the endless tropical downpours sitting in one. Try either a *becak* (a three-wheeled pedicab) or an *ojek* (the motorbike taxi).

Tipping

Tipping is not really part of the scene in Indonesia, but if you leave approximately 5 percent in rupiahs for restaurant, taxi, or porter service, it will be appreciated.

Punctuality

While essentially polychronic, you are expected to be punctual in all situations. Do not arrive more than ten minutes too soon—or more than then minutes late, for that matter. Your Indonesian associates, however, may be late; or if they are already present, they may be deep in side discussions that will require you to wait: do so patiently. You will not be told if your tardiness has caused a problem, of course, but in most cases, it will not help your image.

Dress

The Indonesian standard is more or less fashionable and Western, but the main concern with respect to clothing is the climate: it is hot and tropical most of the year. Therefore, many businessmen wear very lightweight suits, or a dress shirt, either with or without a tie, and no jacket. None of this is an invitation to informality: it is just an adaptation to the weather. Businesswomen wear lightweight skirts and blouses, jackets, or suits. It is best to start out formal, and then you can take your jacket off if you see others without theirs. Wear dress slacks, not jeans or khakis. Social dress is the same, although sometimes clean, pressed jeans are okay with a dress or sport shirt (but no T-shirts!). Sneakers are only for the street or gym (some women do wear sneakers to work, but change just before they enter the office, not after going in); because of the heat, shorts are okay only on the street, with T-shirts (but not at temples). Dress shirts can be short-sleeved, due to the heat. If you are told to wear a "lounge suit," this means a business suit; it is a way of letting you know that the occasion is formal. You may see a very special open-collared men's shirt, often decorated with a batik design the same color and fabric of the background (usually white). This is not an informal shirt: in fact, it is quite traditional, and worn on special occasions (perhaps the signing of your deal). Men wear it outside of their pants, without a jacket and tie. Muslim traditions dictate that women dress so that their legs are covered below the knee, their arms are covered below the elbow, and their torsos are covered from their necks to their waists. Some Muslim women in Indonesia cover their faces; most do not, and nonpracticing Western women need not.

It is inappropriate to wear rubber sandals on the street (although for casual touring about, leather sandals are okay). Remember, if you visit temples, you will need to remove your shoes and walk barefoot while inside.

Seasonal Variations

There are two extreme seasons in Indonesia: wet and hot, and dry and hot. The important thing is to remember the frequent downpours; take an umbrella with you everywhere you go.

Colors

Wear neutral colors whenever possible. Do not wear blue, as it is the color used for mourning; also, black dresses and suits are usually worn only at funerals. Green is the color of Islam, and is appreciated when it is used tastefully.

Styles

For the most part, clothing is simple, adapted to the climate, and meant to keep one looking good and cool. Consider, however, that many public places are air-conditioned to arctic levels, so you might always want to have a lightweight covering available.

Accessories / Jewelry / Makeup

Makeup, hairstyle, and accessories are important for women, but only if they are styled modestly. Perfume and cologne are popular, but usually are not made with alcohol (alcohol is prohibited in Islam).

Personal Hygiene

In Indonesia, personal hygiene is very important. There is a real concern for cleanliness and smelling good, but what smells good and bad to Indonesians may be different from Westerners. Take more than one bath a day, if you need to: Indonesians do, when they can. Throughout the region, the smell of dairy products on individuals is considered offensive, while there is usually no concomitant concern for the smell of other foods, such as garlic or seafood. Do not blow your nose in public: it is considered very rude (if you must blow your nose in public, never use a handkerchief; try disposable tissues). Spitting can occur on the street, however. Muslim and Indian men may sport facial hair, usually in the form of a mustache. At the end of a meal, it is perfectly acceptable to use toothpicks, but you must cover the "working" hand with the other hand, so that others cannot see your mouth.

Dining and Drinking

Mealtimes and Typical Foods

The typical Indonesian diet revolves mainly around the local foods, especially vegetables, seafood, rice, and noodles. Although the Indonesians are becoming increasingly familiar with Western food, they love their own cuisine, and most enjoy a fine Indonesian or Chinese meal (if you are hosting them in your country, unless they directly express an interest in trying a local cuisine, take them to the best local Indonesian or Chinese restaurant you can find, and tell the restaurant manager that you are hosting some visiting Indonesian nationals: they will go out of their way to make the meal very fine for you). Avoid Western food, especially cheese: the taste is generally unpleasant for most Indonesians.

Indonesian food has been influenced by Chinese, Indian, Malaysian, and Dutch traditions, so there are some pretty wonderful combinations of flavors, ranging from mild to very spicy. The Dutch took back many samplings of Indonesian regional cuisine and served it as a special meal called the *rijstafel* (literally, "rice table"): the *rijstafel* has returned to many Indonesian restaurants and makes a wonderful introduction to Indonesian cuisine. It is usually made up of many small dishes, including fish, vegetables, rice, and noodle delicacies, with a variety of spices and sauces that you can add as you wish (peanut and coconut sauces are used in many Indonesian dishes).

Breakfast is served from about 7:30 to 9 A.M., and usually consists of tea and rice; the latter is served either as a porridge-type cereal that can be flavored with any number of ingredients (*nasi gorang*), with eggs in a variety of styles, or with pickled vegetables. Tea in Indonesia, as elsewhere in the region, is usually drunk without sugar, milk, or lemon.

Lunch was traditionally the main meal of the day, and even today, in busy cities, it can still be an elaborate affair with several courses—or it can be a simple noodle dish bolted down in a matter of minutes. Lunch is served from about noon to 1 P.M., and consists of meat, fish, and/or vegetables, with rice and/or noodles. Many dishes can be steamed, stir-fried, or boiled in a variety of different ways, either simply or more elaborately. Typically, the drinks served with lunch and dinner are soft drinks and /or tea (beer is drunk by non-Muslims or nonobservant Muslims).

Dinner is served from 6 P.M. on, with 7 P.M. the customary late time. Even if the main meal of the day was lunch, dinner is only slightly lighter—this is often the case with families at home. The dinner menu is often similar to that of the more formal lunch. If alcohol is being drunk, predinner drinks may begin with beer or rice wine, then move on to beer during the meal, ending with a sweet wine and/or tea.

Regional Differences

Most Indonesian food tastes hot and spicy to Westerners, although the degrees of spice and heat do vary, based on the regions and the foods. You can ask for the heat to be moderated when you order your foods. Indonesian cuisine incorporates and blends hot and bland, sweet and salty, sweet and sour, sometimes all in one dish: the heat helps hold it all together, so that nothing is canceled out, but everything is made that much more intense. Heat tip: don't douse the heat with water, tea, beer, or juice. Liquid only spreads the heat throughout your mouth. Eat rice instead: the rice absorbs the capsaicin, the chemical in chilies and peppers that gives them their bite. Seafood, preserved vegetables, and rice dishes, often mixed with coconut, and, when available, chicken, prepared in a variety of ways, are common everywhere. Islam prohibits the use of pork, so you will find it only in Chinese restaurants; most meats of any kind for Muslims need to be prepared *halal* (the Muslim requirement that the meat be slaughtered as prescribed by certain Islamic codes). Most Hindus are vegetarians; if not, they certainly will avoid beef, as this comes from a cow, an animal held sacred by Hindus. Most food can be spiced up even more with a salty fish sauce that is usually on every table.

Do not eat in front of your Muslim colleagues, or invite them to join you for a meal during the day during Ramadan, as Muslims typically fast (and refrain from drinking and smoking) during the day, and feast with family and friends at night during Ramadan. Ramadan lasts for a lunar month: this is simply not a good time to do business or go out entertaining in Indonesia.

Throughout Southeast Asia, you will find a marvelous dish called *satay:* bits of meat served on small skewers. You usually specify chicken or beef, and in minutes, your skewers arrive along with tart and fiery peanut and tamarind dipping sauces. *Satay* rule: don't dip the skewer and then stick it in your mouth; pull the meat off the skewer onto your plate first. Otherwise you look gauche and run a high risk of puncturing your upper palate.

Typical Drinks and Toasting

The most common alcoholic beverage is beer, generally served cold. Because you must never pour your own drink (be it beer or tea), you must always be alert throughout the meal as to whether your neighbor's cup or glass needs refilling. If it is less than half full, it needs refilling; alternately, if yours is less than half full, your neighbor is obliged to refill it. If he or she does not, do not refill it yourself, for this will cause your neighbor to lose face; instead, diplomatically indicate your need by pouring a little more drink into your neighbor's glass, even if it doesn't really need it.

What to do if you don't drink alcohol? This usually isn't a problem in Muslim Indonesia, but if you are dining with Chinese associates in a Chinese restaurant, they will probably have drinks, and you'll need to provide an explanation if you don't join in. I've heard people say, "My doctor doesn't advise me to drink just now" or "It's my ulcer" (Asians are keenly aware of stomach problems since such ailments are quite common there, and they are receptive to such explanations; however, once such information is shared, be prepared to be offered all sorts of remedies that they absolutely insist will work, and that you probably would want your own doctor to check out before trying), and any number of other little white lies.

If you are the honored guest, you will be expected to make a toast, usually soon after the host does or at the end of the meal, just before everyone departs.

An appropriate toast is to the health of the host and all those present, and to the prosperity of the business under discussion.

Avoid drinking tap water anywhere in Indonesia (this means you should brush your teeth with bottled water and not take ice in any of your drinks; drink only bottled water, or brewed tea or coffee or soft drinks, and avoid getting water from the morning shower into your mouth; and never eat fresh fruits or vegetables that cannot be peeled first, and ideally cooked later before eating). This is a serious matter: there are some very nasty bugs going around in developing countries.

Table Manners and the Use of Utensils

The traditional chopstick cultures are China, Japan, and Korea. They are not used in Indonesia, except when eating Chinese dishes in a Chinese restaurant (for more on chopstick use, see the chapters on Japan and China). In Indonesia, spoons and forks are used (never knives), or no utensils at all (mainly in more traditional Muslim restaurants). If you need to cut things, use the side of your spoon first, then move on to the fork, if necessary (most foods already come precut). Since the spoon is more important than the fork, if you are right-handed, keep the spoon in your right hand and put it down to switch to the fork if you need it. Never use your left hand for eating, especially if you are eating with your hands and not using utensils. Unlike in some rural parts of Asia, bones, gristle, and other remains of your meal do not get scattered on the floor or on the table; these are placed neatly on the side of your plate.

There are times where no utensils are served at all. What to do? Why, eat with your fingers, of course! Many think it makes the experience more fun, maybe because you're adding an extra sense to an already very sensory experience: the sense of touch. This food is known as "banana-leaf" food: wonderful vegetarian or meat curries, served with rice and sauce on a large banana leaf. No plates, no forks, no spoons, no chopsticks. You reach into the rice, take some with your fingers, gently roll it between your index and middle fingers and thumb (not all the fingers on your hands!) into a kind of self-sticking ball, dip it into the sauce on the banana leaf, and mix it with a vegetable or a piece of chicken, then pop the whole thing in your mouth. Most of these hands-on banana-leaf restaurants are Muslim or vegan (Hindu).

Here are some other things to note about eating in such restaurants.

• Wash your hands before you sit down to eat. Many banana-leaf restaurants have washrooms and sinks out in the open specifically for this purpose. (However, you may want to wash your hands with bottled water at the hotel first, since the water at the restaurant may be more hazardous to your health than the germs already on your hands!) You will also need to wash your hands again at the end of the meal, especially after eating the saucy dishes, since you've probably got a good bit of it running down your arm. Don't worry, it's to be expected: don't dress up if you're eating banana-leaf style.

• Use your right hand when picking up and eating food, never your left hand. Keep your left hand at your side. Do not place your left hand on the table, and do not pass food with your left hand.

• Pork will typically not be on the menu.

- Alcohol will usually not be served with the meal.
- Men and women, in some establishments, may be asked to dine separately.
- If you absolutely cannot eat without some kind of utensil, it's usually all right to ask for spoons in such establishments. The proprietors are usually more than pleased to accommodate Westerners.

Rice may be served in separate bowls, or on the same plate with your main dishes. While rice is a staple, it is not necessary to eat every grain; leaving some over is fine. Do not take the last bit of food from a central serving plate; that means there will be none left, in case someone else wants more. Also, a sauce may be mixed with the rice, and the main dish may be eaten with the rice, unlike the practice in Japan. You are not expected to hold the rice bowl (if there is one) by your mouth. Hot tea may be slurped quietly to cool it off as it enters the mouth.

Toothpicks are generally used at the end of the meal. The best way to handle a toothpick is to work away with one hand, while keeping the other hand in front of it over the mouth, as a sort of mask. If you cover the working hand this way, you can join in the toothpick session in public at the end of the meal with the best of them! Just never do it walking down the street: that's simply not done.

A word about smoking: it is ubiquitous throughout Asia, including Indonesia, where a milder, native, clove-scented cigarette is available. Usually, you do not smoke at the table until the meal is over.

Seating Plans

The most honored position is at the middle of the table, with the second most important person seated next. This means that the host will sit at the middle of the table on one side, and the honored guest in the middle on the other side, opposite the host. (Spouses are usually not invited to business meals, and most formal meals in restaurants are business meals. Do not ask if your spouse can join you; it will embarrass your Indonesian colleague into doing something that is uncomfortable for him.) The honored guest sits on the side of the table farthest from the door. (This is the same at business meetings, with the key people sitting in the middle, flanked on either side in descending order by their aides, with the least important people sitting at the ends of the table farthest from the middle, and closest to the door; the arrangement is mirrored on the other side, because the rules of hierarchy demand that everyone must be able to speak with their opposite peers and those who rank below, but those below cannot speak with those above.) Because many tables are round, a curious situation often develops: the least important person from one side ends up sitting next to the host or most important person on the other side. (This is usually not an issue at business meetings, where tables are more often rectangular.) If women are present, they will probably be given the honored positions first, although, practically speaking, there will be far fewer women.

Refills and Seconds

You will always be offered more food. Leave a bit on your plate if you do not want more food. You will be implored to take more two or three times, in the form of a little ritual. The game is as follows: first you refuse, then the host insists, then you refuse again, then the host insists again, and then you finally give in and take a little more. If you really don't want more, take very little and leave it on your plate. You may always have additional beverages; drink enough to cause your cup or glass to be less than half full, and it will generally be refilled. A reminder: never refill your own glass; always refill your neighbor's glass, and he or she will refill yours.

At Home, in a Restaurant, or at Work

Do not begin to eat or drink until the oldest man at the table has been served and has begun. It is appropriate to thank the host at the end of the meal for the fine food.

In informal restaurants, you may be required to share a table. If so, do not force conversation: act as if you are seated at a private table. Waitstaff may be summoned by making eye contact; waving or calling their names is very impolite. The business breakfast is unknown in Indonesia. The business lunch is catching on somewhat, but dinner is the proper venue for business hosting. It is generally not the time to discuss business or make business decisions, however. Take your cue from your Indonesian associates: if they bring up business, then it's okay to discuss it, but wait to take your lead from their conversation. No gum chewing, ever, at a restaurant or on the street (although there is a habit in Indonesia among ethnic Indonesians of chewing betel nut: it is noticeable by the black stain it leaves on the teeth).

When invited to an Indonesian colleague's home for a formal meal, you will be told where to sit, and there you should remain. It is a great honor to be invited into an Indonesian home, because many Indonesians feel that Westerners will find their homes too small and crowded; also, older family members might be living there, and your presence will probably make things uncomfortable for you and them (no mutually intelligible language!). Once invited to enter an Indonesian home, you will need to remove your shoes (this is not the custom in restaurants, however). Once inside the home, do not wander around: much of the house is really off-limits to guests. If you move from room to room in an Indonesian home, be sure to always allow the more senior members of your party to enter the room ahead of you. Be judicious about touching things and moving them about: many items have probably been placed where they are because it is auspicious to do so according to *feng shui,* a common tradition brought to Indonesia from the south of China. Objects are placed, and buildings and rooms designed, so that bad spirits are kept out and good spirits are invited in. The judicious placement of mirrors, which deflect bad spirits, and water, which attracts good spirits, as well as sculptures and other items, is important in *feng shui.* Even the most sophisticated people take this quite seriously. You may be invited to a *selamatan,* a special religious meal given in honor of those in attendance, in an effort to bring good harmony and good fortune to them. Bring a little gift of orchids or some food with you to this event.

Throughout Southeast Asia, people often dine at open-air markets or stalls. In Indonesia, these are called *warung.* The food is almost always totally Indonesian—rice, *satay*—and you can have one dish at one *warung,* and then move on to another dish at another. The tables are usually long and communal, and the dining is completely informal. Walk up to the counter if there are no waiters, order from the stall, wait, and take your dish back to the table and enjoy. (*Warung* coffeehouses, on the other hand, are really gathering places for men to chat and gossip.) The *Rumah makan* (eating house) is a step up from a *warung,* but a rung down from the *restoran* (restaurant): it's inside, but the informality and food are the same. A *Rumah makan padang* tends to serve Sumatran food (a little spicier).

Being a Good Guest or Host

Paying the Bill

Usually the one who does the inviting pays the bill, although the guest is expected to make an effort to pay. Sometimes other circumstances determine the payee (such as rank). Making payment arrangements ahead of time so that no exchange occurs at the table is a very classy way to host, and is very common. When men are at the table, women will not really be able to pay the bill at a restaurant: if you want to, make arrangements ahead of time, and don't wait for the check to arrive at the table. The only time it is considered appropriate for a woman to pay the bill is if she is a businesswoman from abroad.

Transportation

It's a very nice idea, when acting as the host, to inquire ahead of time as to whether the guests will require transportation. If necessary, you should arrange for taxi service at the end of the meal. When seeing your guests off, you must remain at the entrance of the house or the restaurant, or at the site where you deposited your guests into the car, until the car is out of sight: it is very important not to leave until your guests can no longer see you, should they look back. Guests are seated in cars (and taxis) by rank, with the honored guest being placed in the back directly behind the front passenger seat; the next honored position is in the back behind the driver, and the least honored position is up front with the driver.

When to Arrive / Chores to Do

If invited to dinner at a private home, offer to help with the chores, but do not expect to be taken up on your offer. Nor should you expect to visit the kitchen. Do not leave the table unless invited to do so. Spouses might be invited to dinners at a private home, because another person's spouse will probably be there. Be on time. When in someone's home, be careful not to admire things too effusively: Indonesians may feel obligated to give it to you, and you in turn will be required to present them with a gift of equal value. Instead of saying things like "I love that vase," say something like "Vases that beautiful in my country are only found in museums." Your compliments will most likely be dismissed. In Muslim homes, men and women guests will often dine separately, and spend the evening apart.

Gift Giving

In general, gifts are exchanged on many occasions in Indonesia: when one visits a colleague's home, for holidays, to commemorate special events, or to start or seal a business deal. In business settings, this usually takes the form of personal gifts that symbolically say the correct thing about the nature of the relationship. When going to Indonesia on business, you must bring gifts for everyone you will see. The general rule is pastries for the office staff, high-quality corporate logo items (all the same) for business associates, and an especially thoughtful, somewhat personalized gift for the key man you will be working with. Your gifts do not have to be elaborate or expensive; in fact, giving something too overtly costly obligates your Indonesian associates to do the same, something they may not be able to do. You present your gifts at the end of your first meeting in Indonesia, as a sign of your sincerity and best wishes. You will receive a farewell gift at your last meeting in Indonesia before you leave to go home, or when you present your gifts. When Indonesians visit your country, they will bring you a gift, and before they leave, you should give them gifts. Holiday cards are appropriate for the Chinese at the Chinese New Year; they are not very common at other times.

The most appropriate gift for a personal visit to a home, or as a thank-you for dinner, would be a box of fruits, pastries, cakes, cookies, calendars, English-language books about your country, items for the children (games, toys), maps, prints, stamps, tapes and CDs, T-shirts, stationery, and practical houseware (kitchen items). Flowers are typically not given as gifts, except perhaps to Indians (use colored orchids, not white—which is a funeral color). There is no need to send a handwritten thank-you note the day after the dinner party. If you are staying with a family, an appropriate thank-you gift would be a high-quality product that represents your country and is difficult or expensive to get in Indonesia (this is also a good idea for a key business associate). Acceptable gifts include coffee-table books about the United States, or anything that reflects your host's personal tastes (the cap of a famous American team for the football-playing son of the family, for example). Native handicrafts or well-framed and well-mounted photographs of you and your Indonesian business associates are also appreciated. Be sure the gift you give does not have a sticker or tag on it that says it was made in the region. The more you can personalize your "key man" gift, the more it is appreciated.

If your gift consists of several items, and especially if it's for a Chinese Indonesian, be sure that they do not total up to an odd number (bad luck), never four (very bad luck) or nine (also bad luck), and preferably eight (very good luck). Please note that for Indians and Hindus, the reverse is true: land on an odd number, if you can. Do not give the Chinese clocks as gifts, as the Chinese word for clock is similar to the word for death. Also avoid handkerchiefs, as they symbolize sadness, and cutlery, which symbolizes the severing of a relationship. A fine gift for a Muslim would be a silver compass, so that they will always know which direction to face when they say their daily prayers (Muslims must face Mecca no matter where they are when they say their prayers). Be sure not to give pork as a food gift to Muslims; also avoid alcohol, and perfumes and colognes that contain alcohol. Do not give beef as a food gift to Hindus. Because the cow is sacred to Hindus, do not give a gift made of leather (for example, leatherbound portfolios, agendas, or picture frames). Remember, any gift given by a man to a woman must come with the caveat that it is from both him and his wife/sister/mother, or else it is far too personal. For both giving and receiving gifts, two hands are always used. Gifts are typically not opened by the receiver in front of the giver; they are usually received, graciously acknowledged, and placed aside to be opened once the giver is no longer present.

Gifts should be wrapped well. When purchasing any of the previously mentioned items in Indonesia, it will be wrapped beautifully for you, especially if you make it known that it is a gift. Typically, gifts are wrapped in ordinary paper first, and then wrapped again in gold or yellow (royal colors) or pastels and pink (happy colors). Avoid red, unless you are giving a gift to a Chinese Indonesian. Green is appropriate for Muslims; but black and white should both be avoided because they are funeral colors, along with blue, the color used for mourning.

Special Holidays and Celebrations

Major Holidays

The most popular vacation time in Indonesia varies depending on whether one is Buddhist, Muslim, or Hindu. The Indonesian Buddhist New Year (lunar) often falls around the same time as Ramadan, so the period from January through March is not a good time to do business in Indonesia. It is very auspicious if different groups' holidays fall on the same day or around the same time. Hindu holidays are also observed, as listed in the section on holidays in the chapter on India.

January 1 (solar)	New Year's Day
January/February (lunar)	Ramadan (one full lunar month, celebrating when Muhammad received his first revelation)
January/February (lunar)	Chinese New Year (lasts from one to two weeks)
March (lunar)	*Hari Raya Puasa* (end of Ramadan)
May (lunar)	*Hari Raya Haji* (Islamic commemoration of Abraham's sacrifice)
May 1 (solar)	Labor Day
May 31 (solar)	*Awal Muharam* (the Muslim New Year begins)
August 9 (lunar)	The Prophet Muhammad's Birthday
October/November (lunar)	*Deepavali* (a Hindu festival of Thanksgiving)
December 25 (solar)	Christmas

Business Culture

Daily Office Protocols

The traditional Indonesian office has an open design; there are few doors, with the exception of the offices of those holding higher positions, and people work mainly at long, large tables or in individual or shared cubicles. Doors, if they exist, are usually open. The open scheme is similar to the office arrangement described in the chapter on Japan.

In the Indonesian business organization, hierarchy is strictly observed. Executives are usually placed on different floors than those occupied by the rank and file. You probably will not be invited onto the section floors until the proposed project has been set in motion. Because faithful Muslims pray five times a day, you will need to adjust your schedule to accommodate their needs. Usually, prayers are given upon awakening and at noontime, midafternoon, dusk, and before retiring; this means that twice during the workday, there will be time out for prayers. The prayer usually takes a short ten or fifteen minutes or so, and any quiet and private area will usually do. If you accidentally interrupt a Muslim during his prayers, just walk quietly away; there's no need for complicated explanations or apologies. Most organizations have prayer rooms set aside, with carpets. In addition, devout Muslims will not work on Friday (the Muslim Sabbath), and in fact begin to end work early on Thursday, before sundown. They will often return to work on Saturday or Sunday. Because of the Islamic influence, the official Indonesian workweek is Monday through Thursday, plus half a day on Friday and half a day on Saturday.

Management Styles

Because of the rigid rank and hierarchy orientation, titles are very important; the highest ones (e.g., vice president) are usually reserved for very senior, executive-level positions, and should not be used as casually as they are in the United States. Complimenting, rewarding, or criticizing employees publicly is absolutely ineffective. Any criticism must be done very carefully, displaying concern for the feelings of the person you are criticizing, and in private. Deference is shown by subordinates to their seniors; paternalistic concern is often shown by executives to their juniors. As in the case with many bureaucracies, the primary goal may be to protect oneself and one's position vis-à-vis one's superiors (as well as to protect one's superiors), rather than to get immediate goals accomplished. This usually means negotiations or projects can move very slowly at some times, and rapidly at others.

Boss-Subordinate Relations

The decision-making system usually works from the top on down, with key decisions often coming from individuals in high positions of authority. There are formal and informal networking opportunities available in order for the decision maker to build a consensus, but generally, access to power is what determines action.

Conducting a Meeting or Presentation

At your first meeting in Indonesia, you will probably be received in a very comfortable waiting area, which may or may not be where most of the meeting is conducted between yourself and your Indonesian colleague. If this is the case, you are merely being sized up, and your colleague is a gatekeeper. When serving refreshments in the office, be sure they are served in porcelain tea sets: the use of paper or Styrofoam shows disrespect and is very bad form. At meetings of peers, there can be open communication and sharing of ideas: however, most meetings are formalities at which information is exchanged, or decisions that have already been made are confirmed. Meetings are too risky for open problem solving and decision making, given the group and hierarchy orientation in Indonesia. You will probably need to make several visits before things really do start rolling, especially if this is a new venture you are looking to start there. If this is just the beginning of a business relationship, expect to spend most of the time sharing information about your organization with different individuals; you may need to repeat the same things to different people. This is okay; it means your plans are advancing to the right people in the organization, and that those you have previously met with have approved of you and moved you on. Patience and third-party connections are key.

Negotiation Styles

Expect few decisions from Indonesians at the table, and be willing to provide copious amounts of information, to the degree that you can, in response to their questions and in anticipation of their needs. Presentations should be well prepared and simply propounded. Details are best left to questions and backup material, which should be translated into Bahasa Indonesian and left behind. Ideally, you should present your material to the Indonesians for study, along with a proposed agenda, prior to the meeting. Have extra copies available, as you will meet more people than you will expect. You should come with a well-organized team, whose roles have been clearly thought out and defined. Never disagree with each other in front of the Indonesians, or appear uncertain, unsure, not authorized to make a decision, or out of control in any way.

Indonesians generally do not like to bargain, but when they do, they approach it as a win/win possibility (something should be in it for both sides). Although the contract must be legal down to the dotted i's, remember that to the Indonesians it is a piece of paper that merely signifies that an agreement has been reached and which will be followed because of the trust and commitment that has been built between you. Remember, the deal should be finalized with a celebratory meal or round of drinks, and the actual signing might be delayed until an auspicious or lucky day: this might affect your schedule. Keep communications open, especially when at a distance, and stay in touch often with your Indonesian associates: share more information than you normally would, not less; and, because business is so intimately connected with the government and because the political situation is so fluid, try to have a contact on the ground in Indonesia who can always keep you informed of what is really going on, if you can.

Written Correspondence

Your business letters should be very formal and respectful of rank and hierarchy. First names are usually written in uppercase; dates are given in the year/month/day format (with periods in between, not slashes); and an honorific plus the title is as common as an honorific plus the last name. You should write your e-mails, letters, and faxes in a formal, precise way: use a brief but warm introduction, then quickly get down to business. Keep it simple, however, and outline all important matters. In Indonesia, and throughout most of the region, the address is usually given as follows (although there is equal familiarity with the Western format):

Line one: country and postal code
Line two: city (and prefecture)
Line three: street address
Line four: company and/or personal name

The Southeast Asian Cultures: The Philippines

Some Introductory Background on the Philippines and the Filipinos

The Philippines and tiny Macao are the only Latin-based cultures in Asia. The Philippines (named after King Philip II of Spain after Ferdinand Magellan claimed the islands for Spain when he ran aground on them circumnavigating the globe) today is the end result of the blending of three cultures: the native Visayan, the major indigenous Pacific island culture of the archipelago; then Spanish (from Spain); then American. It is said that today's Filipino (Filipina, for a woman) is the result of a culture that began thousands of years ago with farmers and fishermen, and then was influenced by four hundred years of the Spanish Catholic Church and one hundred years of Hollywood. It makes for a very interesting set of behaviors! It also makes it difficult for the country to develop, as there is little tradition of participatory democracy, given that the last two cultures were imposed autocratically. Couple this with the usual burdens of developing nations in this region (coping with natural disasters such as volcanoes, earthquakes, and typhoons; grinding poverty; few resources; and government corruption), and we begin to see the difficulties that Filipinos face in their native land. Add to this the fact that the seven thousand or so islands that make up the archipelago make it difficult to develop a sense of unity among all the people, and the picture becomes clearer. Nevertheless, Filipinos are known for their smiles, their good humor, their sociability and flexibility; they are survivors.

Some Historical Context

Prior to Magellan, the native Visayans, a Malayan people, lived a paradisiacal life of tropical farming and fishing. Their world was ordered according to ancient agrarian myths and belief systems; all that changed dramatically in the sixteenth century when Magellan claimed the territory for Spain, and later explorers began the imposition of Catholicism and Spanish rule, and the exporting of silver and spices. (With both the Philippines and Mexico firmly under Spanish rule, Mexican silver and Southeast Asian foodstuffs formed the core of a transpacific/transatlantic trade route, running from Luzon to Acapulco, across the Mexican mountains, and then from Veracruz onward to Granada.) The imposition of a rigid "conquistador culture," of Catholic dogma and Castilian hierarchies, along with the appropriation and reapportionment of land to Spanish nobles, crushed the indigenous culture and remade the Filipino psyche. When Spain lost the Spanish-American War, the Philippines came under United States control. Many Filipinos, after having resisted the Spanish, continued their resistance against the Americans, and American control was challenged violently, at least at the beginning. Nevertheless, the country developed a culture dependent upon American funds and resources until the Japanese invasion at the beginning of World War II. The Philippines was finally granted its independence in July 1946. Despite the American influence, though, the foundations for the dependency, corruption, and nonrepresentative rule that were to follow were already in place, resulting in, most recently, the unabated corruption of the Marcos regime.

In many ways, the Philippines is still an export economy—but today, of people. There is a large emigration out from the islands of lower- and middle-class people: the lower-class workers fan out across Asia as houseworkers, caregivers (the amahs of the Hong Kong Chinese, for example), factory and piece workers; the middle class attend universities abroad and find work as computer programmers or in other foreign service and professional industries. Large amounts of money are constantly being sent back to the Philippines by overseas Filipinos to help support their poorer families back home.

An Area Briefing

Politics and Government

Today, the Philippines is nominally a democracy, with a representative bicameral legislature and a president, modeled after the U.S. system. There is no monarchy or royalty. However, the political system has been run by the powerful oligarchical elites who own most of the wealth in the country.

Schools and Education

There are Philippine equivalents of high school after grade school, and state-run and private (for the elite) universities are available to those who qualify academically after high school. Education, however, is very difficult for most families to provide, as poverty and daily life make it imperative that children assist in supporting the family. Distance, the lack of government resources, and cultural differences also contribute to reducing the effectiveness of public education. Moreover, where functioning schools exist, education is first made available mainly to boys. Those who can usually advance their education abroad.

Religion and Demographics

Most Filipinos are Roman Catholic; there is a growing Islamic movement (mainly in the southern islands among the poorer agrarian population), which occasionally grows violent. Small percentages of other religions are also represented. Women in the Philippines play a subordinate role to men, in general, and do not have the same business opportunities, although it is common for women to work. Nevertheless, the people's familiarity with modern Western culture enables non-Philippine businesswomen to succeed in the Philippines as long as their authority is established, clear, and maintained. The Philippines is demographically a very young country, with the bulk of its population under the age of thirty.

Fundamental Cultural Orientations

1. What's the Best Way for People to Relate to One Another?

OTHER-INDEPENDENT OR OTHER-DEPENDENT? There is a strong need for all involved in or affected by an action or decision to be consulted. The group-orientation is very strong; individuals typically will not do things, say things, or make decisions until they are sure that those who are affected by a program or a proposal have already bought into it. However, like the conquistadores, self-pride is a powerful element: in the Philippines it is called *hiya,* or self-esteem. It is related to face. When one's *hiya* is high, and one's individual actions benefit the group, one has *amor-propio,* a sense of oneself as an individual who does the right thing and looks good in other's eyes, and this gives one great self-esteem and individual pride. Never do anything to undermine the *hiya* of a Filipino or Filipina. The group of which one is a member (one's *barkada*), along with one's own *hiya,* determines in great part one's *amor-propio.*

HIERARCHY-ORIENTED OR EGALITY-ORIENTED? Structure and hierarchy are critical at all levels—in the home, at school, in the military, and in business. Filipinos must know where you, they, and anyone else they come in contact with fit in the hierarchy of things. Therefore, a strong formality has developed in which people are treated according to their rank and status. However, perhaps because of the American experience, hierarchy is not so much honored as it is needed and expected.

Unlike other hierarchically oriented Asian cultures, this need for structure does not imply the normalcy of unequal relationships: there is the belief that while one needs to understand the roles that people play in society, these roles are changeable, not necessarily fixed or given. This is a subtle but important distinction in the region. Yet those in charge make the decisions, for as long as they are in charge. It is a very autocratic society.

RULE-ORIENTED OR RELATIONSHIP-ORIENTED? Situations, not rules and systems, typically determine action. The particulars of the moment (based on who one is and who the other players in the action are), as opposed to abstract systems and universal rules, will determine what is right and wrong, and what is done, most of the time. *Utang na loob,* or the constant building and fulfilling (not discharging) of obligations between individuals, is the grease that keeps society going.

2. What's the Best Way to View Time?

MONOCHRONIC OR POLYCHRONIC? The Philippines has an extremely polychronic culture: schedules must remain loose, the clock takes a backseat to most other criteria for action. Things do not necessarily flow sequentially: many things can happen simultaneously, and deadlines and schedules are juggled constantly. The workday usually begins around 8 or 8:30 A.M., and ends around 6 P.M. There is usually no work on the weekends, and family time is typically sacred.

RISK-TAKING OR RISK-AVERSE? The Philippines has essentially a risk-avoiding culture, because the social and business hierarchies and individual people's positions must be carefully considered within the larger group context. However, while most Filipinos defer to authority for decision making, they will often go ahead and do things on their own if the expected action is not taken.

PAST-ORIENTED OR FUTURE-ORIENTED? Because the past was one of foreign domination, there is no reason to look back. Filipinos look toward the future, and are frustrated that today's actions do not necessarily affect what happens tomorrow. When things do not work out, it is because of *kinaiya,* or fate. It is an agrarian concept from the indigenous Visayan culture, loosely translated as "That's just the way things are" or "That's just the way we are" (to foreigners).

3. What's the Best Way for Society to Work with the World at Large?

LOW-CONTEXT DIRECT OR HIGH-CONTEXT INDIRECT COMMUNICATORS? Filipinos are very high-context communicators. They avoid confrontation, and will speak in terms that maintain harmony at all costs, even if this results in speech that is indirect, evasive, or contradictory. Because circumstances rather than universal truths or laws determine action, sensitivity to the context is critical if you want accurate information on what is really being meant or done. The use of the word *yes,* even though *no* is meant; the avoidance of explanations and statements that even gently criticize or make someone look bad; the eternal smile, even when things are not going well; the failure to provide bad news or important negative information: all of these are common characteristics in the Philippines, which can ultimately be understood and precluded if one develops the ability to read between the lines. Read the context, not the words. *Pakisisama,* or smooth harmonious relations, is a major priority always.

PROCESS-ORIENTED OR RESULT-ORIENTED? Filipinos, perhaps because of their experience with the West, use a combination of Latin European deductive logic, American inductive logic, and indigenous Philippine associative logic. If things do not fit with their own subjective experiences and beliefs, it may be difficult to get Filipinos to agree to them. The polychronic nature of society additionally provides a holistic approach to problem solving, wherein things may not be looked at systematically or sequentially.

FORMAL OR INFORMAL? Philippine society is very formal, especially when one is on the outside, or beginning to establish relationships with the in-group. Once inside, it is very personal, and sometimes informal.

Greetings and Introductions

Language and Basic Vocabulary

English is the lingua franca, and almost all Filipinos speak it, certainly to English-speaking foreigners. However, the native language is Pilipino (there is no differentiation made between the *p* and *f* sounds), more commonly known as Tagalog, which most Filipinos speak at home. Despite the Spanish influence, Filipinos do not speak Spanish, unless they are intentionally learning it as a second language. It is insulting to begin speaking Spanish to them; use English instead. Because Tagalog stresses the next-to-last syllable, English is often spoken this way, as well, which can occasionally cause some difficulty in comprehension.

Here are some difficult words and phrases to watch out for when using English in the Philippines:

English Word or Phrase	*Philippine Usage*
already	"Let's eat already" (Let's go ahead and eat)
also	"He isn't joining us also" (He isn't joining us, either)
batch	"She was in my batch when I left" (She was in my group when I left)
go down	"Is this where we go down?" (Is this where we get off? E.g., the bus?)
green	"They sat around and told green jokes" (Off-color, in bad taste)
orig	A non-Filipino; a U.S.-born citizen
he/she	Pronoun use is often indiscriminate of gender (Spanish influence): e.g., "Maria, he is a good person"
where are you going?	An incidental greeting meaning "hello": it requires no substantive response

And here are some Pilipino words to become familiar with:

hindi/oo	no/yes
na lang	a term of diminution: e.g., "How are you?" "Okay, *na lang*" ("Okay, sort of")
pinoy	how a Filipino refers to him- or herself
salamat	thank you
sige	sure, or absolutely; e.g., "Do you want to see Maria?" ("*Sige, na!*"; "Sure, why not!")
viand	The food that the rice goes with

Honorifics for Men, Women, and Children

Place these honorifics before the last (family) name of the person:

- mang: Mr. (Mang Suarez)
- aling: Mrs. (Aling Suarez)

Mr. and Mrs./Miss/Ms. are perfectly acceptable forms of address, and should be used whenever people first meet each other. *Mang* and *aling* suggest additional respect, and are most often used with elderly people. In the Philippines, names are often Spanish in origin, but this does not mean those people speak Spanish. However, the Spanish ordering of family and matrilineal names is often followed.

The What, When, and How of Introducing People

Sometimes upon greeting you, Filipinos will simply call you by your first or last name plus your title, or make a comment about the task you are performing: this requires no substantive response.

Always wait to be introduced to strangers; never take that responsiblity upon yourself, as doing so is considered inappropriate most of the time. Filipinos are most comfortable with a third-party introduction whenever one is possible, and will go to great lengths to ensure that you are not left alone to decide this for yourself. Never presume to seat yourself at a gathering; if possible, wait to be told where to sit. The seating arrangements have usually been carefully worked out in advance, and in most cases reflect the status of the individuals in the group, and the honor that is being accorded the guests. When departing, it is important to say farewell to every individual present: the American group wave is not appreciated. Once you greet someone you will encounter later that day in the same circumstances (e.g., at the office), you will need to acknowledge them (without a handshake) whenever you see them again. Seniors, or those who are obviously the oldest in a group, are greeted first, seated first, and allowed to enter a room first (usually at the center of a group, however, and preceded in most cases by their younger aides).

Physical Greeting Styles

Because of their familiarity with Western customs, Filipinos use the handshake as a greeting. It is soft, unlike that in the United States. Men should wait for a woman to extend her hand before reaching to shake it, and many women will shake hands with men. However, Spanish intimacy and physicality is only reserved for individuals of the same sex: in public, women who know each other well may greet each other with a hug and a kiss, but men generally do not (and if they do, only after they have become very close). No slaps on the back, bear hugs, or taps on the shoulder at first: just a good firm handshake will do.

Business introductions also include the exchange of business cards. Always take a large supply of business cards with you: you must give one to every new person you are introduced to (there is no need to provide another business card when you are meeting someone again unless information about you has changed, such as a new address, contact number, or position). Be sure your business cards are in fine shape: they are extensions of you as a person, and must look as good as possible. Never hand out a dirty, soiled, bent, or written-on card. You do not need to have your business card translated from English into Pilipino. When presenting a business card, hold it in the upper right- and left-hand corners, which requires the use of two hands, so that it is readable to the person you are handing it to; you also receive the other person's card with two hands on the upper right- and left-hand corners. The exchange is done quickly, *almost* simultaneously. No bowing, and make eye contact with your colleague before you take a moment to silently read his or her card. Should you meet several people, you will have a handful of cards when the greetings are over.

As this ritual usually precedes a sit-down meeting, it is important to arrange the cards you have received in a little seating plan in front of you along the top of the desk or the table at your seat, reflecting the order in which people are seated. This helps you connect the correct names with the correct individuals throughout the meeting. Do this even if you are just meeting one person; it is expected. During the meeting, it is important never to play with the business cards (do not write on them—ever!); and when the meeting is over, never put them in your back pants pockets: pick them up carefully and respectfully, and place them neatly in your business card holder (a nice-looking leatherbound or brass case would be perfect), then place the card holder in the left inside jacket pocket of your suit (nearest your heart).

Communication Styles

Okay Topics / Not Okay Topics

Okay: anything that reflects your personal interests and hobbies, or your curiosity about things Filipino, like food, songs, the language, and customs. *Not okay:* Politics, current events, relations with the United States, or any subject that might in any way be controversial needs to be avoided at first. Do not inquire about a person's occupation or income in casual conversation, although it may be inquired of you (if so, this is just a way of getting to know more about your country, and not a personal investigation: answer specifically, but fully, with an explanation as to what things cost at home, why you do what you do, etc.). Do not inquire about your colleague's family life. Do not give your opinions about Philippine politics or Imelda Marcos (the extravagant and controversial wife of the former dictator). Do not talk about sex, or tell dirty jokes: it's in very bad taste. Do not complain: things that are annoying are best left ignored by well-bred people; complaining publicly usually brands you as lewd and crass. Sticking to general themes of personal interest or business is fine; it is a way of seeking common ground. There will be no need to begin a conversation with the very American "So, what do you do?" since you already know this from the business card exchange; however, further discussions about your company and its work are very much appreciated, as this gives Filipinos a chance to learn more about you and your firm. The goal of all conversation, at least at the beginning, is to create and maintain a harmonious atmosphere, despite the difficult or confrontational nature of the topic being discussed. At first, speak about things that you believe you have in common, so that you can build a personal connection, which will go far toward maintaining a harmonious bridge between you. This is appropriate for both individuals and organizations.

Tone, Volume, and Speed

Filipinos generally speak in soft, hushed tones. Speak slowly, for the benefit of those translating mentally, in short phrases, and speak clearly. Try to speak expositionally, without emotion, if possible.

Use of Silence

Passive silence—allowing time to pass simply, without words—can be a form of proactive communication in the Philippines. There may be some pauses between comments, but rarely extending over several minutes. When confronted with silence, for whatever reason, the best response is to remain silent yourself, although this may be difficult and appear unproductive for time-conscious Westerners. This is perhaps the most subtle form of communication, yet communication it is. Filipinos are great conversationalists, and there is nothing that they love to do more than talk . . . almost about anything at all. Something that Filipinos spiritedly indulge in is *tsismis,* or gossip. Nevertheless, with an outsider, they will be circumspect, at first. Don't join in the *tsismis;* it will come back to bite you.

Physical Gestures and Facial Expressions

Because of the Filipinos' familiarity with the West, the meaning of every hand and body gesture and facial expression that Americans use is known and equally applied in the Philippines. Be careful. Keep in mind that laughter may or may not be in response to anything humorous; more often, laughter, in the form of giggling, is an expression of embarrassment. The oft-offered smile, however, is a general way of getting through the day, of keeping things pleasant and soft. Practice it. Public displays of familiarity and affection with the opposite sex are expressed only by teenagers and young adults.

Waving and Counting

The pinkie represents the number 1, the forefinger represents the number 4 (the thumb is not used for counting), with everything in between ordered from the pinkie down; however, instead of raising the fingers when counting, the whole hand is exposed, and each finger is depressed as the counting is done. It is very insulting to motion to someone with the forefinger (instead, turn your hand so that the palm faces down and motion inward with all four fingers at once). If you need to gesture for a waiter, very subtly raise your hand. Waving or beckoning is done with the palm down and the fingers moving forward and backward in a kind of scratching motion. It may seem as if the person making this gesture is saying good-bye to you, when in fact you are being summoned over. If you need to point to something or someone, use a full palm motion, or clench your fist as if you were hitchhiking and use the thumb as if it were the index finger to point.

Physicality and Physical Space

Most Filipinos stand, relative to North Americans, about the same distance apart. Never, upon first greeting a Filipino, touch him or her beyond the soft handshake: no backslaps, no hugging, no kissing, *ever.* Never speak with your hands in your pockets: always keep them firmly to your side when standing. If men and women must cross their legs when they sit, it must never be ankle over knee (for women, the preferred style is ankle over ankle). Remember, in public, formal is always better than informal: no gum chewing, *ever;* don't slouch; and don't lean against things. Once close relationships are established, there may be much physicality—touching, for example, or putting arms around other people's shoulders, or holding hands—but generally only between members of the same sex, and not in public between members of the opposite sex except for some teenagers and young adults. About the only time this nonphysicality rule is broken is on public transport, where it is very crowded and touching is unavoidable, or on crowded streets, where you are very likely to be poked and prodded as people jostle by.

Eye Contact

In the Philippines, eye contact can be both direct and indirect. The eyes are used extensively for conveying feelings and thoughts. Tune up your nonverbal antennae. Filipinos usually try to avoid direct eye contact with their superiors. Do not stare at a Filipino/a: it is considered aggressive. Be quick to make eye contact, and move on.

Emotive Orientation

Filipinos are generally restrained; losing one's control is very bad form. There is little emotive expression in business situations that are harmonious and positive, and even when things are not going well, expressions of negativity and displeasure are minimal.

Protocol in Public

Walking Styles and Waiting in Lines

On the street, in stores, and in most public facilities, people generally pay little attention to maintaining orderly lines. Due to the volume of passengers on public transportation, there can be much pushing and jostling. This is not to get into a bus or train ahead of someone else, though; it is merely to get in!

Behavior in Public Places: Airports, Terminals, and the Market

Customer service is a well-developed practice in most stores, because the "other" (in this case, the customer) is so important, and because demonstrating good customer service involves showing deference to the customer. Stores in the cities are open in the evenings and on weekends, as well as during the day. A personal thank-you to store owners, waiters, chefs, and hotel managers for their services is very much appreciated. In food markets, don't worry about touching the produce, since everybody does, and it doesn't obligate you to buy it; in goods stores, if you buy a product and you have problems with it, returning the item is usually difficult. Smoking is endemic, and you may have difficulty finding a no-smoking area on public transportation, in restaurants, and in other public places. Bathroom facilities can range from Western-style toilets to Asian-style toilets (holes in the floor, with buckets of water or hoses attached to a water line for cleanup instead of paper); be prepared.

When answering a telephone, say "Hello" or just your given name. Cell phones are ubiquitous, as the wire networks may be unreliable or nonexistent.

Bus / Metro / Taxi / Car

Driving is on the right, and whether in the country or city, being in a car can be hazardous to your health. The roads are not necessarily in good repair, marked, or where maps say they are; and obtaining fuel when and where you need it can be a problem. The traffic in Manila and other major cities is maddening and chaotic, and construction sites are everywhere. The best way to catch a cab is at designated taxi stands (hotels are good places, but often charge more for the same ride: a hotel surcharge is added to the meter fare, in some cases). When a taxi has been hailed, negotiate the price, as the meter may or may not be working (even if it is, you still should negotiate the price ahead of time).

Tipping

The standard tips are about 10 to 15 percent in restaurants and taxis, and about 5 percent for porters. The tip may or may not appear on the restaurant bill, so ask if you are not sure.

Punctuality

While the Philippines is essentially a polychronic culture, you are expected to be punctual in all situations. Do not arrive more than ten minutes too soon—or more than ten minutes late, for that matter. Your Philippine associates, however, may be late; or if they are already present, they may be deep in side discussions that will require you to wait: do so patiently. For social gatherings the rule is different: being about fifteen minutes late is preferred.

Dress

The Philippine standard is more or less fashionable and Western, but the main concern is the climate: it is hot and tropical most of the year. Therefore, many businessmen wear very lightweight suits, or a dress shirt, either with or without a tie, and no jacket. None of this is an invitation to informality: it is just an adaptation to the weather. Businesswomen wear lightweight skirts and blouses, jackets, or suits. It is best to start out formal, and then you can take your jacket off if you see others without them. Wear dress slacks, not jeans or khakis. Social dress is the same, although sometimes clean, pressed jeans are okay with a dress or sport shirt (but no T-shirts!). Sneakers are only for the street or gym (some women do wear sneakers to work, but change just before they enter the office, not after going in); because of the heat, shorts are okay only on the street, with T-shirts. Dress shirts can be short-sleeved, due to the heat. You may see a very special open-collared men's shirt, often decorated with a batik design the same color and fabric of the background (usually white), called a *barong tagalog*. The long-sleeved version is not an informal shirt: in fact, it is quite traditional and worn on special occasions (perhaps the signing of your deal). Men wear it outside of their pants, without a jacket and tie.

Seasonal Variations

There are two extreme seasons in the Philippines: wet and hot, and dry and hot. The important thing is to remember the frequent downpours; take an umbrella with you everywhere you go.

Colors

Wear neutral colors whenever possible.

Styles

For the most part, clothing is simple, adapted to the climate, and meant to keep one looking good and cool. Consider, however, that many public places are air-conditioned to arctic levels, so you might always want to have a lightweight covering available.

Accessories / Jewelry / Makeup

Makeup, hairstyle, and accessories are important for women. Perfume and cologne are popular.

Personal Hygiene

In the Philippines, personal hygiene is very important. There is a real concern for cleanliness and smelling good. Take more than one bath a day, if you need to: Filipinos do, when they can. Do not blow your nose in public: it is considered very rude (if you must blow your nose in public, never use a handkerchief; try disposable tissues). Spitting can occur on the street, however. At the end of a meal, it is perfectly acceptable to use toothpicks, but you must cover the "working" hand with the other hand, so that others cannot see your mouth.

Dining and Drinking

Mealtimes and Typical Foods

The typical Philippine diet revolves mainly around the local foods, especially vegetables, pork and seafood, and rice and noodles. Filipinos are also very familiar with Western foods, especially fast foods, and the diet of most today is a mixture of all these influences. Westerners familiar with Spanish-influenced cuisine will recognize the Latin-based *menudo*-type stews, the Cuban-style pork dishes, the tapa-like appetizers, but all with native ingredients of Asian and Polynesian origin. On top of this, add the American hamburger, and other types of fast food (which, in all fairness, are found most everywhere around the world), and you have a sense of Filipino cooking. If you are hosting a Filipino in the United States, they will be very comfortable with the local restaurants you choose, but will be especially thrilled if you can locate an authentic Philippine restaurant. If you are with Chinese Filipinos, dine with them at a good Chinese restaurant, whether in the Philippines or abroad; a Chinese banquet is not inappropriate (for a description of a typical one, please see the dining section in the chapter on China).

Breakfast is served from about 7:30 to 9 A.M., and usually consists of tea or coffee and rice; the latter is served either as a porridge-type cereal that can be flavored with any number of ingredients (*nasi gorang*), with eggs in a variety of styles, or with pickled vegetables. Tea may be drunk plain or with lemon, cream, milk, or sugar.

Lunch is traditionally the main meal of the day, and even today, in busy cities, it can still be an elaborate affair with several courses—or it can be a simple noodle dish or fast food bolted down in a matter of minutes. Lunch is served from about noon to 1 P.M., and consists of meat, fish, and/or vegetables, served with rice. Many dishes can be steamed, stir-fried, or boiled in a variety of different ways, either simply or more elaborately. *Lechon,* or pork, is usually roasted or barbecued, and is a very popular meat. You will see *adobo,* a spice, just about everywhere. Fish sauce and fish paste are available with most ethnic Philippine foods, and have very pungent flavors: start out carefully. Filipinos enjoy sweet pastries, so a very sweet dessert of fruits, pudding, or cake is usually available for every meal. Typically, the drinks served with lunch and dinner are soft drinks, beer, and/or tea or coffee.

Dinner is served from 6 P.M. on, with 7:30 P.M. the customary late time. Even if the main meal of the day was lunch, dinner is only slightly lighter—this is often the case with families at home. The dinner menu is often similar to that of the more formal lunch. If alcohol is being served, predinner drinks may begin with beer or rice wine, then move on to beer during the meal, and end with a sweet wine and/or coffee or tea. Western liquors are served in upscale restaurants and at business dinners.

Regional Differences

Seafood is very common everywhere, as are preserved vegetables and rice dishes, mixed often with coconut, pork, and chicken. Restaurants representing various Asian cuisines abound in Manila. There are a few unique Philippine dishes that you will probably be encouraged to try: one of them is *balut,* which is a cooked egg with a half-developed chick or duckling inside.

Typical Drinks and Toasting

The most common alcoholic beverage is beer, generally served cold. Because you must never pour your own drink (be it beer or tea), you must always be alert throughout the meal as to whether your neighbor's cup or glass needs refilling. If it is less than half full, it needs refilling; alternately, if yours is less than half full, your neighbor is obliged to refill it. If he or she does not, do not refill it yourself, for this will cause them to lose face; instead, diplomatically indicate your need by pouring a little more drink into your neighbor's glass, even if it doesn't really need it.

What to do if you don't drink alcohol? This is usually not a problem, since not everyone does, and fruit juices and soft drinks are very popular.

If you are the honored guest, you will be expected to make a toast, usually soon after the host does or at the end of the meal, just before everyone departs. An appropriate toast is to the health of the host and all those present, and to the prosperity of the business under discussion.

Avoid drinking tap water anywhere in the Philippines (this means you should brush your teeth with bottled water and not take ice in any of your drinks; drink only bottled water, or brewed tea or coffee or soft drinks, and avoid getting water from the morning shower into your mouth; and never eat fresh fruits or vegetables that cannot be peeled first, and ideally cooked later before eating). This is a serious matter: there are some very nasty bugs going around in developing countries.

Table Manners and the Use of Utensils

Chopsticks are used to eat Chinese food (for more on chopstick use, see the chapter on China earlier in this book). Otherwise, forks, spoons, and knives are used with Philippine and Western food. In some Philippine restaurants (the more authentic and usually downscale places), no utensils at all are used. Avoid using your left hand for any kind of eating, especially if you are eating directly with your hands and not using utensils.

What do you do when no utensils are offered? Why, eat with your fingers, of course! Many think it makes the experience more fun, maybe because you're adding an extra sense to an already very sensory experience: the sense of touch. This food is known as "banana-leaf" food: wonderful vegetarian or meat curries, served with rice and sauce on a large banana leaf. No plates, no forks, no spoons, no chopsticks. You reach into the rice, take some with your fingers, gently roll it between your index and middle fingers and thumb (not your palm!) into a kind of self-sticking ball, dip it into the sauce on the banana leaf, mix it with a vegetable or a piece of chicken, then pop the whole thing in your mouth. Here are some other things to note about eating in such restaurants:

- Wash your hands before you sit down to eat. Many banana-leaf restaurants have washrooms and sinks out in the open specifically for this purpose. (However, you may want to wash your hands with bottled water at the hotel first, since the water at the restaurant may be more hazardous to your health than the germs already on your hands!) You will also need to wash your hands again at the end of the meal, especially after eating the saucy dishes, since you've probably got a good bit of it running down your arm. Don't worry, it's to be expected: don't dress up if you're eating banana-leaf style.

- Use your right hand when picking up and eating food. Keep your left hand at your side. Do not place your left hand on the table, and do not pass food with your left hand, as the left hand typically is considered the "unclean" hand in Muslim tradition, and many banana-leaf restaurants are Muslim establishments.

- If you absolutely cannot eat without some kind of utensil, it's usually all right to ask for spoons in such establishments. The proprietors are more than pleased to accommodate Westerners.

Do not take the last bit of food from a central serving plate if there is one (more often than not, Philippine meals will be individually served); that means there will be none left in case someone else wants more. Also, a sauce may be mixed with the rice, and the main dish may be eaten with the rice.

Toothpicks are often used at the end of the meal. The best way to handle a toothpick is to work away with one hand, while keeping the other hand in front of it over the mouth, as a sort of mask. If you cover the working hand this way, you can join in the toothpick session in public at the end of the meal with the best of them! Just never do it walking down the street: that's simply not done.

A word about smoking: it is ubiquitous throughout the Philippines. Usually, you do not smoke at the table until the meal is over.

Seating Plans

The most honored position is at the head of the table, as in the western European style, with the honored guest(s) sitting to the right of the host (and hostess):

if there are couples, the honored man sits next to the hostess, and the honored woman sits next to the host. (Spouses are usually not invited to business meals, though, and most formal meals in restaurants are business meals: do not ask if your spouse can join you; it will embarrass your Filipino colleague into doing something that is uncomfortable for him.) The honored guest sits on the side of the table farthest from the door, if possible. (At business meetings, the key people sit in the middle, flanked on either side in descending order by their aides, with the least important people sitting at the ends of the table farthest from the middle, and closest to the door; the arrangement is mirrored on the other side, because the rules of hierarchy demand that everyone must be able to speak with their opposite peers and those who rank below, but those below cannot speak with those above.) Because many tables are round, a curious situation often develops: the least important person from one side ends up sitting next to the host or most important person on the other side. (This is usually not an issue at business meetings, where tables are more often rectangular.) If women are present, they will probably be given the honored positions first, although practically speaking there will be far fewer women.

Refills and Seconds

You will always be offered more food. Leave a bit on your plate if you do not want more food. You will be implored to take more two or three times, in the form of a little ritual. The game is as follows: first you refuse, then the host insists, then you refuse again, then the host insists again, and then you finally give in and take a little more. If you really don't want more, take very little and leave it on your plate. You may always have additional beverages; drink enough to cause your cup or glass to be less than half full, and it will generally be refilled. A reminder: never refill your own glass; always refill your neighbor's glass, and he or she will refill yours.

At Home, in a Restaurant, or at Work

Do not begin to eat or drink until the oldest man at the table has been served and has begun. It is appropriate to thank the host at the end of the meal for the fine food.

In informal restaurants, you may be required to share a table. If so, do not force conversation: act as if you are seated at a private table. Waitstaff may be summoned by making eye contact; waving or calling their names is very impolite. The business breakfast is unknown in the Philippines. The business lunch is very popular, as is the business dinner. Both may be good times to discuss business, but let your Philippine associates take the lead on this: if they bring up business, then it's okay to discuss it.

When invited to a Philippine colleague's home for a formal meal, you will be told where to sit, and there you should remain. It is a great honor to be invited into a Philippine home, and Filipinos may be quick to invite you, as a Westerner, into theirs. Most middle-class households have servants: be aware that they may have prepared the food, not the hostess.

Your spouse may be invited to join you for a meal at your colleague's home (if your spouse is present, very little business will be discussed, however). Once invited to enter the Philippine home, you may need to remove your shoes (this is not the custom in restaurants, however), although Westernization has also changed this, especially in the cities. Once inside the home, do not wander around, unless you are invited to do so: much of the house is really off-limits to guests. If you move from room to room at someone's home, be sure to always allow the more senior members of your party to enter the room ahead of you. If the meal is served "help-yourself" style, be sure not to be the first person to take food; let the host or hostess begin. Be judicious about touching things and moving them about: many items have probably been placed where they are because it is auspicious to do so according to *feng shui,* a common tradition brought to the Philippines from the south of China. (Objects are placed, and buildings and rooms designed, so that bad spirits are kept out and good spirits are invited in.) At the end of the meal, you may be given *pabaon,* a doggie bag with the leftover food in it. This is a common expression of hospitality; make an effort to reject it, but ultimately take it. If you invite someone to an event, you will rarely be turned down directly—people will say things like "Yes, I think I can make it" but this is no guarantee that they will actually come.

Being a Good Guest or Host

Paying the Bill

Usually the one who does the inviting pays the bill, although the guest is expected to make an effort to pay. Sometimes other circumstances determine the payee (such as rank). Making payment arrangements ahead of time so that no exchange occurs at the table is a very classy way to host, and is very common. When men are at the table, women will not really be able to pay the bill at a restaurant: if you want to, make arrangements ahead of time, and don't wait for the check to arrive at the table. The only time it is considered appropriate for a woman to pay the bill is if she is a businesswoman from abroad.

Transportation

It's a very nice idea, when acting as the host, to inquire ahead of time as to whether your guests will require transportation. If necessary, you should arrange for taxi service at the end of the meal. When seeing your guests off, you must remain at the entrance of the house or the restaurant, or at the site where you deposited your guests into the car, until the car is out of sight: it is very important not to leave until your guests can no longer see you, should they look back. Guests are seated in cars (and taxis) by rank, with the honored guest being placed in the back directly behind the front passenger seat; the next honored position is in the back behind the driver, and the least honored position is up front with the driver.

When to Arrive / Chores to Do

If invited to dinner at a private home, do not offer to help with the chores if there is a servant. Offer to help with the chores if there is no servant, but do not expect to be taken up on your offer. Nor should you expect to visit the kitchen. Do not leave the table unless invited to do so. Be about fifteen minutes late to a social dinner at someone's home. When in the home, be careful not to admire things too effusively: Filipinos may feel obligated to give them to you, and you in turn will be required to present them with a gift of equal value. Instead of saying things like "I love that vase," say something like "Vases that beautiful in my country are found only in museums." Your compliments will most likely be dismissed.

Gift Giving

In general, gifts are exchanged on many occasions in the Philippines: when one visits a colleague's home, for holidays, to commemorate special events, to start or seal a business deal, or when someone returns from a trip abroad (this gift is known as *pasalubong:* something brought back from far away). In business settings, this usually takes the form of personal gifts that symbolically say the correct thing about the nature of the relationship. When going to the Philippines on business, you must bring gifts for everyone you will see. The general rule is pastries for the office staff, high-quality corporate logo items (all the same) for business associates, and an especially thoughtful, somewhat personalized gift for the key man you will be working with. Your gifts do not have to be elaborate or expensive; in fact, giving something too overtly costly obligates your Filipino associates to do the same, something they may not be able to do. You present your gifts at the end of the first meeting, as a sign of your sincerity and best wishes. You will receive a farewell gift at your last meeting in the Philippines before you leave to go home, or when you give your gifts. When Filipinos visit your country, they will also bring you a gift, and before they leave, you should give them gifts. Holiday cards are appropriate for any special occasion, as they are in the West.

The most appropriate gift for a personal visit to a home, or as a thank-you for dinner, would be a cut floral bouquet (no chrysanthemums or white lilies: they are used for funeral and religious occasions, and no red roses, as they are too personal), a box of fruits, pastries, cakes, cookies, calendars, items for the children (games, toys, maps, prints, stamps, tapes and CDs, T-shirts), stationery, or practical housewares (simple kitchen items). *Do* send a handwritten thank-you note the day after the dinner party. If you are staying with a family, an appropriate thank-you gift would be a high-quality product that represents your country and is difficult or expensive to get in the Philippines, but remember that items from the United States are usually very familiar or readily available: avoid the coffee-table picture books, sports team paraphernalia, and the like. Instead, bring something that reflects the personality of your host or associate; well-framed and well-mounted photographs of you and your Philippine associates are appreciated. Remember, any gift given by a man to a woman must come with the caveat that it is from both him and his wife/sister/mother, or else it is far too personal. For both giving and receiving gifts, two hands are always used. Gifts are typically not opened by the receiver in front of the giver; they are usually received, graciously acknowledged, and placed aside to be opened once the giver is no longer present. (For Chinese Filipinos, please see the section on gift giving in the China chapter.)

Gifts should be wrapped well. When you purchase any of the previously mentioned items in the Philippines, it will be wrapped beautifully for you, especially if you make it known that it is a gift. Typically, gifts are wrapped in ordinary paper first and then wrapped again in gold or yellow (royal colors) or pastels and pink (happy colors). Avoid red, unless you are giving a gift to a Chinese Filipino, and black, because it is a funeral color.

Special Holidays and Celebrations

Major Holidays

The most popular vacation time in the Philippines varies, but can be March/April, July/August, or November/December.

January 1	New Year's Day
March/April	Easter and Holy Week
April 9	Bataan Day (remembrance day of the battle that led to the fall of Bataan in 1942)
May 1	Labor Day
May 6	National Heroes Day
June 12	Independence Day
July 4	Philippine-American Friendship Day
November 1	All Saints' Day
November 30	Bonifacio Day
December 25	Christmas
December 30	Rizal Day (commemoration of the execution of José Rizal, Philippine national independence hero)

Business Culture

Daily Office Protocols

The traditional Philippine office has an open design; there are few doors, with the exception of the offices of those holding higher positions, and people work mainly at long, large tables or at individual or shared cubicles. Doors, if they exist, are usually open. The open scheme is similar to the office arrangement described in the chapter on Japan. However, in many modern businesses today, the office layout and patterns of day-to-day management follow generally accepted Western organizational designs.

Executives are usually placed on different floors from the rank and file. You will probably meet them either in their offices or in conference rooms.

Management Styles

Because of the rigid rank and hierarchy orientation, titles are very important; the highest ones (e.g., vice president) are usually reserved for very senior, executive-level positions, and should not be used as casually as they are in the United States. Complimenting, rewarding, or criticizing employees publicly is absolutely ineffective. Any criticism must be done very carefully, and in private. Deference is shown by subordinates to their seniors; paternalistic concern is often shown by executives to their juniors. As is the case with many bureaucracies, the primary goal may be to protect oneself and one's position vis-à-vis one's superiors (as well as to protect one's superior), rather than to get immediate goals accomplished. This usually means negotiations or projects can move very slowly at some times, and rapidly at others.

Boss-Subordinate Relations

The decision-making system usually works from the top on down, with key decisions often coming from individuals in high positions of authority. There are formal and informal networking opportunities available in order for the decision maker to build a consensus, but generally, access to power is what determines action. If decision makers do not provide instructions, Filipinos will take it upon themselves to do what they believe needs to be done (they will rarely do nothing): this could have results different from what managers intend. The challenge for Westerners is to provide hands-on management in a caring and involved way—to be decisive, but not authoritarian.

Conducting a Meeting or Presentation

At your first meeting in the Philippines, you will probably be received in a very comfortable waiting area, then move into an office. The meeting is conducted between yourself and most probably, if a first meeting, a "gatekeeper" (not a decision-maker, but someone who will pass you on to higher-ups eventually). Therefore, be sure you start out at the highest level of decision making you can in the organization, or else you will need several meetings to get to the top. When serving any refreshments in the office, be sure they are served in porcelain tea sets and real glasses: the use of paper or Styrofoam shows disrespect and is very bad form. At meetings of peers, there can be open communication and sharing of ideas: however, most meetings are formalities at which information is exchanged, or decisions that have already been made are confirmed. Meetings are too risky for open problem solving and decision making, given the group and hierarchy orientation in the Philippines. If you are with the decision maker, things can move quickly. If not, patience and third-party connections are key.

Negotiation Styles

Expect few decisions from Filipinos at the table, and be willing to provide copious amounts of information, to the degree that you can, in response to their questions and in anticipation of their needs. Presentations should be well prepared and simply propounded. Details are best left to questions and backup material, which should be left behind. English is fine. Ideally, you should present your material to the Filipinos for study, along with a proposed agenda, prior to the meeting. If you have a team (and there need not be), the participants' roles should be well thought out and defined. Never disagree with each other in front of the Filipinos, or appear uncertain, unsure, not authorized to make a decision, or out of control in any way.

Filipinos are very familiar with and very comfortable with the American style of bargaining. Contracts are binding: there is a significant body of contract law in the Philippines that may be used for redress. Keep communications open, especially when at a distance, and stay in touch often with your Filipino associate: share more information than you normally would, not less; and, because business is so intimately connected with the government and because the political situation is so fluid, try to have a contact on the ground in the Philippines who can always keep you informed of what is really going on, if you can.

Written Correspondence

Your business letters should be very formal and respectful of rank and hierarchy. Family names usually are written in uppercase; dates are given in the U.S. style (month/day/year) or the Asian style (year/month/day, with periods in between, not slashes); and an honorific plus the title is as common as the honorific plus the last name. You should write your e-mails, letters, and faxes in a formal, precise way: use a brief, warm introduction, then quickly get down to business. Keep it simple, however, and outline all important matters. Addresses can be formatted either the Western (name, street, city, country + code) or Asian way (country + code, city, street, name).

The Southeast Asian Cultures: Malaysia and Singapore

Note: Malaysia and Singapore share many of the cultural traditions previously discussed in our sections on Indonesia and China. Vietnam, Laos, Cambodia, and Myanmar share many of the cultural traditions previously discussed in our sections on Thailand and China. For this reason, when we discuss these countries, we will be referring to the appropriate source cultures, with additional variations that are unique to the countries being explored.

MALAYSIA

Please refer to the section on Indonesia for appropriate Southeast Asian behaviors and traditions; the information that follows describes additional cultural behaviors that are specific to Malaysia.

Malaysia as a country is a rather new phenomenon. It was created in the early 1960s out of the older Federation of Malaya, a British-sponsored entity that attempted to cobble together the former Islamic sultanates of the region into one organized unit. At one time, it included the current independent city-state of Singapore, and the oil-rich sultanate of Brunei (oil reserves allowed that state to eventually opt out from the organization). Today, the nation-state of Malaysia includes the greater portion of the Malay Peninsula and the Sarawak region on the northwest coast of the island of Borneo. While the indigenous people of this country are the Malay (citizens of the country are called Malaysians, whether they are ethnic Malay or not), many other ethnic groups, such as the Dayaks, Muruts, Kadazans, and Melanaus, have come to inhabit the region. Together, these peoples are referred to as Bumiputras, or the native Malaysians—"Bumis" for short.

Straddling the crossroads of the Straits of Malacca, Malaysia has long attracted the attention of other peoples who were seeking the trade opportunities that this region presented. The Chinese emigrated to the peninsula over two thousand years ago, intermarrying with the Malays and forming, along with powerful trading houses, a new Malay-Chinese culture known as *Perinakan*, or "Straits Chinese"; Indians (southern Tamils, mainly) crossed the Indian Ocean to settle and trade there, establishing powerful Hindu empires; Arabs came from the Middle East spreading Islam and establishing powerful sultanates throughout the straits; and finally the Europeans came, bringing mercantilism and colonizing the region. The British, in an effort to clean up the "pirate trading outposts" of the region, claimed the area that now includes Malaysia and Singapore (while the Dutch claimed Indonesia).

Today, Malaysia reflects the complex interactions of all these cultures. The Bumis themselves are primarily the administrators of the country and the government; the ethnic Straits Chinese, however, pretty much run the economy (along with, and sometimes in conflict with, economically invested Bumis), and Arabs and Tamils generally fill the service and professional niches, respectively. The country is a constitutional monarchy, for alongside the British-modeled parliamentary system, which includes a prime minister and a president, there is a paramount ruler (*yang di-pertuan agong,* in Malay), who is selected by and from the nine hereditary ruling sultans who make up the "monarchy": this ruling sultan is selected for five years, and is the official head of state.

Because of the historic British presence on the peninsula, there is a strong overlay across the entire fabric of the country of British customs. The British left behind them a functioning civil service and infrastructure, as well as English as the lingua franca. This is especially important because of the variety of languages that each of the groups brought with them (even the Chinese often could not speak with each other, since immigrants from one part of China spoke a dialect that was unintelligible to Straits Chinese from another part of China). Bahasa Indonesian and Bahasa Malay are essentially very similar at their core, but differ because in Malaysia, the language was heavily influenced by English, not Dutch. Part of the British infrastructure that has helped Malaysia develop includes the school system, which promoted English and Western ideals as a unifying factor across the various cultures, and gave educational opportunities to many who previously had no access to them.

With the Straits Chinese playing such a marked role in the economics of the country, there is a greater comfort level with risk-taking among them generally than among Bumis. However, the country offers few opportunities for women, for the culture, perhaps as a result of the Islamic influence, is male dominated. Bumis are mainly Muslims, the Chinese are Buddhists, and the Tamils are Hindus. The Malay sultanates play a very significant role in federal and state politics; thus, the Islamic influence in Malaysia is perhaps more powerful than it is in Indonesia.

The honorifics for Bumis, in Bahasa Malay, are:

encik	Mr.
puan	Mrs.
cik	Miss
tuan haji	man who has made the hajj
puan hajjah	woman who has made the hajj

They are placed, as most honorifics are in the region, before the first (given) name.

It should be noted that Indians (particularly Tamils, who make up the general Indian Hindu population in Malaysia) have a nonverbal behavior that can be confusing to Westerners: they "wobble" their head from side to side often in conversation. This is not a disagreement; rather, it usually signifies that they are listening to you as you speak. Muslim women, as well as Indian women, tend to wear saris and sarongs in the street, for social occasions, and at work; additionally, many Muslim women cover their heads, and some, their faces.

Because Islam prohibits alcohol and the region produces an abundance of fruit, fruit juices in all varieties and combinations are widely available, and make for a very refreshing drink. You will be served fruit juices almost everywhere, and certainly with Muslim meals. The unique cuisine that developed in the Peri-nakan culture is called *nonya* cooking, because the original Malay women in the Straits Chinese home were referred to as *nonyas*. The *nonya* kitchen uses lots of indigenous Malay ingredients, blending mild but flavorful spices and sauces with Chinese ingredients, and shows a distinct Indian influence. The food is hearty family fare, with a dark, complex, foresty taste.

Special Holidays and Celebrations

Major Holidays

The most popular vacation time in Malaysia varies depending on whether one is Buddhist, Muslim, or Hindu. The Buddhist New Year (lunar) often falls around the same time as Ramadan, so the period from January through March is not a good time to do business in Malaysia. It is considered very auspicious if different groups' holidays fall on the same day or around the same time of year.

January 1 (solar)	New Year's Day
January/February (lunar)	Ramadan (one full lunar month, celebrating when Muhammad received his first revelation)
January/February (lunar)	Chinese New Year's (lasts from one to two weeks)
February 1 (solar)	Kuala Lumpur City Day
March (lunar)	*Hari Raya Puasa* (end of Ramadan)
May (lunar)	*Hari Raya Haji* (Islam commemoration of Abraham's attempted sacrifice)
May 1 (solar)	Labor Day
May 14 (lunar)	Wesak Day
May 31 (solar)	*Awal Muharam* (the Muslim New Year begins)
June 3 (solar)	Agong's Birthday (Sultan's birthday)
August 9 (lunar)	The Prophet Muhammad's Birthday
August 31 (solar)	National Day
October/November (lunar)	*Deepavali* (a Hindu festival of Thanksgiving)
December 25 (solar)	Christmas

SINGAPORE

Please refer to the sections on Indonesia and China for appropriate Southeast Asian behaviors and traditions; the information that follows describes additional cultural behaviors that are specific to Singapore.

When Sir Thomas Stamford Raffles in 1819 first pulled into the sleepy fishing village that had been renamed Singapura by a Buddhist prince in the thirteenth century (its original name was Temasek), he nearly changed the face of Southeast Asia overnight. The free port he created under British control would eventually rival the duty ports of the Dutch in Indonesia. Almost immediately, trade moved from Batavia (Dutch-controlled Indonesia) to Singapore, thus beginning one of the world's great capitalist endeavors. The city-state became an enclave for Chinese refugees escaping from Manchu rule at the start of the twentieth century; these immigrants added their business savvy and skills to the already thriving port.

In 1965, shortly after the British granted independence to their Malayan Federation, Singapore decided to go it alone. Lee Kwan Yew, the founder of independent, modern-day Singapore, identified the people as the one true asset the country had, and developed a program of socially engineered action that thrust the government into every aspect of daily life, literally molding a nation based on legislating every social behavior within a laissez-faire capitalist structure. In this sense, it was the dream Confucian Chinese society. But in order to jump-start the people into action, Lee needed to find a common entity for them to struggle against, and he found it in Malaysia. By making the larger Asian unknown next door into a danger to be struggled against by tiny Singapore, Lee mobilized the people into coming together in their diversity in a common cause, even if it meant government control of most social activity.

This is the Singapore of today: wildly successful economically (and only more so now that Hong Kong has lost its luster due to the risks that some former Hong Kong–based organizations see associated with keeping their Asian hubs in China), yet restrictive in personal freedoms, only nominally democratic in politics (the PAP—the People's Action Party—the ruling party, is, in effect, the *only* party), and insulated—in part by tightly restricting and controlling the information entering from the outside world. This is a land of contradictions— of gleaming consumer goods, and staggering fines for everything from not flushing public toilets after use to jaywalking to chewing gum in public. Singapore plans to be the first country to ban smoking, flat out. The selling of illegal drugs can result in an immediate death sentence. From time to time, the *Wall Street Journal* Asia edition is banned from the newsstands, and the *Straits Times* has been accused by some of being just a happy sheet for the government. But the complex mixture of people thrive on and Singaporeans are extremely proud of their intensely successful multicultural society.

There are four official languages: Chinese (the official government Chinese is Mandarin, but nearly all Chinese in Singapore speak Cantonese, from southern China), English, Malay, and Tamil. The Chinese majority are at the top of the economic ladder, the Malays in the middle hold the service and professional jobs, and the Indian Tamils and the Arabs are at the bottom (small shopkeepers, etc.), all tied together in an infrastructure heavily influenced by the legacy of the British. The fast-paced life in Singapore today masks ancient cultural influences, which are still evident in the day-to-day drive for success in this small and vibrant country. Curiously, most Singaporeans have bought into the system: legally, they have no choice, and it works very well for most. It is one of the wealthiest nations in the region. Due to the obvious success as well as the lack of a democratic tradition, most Singaporeans only have positive things to say about their country. If you ask them, often you will hear how Singapore is just like the West, only better, safer, cleaner. It is as if Singaporeans will not permit bad news in any form and cannot accept second place; they are seen as overstriving and overcompensating, to insure that their efforts will always succeed.

There is a curious uniquely Singaporean linguistic device, the word *la:* it functions as both an exclamation mark and a question mark, and is used endlessly in conversation—for example, "You need to tell your husband he needs to make more money, la" or "You want to go there tonight for dinner, la?" It is one of the many uniquely Singaporean twists on English, a result of the "Singlish" that resulted from diverse speakers adapting to the English spoken by the British. Invitations are almost never turned down directly: people will always say things like "Yes, I think I can make it," but this is no guarantee that they will actually come. Nevertheless, it is the best that you will get (do not put them on the spot afterward if they do not show up by asking them why or what happened; if the occasion must be mentioned, simply say that they were missed).

Because of the British influence, most of the time dates are written the European way (day.month.year), and addresses are written the Western way, beginning with the name, and working down to the street, city, and country plus postal code. Driving is on the left. It should be noted that Singapore is one of the world's safest cities, and the food, being representative of so many different cultures, is nothing short of glorious. It is safe to eat the food most everywhere, including the ubiquitous street stalls—and the water is safe to drink as well. The Chinese banquet is still a very common business entertainment in Singapore; please see the section on the Chinese banquet in the chapter on China for more information on this wonderful tradition.

Special Holidays and Celebrations

Major Holidays

The most popular vacation time in Singapore varies depending on whether one is Buddhist, Muslim, or Hindu. The Buddhist New Year (lunar) often falls around the same time as Ramadan, so the period from January through March is not a good time to do business in Singapore. It is considered very auspicious if different groups' holidays fall on the same day or around the same time of year.

January (lunar)	*Thaipusam* (Hindu sacrificial worship ceremony)
January 1 (solar)	New Year's Day
January/February (lunar)	Ramadan
January/February (lunar)	Chinese New Year
February (lunar)	*Hari Raya Puasa* (marks end of Ramadan)
March (lunar)	*Qing ming jie* (Chinese Ancestor's Day)
March/April (solar)	Good Friday
March/April (solar)	Easter Sunday
April (lunar)	*Hari Raya Haji* (celebrating the Muslim journey to Mecca)
May (lunar)	Vesak Day
May 1 (solar)	Labor Day
August 9 (solar)	National Day
August/September (lunar)	Feast of the Hungry Ghosts (Chinese: *Zhong yuan jie*)
October/November (lunar)	*Deepavali* (a Hindu festival of thanksgiving)
December 25 (solar)	Christmas
December 31 (solar)	New Year's Eve

CHAPTER EIGHT

The Southeast Asian Cultures of Indochina: Vietnam, Laos, Cambodia, and Myanmar (Burma)

Note: Vietnam, Laos, Cambodia, and Myanmar (Burma) share many cultural traditions related to China and Buddhism; nevertheless, there are some important distinctions. The information that follows describes additional Indochinese cultural behaviors that are specific to these countries.

Some Introductory Background on Indochina and Its People

The region has historically lived in the shadow of China to the north, while suffering the invasions of much of the rest of the world from its vulnerable south. Walking the tightrope between integrating Chinese culture into its own indigenous cultures, while keeping the Chinese politically at bay, has always been a difficult act for the peoples of Indochina. Complicating this picture has been the need to keep the rest of the world, ranging from Arabs to Turks to Tamils to Japanese to Europeans to Americans, from imposing their will. Each country had to find its own path through these struggles, sometimes engendering the enmity of its neighbor in so doing.

Today, while all four nations share much in common, they are in many ways enemies of each other, and within each nation, there are unstable forces that can cause any one fragile sovereignty to crack. Vietnam has only recently been reunified, the latest development in an endlessly repeating cycle of unification and disestablishment between the north and south of this country. Vietnam is the historic enemy of China in the region, and in so doing has made an enemy of its neighbor, Cambodia (Kampuchea), whose own struggle has often been manipulated and controlled by the Chinese, for Chinese benefit. The historic animosity between Vietnam and Cambodia has repeatedly plunged these two countries into conflicts with each other, and kept both weak and unstable, ripe for foreign plundering. Laos has long remained dormant, struggling to regain its footing after years of Western (French) colonialization destroyed this once great "core" empire of central Indochina, while Burma (Myanmar), itself still trying to recover from British imperialist rule, is lost in its efforts to find itself again as the bridge between the Buddhist world of Southeast Asia and the Hindu world of the Indian subcontinent. All of these countries have been heavily influenced by Chinese culture in general, and by Buddhism, Taoism, and Confucianism in particular (the same protocols and behaviors exist in a variety of different cultural forms for all the countries of Indochina; please refer to the chapters on China, Thailand, and Indonesia for generalized Southeast Asian behaviors and values); in fact, *tam giao,* or "triple religion," is a popular belief system in the region that integrates all three philosophies into one. But each of these countries also suffered western European and American colonialization and imperialism (Vietnam, Laos, and Cambodia under the French and, to vary-ing degrees, the United States; Burma under the British), and each has had to reclaim its national identity in the wake of this experience. Finally, and perhaps foremost, these countries also reveal to the world unique indigenous cultures (Lao, Kinh, Hmong, Khmer, Mao, Hoa—each ethnologically connected to China, yet aristocratically independent) which have become part of the mix of what makes up these countries today.

Some Historical Context

The Vietnamese (originally, the Kinh people) have always been seen by others in the region as the "businesspeople" of Southeast Asia. They have worked with, finagled, and survived the Chinese more than once (beginning with the Trung Sisters at the beginning of Vietnamese history about fifteen hundred years ago, who, Joan of Arc–style, cleverly kicked the Chinese out and became Vietnam's first official heroes); they are fishermen and farmers who have kept the sea, and everything it brings to the shore (including unwanted guests from far away), at bay, and have taken from it what they need to survive. But they have only barely survived themselves. Vietnam has forever been breaking in two: the sophisticated, aristocratic, aesthetic cultural heart of the north (Tonkin), threatened by and burdened with the backward, hardworking, independent agri-cultural peasant stock of the south (Cochin), glued together by the practical civic-minded businesspeople of the central region (Annam).

Cambodians (originally the Khmer) developed their own great Buddhist civilizations independent of their Vietnamese neighbors, seeking their roots more from the interior of the peninsula than from the sea. The support that the Chi-nese had traditionally given the Khmer in the development of these civiliza-tions, based as they were so on Chinese culture, only served to isolate the Khmer from their Indochinese neighbors.

But it is the quiet and aristocratic Lao people of Laos (originally mainly the Hoa and Hmong), today the most agrarian and underdeveloped country in the region, that lay claim to being the source of the Indochinese people, from which the Vietnamese, Cambodian, and Burmese civilizations emerged, and whose neu-trality in the political struggles of the region was always fiercely challenged. Even today, Laos is seen as the formative culture, yet it remains isolated and remote from much of the rest of the world.

Finally, the great Burmese civilizations (originally the Mon Meo and Karen peoples), representing an amalgam of Indian and Deccan influences into Indo-chinese Buddhism, remain isolated by the will of a small military elite that is simultaneously trying to fill the vacuum left when the British raj ended, repair the devastation brought by World War II, and retain its authority by keeping its people cut off from the options of global participation.

Greetings and Introductions

Language and Basic Vocabulary

Burmese, Vietnamese, Lao, Khmer, and the various indigenous languages of the region are all different. Because of these differences, be sure to have business cards translated into each language on the back for use in each country. French is the second language of the older generation in Vietnam, Cambodia, and Laos; English is the second language of the younger generation in Vietnam, and it is the second language of older Burmese, so you may also have your business card translated into French (or, accordingly, English) on the back in the appropriate countries. Do not assume English is spoken, even among members of the business communities in any of these countries. Like Chinese, all of these languages are tonal. Each language has a variety of formal and informal forms, based on the gender and the status of both the speaker and the addressee.

As most Americans will have their primary contact in the region with Vietnam, here are some basic Vietnamese phrases to get you started (written Vietnamese contains extensive diacritical marks, which are omitted here):

chao on	hello/good-bye (older man)
chao anh	(a man approximately the same age as the speaker)
chao em	(young boy)
chao ba	hello/good-bye (older woman)
chao co	(a woman approximately the same age as the speaker)
chao em	(young girl)
On/Ba/Co khoe khong?	How are you?
Khoe cam on	I am fine, thanks
cam on	thank you
kon ko chee	you're welcome
Han-han da-gap-on	I am pleased to meet you
phai	yes
khong	no
lam on	please
Sin loi	I'm sorry
toi xin loi	excuse me
khong sao	no problem

Because of the importance placed on avoiding disharmony throughout Southeast Asia, do not use double negatives, and do not ask questions that could result in yes or no answers. In a culture where the emphasis is placed on preserving harmony and face, and where much communication is therefore very high-context and subtle, any answer that could imply difficulty, a rejection of a request, or make the respondent appear uncooperative is usually evaded. This evasion is expressed in a number of ways nonverbally, but often results in unreliable verbal responses. "Yes" more often means "I hear what you are saying, keep talking," not "I agree with what you are saying." Don't complicate the problem, therefore, by asking questions that require yes or no as an answer: the response will give you no reliable information. Instead, ask open-ended questions that require a substantive, informational response. If you know some of the language, use it: your Southeast Asian colleagues will be amazed and charmed!

Honorifics for Men, Women, and Children

Until recently, most Southeast Asian cultures did not use surnames: people were referred to by their given names (their membership in a particular clan was understood). This is still the case for most Indochinese cultures.

In Vietnam, Cambodia, and Laos, use the first name given, preceded by the following honorifics:

u: Mr.
daw: Madame

In Myanmar, you should use all the names that are presented to you, and precede them with the honorifics. In Burmese, the greeting used commonly is *mingala-ba* (much good fortune to you).

Compliments are difficult for people in this region to acknowledge, as they challenge the notion of humility; nevertheless, people love to be complimented, as they do everywhere. Therefore, go ahead and compliment people, but be subtle, sincere, and expect just a smile in return. Occasionally, the Vietnamese and others in the region might cover their mouths when speaking: this is an additional sign of humility. A soft handshake often accompanies a slight bow when people greet each other, and for added sincerity the clasped right hands are gripped softly by the left hand of each person before release. The Indian *namaste,* or Thai *wai,* is done sometimes in Myanmar. Women in Vietnam and Myanmar are often able to hold high positions of authority; Western businesswomen should encounter little resistance if their authority and position is made clear. Throughout the region, once a relationship has been established, people really enjoy good-natured fun between each other, and teasing and ribbing is a way to keep good feelings going; this is especially true in Myanmar. Such playfulness is really a sign of affection, and is usually meant as a compliment. When communicating, be sure not to talk about other groups within the region, as people can be very sensitive about their relationships with their neighbors.

Physical Gestures and Expressions

In addition to the advice given in previous chapters, be sure not to step on a monk's shadow, especially in Burma. Do not touch the top of a person's head (including children), as this is very disrespectful, and women cannot, under any circumstances, touch a monk.

Dining and Drinking

In addition to the information that has been stated in the previous chapter and the chapter on China, it is especially important to remember that you must not eat or drink anything that has been served to you until the oldest person present has also been served and has begun his or her meal. It is proper, if everyone has been served, to ask the oldest person present if you can begin. Never refuse an offer of food or drink, and take very small portions. You may return for seconds if the food is available. In northern Vietnam, the host will place a little bit of each dish available on your plate for you; eat a little, and notice what the rest of the family or guests are eating. If it is only rice, say you are full (there is probably not enough food to go around, and you are getting the best of what there is). In southern Vietnam, you will be free to take food from a central serving plate with a serving spoon (not serving chopsticks); again, take very little at first, and go back for seconds later, if they are available. Green tea is served everywhere, all the time (it is drunk straight: no sugar, no milk). Always thank the person who serves you tea.

Gift Giving

In addition to the gift-giving suggestions made for similar cultures, it is important to consider that gifts in this part of the world also carry symbolic meaning: colors and items each mean something beyond their extrinsic meaning. Here is a short chart to guide you:

Colors:

Red = warm
Purple = feminine, romantic
Green = youth
Blue = freshness, love, hope
Black = mourning
White = death (also purity)
Yellow = betrayal

Animals:

Turtles = endurance, long life
Dragon = good luck, good fortune
Crane = fidelity
Spiders = lucky with money
Buffalo = patience, loyalty
Cow = stupidity
Pig = laziness
Monkey = badness
Raven/owl = omen of death

Special Holidays and Celebrations

Major Holidays

For all cultures in the region, the lunar New Year (Tet in Vietnam, for example) is the preeminent holiday event. It is the one opportunity throughout the year for an extravagant family celebration, with much feasting and observance of ancestor rituals, and can last for a week or more. Please see the China chapter for further information on New Year's celebrations.

Because most Americans will be interacting primarily with Vietnam in the region, the following are the major Vietnamese holidays:

• *Solar holidays* include New Year's Day (January 1); Founding of Communist Party Day (February 3); Liberation of Saigon (from the United States) Day (April 30); International Labor Day (May 1); Ho Chi Minh's Birthday (May 19); War Invalids Day (July 28); National Day (September 2); Ho Chi Minh's Death (September 3); and Christmas Day (December 25).

• *Lunar holidays* include Tet (January/February), the Vietnamese New Year, and the major event; Dong Da Day (January/February), which celebrates the victory over China in the 1700s; Co Loa Festival (January/February); *Le Thuong Nguon,* or the Lantern Festival (January/February); Trung Sisters Day

(February/March); Thanh Minh Day (March/April), which honors the dead; Hung Vuong Kings Day (March/April), which honors the ancient Hung Vuong kings; *Phat Dan* (April/May), the Buddha's birthday; *Tet Doan Ngo* (April/May), which celebrates the summer solstice and the harmony of yin and yang; the Weaver and the Shepherd Reunion (May/June), which celebrates the start of the rainy season; *Trung Nguyen,* or Souls Day (June/July); *Trung Thu* (July/August), the mid-autumn celebration; Tran Hung Dao Day (August/September), celebrating the victory over the Mongols in 1200s); Le Loi Day (September/October), which celebrates the victory over the Chinese Ming invaders; Double Nine Day (October/November), which celebrates the transition from autumn to winter; Anniversary of Confucius's Birthday (November/December); and *Thong Tan Tet,* or the Harvest Festival (November).

The Australasian Cultures: Australia and New Zealand

AUSTRALIA

Some Introductory Background on Australia and the Australians

Australians make Americans feel the way Americans make the rest of the world feel—well, at least when it comes to the issue of informality. While Americans, relative to much of the world, could give two hoots (to use a U.S. expression) about standing on ceremony most of the time, the Aussies (yes, you can call them that; they call themselves that, as a matter of fact) will really knock you off your pedestal if you try. Most of the time, Americans don't realize that they are even standing on a pedestal until the Aussie calls their attention to the fact. This is one of the striking hallmarks of Australian culture, which makes it distinct from most others (and distinguishes it, as one Australian colleague once remarked to me, "from southern California, in addition to being several thousand miles further south").

Yes, there is a definite laid-back feel to the place, with a southern California–esque lifestyle that many Americans recognize; but Americans must also recognize the unique Australian culture that makes this place its own. The similarity with the expansive American continental Wild West, for example, ends about an hour's drive from the coast just about anywhere in Australia. Over 90 percent of all Australians live along the coast; for the most part, the interior being a vast, uninhabited desert island. Australians have a metaphor for this "leveling" informal nature of theirs: "the tall poppy syndrome." Any poppy that grows higher than the others in the field will have its head chopped off. Or put another way, in a famous Australian proverb, "Jack's as good as his master." This is an extremely egalitarian culture, and Australian radar is always on the lookout for anything that smacks of "pulling rank." If so sniffed, you'll be cut down to size. Part of the reason for this particular attribute, and many others, can be found in the historical origins of modern Australia.

Some Historical Context

Although the Aborigines, or indigenous peoples, of the island made it their home for thousands of years, it was Captain James Cook who claimed the territory for

Britain in the eighteenth century, and from that point on began a process of immigration which has yet to stop. During its formative years, Australia was the dumping ground for Pommies, or Prisoners of Her Majesty's Service, eventually used as a term of derogation to describe English immigrants into Australia: the riffraff that the British criminal system found so distasteful that they flung them into the farthest corner of the globe they could find. This ignoble beginning, as a penal colony, formed the basis for the no-nonsense, you're-no-better-than-I attitude still found in Australia today. If you hail a cab in Sydney and hop in the backseat as you would in most places around the world, you run a good risk that the cabdriver will ask you why you won't sit up front with him, like a good mate?

Those who continued to come to Australia after it became a respectable member of the British Commonwealth were often free spirits, investors, adventurers, or immigrants with nothing to lose, looking for some new opportunities in a land that was new, yet familiar; after all, English was (and is) the official language, and the system of education, the government, and the basic social infrastructure were (and are) all British-based. While there is more concern today for the treatment of the Aborigines, and while there has been a recent immigration of other Europeans (Greeks, eastern Europeans, Italians, Spaniards, and Portuguese, mainly) and Asians (mainly Chinese), the culture—despite its increasing resemblance to a melting pot—is, at its core, British with an Australian twist.

An Area Briefing

Politics and Government

Today, Australia is an independent nation. However, it is a member of the British Commonwealth, so the queen of England is, as of this writing, still the head of state (there is a populist movement to have Australia leave the Commonwealth). There is a bicameral legislature, a prime minister, and, of course, a federal judiciary. There are three popular parties (Labor, Liberal, and Australian Democrat), and it is a representative democracy. There is vigorous involvement in politics, and debates are usually founded on social welfare issues.

Schools and Education

Free state-run elementary and high school level education is available and compulsory for all children. There are several fine colleges and universities in the major cities, a combination of state run and private (mainly church affiliated). Students can take either an academic or vocational path in high school, and move onto university or vocational training schools, if they choose. The curriculum is rigorous in high school. Academic track education is based on developing critical Western thinking and delivering specific scientific or technical or professional skills; vocational track education is usually industry specific.

Religion and Demographics

There is no official state religion, but most of the population is Christian, divided mainly between Roman Catholics and Anglicans (members of the Church of England). The culture, however, is very secular, with many people abstaining from identifying themselves with any organized group; there are also minorities of most other religions present. The population is aging, and this fuels many of the concerns around social welfare issues. Women play an active role at work, but struggle for complete equality with men in the business world. Both men and women share in many of the domestic nurturing chores of the household.

Fundamental Cultural Orientations

1. What's the Best Way for People to Relate to One Another?

OTHER-INDEPENDENT OR OTHER-DEPENDENT? Individualism is highly valued in Australia, and personal responsibility is a very important and positive personal characteristic. But for the Australians, like their English cousins, individualism does not mean independence from others, as it does often in the United States. The Australian cowboy, unlike his American counterpart, could not survive out in the barren wilds of the Australian outback without the support of others, his "mates"; this severe topography, coupled with the British tradition of finding one's way within society, not despite it, are the roots of this value. Australians often find Americans too concerned about how they appear, or whether or not they are agreeable, or if they are fitting in okay, or what others think, precisely because the Australian views the American as someone who has had to form his or her identity independent of society and therefore doesn't ever really know who he or she is. Americans, on the other hand, often find Australians to be emotionally unconcerned, almost challenging, cynical, and disrespectful, precisely because, from the Australian point of view, they seem to know exactly who they are and where they fit in society, and don't need to prove anything to anyone.

HIERARCHY-ORIENTED OR EGALITY-ORIENTED? As discussed, this is a very egalitarian-oriented society. There must not be any undue display of unearned deference. People are respected for what they have achieved, and usually this achievement is measured by how it has benefited the majority of other people. Anything else—family, background, wealth, advantage—is not cause, in and of itself, for any display of deference or respect. Subsequently, it is also a very informal culture. It is said that Australia has the world's highest percentage of labor strikes; if you listen to management, this is mainly due to the fact that labor perceives itself as equal to management and doesn't care about what is in the best interests of the general population, that is, a strong economy. Managers simply cannot "tell" workers what to do. Managers must decide, involve, and explain.

RULE-ORIENTED OR RELATIONSHIP-ORIENTED? Australians take great comfort in having designed a system and a society that for them pretty much takes care of most of what a society needs. While there is no doubt that who one knows goes a long way in determining how one lives in the world, the Australian demands the development of and adherence to systems, processes, rules, and regulations that work for most of the people most of the time (aborigines, and perhaps others with non-European backgrounds, excluded). Specific situations generally do not determine right from wrong, nor are they justifiable criteria for decision making.

2. What's the Best Way to VieΩw Time?

MONOCHRONIC OR POLYCHRONIC? Australia is primarily a monochronic culture, especially in business. However, a few minutes late here and there usually is not a problem; and in social situations, being ten minutes late is not a problem. There is a relaxed attitude toward agendas and schedules, which are usually not organized tightly. Australians see Americans as far too eager to live to work, and Americans see Australians as ready, at any moment, to break away from the desk, put on a bathing suit, and throw another "prawn on the barbie" (yes, it's "prawn," not "shrimp," in Australia).

RISK-TAKING OR RISK-AVERSE? As a nation of immigrants without a well-developed hierarchy, there is a high comfort level for risk taking, for living with uncertainty and ambiguity. However, the need to create a smoothly working society that benefits most of the people also serves to keep wayward risk taking in check. There is a balance here.

PAST-ORIENTED OR FUTURE-ORIENTED? The past plays a minimal role in Australia, and no one is that willing to sacrifice a nice sunny day and the good life for an uncertain tomorrow. In this sense, therefore, Australians are rooted in the here and now, pragmatically oriented, and don't get too excited about having to moralize over things or hunker down for a better tomorrow.

3. What's the Best Way for Society to Work with the World at Large?

LOW-CONTEXT DIRECT OR HIGH-CONTEXT INDIRECT COMMUNICATORS? Nothing will get Australians to tell you what's on their minds faster than if you try to tell them what's on your mind first. Australians are usually very direct, and have no problem telling you what they think of just about anything, including you and your country. They do not shy away from confrontation, but react to these things with positive good humor, acknowledging that this stuff can make some people pretty uncomfortable. In fact, a common Australian complaint about Americans is that they don't tell you what's on their mind. Most of the time, Australian directness will take the form of good-natured ribbing or kidding around over a "shout" (that's a round of beers) or two. If you don't get the point that way, however, Australians can also tell you more straightforwardly.

PROCESS-ORIENTED OR RESULT-ORIENTED? Australians are open to evidence that has been reached through empirical research or deductive or inductive methods. They are rational and linear thinkers and rely on logic and proof as criteria for action. There is minimal reliance on subjective experience if facts prove otherwise: in fact, one's subjective experience will be identified and challenged quickly as an insubstantial reason for considering something.

Greetings and Introductions

Language and Basic Vocabulary

The English used in Australia is a combination of British-, American-, and Australianisms. There is a tendency to add the suffixes -ie or -ey to almost any word to make it familiar, unique, accessible, or reduce its "officialness"; usually the word is shortened a bit, as well (e.g., *barbie* for *barbecue*). Other English speakers, including Americans, need to be wary of "*Strine*" (that's Australian for "Australian"). Below are important and unique Strine words.

Australian	*American*
aerial	antenna
arvo	afternoon
barbie	barbecue
biscuit	cookie
billy tea	tea made in a bucket over an open fire
bush	the outback; off the beaten path
corroboree	an aboriginal celebration ceremony
cozzie	bathing suit
crook	to be sick, ill
damper	unleavened bread cooked over an open fire
dill	a dolt
engaged	busy; as in, "the phone is engaged"
entree	an appetizer (*not* the main course)
fair dinkum	the real thing, something honest and true
fascia panel	car dashboard
footpath	sidewalk
fossicking	rock climbing, spelunking
galah	a person acting foolishly (named after a native bird)
g'day	hello, welcome (don't overuse this, foreigner!)
gearbox	automobile transmission
jackeroo	male ranch hand
jillaroo	female ranch hand
lollies	candy
mate	friend
matilda	knapsack
nought	zero
number plate	car license plate
overrider	car bumper
petrol	gasoline
prawn	large shrimp
sandshoes	sneakers
shout	a service you do for others
station	a large ranch (usually in the outback)
sticking tape	cellophane tape
sweets	dessert
ta	thanks
takeaway	food to go

taxi rank	cab stand
tins	canned goods
tinny	a can of soda or beer
toilet	lavatory
tomato sauce	ketchup
torch	flashlight
tube	also a can of beer or soda
windscreen	windshield
wing	car fender
Yank	American

As with British English, there are endless spelling differences between Australian and American English, as well as differences in style, grammar, usage, and syntax.

Honorifics for Men, Women, and Children

Mr/Mrs/Miss are preferred for middle-class Australians today; the term *Ms* is slowly gathering common usage (please note that in written form, Mr, Mrs, and Ms do not have periods—"full stops" in British or Australian English—after them: they are words in and of themselves and not abbreviations). If someone holds a degree or title (e.g., Ph.D., doctor, etc.) it should be used in speech while addressing them, but the holder of the title never uses it when referring to him- or herself (however, such titles and degrees may be written on stationery and the business card). Remember, qualifications and achievement earn respect; mere titles do not. Despite the British crown, there is no titled Australian-based aristocracy! Once the initial business discussions are over, Australians will be comfortable with first names, and you should feel free to refer to others and yourself with given names, and no honorifics. Children are raised to respect adults, but are also encouraged to develop a sense of independence on their own in their teen years; if introduced to a child, use whatever name or honorific is used by the adult. Go ahead and use your business card, but it is not a culture that makes much of a fuss about them: you may have to ask for one in return, or Australians can just as easily write their contact name and phone number down on a piece of paper for you later.

The What, When, and How of Introducing People

It is polite to wait for a third party to introduce you to others, but it may not happen; if, after a few moments, no one steps in to make an introduction for you, feel free to introduce yourself to others without concern for rank or protocol (it is perfectly all right, and quite common). Do not presume to seat yourself at a formal gathering: if possible, wait to be told where to sit, but if there is no immediate information as you approach the table and others are seating themselves, follow suit. If you are acting as the host and would like to maintain a certain seating pattern, you may indicate this to guests as they arrive at the table, or have preset seating cards at each place, if you like (this is considered quite formal, though, in Australia). At the end of an evening, shake hands with everyone before departing if you like, but a group wave is also okay.

Physical Greeting Styles

The handshake is common, but without as much gripping and pumping as the U.S. version. Introductory greetings such as "Pleased to meet you," and "How do you do" are fairly formal; in casual contact, the phrase most often used is the overworked "G'day." It requires no substantive response, except a "G'day" in return. Smiling and other nonverbal indications of informality and casualness will usually accompany the handshake. Men should wait until a woman extends her hand before reaching for it, and women may take the lead in extending their hand or not. However, unless men know each other well, and are genuinely expressing their fondness for the other person, they do not slap each other on the back or hug when greeting; women, however, may kiss each other on the cheek. When being introduced, make immediate eye contact, and maintain general eye contact throughout conversation. The term *mate* means friend or close associate, and can also be used to indicate that more sincerity is required in the relationship: male friends are "mates," emotional partners are also "mates," but male/female business friendships are generally not mates.

Communication Styles

Okay Topics / Not Okay Topics

Okay: the weather (it's usually very pleasant), sports (Aussies can be fanatical about it), the Olympics, and anything related to Australia as a country. *Not okay:* references to Australian stereotypes, like koalas, kangaroos, "Crocodile" Dundee, and the like. Avoid discussions about the Aborigines: as an American, you will be quickly reminded about the treatment of American indigenous peoples; it is a difficult topic. Politics, sex, and religion (the three taboos, which are always spoken about eventually) will engender strong opinions, so be prepared. At the same time, if you know what you are talking about (and that's the important thing), don't be shy about stating an opinion or thought: that is precisely what Australians want. Discussions that are designed to reveal only similarities and like-mindedness are just too plain dull and strike the Australian as superficial. It is acceptable to inquire about a person's occupation in casual conversation.

Tone, Volume, and Speed

In most situations, direct moderate speech is most appropriate. The tone and volume are slightly lower than in American English, and people speak slightly slower.

Use of Silence

There isn't much. This is not a real issue in Australia.

Physical Gestures and Facial Expressions

The "V for Victory" sign must be done with palm facing outward. In most English-speaking countries (with the exception of the United States), making this sign with the palm inward is a vulgar gesture of defiance (it comes from the

British demonstrating at the Battle of Agincourt to the French that they still had two fingers with which to pull the archer's bow). Additionally, the thumbs-up "okay" sign is considered vulgar (the classic forefinger-to-thumb "okay" sign is . . . okay). Winking, whistling, and passing unsolicited comments to strangers, either women or men, are totally unacceptable.

Waving and Counting

The index finger represents the number 1; the thumb represents the number 5. Pointing is usually done with the fingers. The wave is generally done the same way as in the United States.

Physicality and Physical Space

People stand approximately the same distance from each other as North Americans do. Unless they are in an obviously formal situation, men may feel comfortable with their hands in their pockets, and assume relaxed positions (no feet up on the desks, however).

Eye Contact

Eye contact is generally direct; that is, at the beginning of every discussion, make eye contact and maintain it throughout. However, glancing away frequently for a moment (usually as a reaction to gathering information about the environment from time to time, or to think privately) is perfectly acceptable.

Emotive Orientation

No backslapping, no shouting or calling attention to oneself (especially in public), no coarse behavior. Australia is casual and informal, but not loudly so. Keep your hands to your sides, and avoid emphasizing the spoken word with gestures.

Protocol in Public

Walking Styles and Waiting in Lines

Queuing is the norm, but they are generally never really unpleasantly long or bothersome. People walk and drive on the left, and pass on the right: this is true on escalators and moving walkways, as well as roads and streets.

Behavior in Public Places: Airports, Terminals, and the Market

Customer service is similar to most developed English-speaking countries outside of Britain: customers do count, but sales help are not servants. Do as much as you can on your own, and then ask for assistance when required. Smoking in public is on the decline. In public telephones, some coins are still accepted, but many phones only take telecards: get them at local newsstands and kiosks. When answering the telephone, say, "Hello," not "G'day."

Bus / Metro / Taxi / Car

Never break a queue for a bus, train, or taxi; on public transportation, it is polite to surrender your seat to the elderly, women with babies, or the handicapped, but men need not do so for women of the approximate same age. Enter taxis in the front seat next to the driver first.

Tipping

Tips are usually 10 to 15 percent in restaurants and for taxis; more is considered nouveau and gauche. In restaurants, the tip is usually not included on the bill (but it is okay to double-check this with the waiter). Porters and hotel help get a dollar per bag or service rendered.

Dress

Casual Fridays are catching on, but it is still an industry-specific issue: some do, some don't, some will, some won't; take your cue from your colleagues. Most social events do not require dressing up; men may, but typically do not have to, wear a jacket and tie in most restaurants and theaters and at social occasions held in private homes. Office attire is still the business suit or a jacket and tie for men and a dress or a skirt and blouse for women; fashions are usually fairly conservative and not overly stylish.

Seasonal Variations

Australia has four seasons that vary in intensity depending where you are on the island continent. Since it is below the equator, the extremes increase as you head south. The northern part of the island is more or less tropical most of the time, but in the south, the climate is moderately warm in spring and summer, and cool and rainy in fall and winter. Remember also that the times for these seasons are reversed from those north of the equator: summer runs roughly from December through March, and winter lasts from June through September. Seasonal transitions are mild.

Colors

Wear conservative, muted, natural colors; anything that calls attention to oneself may be seen as an attempt at being a "tall poppy," and you know what happens to them.

Styles

"Formal," if indicated on an invitation, means black tie tuxedo, and is usually reserved for very special events only. Conservative is the rule for business settings, while on the street and at home, anything goes, including jeans, sneakers, shorts, and T-shirts. If invited to someone's home for an evening for the first time, men need not wear a jacket and tie; a clean, neat pair of jeans and a sport shirt are usually fine. It is okay to ask the host if you're not sure, but the time will usually tell you how casual it really is (if it is in the afternoon, it is probably a barbecue, and this can be more casual than an evening dinner party).

Accessories / Jewelry / Makeup

Women typically accessorize their clothes for the office, but they still need to be conservative. The idea here is the same as it is for men: modesty is not the driver, but the need not to appear "better" than anyone else *is*. There is an acceptance of facial hair for men, even at higher levels within the business organization.

Dining and Drinking

Mealtimes and Typical Foods

Breakfast can be a quick, U.S.–style toast and coffee, or it can be a more traditional English-style "hearty" affair. It can be held any time from 7 to 9 A.M. Drinks can be tea or coffee (tea is taken usually with milk or cream).

Lunch is served from noon to 1 or 2 P.M., and usually consists of sandwiches or salads. The typical drinks are beer, sodas, or "squash" (usually a carbonated fruit drink). On Sunday, the main meal of the day is supper, which is usually served at lunchtime, but may include full dinner meals, and always features a roast.

Dinner is served from 7:30 to 8:30 P.M. with 8 P.M. the customary time. Dinner usually begins with an alcoholic drink (sherry, gin, or whiskey), plus nuts or other munchies. There is often an appetizer, a main course of seafood, fish, or meat, and vegetables. Desserts are common after dinner. The drinks served with dinner are usually beer, wines, and/or soft drinks. Dinner parties usually end at around 11:30 to midnight.

Tea is a term that is sometimes used interchangeably with *dinner* or *supper,* and refers to a light evening meal, held usually around 5 or 6 P.M., or sometimes slightly later. If you are invited to "tea" at this time, you will be served sandwiches or side dishes, which will constitute your dinner. However, Australians also have "afternoon tea" (which they also refer to as "tea"), which is more or less the daily tea break at around 4 P.M., and does not constitute a full meal. What best distinguishes the two is the time and place: if you are invited to a home for tea at 6 P.M., assume you are there for a light supper. Tea (the drink) is made the English way: after "putting the kettle on" (heating the water on the stove up to and just over the boiling point), one pours the scalding water into the teapot (a ceramic vessel containing the tea leaves), and lets the tea steep for about five minutes. Be sure that the teapot is very near the teakettle when you are ready to pour in the hot water: walking too far from the stove with a hot kettle is not good for the tea (and probably dangerous, as well!). Additional hot water may be added to the teapot as needed until the tea has given all it can. Tea is usually served separately at tea and for breakfast; after lunch and dinner, coffee is the usual drink.

Regional Differences

The "barbie," or barbecue, is a favorite form of home entertaining. It is very similar to the American barbecue, and can be very informal (bathing suits and beer), or more upscale (jackets—not ties—and champagne); the context will determine this (it is perfectly fine to ask if you're not sure when you are invited). Australians love their seafood, and it can be extraordinary: huge shrimps (prawns), lobsters, and a variety of fish abound. Meat—especially lamb, but also chicken, pork, and beef—is a very common main course.

Typical Drinks and Toasting

Mixed drinks before dinner are as common as they are in the States, and mixed drinks are growing in popularity (ask for the American martini if a gin or vodka martini is what you want; if you ask for a "martini" without qualifying it, you will get a Martini and Rossi vermouth). Preprandials can include a short whiskey (Scottish whisky, mainly, and spelled without the *e*; Irish whiskey is spelled with the *e*) usually drunk neat or with water, never over ice; some dry sherry; a gin and tonic; or vermouth. Red and white wines (usually Australian, which are generally quite good) during the meal are common, and port or a sweet sherry at the end of the meal is perfect. Less formal meals, especially at lunch, are washed down with beer or soft drinks, of which there are dozens of fine examples. Australian beer is served cold; English beer is usually served at room temperature.

The most common toasts are "cheers," "to your health," "here's to you," and the like. Toasts are very egalitarian, mainly to a group, and rarely to an individual when a group is present. (If you're at a business meal, a toast to the organization is more appropriate than a toast to an individual, unless you are roasting, not toasting, the individual.) There is a tradition in bars to order "rounds" (or "a shout") of drinks for friends: it is a taking of turns in the buying of drinks for all in the group.

Table Manners and the Use of Utensils

The most important difference is that the Australians do not typically switch knives and forks, as Americans do. The knife remains in the right hand, and the fork remains in the left. When the meal is finished, the knife and fork are laid parallel to one another across the right side of the plate. If you put both utensils down on the plate for any real length of time, it is a sign to the waitstaff that you are finished, and your plate may be taken away from you. In addition, the fork may be held tines down, so that food is "scooped" up onto the backside. At a more formal dinner, there may be additional pieces of cutlery. The knife above the plate is used for butter. If you're unsure of which utensil to use, always start from the outside and work your way in, course by course.

When not holding utensils, your hands are expected to be in your lap at the dinner table. Pass all dishes and serving accessories at the table to your left.

Seating Plans

The most honored position is at the head of the table, with individuals of the greatest importance seated first to the left and then to the right of the head of the table; if there is a hosting couple, one member will be at each end of the table. As is the practice in most of Europe, men and women are seated next to one another, and couples are often broken up and seated next to people they may not have previously known. This is done in the interest of conversation. In informal settings, such as at barbecues, men and women often break up into separate groups (this is never formalized; it's merely a tendency). Men and women do not necessarily rise when newcomers enter a room, nor does gender play much of a role in determining who enters first through doors into rooms, walks ahead, to the left or right or behind, or holds doors for whom: the situation does.

Refills and Seconds

If you are at a private home for dinner, and do not want more food, leave a bit on your plate; you'll be expected to take more, if you like, or not. You may always have additional beverages; drink enough to cause your cup or glass to be less than half full, and it will be refilled by the host, or you may be invited by the host to take some more, and refill it yourself.

At Home, in a Restaurant, or at Work

Dinner is usually served at 8 P.M. Be sure to make reservations (and confirm them) in the most exclusive restaurants, but most establishments can be very informal and casual. Indian and Chinese "takeaway" are very common these days. In informal restaurants, you may be required to share a table; if so, it is perfectly acceptable to get involved in a conversation, as long as it is welcome. Waitstaff may be summoned by making eye contact; waving or calling their names is not done. Business breakfasts are becoming more widespread, though still not as common as in the United States. Australians generally do not like to talk business over a nice meal, so take your cue from them: if they bring it up, okay, but if not, avoid it. More upscale business dining would involve lunch or dinner at a French or Italian restaurant.

Being a Good Guest or Host

Paying the Bill

Usually the one who does the inviting pays the bill, although the guest is expected to make an effort to pay. Making payment arrangements ahead of time so that no exchange occurs at the table is a very classy way to host. Businesswomen who are hosting are expected to pay the bill.

When to Arrive / Chores to Do

If invited to a dinner party at a private home, offer to help with the chores: you will probably be taken up on it. You'll be expected to make yourself at home, and feel comfortable most anywhere, although you will be hosted in the living or dining room. Spouses are often included in business dinners (most commonly if both business associates are married).

Gift Giving

In general, gift giving is generally not done for business purposes; it is best not to send a gift at any time, including the holidays, unless you receive one first from your business associate. However, holiday cards are very appropriate, particularly as a thank-you for your Australian associate's business during the previous year, and should be mailed in time to be received the week before Christmas.

Gifts are not expected for casual social events, but they are as thank-yous for private dinner parties. The best gift in this case is a good bottle of wine, or some chocolates. Flowers are really not necessary. There is no need to send a handwritten thank-you note the next day, nor do you need to phone to say thank you. If you are staying with a family, an appropriate thank-you gift would be a high-quality item that represents your country and is perhaps not easy to get in Australia; gourmet foodstuffs (maple syrup, pralines, etc.) or anything that reflects your host's personal tastes (the cap of a famous American team for the football-playing son of the family, for example) is appropriate. Gifts are usually opened in the presence of the giver.

Special Holidays and Celebrations

Major Holidays

Christmas and New Year's fall in the middle of the summer in Australia, which is high vacation time. Consider this as you make your business travel plans.

January 1	New Year's Day
February 26	Australia Day
March/April	Good Friday, Easter Sunday/Monday
April 25	Anzac Day (Veteran's Memorial Day)
June 5	Queen Elizabeth's Birthday
December 25	Christmas
December 26	Boxing Day

Business Culture

Daily Office Protocols

In general, the business day is carefully defined in Australia, at least for workers and staff: it begins at 9 A.M. and ends at 5 P.M., with senior managers perhaps staying in their offices until 6 P.M. or so. It is not uncommon to socialize for an hour or so in the local bar after the workday with one's office colleagues, but travel time between home and work is a real consideration, and people often head home, or to the gym or the beach, after work.

Management Styles

Among all individuals, regardless of rank, there is much direct and informal communication. While there are hierarchies in the Australian business organization, they exist mainly for clarity of decision making: rank in and of itself has little importance. Managers need to be fair, direct, honest, and involving, although the final decision is theirs. Australians like to get straight down to business and are generally direct, informal, and matter of fact in their discussions.

Conducting a Meeting or Presentation

The facts, details, benefits, and challenges of any proposal should be clearly presented. Anything that even slightly has a whiff of "selling," trying to impress, or assuming acceptance based on reputation or name will be challenged. In fact, you may need to present more facts, and be more open to challenge and questions, if you come in with a reputation or a big name, since the actual here-and-now merits must be established, in spite of the existing reputation.

Negotiation Styles

Once equality is established, Australians will negotiate based on a win/win (that both parties need to achieve their primary objectives) perspective. Do not assume that being an American will automatically make Australians more willing to work with you than with others; you will still need to prove the merits of your organization, product, or service, and demonstrate a real commitment to what will become a joint project. Australians suspect that Americans are inclined to come in with all the answers as they see or want things to be and then step out of the picture. Don't give this impression.

Planning a Project

Decision making can be done at the table, and the meeting is an opportunity for problem-solving and decision-making. Time lines, agendas, and deadlines are all concepts Australians are very comfortable with. They will need assurances that materials and resources are available as stated. Australians will not avoid confrontation or the negative response.

Written Correspondence

Use the word *dear* plus the family name to open a first-time business correspondence—after that, first names are usually okay—and end the correspondence with the matter-of-fact closings "Yours truly" or "Best regards." Dates in Australia are usually in the European style, written day.month.year, and the address is formatted as in the West. E-mails and faxes should be bulletpointed. You can get straight down to the substantive issues after a brief sentence of cordial personal remarks. Addressing is usually done in the following format:

Line 1: name
Line 2: company
Line 3: street address
Line 4: city
Line 5: country and postal code

NEW ZEALAND

Note: New Zealand and Australia share many of the same cultural traditions; nevertheless, there are some important distinctions. The additional information that follows is specific to New Zealand.

Some Introductory Background on New Zealand and the New Zealanders

New Zealanders are not Australians. While the two peoples share British heritage, language, and experience, New Zealanders (or Kiwis: yes, you can use the term, for that is what New Zealanders proudly call themselves) are quick to distinguish themselves from their Australian cousins. Many times it is only out of necessity that Australians and New Zealanders cooperate with each other since their histories, in fact, often placed their forebears in opposition to each other.

The original European Australian settlers were convicted felons, outsiders to British society; New Zealand settlers, however, came of their own free will, often with resources and determination, for they were, more often than not, landed gentry and fully participating members in British society, looking for new or additional opportunities abroad. At home in Britain, the two groups would have been on opposite sides of the bench, if not the law. Nevertheless, when both colonies were settled, New Zealand, being the smaller and younger of the two, was originally part of the Australian colony. Only later did it obtain independence, and in that sense, more from Australia than from the United Kingdom. While Australians debate their connections with the United Kingdom, Kiwis are quite proud of it, apparently very pleased to remain "loyal subjects" of the British Crown. In New Zealand, the queen is the head of state, although there is a parliamentary legislature and a prime minister, and the country is an independent nation.

As a result of the difference in their colonial histories, New Zealanders are a little bit more removed, a little more restrained, than Australians and are not driven by a need to "level" people and relationships in order to work with them. At the same time, because there is a need to be seen as at least equal in weight to their Australian cousins, and as full members of the rest of the very faraway world, and because the original Europeans came to New Zealand in order to achieve a better life, New Zealanders have a strong democratic and humanitarian ethic, perhaps stronger even than the Australians. In fact, this is a criterion that is often used in New Zealand for determining action: what is being considered is usually framed in social and environmental terms.

An Area Briefing

Religion and Demographics

While the European settlers were primarily Anglican, the native people of New Zealand are the Maori, an indigenous Oceanic culture. The Maori have been integrated into New Zealand life more effectively than the Aborigines have in

Australia; in fact, the Maori play a significant role in the politics and business life of New Zealand today. Only Maori who have chosen to do so live according to traditional patterns based on agriculture and communal life. Many interact on a daily basis with *Pakeha,* or white people (referring to non-Maori Europeans). Nevertheless, preserving Maori traditional culture is generally seen as benefiting the entire population, and many Maori traditions remain (such as the *hongi,* the traditional Maori greeting of rubbing noses; you will not see this outside of traditional Maori settings).

The overall New Zealand population is young and growing younger, and there is a high percentage of single-parent households (known as "solo mums") and a strong accompanying social welfare ethic. Nevertheless, while equality is an important issue in this humanitarian culture, it is not an egalitarian culture. Women, while playing an active role in the workplace, do struggle for equality with men in the business world.

Greetings and Honorifics

Greetings in New Zealand can be a bit more reserved than in Australia, and third-party introductions are typical; nevertheless, do feel free to introduce yourself when it becomes clear that you may not be introduced to others in a gathering. New Zealanders may be just a bit more reticent to come forward. When they do, they are warm and friendly. They are open, speak directly, and appreciate opinions, as in Australia. But the tone is more subdued, less teasing, and less driven by underlying leveling requirements. The use of first names is common, but you may want to wait until your New Zealand colleague invites you to do so, or calls you by your first name, before you use his or her first name. In order to indicate that you do not assume they are the same as Australians (and this is an important thing to do as an American), do not use the greeting *g'day* until you hear them do so; it is safer to use the British "How do you do," or simply "Hello, pleased to meet you," at first.

Communication Styles

Okay Topics / Not Okay Topics

Okay: anything that indicates your sincere interest in New Zealand. Be open and inquisitive, but not too gushingly (it will be seen as insincere). *Not okay:* As an outsider, you should do or say nothing that presumes the country is similar to Australia, although there clearly are many cultural similarities; overtly mistaking things Australian as things New Zealand is an automatic, flat-out no-no. It is not okay to speak disparagingly of the British royal family, or of the social welfare and environmental policies of the country: New Zealanders are very sensitive to this. Associated with this is the sensitivity of New Zealanders to their "farawayness" from the rest of the world: they are eager to show you that they have established quite a nicely civilized nation "down here," thank you very much, and that many of the ugly trappings of "northern" Western civilization, such as nuclear bombs, marginalized indigenous peoples, and collapsing infrastructures, are not part of the New Zealand way of life. If you do get into politics, be prepared to hear about this. New Zealanders may seem to speak a bit self-consciously, and while they are very forthright and not reticent in what they say, how they say it may appear grudging and unresponsive to more effusive Americans. People typically stand just a little farther apart from each other than they do in North America.

PART TWO

South Asia, Central Asia, and Eurasia

Intense Incense

An Introduction to the Region

If the Pacific Rim is the economic dynamo of Asia, then Central Asia is perhaps the economic hope. This is the Asian heartland, where economies may not have developed as rapidly as along the Pacific coast, but where there may be the greatest promise for long-term growth. This is also a region of great potential conflict in the twenty-first century, for here the cultures—Muslim, Hindu, Buddhist, and Christian—are colliding along one of the world's great cultural fault lines, in countries beset with enormous economic and social challenges. If the world can contain the differences while nurturing the possibilities, this region holds great promise. The area's central mountain range, the Himalayas, is a metaphor for the region: just as a crush of mighty tectonic plates against each other has produced the world's highest (and youngest) mountains, here in Central Asia cultural tectonic plates—the world's great religions and populations—crush against each other, bringing differing ancient ways into the twenty-first century.

Getting Oriented

South Asia, Central Asia, and Eurasia, for our purposes, can be discussed in terms of the following macrocultural groups:

- South Asia (the subcontinent): India, Pakistan, Bangladesh, Sri Lanka, and the Himalayan Kingdoms (Nepal and Bhutan)
- Central Asia: Afghanistan, Kazakhstan, Uzbekistan, Turkmenistan, Tajikistan, and Kyrgyzstan
- Eurasia: Turkey and the Caucasus (Armenia, Azerbaijan, and Georgia)

<table>
<tr><td>**CHAPTER TEN**</td><td># The South Asian Cultures: India</td></tr>
</table>

Some Introductory Background on India and the Indians

By the end of the first decade of the twenty-first century, the population of India is expected to exceed that of China. Already it is the world's largest democracy, occupying a subcontinent of its own. It is an ancient culture, with one of the world's oldest civilizations. By the time Buddhism had arisen around 600 B.C., Hinduism, the major indigenous religion (known as Brahminism in its earliest forms), was already an old one.

Today, over 90 percent of the world's Hindus are found in India. It has been called, by some, the most spiritual place on earth, where masses of people lead a daily existence dedicated solely to the spirit. The land may barely support its current population, but its natural beauty, from the massive Himalayas in the north to some of the world's most glorious tropical beaches in the south, is all-encompassing. The topography and climate range from cool and dry mountains to sweltering, oppressive humidity and heat, to dust and sand. The weather is equally varied, with the annual monsoons providing a regularity of flood and drought that set the pace and determined the activities of thousands of years of agrarian life.

India's poverty is crushing, its potential astonishing: Asia's Silicon Valley is in the new India, as is the world's largest concentration of squalor and need, centered in the country's great cities. Mumbai (formerly Bombay) is the business center of the country, New Delhi the administrative heart, and Calcutta perhaps its conscience. There are more movies produced in Mumbai (sometimes called "Bollywood") each year than in Hollywood. The people speak a bewildering kaleidoscope of over thirty different major languages, and practice four of the world's major religions, in a delicate mix that is always roiling just below the boiling point. Indians have gained the reputation of being simultaneously charming and infuriating, Asian and Western, skillful businesspeople and hopeless procrastinators, open to investment and closed to new ideas. For most of the post–World War II era, India pursued a nonaligned policy, resulting in a stagnated economy that was closed off to the rest of the world in the misguided idea that by so doing, the country would protect its businesses from the pressures of competition and thus allow them to develop, while keeping decadent aspects of Western culture out. Neither happened. Today, India is opening to outside investment, as it carefully integrates Western ideas into its ancient customs and beliefs.

Some Historical Context

The indigenous peoples of the subcontinent were the Dravidians, who were driven into the south of India by the invasion of Aryan peoples—the Indo-Aryans—from the west (actually from eastern Europe, western Russia, and Iran) around 1500 B.C. The roots of Hinduism go deep into Dravidian culture, and emerge around the time of the Aryan invasions. Like other ethnic groups in the region (Persians, or Iranians; Uzbeks; and Tajiks), Aryan Indians typically have Western physiognomic features, different from the Mongol features of the Pacific Rim.

By 500 B.C., Buddhism had begun to flower, replacing Brahminism (early Hinduism) as the dominant religion. In the fourth century A.D., India's Golden Age began with the establishment of the mighty Buddhist Gupta dynasty. By the tenth century, Islam had arrived and established itself in northern India; and by the fourteenth century, the great Islamic rulers—the Moguls—were clearly in charge. Their rule lasted until the eighteenth century, when the British established their control in the subcontinent. For over two hundred years, the British raj held sway over India.

Finally, in 1947, after much struggle, India became a free and independent nation, and almost immediately was sundered in two by fierce religious conflicts between Hindus and Muslims. The partitioning of India resulted in the creation of Pakistan (itself divided into two regions, west and east) as a homeland for the Muslims. East Pakistan ultimately became the independent state of Bangladesh. Nevertheless, the conflict between Hindus and Muslims continues today, with the tensions inside India (which still has more Muslims than Pakistan) mirroring the underlying hostilities between India and Pakistan.

An Area Briefing

Politics and Government

Today, India is a democracy, with a representative bicameral parliament, modeled after Britain's, and a prime minister. There is no monarchy or royalty. Politics in India has been dominated by the Congress Party, but other factions rise from time to time to form challenging coalitions. The political system is volatile, and the democracy shaky, but in place. In India, politics is always local; it is still a country primarily of rural villages (over 80 percent of the people live outside of the major Indian urban areas). The popular view is that politics is corrupt, and government is a vehicle for jobs and graft.

Schools and Education

Schooling is free and mandatory for all elementary-grade children. The Indian equivalent of high school follows after grade school, and state-run universities are available to those who qualify academically after high school. Education, however, is very difficult for most families to provide, as poverty and daily life make it imperative that children assist in supporting the family. Wealthy Indians usually advance their education abroad, with many returning to India and to the family business. The British left many legacies, for better and for worse; the infrastructure in India, including schools and the civil service, has remained, providing the country with an English-literate, well-educated workforce. This is a powerful reason for the continuing faith in India.

Religion and Demographics

The major religious influences in India are primarily Hinduism and Islam today, although Buddhism had its birth in India, and both Sikhism and Jainism are based in India as secondary major religious groups. Buddhism eventually moved north and east into China and Southeast Asia, and south into Sri Lanka, today a Buddhist enclave off the coast of the subcontinent.

About 80 percent of all Indians are Hindus (Hindi is the language; a Hindu is someone who practices the religion). Hinduism began in India, first as Brahminism and developed over time (incorporating certain elements of Buddhism) to become the unifying religion of the subcontinent. It emphasizes dharma, or right conduct, the four stages of human existence, reincarnation, and a pantheon of gods organized in an eternal hierarchy. The *varnas,* or caste system, reflects in the secular world the stages different souls are at in their cycles of reincarnation. Each of the many gods and goddesses are regarded as a form, with many different aspects, of the one Supreme Being (the three main Hindu gods are Brahma, the Creator; Vishnu, the Preserver; and Siva, the Destroyer). Reincarnation is a central aspect of Hinduism, and faith in the cycles, and the abandonment of secular reality, should be the orientation of individuals if they want to achieve ultimate freedom from the repetition of these cycles, and move onward toward knowing the truth, or the "godhead," and attaining nirvana. How one moves onward in the repetition of reincarnated life cycles is dependent upon one's karma, or destiny, which is influenced by the actions that one takes in each preceding cycle. The *Mahabharata* and the *Ramayana* are two Hindu epics that teach Hindu ideals, and are revered everywhere by Hindus: whenever they are read or performed, they gather large audiences. Many of the original Hindu writings have been compiled into the *Upanishads,* a compilation of Hindu theological writings (or Vedic texts), which is the body of Hindu law and belief that defines the religion.

The caste system, a central idea in Hinduism (and probably earlier Dravidian beliefs, as well), is an integral part of Indian life; although technically now illegal, its influence is felt throughout Indian society. There are four basic castes (or *varnas*), beginning with the princes (or Brahmins), then moving downward to the warriors (who defended the princes), the teachers (or merchants), and the farmers, and finally the laborers and the peasants. All others were outcastes, or "untouchables" (those who were cursed, and performed menial tasks). In today's world, the Brahmins are the leaders of business and politics, the warriors are members of the massive government civil service, the teachers and merchants perform those same roles, and the farmers and peasants are the rural landholders. The untouchables still perform menial labor, but their lot in life has been eased somewhat by social reforms. Every Indian is keenly aware of his or her position in society with reference to others, and all people serve some, and are served by, others. Clearly, this has led to a very stratified society.

Islam is the youngest of the West's three great religious traditions, which began with Judaism and Christianity. As a Western religion, it is linked to the Judeo-Christian belief system and rejects Hinduism as "pagan," and not "of the book," or codified. Incorporating both Judaism and Christianity into its system of beliefs, Islam claims that it is the final revelation of a monotheistic God, as revealed to the world through the prophet Muhammad in the early seventh century, and that previous "messiahs," such as Jesus and Moses, were merely prophets, along with Muhammad, proclaiming the word of God. Muslims do not follow Muhammad (therefore, they are not Muhammadans, a very derogatory term); they believe in Allah, the Arabic term for the same God worshiped by Christians and Jews. Muhammad and his followers wrote down the law of God as revealed to them in the Koran (or Qu'ran), the Islamic holy book. It does not negate the Old or New Testament: it merely provides, in the eyes of the Muslim faithful, the final required text. Islam spread rapidly throughout the Middle East, into Europe, and eastward across Asia, reaching India around the tenth century, and fully flowering into the great Mogul Empires by the fourteenth century. While Islam underwent a serious split almost immediately following Muhammad's death (two major camps emerged, the Shia and the Sunni, in an effort to decide how to continue the faith), it nevertheless rapidly gathered huge followings. Sunni Muslims believe that the caliphs (or religious leaders who took control after Muhammad's death) were legitimate descendents of Muhammad; Shiite Muslims believe that the caliphs that took control after Muhammad's death were usurpers, and therefore reject Sunni authority. All Muslims must abide by five basic tenets, or Pillars of Faith:

- Proclaim the supremacy of the one true God, Allah, above all others
- Pray to Allah five times daily
- Observe Ramadan, the holy month, the ninth month of the Islamic calendar, which is essentially a celebration of the first time God revealed his word to Muhammad
- Give alms to the poor and needy
- Perform the hajj, or spiritual (and physical) journey to Mecca, at least once in their lifetime if they are capable of doing so

Specific codes of conduct have developed over time, and have been codified into Islamic law, known as the *Shariah*. The degree to which one follows these scriptures often determines how devoutly one applies the Islamic ethical code to day-to-day life, and in India, Muslims run from very devout to lax.

Sikhism was founded in the late 1400s and early 1500s by Guru Nanak, who was attempting to build a religion based on bridging the differences between Muslims and Hindus: Sikhism attempts to be a synthesis of the two religions. As an example, Sikhs actively fought against Mogul rule, yet today fiercely defend Islam, its traditions, holy sites, and lands, as well as their own beliefs and holy sites (The Golden Temple of Amritsar, Sikhism's holiest site, is often a source of clashes between Sikhs and Hindus) against Hindus. Sikhs are generally known as fierce warriors, skilled businesspeople, and defenders of many Indian traditions. They originally sought an independent state, Kalistan, and today there is a strong Sikh independence movement. The fifth guru, or leader, Arjun, compiled Sikh thought into the *Granth Sahib* (the Sikh "Bible") in the sixteenth century. Sikhs wear turbans, do not cut their hair or beard, do not smoke or drink alcohol, and wear a comb in their hair, a steel bracelet on their right wrist, and a small sword. There is no caste system; the religion is essentially egalitarian in nature.

Jainism: Founded by Mahavira (or Vardhamana), a contemporary of the Buddha, who was also looking for a more effective way to realize essential Hindu ideals, Jainism does not recognize any one God or supreme creator. Instead, there are considered to be twenty-four "founders" (*tirthankaras*), or masters. Mahavira, in fact, was the last of these, and all *tirthankaras* are worshiped as saints. In Jain thought, *moksha* is the highest state one can attain: it is the ultimate enlightenment, achievable through supreme sacrifice and a total rejection of anything that is an earthly attachment (including clothing, which is why many Jains are nude). *Moksha* results as the total "unbonding" of one's soul from *karman,* the nonliving matter of the earth. Mahavira's writings are compiled in the *Angas,* the Jain "Bible." As with Buddhism, there are two sects: the *Digambaras,* the more conservative, does not permit women access to *moksha* until they are reincarnated into men first; and the *Svetambaras,* which allows women to become *tirthankaras.*

Women in India, subsequently, have an unequal role with men in society; their traditional role as homemaker and nurturer is often seen as subordinate to the male provider role (despite the fact that there is a very special bond between Indian men and their mothers). Indian women have some professional opportunities in education, in medicine, and in politics, but usually not in business. It might be difficult for non-Indian businesswomen who do not establish their authority ahead of time to be effective in the male-dominated Indian work environment.

Fundamental Cultural Orientations

1. What's the Best Way for People to Relate with One Another?

OTHER-INDEPENDENT OR OTHER-DEPENDENT? There is a combination of deep concern for family, clan, and other membership groups that define an individual (such as work and religion), and individual expression. Individuals are responsible for themselves, within their group, and are expected to use their resources to advance their own agendas. Yet, individual initiative, while important, must be justified as producing results that will benefit others, and must ultimately involve others if it is to succeed.

HIERARCHY-ORIENTED OR EGALITY-ORIENTED? Individual expression, however, is not the same as individual empowerment, which is defined solely by one's position in society. The caste system has laid down a rigid hierarchy as a way of organizing society at all levels—in the home, at school, on the streets, and at work. Always start at the highest possible levels, and be sensitive to the fact that your position and authority are being judged. A strong formality has developed in which people are treated according to their rank and status. Unlike the Pacific Rim countries, where the emphasis is on humility, one's rank in the system in India is demonstrated by the expression of authority from above and the deference shown to such authority from below. There is little concern for face: there is great concern for knowing one's place and acting accordingly. This emphasis on hierarchy also normalizes unequal relationships: it is, after all, natural that some be in charge and others not, that some have power and others not, that some dictate and others follow. Those above absolutely make the decisions for those below.

RULE-ORIENTED OR RELATIONSHIP-ORIENTED? Practically, immediate situations determine decisions and action; this means that there is a strong dependence on knowing the right people and on accepting the benefits of influence. However, there is also an understanding that this may not be morally correct, and as such, there is much concern whenever such behavior becomes apparent, as universal rules and systems are held in high moral regard.

2. What's the Best Way to View Time?

MONOCHRONIC OR POLYCHRONIC? India is essentially a polychronic culture in that the clock is usually not the determinant of action; it most certainly plays a role, particularly in the larger, more modern urban areas, and there is an acceptance of Western organizational ideas. Nevertheless, there is forgiveness for the inevitable delays, and understanding when things don't go as planned or scheduled; people may or may not show up at scheduled events, meetings and projects may or may not happen as planned. India is forever acting Indian, but judging itself by Western standards of universal morality, resulting in a kind of self-consciousness that swings between superiority and inferiority.

Daily life in India has historically been arranged according to vast, agriculturally based blocks of time, over which no individual or government had control, for example, the seasons, day and night. This tradition has been spiritually justified by the tenets of Hinduism and Buddhism, which emphasize vast cycles of life and reincarnation. Even today, schedules tend to be loose and flexible; the workday begins around 9 A.M., and ends around 4 P.M. Most workers take an hour break and a midafternoon nap after lunch.

RISK-TAKING OR RISK-AVERSE? Indians are prone to taking risks when in positions of authority, and avoiding risks when not. Within castes, families, and organizations, the decision makers can be bold, even reckless, but subordinates generally are not, and take action only when instructed to do so and only when they are sure that all "i"s are dotted and all "t"s are crossed. Therefore, comfort with uncertainty, in general, is low, and much information may need to be exchanged with different people before decisions can be made; however, this is rarely to develop consensus, but rather to force the correct individual to make the ultimate decision. Because this is often being done with individuals who have no incentive to facilitate the business themselves, this can be a slow and frustrating experience.

PAST-ORIENTED OR FUTURE-ORIENTED? All Indian religious traditions emphasize the fatalistic nature of the universe; from reincarnation to karma, there is a distinct and inherent fatalism assigned to the effect of human action. Nevertheless, those empowered by virtue of their caste position are expected to make the decisions that keep this secular world running, as a reflection of their higher ranking in the universal order of things. Therefore, future benefits often do not motivate Indians; doing nothing, or doing things for the here and now, are sometimes more relevant, and if things do not work out, that is to be expected—no one controls the universe, and all is determined. Hindus see both the future and the past as part of the same repeating cycles of history, and some more devout Muslims find it heretical that mere mortals can presume to know or alter Allah's will by planning far into the future.

3. What's the Best Way for Society to Work with the World at Large?

LOW-CONTEXT DIRECT OR HIGH-CONTEXT INDIRECT COMMUNICATORS? Indians can be very direct. Since individuals have unquestioned authority based on their positions, and one of the reasons for the caste system was to make clear and explicit rules of behavior between these levels, Indians do not hesitate in saying what they believe their position entitles them to say. They do not necessarily avoid confrontation. Nevertheless, with outsiders, particularly Westerners, Indians forego some of these rank entitlements, and can be more discreet in their communication styles. While context will convey some information, direct communication is the rule between peers or from superiors down to subordinates, and indirect communication is the rule from subordinates up to their superiors, or between individuals whose rank and influence is unknown.

PROCESS-ORIENTED OR RESULT-ORIENTED? Associative and subjective experience-based logic predominates in most situations, but Indians often judge results according to the processes of Western logic that have become ingrained in the culture since the British were in control. This can result in much examination of issues, the outcome of which will still often be based on intuition, personal beliefs, and past personal experience.

FORMAL OR INFORMAL? Indian society is formal and ritualized; each group has its own way of honoring the hierarchies, establishing respect and deference, and following (or not following) through on their responsibilities. It is even more formal when one is on the outside, or just beginning to establish relationships with the in-group.

Greetings and Introductions

Language and Basic Vocabulary

There are two main official languages, Hindi and English, although there are scores of local languages spoken throughout the country, the major ones being Gujarati in the west, Bengali in the east, and Tamil in the south. Most of the indigenous languages are written in a version of printed Sanskrit (Sanskrit is no longer a spoken language); many are written with roman letters. Because English is taught and spoken by most people in business, it is the lingua franca for visitors in India. Be aware that the English is British English, and the differences between British English and the English spoken by other English speakers, particularly Americans, can be considerable.

Honorifics for Men, Women, and Children

It is important to identify Hindus and Muslims correctly, as the honorifics and greeting forms will be different. Generally speaking, Muslims can be identified first by their names, for they often incorporate Arabic names or Arabic forms into their own names (because Arabic was the language in which the Koran was written, it is considered by many to be a holy language). Moreover, many Hindu names are characteristically long and multisyllabic, or have Hindu or Buddhist terms included (e.g., Subramanian, Prabuddha).

FOR HINDU INDIANS. Many Hindu Indian businesspeople today use Westernized versions of their names. Many retain the traditional Indian form, in which no surname (family name) is used, just a given name plus an honorific. Both men and women simply put the first initial of their father's first (given) name before their own given (first) name. For example, in the name R. Sarinda, Sarinda is the person's first (given) name, and R. is the initial of his father's first name (Ravi); the proper form of address is Mr. Sarinda. If a woman named K. Sardar marries M. Sarinda, she would properly be addressed as Mrs. Sardar Sarinda.

The word for "Mr." in Hindi is *sri,* and often precedes the given (first) name: for example, Sri R. Sarinda (or Mr. Sarinda, where Sarinda is the first— or given—name, and R. is the first initial of his father's first name).

Titles are very important, so if an individual has one (e.g., lawyer), it needs to come immediately after the honorific, followed by the full or first name: for example, Sri Dr. R. Sarinda.

FOR MUSLIM INDIANS. *For men,* use the first (given) name plus *bin* (meaning "son of") plus the father's given (first) name (e.g.: Ali bin Muhammad). The proper form of address is Mr. Ali.

For women, use the first (given) name plus *binti* or *binte* (meaning "daughter of") plus the father's given (first) name (e.g.: Asmah binti Naguib). The proper form of address is Mrs./Miss/Ms. Asmah.

If Asmah and Ali were married, she might also be referred to by her husband's first name after her first name: thus, the proper form of address is Mrs. Asmah Ali.

If someone's titles are known, all the titles come before the entire name (e.g.: Mr. Dr. Ali bin Muhammad).

Muslim men who have made the hajj often use the honorific *hajji* as a title before the name (e.g.: Hajji Ali bin Muhammad).

Muslim women who have made the hajj often use the honorific *hajja* as a title before the name (e.g.: Hajja Asmah binti Naguib; or, if married, Hajja Asmah Ali).

FOR SIKH INDIANS. Sikhs use their given name preceded by *singh* if male, or *kaur* if female: for example, Singh Ali, or Kaur Asmah.

Again, married Sikh women use their given (first) name plus their husband's given (first) name as a last name, as in the Muslim example above. Do not use the honorific *singh* as a last name or call someone Mr. Singh—as you are really then saying "Mr. Mr."

The What, When, and How of Introducing People

Indians may, upon greeting you, simply call you by your first or last name, plus your title, or make a comment about the task you are performing: this requires no substantive response. This use of the first name is not informal, as first names are the correct way to greet people in India.

Always wait to be introduced to strangers; never take that responsibility upon yourself, as doing so is considered inappropriate most of the time. Indians absolutely insist on third-party introductions, to ensure that people from different castes are not being introduced to each other. Never presume to seat yourself at a gathering: if possible, wait to be told where to sit. The seating arrangements have usually been carefully worked out in advance, and in most cases reflect the status of the individuals in the group, and the honor that is being accorded the guests. When departing, it is important to say farewell to every individual present: the American group wave is not appreciated. Once you greet someone you will encounter later that day in the same circumstances (e.g., at the office), you do not need to greet them when you see them again. Seniors, or those who are obviously the oldest in a group, are greeted first, seated first, and allowed to enter a room first (usually at the center of a group, however, and preceded in most cases by their younger aides).

Physical Greeting Styles

HINDU AND SIKH INDIANS. Like many Asian cultures, India is essentially a nontouching culture—at least at first. Only the most intimate of friends (mainly young people) will touch each other casually. The handshake is a Western custom, and not native to the region, but because of the significant Western influences in India, it is sometimes used with Westerners after the traditional greeting, the *namaste* (literally, "I honor the godhead within you"). The *namaste* requires that you put your hands in a prayer position, and place them at chest level so that if you bend your head, your chin almost touches the tips of your fingers. As you bend your head and raise your hands together in this position, you say, "Namaste." If a handshake follows, it is usually very soft, almost limp. This does not signify insincerity; rather, it is an accommodation to the Westerner. For extra sincerity after the handshake, you may bring your hand back and touch your heart. Let your Indian colleague initiate any handshakes after the *namaste,* if there are any at all (typically, they will not occur between men and women; if they do, the woman must extend her hand first). Remember that it may still be uncomfortable for many to touch or shake hands with people from other castes, especially the untouchables. In very formal situations, it is traditional after greeting someone to place a garland of flowers (similar to the Hawaiian lei) around their neck as a sign of welcome. If you should receive such a garland, accept it humbly, and then, when seated, be sure to remove it and place it to your right on the table. Do not remain seated with the garland on your neck. It is merely a welcome sign, not a bit of fashion.

MUSLIM INDIANS. Typically, the greeting here is the salaam, which involves softly shaking hands with your right hand, and then bringing the hand back to your heart and touching it. Traditionally, the salaam was performed by quickly touching your forehead first, then your heart, then the front of the abdomen with your right hand as you bowed slightly; this is still done on very formal occasions. Muslim women and men do not touch or shake hands (unless the woman is very Westernized).

The traditional Indian business introduction also includes the exchange of business cards. Always take a large supply of business cards with you: you must give one to every new person you are introduced to (there is no need to provide another business card when you are meeting someone again unless information about you has changed, such as a new address, contact number, or position).

Be sure your business cards are in fine shape: they are extensions of you as a person, and must look as good as possible. Never hand out a dirty, soiled, bent, or written-on card. You do not need to translate your business card into Hindi or any other Indian language, as English is well understood. When presenting your business card, you give it to your Indian associate so that it is readable for them as you hold it (they will, in turn, present their card so that it's readable for you); you need not hold the card with two hands. Do not worry too much about who receives and gives their business card first: the exchange is very quick, and because you would probably not be introduced to that first person in the first place if you were not already seen as having an equivalent rank, there is no need to show deference. There is also no need for bowing in India.

Smiling and other nonverbal forms of communication usually accompany the card exchange; it is appropriate to appear genuinely pleased to meet the other person. Information about each other's status is the most important information to be exchanged, and this is provided directly on the business card, as well as indirectly through a number of high-context indicators, such as gray hair (indicating older age), gender (usually male), and the number of people surrounding and assisting the other person (important people usually have assistants). Should you meet more than one Indian at a reception, you will have a handful of cards when the greetings are over.

As the business card exchage usually precedes a sit-down meeting, it is important to arrange the cards you have received in a little seating plan in front of you along the top of the desk or the table at your seat, reflecting the order in which people are seated. This will help you connect the correct names with the correct individuals throughout the meeting. Do this even if you are just meeting one person; it is expected. During the meeting, it is important never to play with the business cards (do not write on them—ever!); and when the meeting is over, never put them in your back pants pockets: pick them up carefully and respectfully, and place them neatly in your cardholder (a nice-looking brass—*never* leather!—card case would be perfect), then place the cardholder in the left inside jacket pocket of your suit (nearest your heart).

Communication Styles

Okay Topics / Not Okay Topics

Okay: anything that reflects your personal interests and hobbies, or your curiosity about things Indian, like its food or its history. *Not okay:* Politics, current events, or any subject that might in any way be controversial needs to be avoided at first. Do not inquire about a person's occupation or income in casual conversation, although it may be inquired of you (if so, this is just a way of getting to know more about your country, and not a personal investigation: answer specifically, but fully, with an explanation as to what things cost at home, why you do what you do, etc.). Do not inquire about your colleague's family life, or the role of servants and household help. Do not give your opinions about the Gandhi family or political corruption. Do not talk about sex or tell dirty jokes (they are generally not understood and in very bad taste). *Never* discuss religion, and do not disparage any particular group. Discussions about your company and its work are very much appreciated, as it gives the Indians a chance to learn more about you and your firm. The goal of all conversation, at least at the beginning, is to create and maintain a harmonious atmosphere, despite the difficult or confrontational nature of the topic being discussed. At first, speak about things that you believe you have in common, so that you can build a personal connection that will go far toward maintaining a harmonious bridge between you. This is appropriate for both individuals and organizations.

Tone, Volume, and Speed

Indians generally speak in soft, hushed tones, at least at first. However, they may become animated and very direct. They tend to speak in voices that are pitched slightly higher than typical Western speakers, and may speak rapidly. If you, in turn, speak rather slowly, they may get the hint and slow down.

Use of Silence

Passive silence—allowing time to pass simply, without words—can be a form of proactive communication, but is not that common in India.

Physical Gestures and Facial Expressions

In India, a wobbling type of head motion, is prevalent, particularly in the south, which may appear to the Westerner as if the Indian is shaking their head from side to side indicating negativity or disapproval. This is not the case. This motion simply indicates that the Indian is listening to what you have to say and that you should continue. Winking, whistling, and similar displays are considered very vulgar. Public displays of familiarity and affection with the opposite sex are expressed only by teenagers. Never touch anyone, including small children, on his or her head: this is considered the holiest part of the body. Do not point with or intentionally show the sole of your shoe to anyone: this is considered vulgar, as the bottom of the shoe touches the ground, and is therefore the dirtiest part of the body. Standing with your hands on your hips is considered very aggressive and should always be avoided. Do not give donations to anyone on the street, as this generally only encourages throngs more. Philanthropic intentions should be expressed by making donations to reputable local charities.

For any action or gesture that would naturally be done only with one hand, do not use your left hand, especially in the presence of Muslims, as the left hand is considered the unclean hand (the hand used for personal hygiene). Pass all documents, food, and money *only* with your right hand (if you're a southpaw, you will have to practice this). You must remove your shoes before entering a Hindu temple; you will also need to wash your feet and hands before entering the temple, as well as a Muslim mosque. Both men and women are most welcome in Hindu temples, but women may be restricted to specific areas and times when visiting mosques. Women entering both temples and mosques need to have their heads covered, their legs covered below the knees, and their arms covered below the elbows.

Waving and Counting

The pinkie represents the number 1, the thumb represents the number 5, with everything in between ordered from the pinkie down; however, instead of raising the fingers when counting, the whole hand is exposed, and each finger is depressed as the counting is done. It is very insulting to motion to someone with the forefinger; instead, turn your hand so that the palm is facing down and motion inward with all four fingers at once. If you need to gesture for a waiter, very subtly raise your hand. Waving or beckoning is done with the palm down and the fingers moving forward and backward in a kind of scratching motion. It may seem as if the person making the gesture is saying good-bye to you, when in fact you are being summoned over. If you need to point to something or someone, use a full open palm motion, not the index finger.

Physicality and Physical Space

Most Indians stand, relative to North Americans, just a little farther apart; resist the urge at first to move in closer. Never, upon first greeting an Indian, touch him beyond the soft handshake: no backslaps, no hugging, no kissing, *ever.* Never speak with your hands in your pockets: always keep them firmly to your side when standing. If men and women must cross their legs when they sit, it must never be ankle over knee (for women, the preferred style is to cross ankle over ankle; the bottoms of the shoes must not show to the other person). Remember, in public, formal is always better than informal: no gum chewing, *ever;* don't slouch; and don't lean against things. About the only time the nonphysicality rule is broken in India is on public transport, where it is very crowded and touching is unavoidable, or on crowded streets, where you are very likely to be poked and prodded as people jostle by.

Eye Contact

In India, eye contact is very indirect between classes; but it can be direct among equals. Interest in what one's supervisor is saying is shown by averting the eyes, not by making eye contact. The eyes are used extensively to convey true feelings in formal situations where it may be difficult to express your thoughts verbally. Tune up your nonverbal antennae.

Emotive Orientation

Indians may be very restrained when they are with people from another class or with people whose class and authority are unknown. They can be very emotive with familiars or peers, however.

Protocol in Public

Walking Styles and Waiting in Lines

On the street, in stores, and in most public facilities, people pay little attention to maintaining orderly lines. Due to the volume of passengers on public transportation, there can be much pushing and jostling. This is not to get into a train or a bus ahead of someone else, though; it is merely to get in!

Behavior in Public Places: Airports, Terminals, and the Market

Customer service is not as well developed as one might expect in such a rank-oriented culture, perhaps because serving is so rank associated, and therefore just another role to play in life. It is a servile-oriented culture, not a service-oriented culture. Service is perfunctory, at best, in most stores and restaurants, or obsequiously fawning in the high-end establishments. Stores in the cities are open in the evenings and on weekends, as well as during the day. A personal thank-you to store owners, waiters, chefs, and hotel managers for their services is not always necessary. In food markets, don't touch the produce, as you may make it "unclean" for the next person; in goods stores, if you buy a product and have problems with it, returning the item can be difficult. Smoking is endemic, and you may have difficulty finding a no-smoking area on public transportation, in restaurants, and in other public places (be sure not to smoke in front of Muslims during Ramadan, when they abstain). Bathroom facilities can range from Western-style toilets to Asian-style toilets (holes in the floor, with buckets of water or hoses attached to a water line for cleanup instead of paper); be prepared.

Unless they are in the company of other women or close male relatives, women generally do not go out in public. Western women traveling alone in the country will place an unusual burden on the behavior of others toward them: many Indians won't know what to do or how to act toward them; other women will want to assist them; and certain men, no doubt, will try to take advantage of them. Traveling alone in India is not a good idea for women.

When answering a phone, say "Hello" or just your given name. Cell phones are ubiquitous, as the wire networks may be unreliable or nonexistent.

Bus / Metro / Taxi / Car

Driving is on the left, and whether in the country or city, being in a car can be hazardous to your health. The roads are not necessarily in good repair, marked, or where maps say they are; and obtaining fuel when and where you need it can be a problem. The traffic in Mumbai, New Delhi, and other major cities is maddening and chaotic, and construction sites are everywhere.

The best way to catch a cab is at designated taxi stands (hotels are good places, but often charge more for the same ride: a hotel surcharge is added to the meter fare, in some cases). When a taxi has been hailed, negotiate the price, as the meter may or may not be working (even if it is, it is important to negotiate the fare ahead of time). Whenever possible, have the address you need to get to written down on a piece of paper (or use the business card of the person you are going to see, if you can) before you hail the cab. A small map outlining the route is great, if you can have one prepared before you go. Taking open motorbikes may not be a good idea, as sudden downpours will drench you, and motorbikes can be dangerous in the congestion and traffic.

Tipping

Tipping is universally required, everywhere you can imagine—and then some. Tips in restaurants run about 10 percent, and are typically not included in the bill (but double-check to be sure); a separate tip is not necessary if you have negotiated the fare for the taxi ahead of time, and already figured in the tip. For everything else, a few rupees is all that is needed, but you should always have a lot of spare change handy to see you through the day. Be careful walking in front of temples: people may approach you and offer you a *prasad* (an offering from the gods) in the form of a garland of flowers or a bracelet, by thrusting it in your hands or on your wrist; you are then obligated to pay for it. It is difficult to return.

Punctuality

Punctuality is valued, perhaps because it is not as common in India as it should be. For business meetings, be on time if you can, but don't worry if you are five or ten minutes late; for social occasions, being up to twenty minutes late is okay. Making a general comment about the weather, the traffic, or something else is generally all you need to do to get off the hook for being late.

Dress

The Indian standard is more or less Western, but the main concern is the climate: it is hot and tropical most of the year. Therefore, many businessmen wear very lightweight suits, or a dress shirt (sometimes short-sleeved), either with or without a tie, and no jacket. None of this is an invitation to informality: it is just an adaptation to the weather. Businesswomen wear lightweight skirts and blouses, jackets, or suits. It is best to start out formal, and take your jacket off only if you see others without theirs. Wear dress slacks, not jeans or khakis. Social dress is the same, although sometimes clean, pressed jeans are okay with a dress or sport shirt (but no T-shirts!). Sneakers are only for the street or gym (few women wear sneakers to work); because of the heat, shorts are okay on the street, with T-shirts (but not at temples, ever). Muslim traditions dictate that women dress so that their legs are covered below the knee, their arms are covered below the elbow, and their torsos are covered from their necks to their waists. Some Muslim women in India cover their faces, but most do not; and nonpracticing Western women need not. Most Hindu women wear the sari, and it is appropriate for Western women to do the same, if they know how.

Remember, if you visit temples, you will need to remove your shoes and walk barefoot while inside. Avoid wearing leather, which is made from cows; as cows are sacred to Hindus, some may be offended if you do.

Seasonal Variations

There are two extreme seasons in India: wet and hot, and dry and hot (with the exception of the hill station towns in the mountains in the north, where the weather can be temperate to cool). The important thing is to remember the frequent downpours and periodic monsoons; take an umbrella with you everywhere you go.

Colors

Wear neutral colors whenever possible. Do not wear white or black only, as to do so indicates you are in mourning or going to a funeral. Orange-yellow (or saffron) is a preferred color in India. Green is the color of Islam, and is appreciated when it is used tastefully.

Styles

For the most part, clothing is simple, adapted to the climate, and meant to keep one looking good and cool. Consider, however, that many places are air-conditioned to arctic levels, so you might always want to have a lightweight covering available.

Accessories / Jewelry / Makeup

Makeup, hairstyle, and accessories are important for women, but only if they are styled modestly. Perfume and cologne are popular, but usually are not made with alcohol (alcohol is prohibited in Islam). Among Hindu women, the *bindi,* or beauty dot in the middle of the forehead between and slightly above the eyebrows, is a cosmetic addition designed to enhance beauty; in and of itself, it is not a mark of rank or status.

Personal Hygiene

In India, cleanliness is associated with purity, and is therefore important. Washing both hands and feet more than once a day is very common. There is a real concern for smelling good, but what smells good and bad to Indians may be different from Westerners. Throughout the region, the smell of meat (particularly red meat) on individuals is offensive, while there is usually no concomitant concern for the smell of other foods, such as garlic or seafood, or natural human body odors. Do not blow your nose in public: it is considered very rude. Spitting may occur on the street. Muslim and Indian men may sport facial hair, usually in the form of a mustache. At the end of a meal, it is perfectly acceptable to use toothpicks, but you must cover the "working" hand with the other hand, so that others cannot see your mouth. Remember that Muslims consider dogs very unclean; therefore, do not refer to them or bring them along with you.

Dining and Drinking

Mealtimes and Typical Foods

The typical Indian diet is a varied and multifaceted treat. (Of course, there are millions in India who subsist on the slimmest diets of grain, rice, or yogurt.) Indian cuisine revolves mainly around the local foods, especially fresh vegetables (including lentils, cauliflowers, and beans), pickled and preserved vegetables (in the form of pickles, chutneys, and curries, etc.), seafood, rice, and breads. Although Indians are becoming increasingly familiar with Western food, they love their own cuisine, and most will enjoy a fine Indian meal (if you are hosting them in your country, unless they directly express an interest in trying a local cuisine, take them to the best local Indian restaurant you can find, and tell the restaurant manager that you are hosting some visiting Indian nationals, as well as the region they are from: the restaurant management will usually go out of its way to make the meal very fine for you). Avoid Western food, especially cheese: the taste is unpleasant for Muslims. Indian foods are not always spicy and hot (although there is a tendency to use more spices the farther south one goes—this is in direct proportion to the need to preserve food in a hot climate; in the same line, more dairy products, in the form of yogurt and milk, are used in the north, as it is easier to preserve these foods in the cooler climates). Fresh-baked breads of all kinds are ubiquitous (*papadams,* nans, etc.). Baked or fried filled dumplings called *samosas* are typically served at the beginning of the meal as an appetizer.

Breakfast is served from about 7:30 to 9 A.M., and usually consists of tea and rice; the latter is usually served as a porridge-type cereal that can be flavored with any number of ingredients. Tea in India is usually drunk with milk and sugar: if you want it plain, you should request it that way when you order it. Yogurt and fruit drinks are sometimes served for breakfast.

Lunch was traditionally the main meal of the day—and even today in busy cities, it can still be an elaborate affair with several courses—or it can be a simple snack prepared and eaten in a matter of minutes. Lunch is served from about noon to 1 P.M., and consists of meat, fish, and/or vegetables, with rice. Many dishes can be steamed, stir-fried, baked, or boiled in a variety of different ways, either simply or more elaborately. Typically, the drinks served with lunch and dinner are soft drinks and/or tea (beer is often drunk by non-Muslims or non-observant Muslims).

Dinner is served from 6 P.M. on, with 7 P.M. the customary late time. Even if the main meal of the day was lunch, dinner is only slighter lighter—this is often the case with families at home. The dinner menu is often similar to that of the more formal lunch. If alcohol is being drunk, predinner drinks may begin with a beer, then move on to beer during the meal, and end with tea. Indians love sweets, and serve them before meals, as well as after. When you come to an Indian home, even for just a brief visit, you will be served some sweet delicacy plus a cool drink (usually iced water, lemonade, or fruit juice) and/or tea. The sweet is not dessert; you will get that as well at the end of the meal. In fact, sweets are so loved in India that sweet pickles, chutneys, and sweet pastries are sold in sweet shops (*shwarma*), where one can go for tea or coffee and a sweet at any time.

Regional Differences

Most Indian food tastes hot and spicy to Westerners, although the degrees of spice and heat do vary, based on the regions and the foods. You can ask for the heat to be moderated when you order your foods. Indian cuisine incorporates hot and bland, sweet and salty, sweet and sour, with blends of textures as well—cool and creamy, crunchy and hot. Heat tip: don't douse the heat with water, tea, beer, or juice. Liquid only spreads the heat throughout your mouth. Eat rice instead: the rice absorbs the capsaicin, the chemical in chilies and peppers that gives them their bite. Seafood is very common along the coasts, and preserved vegetables and rice dishes, often mixed with coconut, and, when available, chicken, are prepared in a variety of different ways throughout the country. Remember, Islam prohibits the use of pork, and Hindus do not eat beef (most Hindus, in fact, are vegetarians, and avoid all animal meats; some avoid all animal products, such as eggs). Most meats of any kind for Muslims need to be prepared *halal* (according to Islamic dietary code). Do not eat in front of your Muslim colleagues, or invite them to join you for a meal, during the day during Ramadan, as Muslims typically fast (and restrain from drinking and smoking) during the day, and feast with family and friends at night. Ramadan lasts for a lunar month: this is simply not a good time to do business or go out entertaining in India.

Typical Drinks and Toasting

The most common alcoholic beverage is beer, generally served cold. Because you must never pour your own drink (be it beer or tea), you must always be alert throughout the meal as to whether your neighbor's cup or glass needs refilling. If it is less than half full, it needs refilling; alternately, if yours is less than half full, your neighbor is obliged to refill it. If he or she does not, do not refill it yourself, for this will cause your neighbor to lose face; instead, diplomatically indicate your need by pouring a little more drink into your neighbor's glass, even if it doesn't really need it.

What to do if you don't drink alcohol? This usually isn't a problem with Muslims, but if you are dining with associates who drink, you'll need to provide an explanation if you don't join in. I've heard people say, "My doctor doesn't advise me to drink just now" or "It's my ulcer," and any number of other little white lies.

If you are the honored guest, you will be expected to make a toast, usually soon after the host does or at the end of the meal, just before everyone departs. An appropriate toast is to the health of the host and all those present, and to the prosperity of the business under discussion.

Avoid drinking tap water anywhere in India (this means you should brush your teeth with bottled water and not take ice in any of your drinks; drink only bottled water, or brewed tea or coffee or soft drinks, and avoid getting water from the morning shower into your mouth; and never eat fresh fruits or vegetables that cannot be peeled first and, ideally, cooked later before eating). This is a serious matter: there are some very nasty bugs going around in developing countries. Also avoid all dairy products except in the finest hotels, as the required refrigeration may be questionable.

Table Manners and the Use of Utensils

Chopsticks are not used with Indian food. In India, spoons, forks, and knives are used, if necessary, or no utensils at all (mainly in more traditional Muslim restaurants). Since the spoon is more important than the fork, if you are right-handed, keep the spoon in your right hand, and put it down to switch to the fork if you need it. Never use your left hand for eating, especially if you are eating directly with your hands.

What do you do when no utensils are available? Why, eat with your fingers, of course! Many think it makes the experience more fun, maybe because you're adding an extra sense to an already very sensory experience: the sense of touch. The type of food eaten with the hands is known as "banana-leaf" food: wonderful vegetarian or meat curries, served with rice and sauce on a large banana leaf. No plates, no forks, no spoons, no chopsticks. You reach into the rice, take some with your fingers, gently roll it between your index and middle fingers and thumb (not in your palms!) into a kind of self-sticking ball, dip it into the sauce on the banana leaf, mix it with a vegetable or a piece of chicken, then pop the whole thing in your mouth. Most of these hands-on banana-leaf restaurants are Muslim or vegan (Hindu).

Here are some other things to note about eating in such restaurants:

• Wash your hands before you sit down to eat. Many banana-leaf restaurants have washrooms and sinks out in the open specifically for this purpose. (However, you may want to wash your hands with bottled water at the hotel first, since the water at the restaurant may be more hazardous to your health than the germs already on your hands!) You will also need to wash your hands again at the end of the meal, especially after eating the saucy dishes, since you've probably got a good bit of it running down your arm. Don't worry, it's to be expected: don't dress up if you're eating banana-leaf style.

• Use your right hand when picking up and eating food, never your left hand. Keep your left hand at your side. Do not place your left hand on the table, and do not pass food with your left hand.

• Pork will typically not be on the menu.

• Alcohol will usually not be served with the meal.

• Men and women, in some establishments, may be asked to dine separately.

• If you absolutely cannot eat without some kind of utensil, it's usually all right to ask for one in such establishments. The proprietors are usually more than pleased to accommodate Westerners.

Rice may be served in separate bowls, or on the same plate with your main dish. While rice is a staple, it is not necessary to eat every grain; leaving some over is fine. Do not take the last bit of food from a central serving plate; that means there will be none left, in case someone else wants more. Also, a sauce may (in fact, should) be mixed with rice, and eaten together with the main dish. You are not expected to hold the rice bowl (if there is one) up by your mouth. Hot tea (*cha*) may be slurped quietly to cool it off as it enters the mouth.

When dining with Hindus, it is especially important not to touch directly any food that is being served to others, and this is especially the case between men and women: this makes it impure. When dining with devout Muslims, it is especially important for women not to touch directly any food that is being served to men: this also makes it impure.

A word about smoking: it is ubiquitous throughout Asia, including India. Usually, at the table, you do not smoke until the meal is over. At the end of some meals, fresh mints, caraway seeds, or betel nuts may be offered as a special treat after dessert (betel nuts produce, over time, a dark stain on the teeth).

Seating Plans

The host sits at the head of the table, with the honored guest seated next to the host. (Spouses are usually not invited to business meals in restaurants. Do not ask if your spouse can join you: it will embarrass your Indian colleague into doing something that is uncomfortable for him; however, your spouse might be invited to a meal at your colleague's home, especially if the spouse of the host will be there, which will probably be the case.) In addition, the honored guest sits on the side of the table farthest from the door. (In business meetings, the key people sit in the middle, flanked on either side in descending order by their aides, with the least important people sitting at the ends of the table farthest from the middle, and closest to the door; the arrangement is mirrored on the other side.) Men and women eating at someone's home may dine in separate areas (and spend the entire evening separated) or at separate times, with the men dining first.

Refills and Seconds

You will always be offered more food. Leave a bit on your plate if you do not want more food. You will be implored to take more two or three times, in the form of a little ritual. The game is as follows: first you refuse, then the host insists, then you refuse again, then the host insists again, and then you finally give in and take a little more. If you really don't want more, take very little and leave it on your plate. You may always have additional beverages; drink enough to cause your cup or glass to be less than half full, and it will generally be refilled. A reminder: never refill your own glass; always refill your neighbor's glass, and he or she will refill yours.

At Home, in a Restaurant, or at Work

The honored guest is served first, then the oldest man, then the rest of the men, then children, and finally women. Do not begin to eat or drink until the oldest man at the table has been served and has begun. At the end of the meal, it is considered unnecessary and in bad taste to thank the host or hostess for the meal; this is perceived as a "payment" for the meal, and as a guest, you should not do that. Instead of thanking the host vocally when you are finished, just perform a *namaste* at your seat.

In informal restaurants, you may be required to share a table. If so, do not force conversation: act as if you are seated at a private table. Waitstaff may be summoned by making eye contact; waving or calling their names is very impolite. The business breakfast is unknown in India, and most business meals are lunches. Business meals are generally not good times to discuss business or make business decisions, however. Take your cue from your Indian associates: if they bring up business, then it's okay to discuss it, but wait to take your lead from their conversation.

When invited to a colleague's home for a formal meal, you will be told where to sit, and there you should remain. It is a great honor to be invited into an Indian home. Once inside, you may need to remove your shoes (this is not the custom in restaurants, however). You will know when you approach the home and see a row of shoes at the door (keep your socks in good shape, and wear comfortable but well-made, nonleather slip-ons for such occasions). Once inside the home, do not wander around: much of the house is really off-limits to guests. If you move from room to room in an Indian home, be sure to always allow the more senior members of your party to enter the room ahead of you. Servants and household help are very common in middle- and upper-class Indian homes; do not comment on them (or on how they are treated, as you might be shocked at how they seem to be ordered about), and do not offer to help: they are there to serve.

Being a Good Guest or Host

Paying the Bill

Usually the one who does the inviting pays the bill, although the guest is expected to make an effort to pay. Sometimes other circumstances determine the payee (such as rank). Making payment arrangements ahead of time so that no exchange occurs at the table is a very classy way to host, and is very common. Western businesswomen will not have a problem paying the bill at a restaurant, but to be sure, make payment arrangements ahead of time, and don't wait for the check to arrive at the table.

Transportation

It's a very nice idea, when acting as the host, to inquire ahead of time as to whether your guests will require transportation. If necessary, you should arrange for taxi service at the end of the meal. When seeing your guests off, you must remain at the entrance of the house or the restaurant, or at the site where you deposited your guests into the car, until the car is out of sight: it is very important not to leave until your guests can no longer see you, should they look back. Guests are seated in cars (and taxis) by rank, with the honored guest being placed in the back directly behind the front passenger seat; the next honored position is in the back behind the driver, and the least honored position is up front with the driver.

When to Arrive / Chores to Do

If invited to dinner at a private home, do not offer to help with the chores: you are a guest, and the servant performs such tasks. You should not expect or ask to visit the kitchen. Do not leave the table unless invited to do so. When in the home, be careful not to admire a thing too effusively: Indians may feel obligated to give it to you, and you in turn will be required to present them with a gift of equal value. Instead of saying things like "I love that vase you have," say something like "Vases that beautiful in my country are only found in museums." Your compliments will most likely be dismissed.

Gift Giving

In general, gift giving is common in many situations in India. It is not only done as a gesture of thanks, but as a way of helping to ensure good business relations in the future (be careful not to go overboard here, as a gift that looks like graft is not appreciated, and may land you in quite a bit of trouble). In business settings, this usually takes the form of a personal gift that symbolically says the correct thing about the nature of the relationship. When going to India on business, bringing a personalized gift for the key decision maker is enough. Your gift does not have to be elaborate or expensive. You present your gift before you leave to return home; you will receive a farewell gift at this last meeting as well. When Indians visit your country, they will bring you a gift, and before they leave, you should give them gifts. Holiday cards are not that common.

The most appropriate gift for a personal visit to a home, or as a thank-you for dinner, would be a box of fruits, pastries, cakes, cookies, or other sweets. Flowers are typically not given as gifts, but if you must, avoid frangipani flowers, as these are used almost exclusively for funerals, or any flowers that are white, which is a funeral color. It is appropriate to send your hosts a handwritten thank-you note the day after the dinner party. If you are staying with a family, an appropriate thank-you gift would be a high-quality item that represents your country and is difficult or expensive to get in India; this is also a good idea for a key business associate. Acceptable gifts include coffee-table books about the United States, or anything that reflects your host's personal tastes (the cap of a famous American team for the football-playing son of the family, for example). Native handicrafts or well-framed and well-mounted photographs of you and your Indian associates are also appreciated. Be sure the gift you give does not have a sticker or tag on it that says it was made in the region.

If your gift consists of several items, be sure that the total number is an odd number. Avoid handkerchiefs, as they symbolize sadness, and cutlery, which symbolizes the severing of a relationship. A fine gift for a Muslim would be a silver compass, so that they will always know which direction to face when they say their daily prayers (Muslims must face Mecca no matter where they are when they say their prayers). Be sure not to give pork as a food gift to Muslims; also avoid alcohol, and perfumes and colognes that contain alcohol. Do not give beef as a food gift to Hindus. Because the cow is sacred to Hindus, do not give a gift made of leather: leatherbound portfolios, agendas, or picture frames are not appropriate. Remember, any gift given by a man to a woman must come with the caveat that it is from both him and his wife/sister/mother, or else it is far too personal. For both giving and receiving gifts, two hands are always used. Gifts are typically not opened by the receiver in front of the giver; they are usually received after much imploring by you, graciously acknowledged, and placed aside to be opened once the giver is no longer present.

Gifts should be wrapped well. Typically, gifts are wrapped in ordinary paper first then wrapped again in green, saffron, or red; black and white both should be avoided because they are funeral colors (blue has little significance, but is simply not used very much).

Special Holidays and Celebrations

Major Holidays

April through October is not a good time to do business in India, primarily due to the weather. Avoid the entire month of Ramadan if working with Muslims. Many cities have different local holidays as well, so double-check with your associates in India before making final plans.

January 26 (solar)	Republic Day
January/February (lunar)	Ramadan (one full lunar month, celebrating when Muhammad received his first revelation)
March (lunar)	*Hari Raya Puasa* (end of Ramadan)
May (lunar)	*Hari Raya Haji* (Islamic commemoration of Abraham's sacrifice)

May 1 (solar)	Labor Day
May 31 (solar)	*Awal Muharam* (the Muslim New Year begins)
June 30 (solar)	Bank holiday
August 9 (lunar)	The Prophet Muhammad's Birthday
August 15 (solar)	Independence Day
October 2 (solar)	Mahatma Gandhi's Birthday
October/November (lunar)	*Deepavali* (a Hindu festival of Thanksgiving)
December 25 (solar)	Christmas

Business Culture

Daily Office Protocols

The traditional Indian office has an open design; there are few doors, with the exception of the offices of those holding higher positions, and people work mainly in individual or shared cubicles. Doors, if they exist, are usually open. In the Indian business organization, hierarchy is strictly observed. Executives are usually placed on different floors than the rank and file. You probably will not be invited onto the working floors until the proposed project has been set in motion. Because faithful Muslims pray five times a day, you will need to adjust your schedule to accommodate their needs. Usually, prayers are given upon awakening, and at noontime, midday, dusk, and before retiring; this means that twice during the workday, there will be time out for prayers. The prayers usually take a short ten or fifteen minutes or so, and any quiet area will do. If you accidentally interrupt a Muslim during his prayers, just walk quietly away; there's no need for complicated explanations or apologies. Most organizations have prayer rooms set aside, with carpets. In addition, devout Muslims will not work on Friday (the Muslim Sabbath), and, in fact, begin to end work early on Thursday, before sundown. They will often return to work on Saturday or Sunday.

Management Styles

Because of the rigid rank and hierarchy orientation, titles are very important; the highest ones (e.g., vice president) are usually reserved for very senior, executive-level positions, and should not be used as casually as they are in the United States. Complimenting, rewarding, or criticizing employees publicly is often done, but Westerners should abstain from this practice. Any criticism by them must be done very carefully, even privately. Deference is shown by subordinates to their seniors; paternalistic concern is often shown by executives to their juniors. As in many bureaucracies, the primary goal may be to protect oneself and one's position vis-à-vis one's superiors (as well as to protect one's superior) rather than to get immediate goals accomplished. This usually means negotiations or projects can move very slowly at some times, and rapidly at others.

Boss-Subordinate Relations

The decision-making system usually works from the top on down, with key decisions often coming from individuals in high positions of authority. While bosses do solicit input from trusted subordinates, this is strictly information gathering, and not consensus building. Superiors are expected to provide clear and fully informed sets of instructions: that is their responsibility, and it is the responsibility of subordinates to carry out those instructions. Consequently, "management by objective" and other egalitarian and individually empowered management styles often may not work in this environment: without clear instruction from above, subordinates usually will do nothing. They also lose respect for the manager for not making the decisions he or she should be making.

Conducting a Meeting or Presentation

At your first meeting in India, you will probably be received in a very comfortable waiting area, which may or may not be where most of the meeting is conducted between yourself and your Indian colleague. If this is the case, you are merely being sized up, and your colleague is a gatekeeper. There may be several people in the room with you and your Indian contact whom you may or may not be introduced to. These "ghost people" are probably trusted friends or relations of your Indian colleague, and he will no doubt want their input after the meeting. If you are not introduced to them, do not ask to be: acknowledge them with a smile and a nod, and proceed with your meeting. If you are meeting with a decision maker, the discussions will probably be direct, forthright, and businesslike. If this is just the beginning of a business relationship, expect to spend most of the time sharing information about your organization with different individuals: you may need to repeat the same things to different people. This is okay; it means your plans are advancing to the right people in the organization, and that those you have previously met with have approved of you and moved you on. Patience and third-party connections are key. This also means that you should start as high up in the organization as you possibly can. When serving refreshments in the office, be sure they are served in porcelain tea sets: the use of paper or Styrofoam shows disrespect and is very bad form.

Negotiation Styles

Expect few decisions from Indians at the table at first, and be willing to provide copious amounts of information, to the degree that you can, in response to their questions and in anticipation of their needs. Presentations should be well prepared and simply propounded. Details are best left to questions and backup material, which can be written in English and left behind. Ideally, you should present your material to the Indians for study, along with a proposed agenda, prior to the meeting. Have extra copies available, as you might meet more people than you will expect. Should you come with other associates or as a team, make sure that your roles are well coordinated. Never disagree with each other in front of the Indians, or appear uncertain, unsure, not authorized to make a decision, or out of control in any way.

Indians generally like to bargain and approach it as a win/lose possibility, at first. Your job is to make it a win/win situation as you build trust and credibility. Contracts and contract law are well known in India, so expect and insist on well-executed documents to finalize an agreement; there is a dependable legal system for redress. Remember, the deal should be sealed with a celebratory meal. Keep communications open, especially when at a distance, and stay in touch often with your Indian associates: share more information than you normally would, not less; and, because business is so intimately connected with the government bureaucracy and because the political situation is so fluid, try to have a contact on the ground in India who can always keep you informed of what is really going on, if you can.

Written Correspondence

Your business letters should be very formal and respectful of rank and hierarchy. First names usually are written in uppercase; dates are given in the day/month/year format (with periods in between, not slashes); and an honorific plus the title is as common as an honorific plus the last name. You should write your e-mails, letters, and faxes in a formal, precise way: use a brief but warm introduction, then get down to business. Keep it simple, however, and bulletpoint or outline all important matters. In India, use the Western formatting of the address.

Line one: country and postal code
Line two: city (and prefecture)
Line three: street address
Line four: company and/or personal name

The South Asian Cultures: Pakistan and Bangladesh

Some Introductory Background on Pakistan and the Pakistanis and Bangladesh and the Bangladeshis

Pakistanis and Bangladeshis are not Indians; moreover, they are not like each other (although there are similarities between them, especially when compared with Indians). Both Pakistan and Bangladesh were part of India when that country obtained its independence from Britain in 1947. At that time, Pakistan was divided into several states, including Kashmir and the Punjab; and Bangladesh was known as East Bengal. However, these regions were primarily Muslim, while India is primarily Hindu, and therein lay the problem. And although Bengalis were Muslims like their Western cousins, life in the eastern, tropical region of Bengal, on the border of Burma (now Myanmar) and Southeast Asia, was very different from the more central Asian world of the Pakistani, and East Pakistanis often felt like second-class Muslims when compared with their West Pakistani cousins. Pakistan and Bangladesh today are independent countries, different politically, but culturally similar, and united in their Islamic difference with regard to Hindu India.

Some Historical Context

The major river that runs through Pakistan, from the mountains in the north to the Arabian Sea in the south, is the Indus; and its valley has been the source of civilizations for thousands of years. After 700 A.D., waves of Arabs brought Islam to the area, establishing it in the southern and western Sind region. Islam spread rapidly, and has been the predominant religious and cultural influence ever since. As Islam moved eastward across the subcontinent, it also took root in eastern Bengal through the Sufi sect (a mystical wing of Islam that seeks a more spiritual knowledge of Allah, in addition to a cognitive understanding of the Koran), which became a small enclave of Muslim life in the otherwise Hindu Indian world. Once India was independent, Muslims demanded their own independent homeland (no doubt in fear of being dominated by the vastly larger Hindu population, and against the wishes of Mahatma Gandhi, who fervently believed in an India that would allow for a diversity of religious beliefs under the protective umbrella of a secular, modern republic—it was not to be). Pakistan was created with Bengal forming its eastern province. However, Bengalis, while united in many ways with their West Pakistani cousins, chafed under the political thumb of Islamabad, and rejected West Pakistani rule in 1971. A fierce civil war ensued, and millions of Muslim Bengalis fled back into India, which used the situation to enter the war on the side of East Pakistan and routed the West Pakistani troops. The new People's Republic of Bangladesh was then created as a Muslim homeland in the east. Today, both Bangladeshis and Pakistanis share many common Islamic customs and cultural characteristics, but Bangladeshis have a special relationship with India and are, in many ways, dependent on their Indian neighbors. Pakistanis, on the other hand, are fierce enemies of the Hindu-led Indian state. When Muslims and Hindus rattle their sabers, it is mainly Pakistani Muslims and Indian Hindus, with the Bangladeshis in an ambivalent middle ground. Sikhs and other groups sometimes use the Hindu-Muslim conflict in the region as an excuse to advance their own causes, throwing their weight in the direction of one side or the other—and sometimes neither—as their self-interest dictates.

An Area Briefing

Politics and Government

Today, Pakistan is technically a democracy, but one which is legally, culturally, and politically subordinate to the law of Islam, as interpreted by Islamic leaders. The government is comprised of a nominally representative bicameral parliament, modeled after Britain's, and a prime minister. There is no monarchy or royalty. Islamic law is supreme in Pakistan, and has effectively limited the role of democratic government. Further destabilizing any hopes for democracy, Pakistan has depended on its military to solve serious sovereignty issues ever since its inception, ranging from the continuing preoccupation with the perceived threat of an Indian invasion, to territorial disputes with both India and China over the Punjab region, to apprehension and then involvement with Afghan rebels. Politics is always local, and is rife with corruption; the country has become the domain of a few powerful families. Economically, the country is in a state of collapse for a variety of reasons (many of which were exacerbated by Western exploitation, or so many Pakistanis believe). Banking scandals brought the financial system to a halt in recent years, and with the imposition of Islamic law (which prohibits the practice of charging interest), the system remains closed to global finance options. Bangladesh has not fared much better, often being the unfortunate target of nature's fury (topographically, it is a nation under water, as it is mainly the basin for the mouth of the Ganges River as it flows into the Bay of Bengal) in the form of torrential tropical cyclones and massive flooding, and the accompanying hardships that a developing agrarian nation must endure in the face of such calamities. Bangladesh, however, has developed cultural, economic, and social relationships with India and its other neighbors, so that it is not isolated in the way Pakistan has become, and is singularly less involved with military defensiveness and saber rattling.

Schools and Education

Although schooling is free and mandatory for all elementary-grade children, and there are local equivalents of high school after grade school, education is not a practical option for the majority of the people in either state at this time. Poverty and daily life make it imperative that children assist in supporting the family, and the educational system in Pakistan does little more than provide basic literacy and math tools in the context of Islamic religious catechism. Wealthy Pakistanis and Bangladeshis usually advance their education abroad, with some returning home to the family business. English is the language taught in schools; Arabic is taught as well in Pakistan.

Religion and Demographics

The religious influence in both countries is overwhelmingly Islam, and both Sunni and Shiite believers are represented. There is a small minority of Hindus, Christians, and other religious groups in both countries. Bengalis are the major ethnic group in Bangladesh, while in Pakistan, the ruling majority group has always been the Punjabis (they are usually the leaders of business and government). In Pakistan, there are also Sinds and Baluchis.

Islam is the youngest of the West's three great religious traditions, beginning with Judaism and Christianity. As a Western religion, it is linked to the Judeo-Christian belief system and rejects Hinduism as "pagan" and not "of the book," or codified. Incorporating both Judaism and Christianity into its system of beliefs, Islam claims that it is the final revelation of a monotheistic God, as revealed to the world through the prophet Muhammad, and that previous "messiahs," such as Jesus and Moses, are merely prophets, along with Muhammad, proclaiming the word of God. Muslims do not follow Muhammad (therefore, they are not Muhammadans, a derogatory term created by Westerners who did not understand Islam); they follow Allah, the Arabic term for the same God worshiped by Christians and Jews. Muhammad and his followers wrote down the law of God as revealed to them in the Koran (or Qu'ran), the Islamic holy book. It does not negate the Old or New Testaments: it merely provides, in the eyes of the Muslim faithful, the final required text. Islam spread rapidly throughout the Middle East, into Europe, and eastward across Asia, reaching India around the tenth century, and fully flowering into the great Mogul Empire in India around the fourteenth century. In Pakistan, it entered the Indus Valley region soon after its beginnings in Mecca, and established itself in the Sind area. While Islam underwent a serious split almost immediately following Muhammad's death (two major camps emerged, the Shia and the Sunni, in an effort to decide how to continue the faith), it nevertheless rapidly gathered huge followings. Sunni Muslims believe that the caliphs, or religious leaders, who took control after Muhammad's death are legitimate. Shiite Muslims believe that the caliphs who took control after Muhammad's death were usurpers, and therefore reject Sunni authority. All Muslims must abide by five basic tenets, or Pillars of Faith:

- Proclaim the supremacy of the one true God, Allah, above all others
- Pray to Allah five times daily
- Observe Ramadan, the holy month, the ninth month of the Islamic calendar, which is essentially a celebration of the time when God revealed his word to Muhammad

- Give alms to the poor and needy
- Perform the hajj, or spiritual (and physical) journey to Mecca at least once in their lifetime, if they are capable of doing so

Specific codes of conduct have developed over time, and have been codified into Islamic law, known as the Shari'a. The degree to which one follows these scriptures often determines how devoutly one applies the Islamic ethical code to day-to-day life. Generally, Pakistan applies Islamic law more fundamentally and Bangladesh applies it more liberally.

Women in both countries have an unequal role with men in society; their traditional role as homemaker and nurturer is often seen as superior to the man's role at home, but subordinate to men in the public world. Educated and Westernized Pakistani and Bangladeshi women might have some professional opportunities in education, in medicine, and in politics, but typically not in business. It can be difficult for Western businesswomen who do not establish acceptance of their authority ahead of time to be effective in this male-dominated business environment.

Fundamental Cultural Orientations

1. What's the Best Way for People to Relate to One Another?

OTHER-INDEPENDENT OR OTHER-DEPENDENT? There is a combination of deep concern for family, clan, and other membership groups that defines an individual (such as work and religion), and individual expression. Individuals are responsible for themselves, within their group, but individual initiative must be justified as producing results that will benefit others, and must ultimately involve others if it is to succeed. All action should conform with essential Islamic ideas.

HIERARCHY-ORIENTED OR EGALITY-ORIENTED? Individual expression, however, is not the same as individual empowerment, which is defined solely by one's position in society. The caste system was prominent in this region historically and, even though it is not acknowledged in this non-Hindu culture, has laid down traditions of rigid hierarchy, as a way of organizing society, that have been subsequently supported by Islamic beliefs. This hierarchical orientation is mirrored at all levels of society: in the home, at school, on the streets, and at work. It does not require deference to individuals, but it does require submission to authority, be it organizational or religious. Always start at the highest possible levels, and be sensitive to the fact that your position and authority are being judged. Bureaucracies in both countries are labyrinthine and can be mystifying and ultimately frustrating. Historically, the government in both countries is the biggest employer and biggest customer; you will have to deal with bureaucrats and the resulting army of entrepreneurs who will, for a fee (known as *basket*), guide you through the maze. A strong formality has developed in which people are treated according to their rank and status. Unlike the Pacific Rim countries, where the emphasis is on humility, one's rank in the system in

Pakistan (and slightly less so in Bangladesh) is demonstrated by the expression of authority from above and the deference shown to such authority from below. There is less concern for face: there is greater concern for knowing one's place and acting accordingly. This emphasis on hierarchy also normalizes unequal relationships: it is, after all, natural that some be in charge and others not, that some have power and others not, that some dictate and others follow. Those above absolutely make the decisions for those below, and those ultimately in charge in Pakistan currently are Islamic mullahs, or priests, and the military.

RULE-ORIENTED OR RELATIONSHIP-ORIENTED? Practically, immediate situations determine decisions and action; this means that there is a strong dependence on knowing the right people, and on accepting the benefits of influence. Many of the Western codes, structures (legal, political, and education systems, for example), and standards by which behaviors were to be judged have been replaced in Pakistan by Islamic standards and codes (somewhat less so in Bangladesh). Essentially, subjective behavior based on personal relationships is the typical orientation, justified against Islamic codes of behavior.

2. What's the Best Way to View Time?

MONOCHRONIC OR POLYCHRONIC? Both countries are essentially very polychronic, due to the influence of both agrarian and religious traditions, and the difficulties in effective control and organization posed by the general environment in developing nations. The clock is definitely not the determinant of action, although it plays a role, most certainly, particularly in the larger, more modern urban areas, and there is an acceptance of Western organizational ideas. Nevertheless, there is forgiveness for the inevitable delays and understanding when things don't go as planned or scheduled; people may or may not show up at invited events, things may or may not happen as planned. Muslim laws can even view planning too far into the future as heretical, for it presumes that individuals can control events that are essentially in the hands of Allah. Even today, schedules tend to be loose and flexible; the workday begins around 9 A.M. and ends around 4 P.M. Most workers take an hour break and a midafternoon nap after lunch.

RISK-TAKING OR RISK-AVERSE? Pakistanis and Bangladeshis can take risks when in positions of authority, but avoid them when they are not. Within castes, families, and organizations, the decision makers can be bold, even reckless, but subordinates generally are not, and take action only when instructed to do so, making sure every detail is in place before moving forward. Therefore, comfort with uncertainty, in general, is low, and much information may need to be exchanged with different people before decisions can be made; however, this is rarely to develop consensus but rather to force the appropriate individual to make the ultimate decision. Because this may be done with individuals who have no incentive to facilitate the business themselves, this can be a slow and frustrating experience.

PAST-ORIENTED OR FUTURE-ORIENTED? There is a distinct and inherent fatalism regarding the effect of human action. Nevertheless, those empowered by virtue of their position are expected to make the decisions that keep the world running. Therefore, future benefits often do not motivate most Pakistanis or Bangladeshis; doing nothing, or doing things for the here and now, are more relevant, and if things do not work out, that is to be expected—no one controls the universe, and all is ultimately determined. As a Westerner, however, you will be seen as someone who does have resources at your command, and you will be expected to provide them in order to assist in the progress of a particular project. There is a deep belief that things will take the time they need to take, and that ultimately only Allah knows what that is.

3. What's the Best Way for Society to Work with the World at Large?

LOW-CONTEXT DIRECT OR HIGH-CONTEXT INDIRECT COMMUNICATORS? Pakistanis and Bangladeshis are generally indirect in their communication styles, with both outsiders and insiders. They generally avoid direct confrontation, and believe it is unseemly for individuals to act emotionally. Much information is conveyed, therefore, in the context in which a situation occurs, rather than in the words that are spoken. There is much use of symbolic speech. Occasionally, when authority and context permit, those in charge can be very direct with subordinates, but never the other way around.

PROCESS-ORIENTED OR RESULT-ORIENTED? Associative and subjective experience-based logic predominates in most situations, judged against a backdrop of Islamic codes of behavior.

FORMAL OR INFORMAL? Both societies are formal and ritualized, and each group has its own way of honoring the hierarchies, establishing respect and deference, and following (or not following) through on their responsibilities. They are even more formal when one is on the outside or beginning to establish relationships with the in-group.

Greetings and Introductions

Language and Basic Vocabulary

There are two official languages—Urdu and English—in Pakistan, with Punjabi, Pashtu, Baluchi, Sind, and others spoken locally; in Bangladesh, the two official languages are English and Bengali. In both countries, most businesspeople speak English, although the English they learned is British English, not American English in most cases; the differences between British English and the English spoken by other English speakers, particularly Americans, can be considerable (please see the chapter on England in *The Global Etiquette Guide to Europe* for further language information).

Here are some basic Urdu phrases (the *x* is pronounced like a guttural *ch*):

Salaam alayekum	Greetings! And peace be with you.
Wa alayekum salaam	And peace be with you.
Aap ka kaisa mizaaj hai?	How are you? (formal)
Kyaa haal hai?	How are you? (informal)

Aap se mil kar bardi xushi hui?	I am very pleased to meet you (formal)
Inshallah	God willing (this is a very common expression, used after most responses to questions: it indicates one's submission to greater will)
Aap ka isme-e sharif kyaa hai?	What is your name? (formal)
ji ha-a	yes, or a general affirmative
ji nah-i	no, or a general negative
ji?	excuse me
ma-af kijiye	pardon me, please
koi baat nah-i	you're welcome; that's okay
xuda hafez	God be with you; good-bye

Honorifics for Men, Women, and Children

Because Arabic was the language in which the Koran was written, it is considered by many to be a holy language. In both countries, but particularly in Pakistan, names will be Arabic in content, but structured according to the fairly complex and sometimes differing regional traditions. In Bangladesh, names may contain Indian-sounding elements, as well as clearly Arabic elements.

Most people have several names, with the family name (surname) being placed either first or last. Other names used may refer to one's role in the family (such as son) or an honorary association with an important or meaningful person (often a reference to an important person in Islamic history). It is important to address Pakistanis by their surnames, not their given or any other relational names, only. When introduced, you will generally be told whether the surname is the first or last. If you do not know, use the first and last name together when referring to an individual (in most cases, a full name will contain no more than three customary names).

The honorific *sahib* (Mr.) is placed after the surname: for example, Ali Muhammad Rahman is referred to as Rahman Sahib. The honorific *begum* (Mrs.) is placed after the surname: for example, Benazir Asmah Azi is referred to as Azi Begum.

If Benazir marries Ali, she would be referred to either by her current family name plus *begum*, not indicating marital status, or, if she wanted to indicate her marital status, as Mr. Rahman's Begum.

Muslim males who have made the hajj often use the honorific *hajji* as a title after the surname, replacing or preceding *sahib*. A similar pattern occurs if there are titles, such as doctor (although Pakistanis and Bangladeshis will rarely introduce themselves with their titles: you might see this on their business cards, however). For example, Rahman Hajji Sahib, or Rahman Hajji, may also be called Rahman Doctor Sahib.

Muslim females who have made the hajj often use the honorific *hajja* as a title after the surname, replacing or preceding *begum*. For example, Azi Hajja Begum, or Azi Hajja, may also be called Azi Doctor Begum.

The What, When, and How of Introducing People

Pakistanis may, upon greeting you, call you by your last or first name, with or without your title. Always wait to be introduced to strangers; never take that responsibility upon yourself, as doing so is considered inappropriate most of the time. Pakistanis and Bangladeshis are most comfortable with third-party introductions, and because business is typically very personal, you will need an individual to connect you to the people you need to meet. Never presume to seat yourself at a gathering: if possible, wait to be told where to sit. The seating arrangements have usually been carefully worked out in advance, and in most cases reflect the status of the individuals in the group and the honor that is being accorded the guests. When departing, it is important to say farewell to every individual present: the American group wave is not appreciated. Once you greet someone you will encounter later that day in the same circumstances (e.g., at the office), you do not need to greet them when you see them again. Seniors, or those who are obviously the oldest in a group, are greeted first, seated first, and allowed to enter a room first (usually at the center of a group, however, and preceded in most cases by their younger aides).

Physical Greeting Styles

Like many Asian cultures, both countries are essentially nontouching cultures at first with Westerners. Only the most intimate of friends (mainly young people) will touch each other casually. Close associates and businesspeople who have developed intimate working relationships often greet each other warmly, with hugs and kisses; this is never done between men and women, however. Wait until your Pakistani or Bangladeshi host initiates this behavior before responding. Typically, the greeting here is the *salaam*, which involves a soft handshake with the right hand, after which you may bring your hand back to your heart and touch it, for an extra sign of sincerity. Traditionally, the salaam was performed by quickly touching your forehead first, then your heart, then the front of your abdomen with your right hand as you bowed slightly; this is still done on very formal occasions. Muslim women and men do not touch or shake hands (unless the woman is very Westernized). The handshake, which was introduced to the region by the British, is soft, almost limp sometimes. This does not signify insincerity; rather, it is an accommodation to the Western tradition while indicating humility. Let your Pakistani or Bangladeshi colleague initiate any handshakes. A version of the Indian *namaste* is sometimes used in more formal, conservative situations, but instead of saying *"Namaste,"* the Urdu word, *"Namaskaran,"* is used. You are advised not to initiate this, but merely respond to it if it is done to you first; as a Westerner from abroad, if you initiate this, the locals may think you do not know the difference between Hindu and Muslim customs. Never greet Pakistanis or Bangladeshis with a *namaste*.

The traditional Pakistani or Bangladeshi business introduction also includes the exchange of business cards. Always take a large supply of business cards with you: you should give one to every new person you are introduced to (there is no need to provide another business card when you are meeting someone again unless information about you has changed, such as a new address, contact number, or position). Be sure your business cards are in fine shape: they are extensions of you as a person, and must look as good as possible. Embossed cards are extremely impressive. Never hand out a dirty, soiled, bent, or written-on card. You do not need to translate your business card into Urdu or Bengali in either country, as English is well understood.

When presenting a business card, you give it to your Pakistani or Bangladeshi colleague so that it is readable for him as you hold it (he, in turn, will present his card so that it is readable for you); you should hold the card with two hands in the upper corners as you present it. Do not worry too much about who receives and gives their business card first: the exchange is very quick, and because you would probably not be introduced to that person in the first place if you were not already seen as having an equivalent rank, there is no need to show deference. There is also no need for bowing.

Smiling and other nonverbal forms of communication usually accompany the card exchange in Bangladesh, but this is not necessarily the case in Pakistan; Pakistani businesspeople are known as having a serious demeanor. Information about each other's status is the most important information to be exchanged, and this is provided directly on the business card, as well as indirectly through a number of high-context indicators, such as gray hair (a sign of age and seniority), gender (male), and the number of people surrounding and assisting the other person (usually, more important people have assistants). Should you meet more than one individual at a reception, you will have a handful of cards when the greetings are over.

As the business card exchange usually precedes a sit-down meeting, it is important to arrange the cards you have received in a little seating plan in front of you along the top of the desk or the table at your seat, reflecting the order in which people are seated. This will help you connect the correct names with the correct individuals throughout the meeting. Do this even if you are just meeting one person; it is expected. During the meeting, it is important never to play with the business cards (do not write on them), and when the meeting is over, never put them in your back pants pockets: pick them up carefully and respectfully, and place them neatly in your cardholder (a nice-looking brass card case would be perfect), then place the cardholder in the left inside jacket pocket of your suit (nearest your heart).

Communication Styles

Okay Topics / Not Okay Topics

Okay: anything that reflects your personal interests and hobbies, and your curiosity about things native to the region, like its food or its history. *Not okay:* Politics, current events, or any subject that might in any way be controversial needs to be avoided at first. Do not inquire about a person's occupation or income in casual conversation, although it may be inquired of you (if so, this is just a way of getting to know more about your country, and not a personal investigation: answer specifically, but fully, with an explanation as to what things cost at home, why you do what you do, etc.). Do not inquire about your colleague's family life, especially spouses or the role of servants and household help. Do not give your opinions about Indians, Arabs, Jews, important families, or political corruption. Do not talk about sex, or tell dirty jokes: it is in very bad taste. Never discuss religion, and be very careful to eliminate all casual references to God or other religious figures from your vocabulary ("God, it's a hot day!" is *not* good). Discussions about your company and its work are very much appreciated, as it gives the Pakistanis and Bangladeshis a chance to learn more about you and your firm. The goal of all conversation, at least at the beginning, is to create and maintain a harmonious atmosphere, despite the difficult or confrontational nature of the topic being discussed. At first, speak about things that you believe you have in common, so that you can build a personal connection that will go far toward maintaining a harmonious bridge between you. This is appropriate for both individuals and organizations.

Tone, Volume, and Speed

The people of these cultures generally speak in soft, quiet, and restrained tones. Pakistanis tend to speak in voices that are pitched slightly lower than their Indian neighbors. They may speak rapidly, but if you, in turn, speak rather slowly, they may get the hint and slow down.

Use of Silence

Passive silence—allowing time to pass simply, without words—can be a form of proactive communication, and is used as a nonverbal way of avoiding confrontation, disagreement, or an unpleasant subject. If confronted with an unexplainable silence, gently coax the conversation in a different direction, one that is more mutually harmonious.

Physical Gestures and Facial Expressions

You are advised to reduce the amount of body language you use. Winking, whistling, and similar displays are considered very vulgar. Public displays of familiarity and affection with the opposite sex are rarely if ever expressed. Never touch anyone, including a child, on his or her head: this is considered the holiest part of the body. Do not point with or intentionally show the sole of your shoe to anyone: this is considered vulgar, as the bottom of the shoe touches the ground, and is therefore the dirtiest part of the body. Any gesture involving a closed fist is considered quite vulgar. Standing with your hands on your hips is considered very aggressive and should always be avoided. Do not give donations to anyone on the street, as this only encourages others. Philanthropic intentions should be expressed by making donations to reputable local charities.

For any action or gesture that would naturally be done only with one hand, do not use your left hand, as this is considered the unclean hand (the hand used for personal hygiene). Pass all documents, food, and money *only* with your right hand (if you're a southpaw, you will have to practice this). You must remove your shoes before entering a mosque, and you will need to wash your feet and hands at the ground fountain provided before entering as well. Women may be restricted to specific areas and times when visiting mosques. Women entering mosques need to have their heads covered, and their legs covered below the knees, and their arms covered below the elbows; Western women do not need to have their faces covered.

Waving and Counting

The pinkie represents the number 1, the thumb represents the number 5, with everything in between ordered from the pinkie down; however, instead of raising the fingers when counting, the whole hand is exposed, and each finger is depressed as the counting is done. It is very insulting to motion to someone with the forefinger (instead, turn your hand so that your palm is facing down and motion inward with all four fingers at once). If you need to gesture for a waiter, very subtly raise your hand. Waving or beckoning is done with the palm down and the fingers moving forward and backward in a kind of scratching motion. It may seem as if the person making this gesture is saying good-bye to you, when in fact you are being summoned over. If you need to point to something or someone, close your fingers, open your palm and face it upward, and pass your hand in the direction you want to indicate.

Physicality and Physical Space

Most Pakistanis and Bangladeshis stand just a little closer than North Americans typically do; resist the urge to move back. Never, upon first greeting someone, touch him or her beyond the soft handshake: no backslaps, no hugging, no kissing, ever. Never speak with your hands in your pockets: always keep them firmly at your side when standing. If men and women must cross their legs when they sit, it must never be ankle over knee (for women, the preferred style is to cross ankle over ankle) and the bottoms of the shoes must not show to the other person. Remember, in public, formal is always better than informal: no gum chewing, *ever;* don't slouch; and don't lean against things. About the only time the nonphysicality rule is broken in Pakistan is on public transport, where it is very crowded and touching is unavoidable, or on crowded streets, where you are very likely to be poked and prodded as people jostle by.

Eye Contact

Eye contact is very indirect, especially between strangers. Interest in what one's supervisor is saying is shown by averting the eyes, not by making eye contact. The eyes are used extensively to convey true feelings in formal situations where it may be difficult to express your thoughts verbally. Tune up your nonverbal antennae.

Emotive Orientation

Pakistanis and Bangladeshis are seen as restrained and serious at first; perhaps even stern. This does not mean they are not warm or caring, but feelings are not demonstrated on the outside immediately around people one does not know.

Protocol in Public

Walking Styles and Waiting in Lines

On the street, in stores, and in most public facilities, little attention is paid to maintaining orderly lines. Due to the volume of passengers on public transportation, there can be much pushing and jostling. This is not to get into a train or a bus ahead of someone else, though; it is merely to get in!

Behavior in Public Places: Airports, Terminals, and the Market

Customer service is not a well-developed practice; unless and until you establish a personal relationship with a shopkeeper, you can expect little assistance as a newcomer. Service is perfunctory, at best, in most stores and restaurants. Stores in the cities are open in the evenings and on weekends, as well as during the day, but are closed during the Muslim Sabbath (Friday) and in preparation for it (Thursday nights), and on all Muslim holidays. A personal thank-you to store owners, waiters, chefs, and hotel managers for their services is important, as it will help establish the relationship you need to get good service the next time. In food markets, do not touch the produce unless you intend to buy it; in goods stores, if you buy a product and have problems with it, returning the item is usually difficult. Smoking is endemic, and you may have difficulty finding a no-smoking area on public transportation, in restaurants, and in other public places (be sure not to smoke during Ramadan, when Muslims abstain; this is true for eating and drinking during the day during Ramadan, as well, when in the presence of observant Muslims). Bathroom facilities can range from Western-style toilets to Asian-style toilets (holes in the floor, with buckets of water or hoses attached to a water line for cleanup instead of paper); be prepared.

Unless they are in the company of other women or close male relatives, women generally do not go out in public. Western women traveling alone in these countries will place an unusual burden of consideration on the behavior of others toward them: If you are a Western woman, many Muslims won't know what to do or how to act toward you; other women will want to assist you; and certain men, no doubt, will try to take advantage of you. Traveling alone in Pakistan and Bangladesh is not a good idea for women.

When answering a telephone, say "Hello" or just your given name. Cell phones are ubiquitous, as the wire networks may be unreliable or nonexistent.

Bus / Metro / Taxi / Car

Driving is on the left, and whether in the country or city, being in a car can be hazardous to your health. The roads are not necessarily in good repair, marked, or where maps say they are; and obtaining fuel when and where you need it can be a problem. There are dangerous areas in the major cities and in the countryside, where guerrillas (in Pakistan) may be active. Driving in the countryside puts you at risk for being stopped, ambushed, or mugged. City traffic is maddening and chaotic, and construction sites (and the occasional monsoon flood) are everywhere.

Buses usually stop running after 11 P.M. or midnight. The best way to catch a cab is at designated taxi stands (hotels are good places, but often charge more for the same ride: a hotel surcharge is added to the meter fare, in some cases). When a taxi has been hailed, negotiate the price, as the meter may or may not be working (even if it is, it doesn't always matter). Whenever possible, have the address you need to get to written down on a piece of paper (or use the business card of the person you are going to see, if you can) before you hail the cab. A small map outlining the route is great, if you can have one prepared before you go. Taking open motorbikes is not a good idea.

Tipping

Tipping is universally required, everywhere you can imagine—and then some. Tips in restaurants run about 10 percent and are typically not included in the bill (but double-check to be sure); a separate tip is not necessary if you have negotiated the fare for the taxi ahead of time and already figured in the tip. For everything else, a few coins is all that is needed, but you should always have a lot of spare change handy to see you through the day.

Punctuality

Punctuality is valued, but not required. For business meetings, be on time if you can, but don't worry if you are ten or fifteen minutes late; for social occasions, being up to a half hour late is fine. Making a general comment about the weather or the traffic is all you need to do to get off the hook for being late.

Dress

The standard in both countries for business is more or less Western, but the main concern is the climate: it is hot and tropical most of the year. Therefore, many businessmen do not wear suits or jackets during the summer months, and a lightweight suit, or a jacket with tie, is fine at other times, although a dark business suit is required for formal events. Short-sleeved dress shirts are also acceptable. None of this is an invitation to informality: it is just an adaptation to the weather. Businesswomen wear lightweight skirts and blouses, or long pants. Women need to be especially careful not to wear skirts that are too short: they need to go clearly below the knees. Wear dress slacks, not jeans or khakis. Social dress is the same, although sometimes clean, pressed jeans are okay with a dress or sport shirt (but no T-shirts!). Sneakers are only for the street or gym; shorts are never okay, on the street or elsewhere. Muslim traditions dictate that women dress so that their legs are covered below the knee, their arms are covered below the elbow, and their torsos are covered from their necks to their waists. Some Muslim women cover their faces, others do not; nonpracticing Western women need not cover their faces. Wearing the *salwar kameez,* a traditional Pakistani dress for women, is perfectly fine for Western women as well (it is similar to an Indian sari).

Remember, if you visit mosques, you will need to remove your shoes and walk barefoot while inside.

Seasonal Variations

There are two extreme seasons in Pakistan and Bangladesh: wet and hot, and dry and hot (with the exception of the towns in the mountains in the north, where the weather can be temperate to cool). The important thing is to remember the frequent downpours and the periodic monsoons; take an umbrella with you everywhere you go.

Colors

Wear neutral colors whenever possible. Do not wear white or black only, as to do so indicates you are in mourning or going to a funeral. Orange-yellow (or saffron) is a preferred color, as is green, the color of Islam, when it is used tastefully.

Styles

For the most part, clothing is simple, adapted to the climate, and meant to keep one looking good and cool. Consider, however, that some places may be air-conditioned to arctic levels, so you might always want to have a lightweight covering available.

Accessories / Jewelry / Makeup

Makeup, hairstyle, and accessories are important for women, but only if they are used modestly. Perfume and cologne are popular, but usually are not made with alcohol (alcohol is prohibited in Islam).

Personal Hygiene

In this part of the world cleanliness is associated with purity. Washing both hands and feet more than once a day is very common. There is a real concern for smelling good, but what smells good and bad to the locals may be different from the Westerners. Throughout the region, the smell of meat (particularly red meat) on individuals is offensive, while there is usually no concomitant concern for the smell of other foods, such as garlic and seafood, or natural human body odors. Do not blow your nose in public: it is considered very rude. Spitting does occur on the street, but it is also regarded as rude. Muslim men may sport facial hair, usually in the form of a mustache. At the end of a meal, if you use a tooth-pick, you must cover the "working" hand with the other hand, so that others cannot see your mouth. Remember that Muslims consider dogs very unclean; therefore, do not refer to them or bring them along with you.

Dining and Drinking

Mealtimes and Typical Foods

The typical diet in these countries is similar to the rest of the subcontinent, with an emphasis on grains, breads, and yogurts in Pakistan, and an emphasis on spiced and sweetened foods in Bangladesh. Meats will include lamb, goat, and chicken. The cuisine revolves mainly around the local foods, especially fresh vegetables (including lentils, cauliflowers, and beans), pickled and preserved vegetables (in the form of pickles, chutneys, curries, etc.), seafood, rice, and breads. Although people in this region are becoming increasingly familiar with Western food, Pakistanis and Bangladeshis love their own cuisine, and most enjoy a fine local meal (if you are hosting them in your country, unless they directly express an interest in trying a local cuisine, take them to the best local Indian-Pakistani restaurant you can find, and tell the restaurant manager that you are hosting some Pakistani or Bangladeshi nationals: the restaurant management will usually go out of its way to make the meal very fine for you). Avoid Western food, especially hamburgers and cheese: the tastes are unpleasant for many Muslims. You, as a guest, may be rewarded with favored parts of the animal, such as the goat's eye or head: this is an honor that needs to be acknowledged before the food is rejected (if you cannot bring yourself to partake, acknowledge the honor, and suggest that while you will always hold the honor in your heart, you in turn will bestow it on someone who can better appreciate it in their belly: then pass the honored dish on to a Pakistani or Bangladeshi). Not all foods are spicy and hot; more dairy products, in the form of yogurt and milk, are used in northern Pakistan. Fresh-baked breads of all kinds are ubiquitous. Most meals begin with tasty appetizers of fried dumplings and vegetables with associated dipping sauces.

Breakfast is served from about 7:30 to 9 A.M., and usually consists of tea and rice; the latter is usually served as a porridge-type cereal that can be flavored with any number of ingredients. Tea is usually drunk plain, but if you ask for milk or sugar, you will generally get some. But be careful not to request them in remote locations where they may be difficult to obtain: in this case, you run the risk of insulting your host's hospitality, and that is not a good thing. Yogurt and fruit drinks are sometimes served for breakfast.

Lunch was traditionally the main meal of the day, and even today in busy cities, it can still be an elaborate affair with several courses, or it can be a simple snack prepared and eaten in a matter of minutes. Lunch is served from about noon to 1 P.M., and consists of meat, fish, and/or vegetables, with rice or yogurt. Main dishes can be steamed, stir-fried, or boiled in a variety of different ways, either simply or more elaborately. Typically, the drinks served with lunch are soft drinks, fruit juices, and/or tea.

Dinner is served from 6 P.M. on, with 7 P.M. the customary late time. Even if the main meal of the day was lunch, dinner is only slightly lighter—this is often the case with families at home. The dinner menu is often similar to that of the more formal lunch. Dinner drinks are similar to those served at lunch. When you come to a Pakistani or Bangladeshi home, even for a brief visit, you will be served some sweet delicacy plus a cool drink (usually iced water, lemonade, or fruit juice) and/or tea. The sweet is not a dessert; you will get that at the end of the meal as well. In fact, sweets are so loved here that sweet pickles, chutneys, and sweet pastries are sold in sweet shops, where one can go for a tea or coffee and a sweet most any time.

Regional Differences

Most food on the subcontinent tastes hot and spicy to Westerners, although the degrees of spice and heat do vary, based on the regions and the foods. You can ask for the heat to be moderated when you order your foods. Pakistani and Bangladeshi cuisine incorporates hot and bland, sweet and salty, sweet and sour, with blends of textures as well—cool and creamy, crunchy and hot. Heat tip: don't douse the heat with water, tea, or juice. Liquid only spreads the heat throughout your mouth. Eat rice instead: the rice absorbs the capsaicin, the chemical in chilies and peppers that gives them their bite. Seafood is very common along the coasts, and preserved vegetables and rice dishes, often mixed with coconut, and, when available, chicken, are combined to create a variety of regional dishes. Remember, Islam prohibits the use of pork, and most meats of any kind for Muslims need to be prepared *halal* (according to Islamic health prescriptions). Do not eat in front of Muslim colleagues, or invite them to join you for a meal, during the day during Ramadan, as Muslims typically fast (and refrain from drinking and smoking) during the day, and feast with family and friends at night. Ramadan lasts for a lunar month: this is simply not a good time to do business or go out entertaining in either country.

Typical Drinks and Toasting

Tea is served everywhere, all the time. Sometimes it is boiling hot; sometimes it is lukewarm; most of the time it is served without milk or sugar. Always take the tea, even if you only put it to your lips or just take a few sips. Your cup will always be refilled if it is less than half full. Typically, beer and other alcoholic drinks are not served: fruit juices and lemonades, along with tea, accompany most meals. Because you must never pour your own drink (be it juice or tea), you must always be alert throughout the meal as to whether your neighbor's cup or glass needs refilling. If it is less than half full, it needs refilling; alternately, if yours is less than half full, your neighbor is obliged to refill it. If he or she does not, do not refill it yourself, for this will cause your neighbor to lose face; instead, diplomatically indicate your need by pouring a little more drink into your neighbor's glass, even if it doesn't really need it.

If you are the honored guest, you will be expected to make a toast, usually soon after the host does or at the end of the meal, just before everyone departs. An appropriate toast is to the health of the host and all those present, and to the prosperity of the business under discussion.

Avoid drinking tap water anywhere in Pakistan and Bangladesh (this means you should brush your teeth with bottled water and not take ice in any of your drinks; drink only bottled water, or brewed tea or coffee or soft drinks, and avoid getting water from the morning shower into your mouth; and never eat fresh fruits or vegetables that cannot be peeled first, and ideally cooked later before eating). This is a serious matter: there are some very nasty bugs going around in developing countries. Also, avoid all dairy products except in the finest hotels, as the required refrigeration may be questionable.

Table Manners and the Use of Utensils

Pakistani or Bangladeshi food is eaten with spoons, forks, and knives, if necessary, or with no utensils at all (mainly in more traditional Muslim restaurants). Since the spoon is more important than the fork, if you are right-handed, keep the spoon in your right hand, and put it down to switch to the fork if you need it: never use your left hand for eating, especially if you are eating directly with your hands.

What do you use at those times when no utensils are available? Why, eat with your fingers, of course! Many think it makes the experience more fun, maybe because you're adding an extra sense to an already very sensory experience: the sense of touch. The type of food eaten with the hands is known as "banana-leaf" food: wonderful vegetarian or meat curries, served with rice and sauce on a large banana leaf. No plates, no forks, no spoons, no chopsticks. You reach into the rice, take some with your fingers, gently roll it between your index and middle fingers and thumb (not your palms!) into a kind of self-sticking ball, dip it into the sauce on the banana leaf, mix it with a vegetable or a piece of chicken, then pop the whole thing in your mouth. Most of these hands-on banana-leaf restaurants are also vegan.

Here are some other things to note before eating in such restaurants:

• Wash your hands before you sit down to eat. Many banana-leaf restaurants have washrooms and sinks out in the open specifically for this purpose. (However, you may want to wash your hands with bottled water at the hotel first, since the water at the restaurant may be more hazardous to your health than the germs already on your hands!) You will also need to wash your hands again at the end of the meal, especially after eating the saucy dishes, since you've probably got a good bit of it running down your arm. Don't worry, it's to be expected: don't dress up if you're eating banana-leaf style.

• Use your right hand when picking up and eating food, never your left hand. Keep your left hand at your side. Do not place your left hand on the table, and do not pass food with your left hand.

• Pork will typically not be on the menu.

• Alcohol will usually not be served with the meal.

• Men and women, in some establishments, may be asked to dine separately.

• If you absolutely cannot eat without some kind of utensil, it's usually all right to ask for one in such establishments. The proprietors are usually more than pleased to accommodate Westerners.

Rice may be served in separate bowls, or on the same plate with your main dish. While rice is a staple, it is not necessary to eat every grain; leaving some over is fine. Do not take the last bit of food from a central serving plate; that means there will be none left in case someone else wants more. Also, a sauce may (in fact, should) be mixed with rice, and eaten together with the main dish. You are not expected to hold the rice bowl (if there is one) up by your mouth. Hot tea (*cha*) may be slurped quietly to cool it off as it enters the mouth.

Women should be careful not to directly touch food that is being served to a Muslim male, other than those who are her immediate relatives.

A word about smoking: it is ubiquitous throughout Asia, including Pakistan and Bangladesh. Usually, you do not smoke until the meal is over. In addition, at the end of some meals, fresh mints, caraway seeds, or betel nuts may be offered as a special treat after dessert (betel nuts produce, over time, a dark stain on the teeth).

Seating Plans

The host sits at the head of the table, with the honored guest seated next to the host. (Spouses are usually not invited to business meals in restaurants. Do not ask if your spouse can join you; it will embarrass your Pakistani or Bangladeshi colleague: however, your spouse might be invited to a meal at your colleague's home, especially if the spouse of the host will be there, which will probably be the case.) In addition, the honored guest sits on the side of the table farthest from the door. (At business meetings, the key people sit in the middle, flanked on either side in descending order by their aides, with the least important people sitting at the ends of the table farthest from the middle, and closest to the door;

the arrangement is mirrored on the other side.) Men and women eating at someone's home may dine in separate areas (and may spend the entire evening separated) or at separate times, with the men dining first.

Refills and Seconds

You will always be offered more food. Leave a bit on your plate if you do not want more food. You will be implored to take more two or three times, in the form of a little ritual. The game is as follows: first you refuse, then the host insists, then you refuse again, then the host insists again, and then you finally give in and take a little more. This is known as the *uzooma* (the seesaw dialogue of imploring, rejecting, and finally submitting). If you really don't want more, take very little and leave it on your plate. You may always have additional beverages; drink enough to cause your cup or glass to be less than half full, and it will generally be refilled. A reminder: never refill your own glass; always refill your neighbor's glass, and he or she will refill yours.

At Home, in a Restaurant, or at Work

The honored guest is served first, then the oldest man, then the rest of the men, then children, and finally women. Do not begin to eat or drink until the oldest man at the table has been served and has begun. At the end of the meal, it is appropriate to thank the host or hostess for a wonderful meal.

In informal restaurants, you may be required to share a table. If so, do not force conversation: act as if you are seated at a private table. Women should be sensitive to the fact that they may be seated only with other women. Waitstaff may be summoned by making eye contact; waving or calling their names is very impolite. The business breakfast is generally unknown in Pakistan or Bangladesh, and most business meals are lunches. Business meals are generally not good times to discuss business or make business decisions, however. Take your cue from your Pakistani or Bangladeshi associates: if they bring up business, then it's okay to discuss it, but wait to take your lead from their conversation.

When you are at a colleague's home for a formal meal, you will be invited to sit anywhere you like at the table; resist the impulse to sit down, and wait until your host gives you further instructions. These will generally come after the host or the oldest male is seated, and often you will be placed at his side. It is a great honor to be invited into a Pakistani or Bangladeshi home. Once invited in, you may need to remove your shoes (this is not the custom in restaurants, however). You will know when you approach the home and see a row of shoes at the door (keep your socks in good shape, and wear comfortable but well-made slip-ons for such occasions). Once inside the home, do not wander around: much of the house is really off-limits to guests. If you move from room to room in someone's home, be sure to always allow the more senior members of your party to enter the room ahead of you. Servants and household help are very common in middle- and upper-class homes; do not comment on them (or on how they are treated, as you might be shocked at how they seem to be ordered about), and do not offer to help: they are there to serve.

Being a Good Guest or Host

Paying the Bill

Usually the one who does the inviting pays the bill, although the guest is expected to make an effort to pay. Sometimes other circumstances determine the payee (such as rank). Making payment arrangements ahead of time so that no exchange occurs at the table is a very classy way to host, and is very common. Western businesswomen will not have a problem paying the bill at a restaurant, but be sure to make payment arrangements ahead of time, and don't wait for the check to arrive at the table.

Transportation

It's a very nice idea, when acting as the host, to inquire ahead of time as to whether your guests will require transportation. If necessary, you should arrange for taxi service at the end of the meal. When seeing your guests off, you must remain at the entrance of the house or the restaurant, or at the site where you deposited your guests into the car, until the car is out of sight: it is very important not to leave until your guests can no longer see you, should they look back. Guests are seated in cars (and taxis) by rank, with the honored guest being placed in the back directly behind the front passenger seat; the next honored position is in the back behind the driver, and the least honored position is up front with the driver.

When to Arrive / Chores to Do

If invited to dinner at a private home, do not offer to help with the chores: you are a guest, and the servant performs such tasks. You should not expect or ask to visit the kitchen. Do not leave the table unless invited to do so. When in the home, be careful not to admire something too effusively: Pakistanis and Bangladeshis may feel obligated to give it to you, and you in turn will be required to present them with a gift of equal value. Instead of saying things like "I love that vase," say something like "Vases that beautiful in my country are found only in museums." Your compliments will most likely be dismissed.

Gift Giving

In general, gift giving is common in many situations in Pakistan. It is not only done as a gesture of thanks, but as a way of helping to ensure good business relations in the future (be careful not to go overboard here, as a gift that looks like a bribe is not appreciated, and may land you in quite a bit of trouble . . . with the authorities in your home country, more than likely). Gift giving is not formal, but is common. In business settings, this usually takes the form of a personal gift that symbolically says the correct thing about the nature of the relationship. When going to Pakistan or Bangladesh on business, bringing a personalized gift for the key decision maker is enough. Your gift does not have to be elaborate or expensive. You present your gift when you arrive in the country;

before you leave to return home, you will receive a farewell gift at the last meeting. When Pakistanis or Bangladeshis visit your country, they will bring you a gift, and before they leave, you should give them gifts. Holiday cards are not that common.

The most appropriate gift for a personal visit to a home, or as a thank-you for dinner, would be a box of fruits, pastries, cakes, cookies, or other sweets. Flowers are typically not given as gifts, but if you must, avoid frangipani flowers, as these are used almost exclusively for funerals, or any flowers that are white, which is a funeral color. It is not necessary to send a handwritten thank-you note the day after the dinner party. If you are staying with a family, an appropriate thank-you gift would be a high-quality product that represents your country's culture and is difficult or expensive to get in these countries; this is also a good idea for a key business associate. Avoid gifts that carry political messages from or about the United States, as relations between the United States and these countries have been strained (the political and economic policies of the West are currently often seen as one of the reasons for these countries' dismal financial states). Practical but thoughtful gifts are most appreciated (stationery, kitchen/office gadgets, etc.). Be sure the gift you give does not have a tag or sticker on it that says it was made in the region.

If your gift consists of several items, be sure that the total number is an odd number. Avoid handkerchiefs, as they symbolize sadness, and cutlery, which symbolizes the severing of a relationship. A fine gift for a Muslim would be a silver compass, so that he will always know which direction to face when he says his daily prayers (Muslims must face Mecca no matter where they are when they say their prayers). Be sure not to give pork as food gifts to Muslims; also avoid alcohol, and any products that contain alcohol, including perfumes and colognes. Remember, any gift given by a man to a woman must come with the caveat that it is from both him and his wife/sister/mother, or else it is far too personal. For both giving and receiving gifts, two hands are always used. Gifts are typically not opened by the receiver in front of the giver; they are usually received after much imploring by you, graciously acknowledged, and placed aside to be opened once the giver is no longer present.

Gifts should be wrapped well. Typically, gifts are wrapped in ordinary paper first then wrapped again in green, saffron, or red; black and white both should be avoided because they are funeral colors (blue has little significance, but is simply not used very much).

Special Holidays and Celebrations

Major Holidays

April through October is not a good time to do business in Pakistan or Bangladesh, primarily due to the weather. Avoid the entire month of Ramadan. Many cities have different local holidays, as well, so double-check with your associates in these countries before making final travel plans.

January/February (lunar)	Ramadan (one full lunar month, celebrating when Muhammad received his first revelation)
March (lunar)	*Hari Raya Puasa* (end of Ramadan)
March 23 (solar)	Pakistan Day

May (lunar)	*Hari Raya Haji* (Islam commemoration of Abraham's sacrifice)
May 1 (solar)	Labor Day
May 31 (solar)	*Awal Muharam* (the Muslim New Year begins)
July 1 (solar)	Bank holiday
August 9 (lunar)	The Prophet Muhammad's Birthday
August 14 (solar)	Independence Day
September 6 (solar)	Defense of Pakistan Day
September 11 (solar)	Anniversary of the Death of Muhammad Ali Jinnah, founding father of Pakistan
November 9 (solar)	Igbal Day (birthday of the Pakistani poet Igbal, who was instrumental in Pakistan's independence)
December 25 (solar)	Birthday of Muhammad Ali Jinnah
December 31 (solar)	Bank holiday

Business Culture

Daily Office Protocols

The traditional Pakistani and Bangladeshi office has an open design; there are few doors, with the exception of the offices of those holding higher positions, and people work mainly in individual or shared cubicles. Doors, if they exist, are usually open. In the Pakistani/Bangladeshi business organization, hierarchy is strictly observed. Executives are usually placed on different floors from the rank and file. You probably will not be invited onto the working floors until the proposed project has been set in motion. Because faithful Muslims pray five times a day, you will need to adjust your schedules to accommodate their needs. Usually, prayers are given upon awakening and at noontime, midday, dusk, and before retiring; this means that twice during the workday, there will be time out for prayers. The prayer usually takes a short ten or fifteen minutes or so, and any quiet area will do. If you accidentally interrupt a Muslim during his prayers, just walk quietly away; there's no need for complicated explanations or apologies. Most organizations have prayer rooms set aside, with carpets. In addition, devout Muslims will not work on Friday (the Muslim Sabbath), and in fact begin to end work early on Thursday, before sundown. The official workweek is Saturday though Thursday, 9 A.M. to 4 P.M.

Management Styles

Because of the rigid rank and hierarchy orientation, titles are very important; the highest ones (e.g., vice president) are usually reserved for very senior, executive-level positions, and should not be used as casually as they are in the United States. Complimenting, rewarding, or criticizing employees publicly is done, but Westerners should abstain from this practice. Any criticism by Westerners must be done very carefully, even privately. Deference is shown by subordinates to their seniors; paternalistic concern is often shown by executives to their subordinates. As in many bureaucracies, the primary goal may be to protect oneself and one's position vis-à-vis one's superiors (as well as to protect one's superior) rather than to get immediate goals accomplished. This usually means that negotiations or projects can move very slowly at some times and rapidly at others.

Boss-Subordinate Relations

The decision-making system usually works from the top on down, with key decisions often coming from individuals in high positions of authority. While bosses do solicit input from trusted subordinates, this is strictly information gathering, and not necessarily consensus building. Superiors are expected to provide clear and fully informed instructions: that is their responsibility, and it is the responsibility of subordinates to carry out those instructions. Consequently, "management-by-objective" and other egalitarian and individually empowered management styles often may not work in this environment: without clear instruction from above, subordinates usually will do nothing. They also lose respect for the manager for not making the decisions he or she should be making.

Conducting a Meeting or Presentation

At your first meeting in these countries, you will probably be received in a very comfortable waiting area, which may or may not be where most of the meeting is conducted between yourself and your Pakistani or Bangladeshi colleague. If this is the case, you are merely being sized up, and your colleague is a gatekeeper. When serving refreshments in the office, be sure they are served in porcelain tea sets: the use of paper or Styrofoam shows disrespect and is very bad form. There may be several people in the room with you and your contact whom you may or may not be introduced to. These "ghost people" are probably trusted friends or relations of your Pakistani or Bangladeshi colleague, and he will no doubt want their input after the meeting. If you are not introduced to them, do not ask to be: acknowledge them with a smile and a nod, and proceed with your meeting. If you are meeting with a decision maker, the discussions will probably be direct, forthright, and businesslike. If this is just the beginning of a business relationship, expect to spend most of the time sharing information about your organization with different individuals, or repeating the same things to the same individual. This is okay; it means that your plans are advancing to the right people in the organization, and that those you have previously met with have approved of you and moved you on, and that you are building personal trust with the key decision maker. Business is personal in Pakistan: decision makers have got to know your face. Patience and third-party connections are key. This also means that you should start as high up in the organization as you possibly can.

Negotiation Styles

At first, expect few decisions from your colleagues at the table, and be willing to provide copious amounts of information, to the degree that you can, in response to their questions, and in anticipation of their needs. Presentations should be well prepared and simply propounded. Details are best left to questions and backup material, which can be written in English and left behind. Ideally, you should present your material to your colleagues for study, along with a proposed agenda, prior to the meeting. Have extra copies available, as you might meet more people than you will expect. Should you come with other team members, make sure that your roles are well coordinated. Never disagree with each other in front of Pakistanis or Bangladeshis, or appear uncertain, unsure, not authorized to make a decision, or out of control in any way.

Both Pakistanis and Bangladeshis love to bargain, and see this process as a way of getting to know you: it does not imply insincerity to offer one price and then change one's mind later (as it often does with Pacific Rim cultures). In fact, avoiding this process will generate suspicion. Final terms must be fair to all (win/win). Contracts and contract law are well known and understood; it is just that the infrastructure is not really in place to enforce this, and some disreputable groups might try to take advantage of this situation. Nevertheless, expect and insist on well-executed documents to finalize an agreement. Remember, the deal should be sealed with a celebratory meal. Keep communications, especially when at a distance, open and stay in touch often with your Pakistani or Bangladeshi associates: share more information than you normally would, not less; and, because business is so intimately connected with the government bureaucracy and because the political situation is so fluid, try to have a contact on the ground in Pakistan or Bangladesh who can always keep you informed of what is really going on, if you can.

Written Correspondence

Your business letters should be very formal and respectful of rank and hierarchy. Surnames usually are written in uppercase; dates are given using the day/month/year format (with periods in between, not slashes); and an honorific plus the title is as common as the honorific plus the last name. You should write your e-mails, letters, and faxes in a formal, precise way: open with a brief but warm introduction, then get down to business. Keep it simple, however, and outline all important matters. In Pakistan, you may use either the Asian or the Western format for addresses.

CHAPTER TWELVE

The South Asian Cultures: Sri Lanka and the Himalayan Kingdoms

SRI LANKA

Note: Please refer to the chapter on India for general South Asian behaviors and traditions; the additional information that follows describes specific Sri Lankan variations on these cultural behaviors.

Some Introductory Background on Sri Lanka and the Sri Lankans

Sri Lanka hangs like a small jewel at the tropical tip of India; but it is cracked and tarnished by a vicious ethnic division that has split the cultural patterns of this island country in two. The indigenous peoples, the Veddas, have fully blended into the larger society, so that their numbers are insignificant today, and there are small percentages of Christians and Catholics (remnants from European colonialism), and Muslim Moors. The majority of the people in Sri Lanka are Sinhalese, who are Buddhists. The northern part of the island—the tea country—is inhabited primarily by the Tamils, who are Hindus. And therein lies the essential division of the country. Using ancient differences as reasons for maintaining inequality and hatred, the Sinhalese and Tamils are classic enemies, and violence between the two groups erupts with unfortunate regularity. Visitors to this beautiful island, however, can enjoy themselves and develop positive relationships with all Sri Lankans by a careful observance of the customs and protocols of each group. By referring to the cultural patterns of Buddhists that can be found in the chapter on China, and by referring to the cultural patterns of Hindus that can be found in the section on India, one can obtain a detailed cultural road map for working effectively with both the Sinhalese and the Tamils.

Some Historical Context

Prince Vijaya, leading a group of Indo-Aryans from mainland India, established the first Sri Lankan empire in about 500 B.C., supplanting the indigenous Veddas. About seven hundred years later, Prince Mahinda introduced Buddhism to the island, which became a Buddhist bastion in South Asia even though Buddhism itself was driven out by the more powerful Hindus in India. The fact that Buddhism remained in Sri Lanka has always been a justification for Hindu reaction. In fact, a major Sri Lankan holiday celebrates a relic of the Buddha himself: his tooth is kept carefully preserved in a Buddhist shrine on the island. By the fifteenth century, the Europeans had discovered the island. The Catholic Portuguese came first, then the Dutch, and finally the English, which made Sri Lanka, then known as Ceylon, a British crown colony. After World War II, Ceylon was granted its independence. In 1972, the Republic of Sri Lanka was proclaimed.

However, during the period of British rule (and even before), ethnic Tamil Hindus from south India were brought into northern Sri Lanka to work the plantations. When Sri Lanka became independent, both the Tamils and the Sinhalese felt immensely threatened by the other, based on ancient religious rivalries and their historic economic relationship. Today, Sri Lanka has a parliamentary system of government, with no monarchy or royalty; yet it functions with difficulty at best, due to the problems between the Tamils and the Sinhalese. Recent events have scarred the island with violence: currently the Tamils are seeking an independent state of their own in northern Sri Lanka, and the Sinhalese oppose such a political division.

The British influence has made English the lingua franca for business, although most people on the street, Sinhalese or Tamil, do not use English on a day-to-day basis. Tamils speak Tamil, and Sinhalese speak Sinhalese; the two groups do not speak the other's language to each other. Written forms of both may appear similar to the illiterate eye: they are not. Do not present a business card translated into Tamil to a Sinhalese, or vice versa: unless you have two distinctly different sets of translated cards, use only English-language business cards. The Sinhalese are generally seen as the more individualistically minded of the two groups, with the Tamils being far more group oriented; both groups, for various reasons, subscribe to strong hierarchical values, with Tamils perhaps more inclined to such social organization due to the Hindu caste traditions. Sinhalese are seen more as the risk takers, with ethnic Tamils regarded by many Sinhalese as less capable usurpers. For both groups, subjective relationships and past personal experiences determine action, justified by each group's dislike for the other. Sri Lankan society is extremely polychronic: business appointments are often reduced to just one or two per day, and schedules and timetables are very fluid. Westerners, however, should be punctual, but must be prepared to wait; in this kind of polychronic environment, be sure to confirm appointments as often as possible. Both groups are extremely fatalistic, and it may be slicing hairs to say that the Buddhist Sinhalese have a slightly greater tendency to believe in their ability to control events.

Greetings and Introductions

Sri Lankan names are often multisyllabic and long. The name arrangements can be complex, as they involve both surnames (at either the beginning or end) or given names (usually in the middle); in addition, as is the case in Pakistan and elsewhere in Asia, certain names in the name set refer to the relationship between the individual and other individuals. You are usually safe in referring to either the first or the last name given, and it is perfectly acceptable to ask your Sri Lankan associate how he or she would prefer to be called. Alternatively, you may use the following honorifics independent of any name given, and it would be acceptable.

Sinhalese

• *Mahataya* (Sir) goes after the last name used: for example, Ranasinghe Premadasa is referred to as Premadasa Mahataya.
• *Nona* (Madame) goes after the last name used: for example, Sirima Bandaranaike is referred to as Bandaranaike Nona.

Tamil

• *Aiyaa* (father) goes after the last name, or stands alone without the name.
• *Ammaa* (mother) goes after the last name, or stands alone without the name.

In addition, Tamils may retain the honorific patterns of other Hindus in India, referring to themselves with one name, and preceding it with the initial of their father's first name.

The traditional Sri Lankan greeting is the *namaste,* which is used by all groups; however, while Tamils will say *"Namaste,"* Sinhalese will use the *namaste* gesture and say, in Sinhalese, *"Aibowan."*

Do not talk about one group with the other. In Sri Lanka, it is generally safe to reverse the meanings of head gestures, so that moving the head from left to right and back again, as in the Indian "wobble," is an affirmative gesture, while nodding the head up and down is a negative gesture (the chin is leading, while the head moves upward once or twice in a disparaging fashion). Be careful about smiling, as neither the Sinhalese nor the Tamils generally smile as much as many other Asians in casual contact. Casual smiles do not indicate the desire for smooth relationships, as they do, say, in Southeast Asia; in Sri Lanka, a casual smile exchanged with a stranger often indicates a desire for far more.

Dress

The Sri Lankan standard is very casual: suits and ties are rarely worn, but clothes must be clean and neat. Open-collared dress shirts for men and pants with a blouse for women are fine in business settings. This is due mainly to the intensely humid and hot climate, and is not a fashion statement. The style of both men's and women's clothing is very conservative in cut, color, and fabric. There is little that is excessive or striking about it.

Dining and Drinking

There are several dishes that are uniquely Sri Lankan, and that blend the native cuisines of India and the rest of neighboring Asia with those brought by the Europeans (particularly the British). Try the breads and pudding-style entrees made with grains and baked like a casserole. They strike most Westerners as surprisingly mild. Most dishes will be served without utensils, "banana-leaf" style. Remember, Hindus (Tamils) do not eat beef, while Buddhists (Sinhalese) have no such prohibitions. Tea is served throughout the day; in the workplace, there can be several tea breaks during the day (and they really are "breaks"—these are not cups of tea taken at the desk). Food is generally served from a central serving dish at mealtime; because of Hindu purity concerns, it is especially important with Tamils not to allow the serving utensil from the central serving dish to touch your plate. Never directly touch food that others might also partake of. Having seconds and thirds is much more preferable than serving yourself a great deal of food at once: to do so looks overwhelming and gross from the Sri Lankan perspective.

Gift Giving, Special Holidays and Celebrations, and Business Culture

Most holidays in Sri Lanka are religious festivals, either Hindu or Buddhist (please see the China and India chapters for more details); in most cases, they are celebrated only by the appropriate group. Recognize that Buddhist traditions will influence gift giving accordingly (please see the Buddhist gift-giving protocols in the China and Southeast Asia chapters); the same is true for Hindu traditions. Buddhist traditions also influence business decisions and behaviors (for example, there is a strong tendency among most Sri Lankans—Sinhalese Buddhists—to do things only at fortuitous times, in fortuitous places, with much concern placed upon numerology and astrology: you may have to wait for an auspicious time before your deal is signed, sealed, and delivered!). The Sri Lankan workday is typically Monday through Friday, from 8:30 or 9 A.M. to 4 or 4:30 P.M., but it is very flexible, and because there is no Hindu or Buddhist Sabbath, there is no one day that businesses are necessarily closed.

NEPAL AND BHUTAN

The mountain kingdoms of Nepal and Bhutan have been hidden from the rest of the world until very recently, not just by the topography, but also by the cultural distance of these lands. They are still remarkably agrarian, with no modern business organizational forms, except perhaps for tourism. Both are monarchical kingdoms (although there is a parliamentary system in place in Nepal), and both are ruled by kings. Both are just recently entering developing-nation status, emerging out of the mists of ancient agrarian patterns.

Culturally, they are intriguing, for they represent a blend of both Indian and Chinese cultures, Hindu and Buddhist. While there are indigenous languages (Nepali being the major language in the region), the roots of these cultures go back to Hinduism and Buddhism. By blending the two, and through a complex interweaving of many different offshoots of both, we arrive at the major version of Himalayan Buddhism—Tantrism. Mystical in nature, it is more animist than either, with a pantheon of Hindu gods and a Buddhist theology. In Tantrism, Buddhist and Hindu hierarchies converge to create very rigid social organizational patterns; erotic Hindu ideas influence static and authoritative Buddhist teachings and philosophy; Hindu patterns of individual paths to enlightenment mix with Buddhist notions of the power of many.

Daily life in both countries, with the exception of Kathmandu and certain tourist areas, has not changed from the way it has always essentially been, and the protocols and etiquettes of both Hindu and Buddhist cultures overlap and influence each other in a fabric of repeating agrarian cycles. It should be noted that aspects of both Hinduism and Buddhism, in the face of being integrated into one another in these agrarian cultures, are often exaggerated; for example, in Nepal, the Hindu concern for making food impure by touching it is exaggerated so that when drinking from a cup, one should hold it so that the fluid goes into the mouth, but the lips never touch the cup rim (this may be difficult to master at first). While tea is the local daily drink, *chang* (a fermented version of millet) is the local brew. One must take special care not to cause the members of one caste or sect to socialize or come in contact with members of another in typical daily activities. Fire is sacred, so, as a guest in a home, you will never be invited into the kitchen, and you must never casually toss anything into a flame. Because spirituality rules all aspects of life, consider the following: when walking into and through a temple, one must always walk in a clockwise direction. White scarves, called *khati,* are exchanged between people as signs of welcome, or as an indication of a donation made at a temple. You will see them available everywhere for purchase: do so often. Monks must never be touched by men or women, and the highest title one can bestow on someone is *rimpoche,* or holy monk. It is used after the person's name (usually a given name).

The Central Asian Cultures: Kazakhstan, Uzbekistan, Turkmenistan, Tajikistan, Kyrgyzstan, and Afghanistan

Note: As these cultures incorporate many Turkish and Islamic South Asian cultural attributes, this chapter will identify only those aspects of Central Asian cultural behaviors that may differ from Turkish and Islamic South Asian cultures. Please refer to the chapters on Turkey and South Asia in this book for further information.

Some Introductory Background on the Region and Its Peoples

Prior to the breakup of the Soviet Union, the only independent country in the region was Afghanistan, and toward the end of the Soviet empire, even that was questionable (the Soviet invasion of Afghanistan attempted, among other things, to turn it into a Soviet satellite; the invasion backfired, and became one of the sparks that set in motion the dissolution of the Soviet Union itself); the other five countries of the region had already been incorporated into the greater Soviet Union for much of the century. However, these countries represented empires and cultures that reached back several millennia. The entire region is Muslim, to greater or lesser extent depending upon the country, and this provides an immediate set of behaviors that non-nationals need to consider (please see the chapters on Pakistan and Bangladesh and the Arab world for more information on Islamic protocol and behaviors). This is the region where three great cultures met, fought with each other, and became integrated, with the current countries representing the resulting cultural variations. The three great cultures were the Turkish (in the west), the European (Russian primarily), and the Mongol (in the east). Each of these countries has experienced a great amount of Russification, due to the recent Soviet rule, and experienced British influence in the nineteenth century. This has resulted, among other things, in a very mild version of Islam in the region: not the fundamentalist, theologically rooted Islam of the Gulf States, for example, but a less rigid Islam, one possessing a greater tolerance for other, non-Islamic cultural influences.

Islam came to the region primarily through two sources: from the Turks (the Osmanis—the forerunners of the Turkish Ottoman Empire—and the Seljuks—the formative Muslim group in the area of Turkey), who were primarily Sunni and practiced a moderate form of Islam, and the Iranians (Shiite, and more fundamentalist). Iran had great influence in the region in the past, but recent regional Russification and association with Turkey and the Turkish language and culture has reduced the Iranian influence. Kazakhstan, for example, is half Russian, with Russians primarily in the north and Kazakhs in the south. The Islam practiced in Kazakhstan is a mild form; alcohol is common, women need not cover their faces, and many other aspects of Muslim life have been modified by the Western influence. Turkish culture is found primarily in Turkmenistan (ethnically, Turks and Turkomans are the result of Mongols and Europeans); Turkish culture, in turn, mixed with Mongol culture to produce the Kazakh and Kirghiz peoples. The interplay between Turks and Iranians resulted in the Uzbekistani culture; the mingling of Mongol and Iranian customs resulted in the Tajikistani culture.

Kazakh culture, spanning the largest geographic area, and bridging Europe with Asia, has interfaced with both Mongols (the first khan—or Kazakh leader—was Genghis Khan) and Russians (the three major Mongol groups of the central steppes—the Small Horde in the west, the Middle Horde between the Caspian and Aral Seas, and the Great Horde in the east; all three in turn succumbed over the centuries to the domination of the invading Russians) to a greater degree than any other country in the region. Kazakh culture is one of nomadic agricultural traditions, most vulnerable to outside influences, and least amenable to strictly defined codes of conduct. The Kazakhs and the Kirghiz are cousins, only the Kirghiz are on the eastern side—and here, too, because of the strong influence of Mongol culture, and the distance from both Turkish Islam and Iranian Islam, Islamic roots are deep but not binding.

Turkoman culture is rooted in the eastern, or Turkmen, tradition of Turkish culture; it loosely adopted Islam (being more concerned about its Turkishness than its association with a strange, Iranian form of Islam that differed from that of its Turkish cousins); in this sense, it is not Turkish, but Turkic (as is the language). In addition, its strong association with Russia, being the most western of all the central Asian republics, provided Turkmenistan with an autocratic government, most closely associated with the Soviets than any of the other republics of the region.

Among those central Asian republics most heavily influenced by Iran (non-Turkish cultures), Uzbekistan is the one most associated with trade, business, and development in the region. This is not surprising, since Uzbekistanis historically have played the role of traders, brokers, and businesspeople along the Silk Road, the caravan trails, and the overland spice routes between east and west. Uzbekistanis long ago learned how to do business with foreigners, and today are the most tuned to working with the West, and adapting to Western influences that go beyond just Russia. Most non-nationals find Uzbekistanis to be the most comfortable to work with of all central Asians. Tajikstanis, being a mix of Iranians and Mongols, have long endured a fragmented and fragile existence, where the mixtures of differences so vast in so small a country have resulted in the most balkanized nation in central Asia.

Finally, Afghans, being able to retain their independence from Russia and Europe in general, were also able to advance the cause of Islam most dramatically, and have, for all intents and purposes, become an Islamic country, with rules of Islam fundamentally entrenched. The Islam of Afghanistan is Sunni, although it is near Iran, which is Shiite: there is always the potential in this division for conflict between the two—another reason for the circumspect position toward Islam taken in the remaining five republics.

Be careful when referring to someone's nationality in the region: Uzbek and Turkoman citizens are identified with the full name of their country plus the letter *i* (for example, Uzbekistani); however, only someone ethnically identified as an Uzbek can be called Uzbeki, and they may or may not be Uzbekistani. All central Asians are generally clan oriented and group focused, with Uzbekistanis and Kazakhs, for their own unique reasons, perhaps being more individualist than the others. All are strongly hierarchically oriented, perhaps Turkomans and Kazakhs more strongly than the others (Uzbekistanis, the least), including the subordination of the woman's role. The immediate face-to-face relationship is the determining factor for most action among all these cultures, and rules take a backseat to subjective obligations. Most are very polychronic, emerging in various degrees, out of agrarian existences (Uzbekistan and Turkmenistan, for example, were the vegetable and cotton baskets for all of Russia), and most are highly risk averse (with Uzbekistanis being slightly less so). Fatalism is not as strong a force as one might expect (least so in Uzbekistan, most marked in Turkmenistan and Tajikistan). All the cultures are generally high-context and formal (especially with outsiders).

Greetings and Introductions

Language and Basic Vocabulary

The languages of the region fall into three basic indigenous groups: Turkic (Turkmen, Kazakh, Uzbek), Mongol (Tajik, Kirghiz), and Urdu (Afghan): as the cultures mix in the region, so do the languages. Russian may be the second language spoken most often. English is not well understood or spoken, even among businesspeople. Translators are required. Because of both the Iranian and Turkish vectors for Islam in the region, even today, the breakup of the Soviet Union has forced the local countries to rethink their cultural Islamic roots: Turkish or Persian? For example, while Russified, all languages were written in Cyrillic; now, with the exception of the significant Russian populations in most of these countries that still desire to retain the Cyrillic alphabet, there is a choice of using either Arabic or Turkish (which is written in Roman letters): predictably, Turkmenistan and Kazakhstan lean toward Latinizing; Uzbekistan toward Arabic; and Kyrgyzstan and Tajikistan undecided.

Honorifics and Basic Greetings

Because Arabic is the language in which the Koran was written, it is considered by many to be a holy language. In all these countries, the names will mainly be Arabic in content, but with Turkic or Persian suffixes; they may also be heavily Russified (with Russian suffixes added). For example:

Russified	*Arabic*	*Turkic*	*Persian*
Yusupov	Yusuf	Evren	Abdul

Suffixes (after the given/family name):

-vich (son of)	-al Din (of faith)	-oglu (son of)	-zad/zadeh (son of)
Yusupovich	Yusuf al-Din	Evren-oglu	-Abdullazadeh

Identifying someone as hajj or hajja is not as common a prefix, but it does occur; using the suffix *-bey* after a name indicates great respect in the Turkic cultures.

Communication Styles

It is important not to discuss Russia and Russification, as you may be speaking with Russians or nationals with strong feelings about Russia. In addition, do not seem as if you are unaware of the ethnic and cultural differences in the region: it will earn you great respect if you demonstrate sensitivity to its complexities. Most Turkic central Asians speak louder and more boldly than do Mongol central Asians.

Being a Good Guest or Host

Tea, or *cha,* is served everywhere and at every possible time. Always accept the tea, and be careful not to reject the hospitality of your hosts. The tea can be served unsweetened, or sometimes with a great deal of sugar already added; it can be served plain, or with a fermented kind of butter or milk added (usually from yak; this can give it a salty, fatty taste that may take some getting used to). Beer and other plant fermentations (some very interesting and potent concoctions!) are the standard alcoholic beverages (usually drunk only on special occasions); be sure to make a toast when toasts are made, maintaining strong eye contact (eye contact is usually fairly direct among the Turkmenistanis, the Kazakhs, and the Kirghiz; less so among the Tajikstanis and the Afghans; moderate among Uzbeks). Many foods have symbolic meaning, especially special foods that are served to honor someone: in Kazakhstan, a sheep or goat is typically slaughtered for a feast in honor of a special guest, and the head of the sheep is the most honored part. In addition, meat from various parts of the head indicate different aspects of the person you serve it to; for example, the tongue means the person is talkative, the ears, that he listens well. These meanings serve as vehicles for providing compliments, but may also be taken as insults. Be careful!

The Eurasian Cultures: Turkey and the Caucasus

TURKEY

Some Introductory Background on Turkey and the Turks

Turkish culture once ruled from central Europe across the Middle East to the borders of China. It has been indigenous, Christian, Islamic, and secular. Today, Turkey is a secular nation placed strategically at one of the most geographically important areas of the world, the straits that connect the Black Sea and the Mediterranean Sea, standing watch over the trade for most of eastern Europe and Russia. Having modernized itself into a secular republic, Turkey stands as a buffer to fundamentalist Islam, but is itself neither East nor West, which defines both its problem and its blessing: its heart is Asia (Ankara), but its face is Europe (Istanbul).

Some Historical Context

The ancient Hittites created an empire on this peninsula of Asia (Anatolia) long before it became the site of the Eastern Orthodox Church. After the great schism in Christianity led to the establishment of the Eastern pope in Constantinople (named after Constantine the Great, who extended the Roman Empire at the time throughout the Middle East), the Byzantine Empire stood as an equal to Rome. By 1000, however, Muslims began knocking at the door of Byzantium—first the Seljuks, and later the Osmani, who eventually became the Ottomans—and the struggle for supremacy in the region raged for hundreds of years. Eventually the Ottomans toppled Byzantium. By the middle of the 1500s, Süleyman the Magnificent ruled an empire that stretched from eastern Europe to India, and down through the Holy Lands. But European conquests and incursions from the outside, and corruption and indifference from within, combined to weaken the Ottoman rule. By the end of World War I, the Ottoman Empire had been dissolved and cut up into myriad European administrative regions. Under the leadership of Kemal Ataturk (a name given to him later by the country, meaning "Father of Turkey"), Turkey waged wars of independence against the Europeans (and other neighbors), and became a free republic in the early 1920s. Ataturk then set about modernizing Turkey in a frenzy of Westernization, the result of which can be seen today in a country that combines both Islamic and Christian, Ottoman and Byzantine, Western and Eastern forms in an unsteady but relatively balanced harmony.

An Area Briefing

Politics and Government

Today Turkey is a representative democratic republic, with a parliament, a prime minister, and a president. Nevertheless, there is strong pressure from Islamic fundamentalist forces to influence, if not replace, secular law with Islamic law. In addition, Turkey struggles constantly with internal conflicts (most noteworthy, the Kurdish insurgency in southeastern Turkey, where the ethnic Kurds seek an independent homeland) and external enemies (historically, Greeks, Russians, Arabs, and Iranians), as well as playing a significant role as supporter of all Turks and Turkish causes (most notably, the current struggle of Turks in the Caucasus and throughout all of central Asia). The sense of constant political crisis, real or imagined, has often led to government crackdowns, and Turkey has a reputation as an abuser of civil and human rights.

Schools and Education

Modernization has meant that all schooling is free and mandatory for all elementary-grade children, and that there are the equivalents of high school after grade school. The literacy rate is about 80 percent. Many wealthy Turks go to school in Europe and the United States, but there are several fine universities in Turkey, and education is emphasized as a route toward a better life. English is the language taught in schools; Arabic is also taught, but is usually done so in association with Islamic studies.

Religion and Demographics

Turkey is a Muslim nation, but because of its Byzantine roots, close proximity to the West, and conscious efforts at modernization and maintaining a secular government, many of the traditions of Islam are manifested in "softer" or Westernized versions. For example, alcohol is permitted in Turkey, and the government remains, despite intense pressure, a secular institution with its own laws. Women do have opportunities in business and in public life in Turkey; and the people's clothing, eating habits, and daily life can look, feel, and taste distinctly Western. However, Islamic traditions remain, and Islam is a potent background force to the way Turks see the world and behave toward each other and outsiders.

Islam is the youngest of the West's three great religious traditions, which began with Judaism and Christianity. As a Western religion, it incorporates both Judaism and Christianity into its system of beliefs, claiming to provide the final revelation of a monotheistic God, as revealed to the world through the prophet Muhammad. Previous "messiahs," such as Jesus and Moses, according to Islam, were merely prophets, along with Muhammad, all of them proclaiming the word of God. Muslims do not follow Muhammad (therefore, they are not Muhammadans, a very derogatory term created by Westerners who did not understand Islam); they believe in Allah, the Arabic term for the same God worshiped by Christians and Jews. Muhammad and his followers wrote down the law of God as revealed to them in the Koran (or Qu'ran), the Islamic holy book. It does not negate the Old or New Testament: it merely provides, in the eyes of Muslim faithful, the final required text. Islam spread rapidly into Turkey from Arabia by the tenth century. While Islam underwent a serious split almost immediately following Muhammad's death (two major camps emerged, the Shia and the Sunni, in an effort to decide how to continue the faith), it nevertheless rapidly gathered huge followings. Sunni Muslims believe that the caliphs, or religious leaders who succeeded Muhammad, were the legitimate leaders; Shiite Muslims believe that the caliphs who succeeded Muhammad were usurpers, and they therefore reject Sunni authority. Sunni Muslims dominate in Turkey. All Muslims must abide by five basic tenets, or Pillars of Faith:

- Proclaim the supremacy of the one true God, Allah, above all others
- Pray to Allah five times daily
- Observe Ramadan, the holy month, the ninth month of the Islamic calendar, which is essentially a celebration of the first time God revealed his word to Muhammad
- Give alms to the poor and needy
- Perform the hajj, or spiritual (and physical) journey to Mecca, at least once in their lifetime if they are capable of doing so

Specific codes of conduct have developed over time, and are codified into Islamic law, known as the Shariah. The degree to which one follows these scriptures often determines how devoutly one applies the Islamic ethical code in day-to-day life.

Women in Turkey have access to careers in medicine, teaching, government service, and, to a lesser degree, business. Western businesswomen should have little problem in Turkey as long as their authority has been established. Turkey is a demographically young country, with a significant percentage of its population under the age of thirty.

Fundamental Cultural Orientations

1. What's the Best Way for People to Relate to One Another?

OTHER-INDEPENDENT OR OTHER-DEPENDENT? The family and one's membership in other groups is the first concern for most Turks. Family and personal life determine one's standing in society, and the actions that one subsequently takes are often prescribed by how others will view them. Individuals are responsible for their acts and decisions, but mainly as they are viewed by others.

HIERARCHY-ORIENTED OR EGALITY-ORIENTED? Most organizations are highly structured, and it is important for rank and titles to be so honored. Perhaps no one aspect of orientation toward status and rank is more important than age: the older person is eminently respected in Turkish society, and demonstrations of such respect are shown everywhere in daily life. Women and men have separate roles at home and at work, but the differences are not as severe as they are in many other Islamic cultures.

RULE-ORIENTED OR RELATIONSHIP-ORIENTED? While Turks have been influenced strongly by the West, this influence is not as profound when it comes to criteria for decision making. Practically, immediate situations determine decisions and action; this means that there is a strong dependence on knowing the right people, and on accepting the benefits of influence. Rules are made to be broken, depending upon the immediate and subjective circumstances. Systems and processes, therefore, are often unreliable, and circumvented in various ways. This means that Turks need to get to know the flesh-and-blood person: business relationships will determine the success of the business deal, not just the terms of the agreement, and building relationships can take time (and more than one trip!).

2. What's the Best Way to View Time?

MONOCHRONIC OR POLYCHRONIC? Turkish culture is essentially polychronic. The clock is definitely not the determinant of action; it plays a role, most certainly, particularly in the larger, more modern urban areas, and there is an acceptance of Western organizational ideas. Nevertheless, there is forgiveness for the inevitable delays, and understanding when things don't go as planned or scheduled; people may or may not show up at scheduled events, meetings and projects may or may not happen as planned. Even today, schedules tend to be loose and flexible; the workday begins around 9 A.M., and ends around 4 P.M. Most workers take an hour break, as well as many tea and smoke breaks throughout the day.

RISK-TAKING OR RISK-AVERSE? Turks are prone to taking risks when in positions of authority, and avoiding risks when not. Within organizations, the decision makers can be bold, even reckless, but subordinates generally are not, and take action only when instructed to do so. If individuals do not receive instructions from their superiors, however, there is a strong tendency to take control in what is interpreted as a power vacuum; then people may appear to be authoritative, when they are merely acting in response to real or perceived inaction by superiors.

PAST-ORIENTED OR FUTURE-ORIENTED? In Turkey, there is a distinct and inherent fatalism assigned to the effect of human action. Nevertheless, those empowered by virtue of their position are expected to make the decisions that keep the world running. Therefore, future benefits often do not motivate the Turks; doing nothing, or doing things for the here and now, are more relevant, and if things do not work out, that is to be expected: no one controls the universe.

3. What's the Best Way for Society to Work with the World at Large?

LOW-CONTEXT DIRECT OR HIGH-CONTEXT INDIRECT COMMUNICATORS? Turks are high-context communicators. They are generally indirect in their communication style, and use much nonverbal behavior. They generally avoid direct confrontation, and believe it is unseemly for individuals to act emotionally. They will go out of their way not to bring bad news forward. Much information is conveyed, therefore, in the context in which a situation occurs, rather than in the words that are spoken. There is much use of symbolic speech. Occasionally, when authority and context permit, those in charge can be very direct with subordinates, but rarely the other way around.

PROCESS-ORIENTED OR RESULT-ORIENTED? Associative and subjective experience-based logic predominates in most situations, but is judged against a backdrop of Islamic codes of behavior.

FORMAL OR INFORMAL? Turks are formal, and act in a ritualized fashion with people on the outside, and informal and relaxed with those on the inside (but still with an important emphasis on formal respect for rank, age, and hierarchy).

Greetings and Introductions

Language and Basic Vocabulary

The official language is Turkish, which is not related to any other western European language (it is Ural-Altaic in origin, not Latin or Anglo-Saxon). Businesspeople are likely to speak some English, but more likely to speak Arabic, German, or French as a second language; if they do speak some English, it is likely to be British English, and the differences between British English and the English spoken by other English speakers, particularly Americans, can be considerable (please see the chapter on England in *The Global Etiquette Guide to Europe* for further information).

Here are some Turkish basics (*c* = *j*, as in *just;* *ç* (with a cedilla) = *ch* as in *church;* and *s* = *sh* as in *shoe*):

meerh'aba	hello
gunaydin	good morning
iyi gunler	good day
iyi aksamlar	good evening
memnum oldum	pleased to meet you
lutfen	please
tesekkur	thank you
hos geldiniz	you're welcome
affedersiniz	excuse me
allah ismarladik (spoken by the one who leaves)	good-bye
gule gule (spoken by the person who remains behind)	good-bye
evet	yes
hayir	no
Nasilsiwiz?	How are you?

Honorifics for Men, Women, and Children

Because Arabic is the language in which the Koran was written, it is considered by many to be a holy language. In Turkey, some people use Arabic-derived names, but most use Turkish names.

Prior to Ataturk, the tradition was to mainly use one's given (first) name, with the family name being of secondary importance. After Ataturk, Turkey legally required people to use the Western form, with given names first and family names last. Therefore, if addressing or being addressed by older Turks, the older tradition may be used; younger Turks, and certainly businesspeople, usually arrange their names the Western way.

The traditional honorifics are *bey* (Mr.; placed after the first or given name), and *hanim* (Mrs./Miss; placed after the first or given name): for example, Ismail Bey; Leyla Hanim.

The modernized honorifics are *bay* (Mr.; placed before the surname or the full name), and *bayam* (Mrs./Miss; placed before the surname or the full name): for example, Bay Ismail Erbekan; Bayam Leyla Erbekan.

Married women typically take their husbands' family names, as in the West. Degrees and titles are listed as they are in the West.

The What, When, and How of Introducing People

Modern Turks will refer to foreigners by their full Western names, and use Mr. or Mrs./Miss (Ms. is not well understood). Turks will use titles and degrees; if you have them, put them on your business card.

Always wait to be introduced to strangers; never take that responsibility upon yourself, as doing so is considered inappropriate most of the time. Turks are most comfortable with third-party introductions, and because business is very personal, you will need an individual to introduce you to the required people. Never presume to seat yourself at a gathering: if possible, wait to be told where to sit. The seating arrangements have usually been carefully worked out in advance, and in most cases reflect the status of the individuals in the group, and the honor that is being accorded the guests. When departing, it is important to say farewell to every individual present: the American group wave is not appreciated. Once you greet someone you will encounter later that same day in the same circumstances (e.g., at the office), you do not need to greet them when you see them again. Seniors, or those who are obviously the oldest in a group, are greeted first, seated first, and allowed to enter a room first (usually at the center of a group, however, and preceded in most cases by their younger aides).

Physical Greeting Styles

Turks greet each other with the Western handshake, and it can be firm. Extra sincerity is sometimes demonstrated by clasping the hand being shaken with two hands. Sometimes, after the handshake, one's own hand is brought back to touch one's heart. Occasionally, with much older, well-known people, the hand is kissed, and then raised to touch the forehead of the one who kissed the hand. There can be much physical greeting between two men and two women, but never between the sexes in public. Close associates and businessmen (the operative part of the word is *men,* as this is done only between men, and never between men and women) who have developed intimate working relationships often greet each other warmly with hugs and kisses. Muslim women and men typically do not touch or shake hands (unless the woman is very Westernized), so always let a woman extend her hand first.

The traditional Turkish business introduction also includes the exchange of business cards. Always take a large supply of business cards with you: you should give one to every new person you are introduced to (there is no need to provide another business card when you are meeting someone again unless information about you has changed, such as a new address, contact number, or position). You will be asked to provide business cards to receptionists, so be prepared to present another to your colleague when you meet. Be sure your business cards are in fine shape: they are an extension of you as a person, and they must look as good as possible. Embossed cards are extremely impressive. Never hand out a dirty, soiled, bent, or written-on card. You do not need to translate your business card into Turkish on the reverse side, but if you do, it's a nice touch. Present your card so that it is readable for your Turkish colleague as you hold it (he will, in turn, present his card so that it is readable for you); you should hold the card with two hands in the upper corners as you present it. Do not worry too much about who receives and gives the business card first: the exchange is very quick, and because you would probably not be introduced to that person in the first place if you were not already seen as having an equivalent rank, there is no need to show deference. There is also no need for bowing.

Smiling and other nonverbal forms of communication usually accompany the card exchange. Information about each other's position and role in the organization is the most important information to be exchanged, and this is provided directly on the business card, as well as indirectly through a number of high-context indicators, such as gray hair (indicating age and seniority), gender (male), and the number of people surrounding and assisting the other person (important ranking people tend to have assistants). Should you meet more than one individual at a reception, you will have a handful of cards when the greetings are over.

As the business card exchange usually precedes a sit-down meeting, it is important to arrange the cards you have received in a little seating plan in front of you along the top of the desk or the table at your seat, reflecting the order in which people are seated. This will help you connect the correct names with the correct individuals throughout the meeting. Do this even if you are just meeting one person; it is expected. During the meeting, it is important never to play with the business cards (do not write on them—ever!); and when the meeting is over, never put them in your back pants pockets: pick them up carefully and respectfully, and place them neatly in your cardholder (a nice-looking brass card case would be perfect), then place the cardholder in the left inside jacket pocket of your suit (nearest your heart).

Communication Styles

Okay Topics / Not Okay Topics

Okay: anything that reflects your personal interests and hobbies, or your curiosity about things native to Turkey, like its food or its history. Discussions about your company and its work are very much appreciated, as it gives the Turks a chance to learn more about you and your firm. The goal of all conversation, at least at the beginning, is to create and maintain a harmonious atmosphere, despite the difficult or confrontational nature of the topic being discussed. At first, speak about things that you believe you have in common, so that you can build a personal connection that will go far toward maintaining a harmonious bridge between you. This is appropriate for both individuals and organizations. *Not okay:* Politics, current events, or any subject that might in any way be controversial needs to be avoided at first. Turks do not like to talk about unpleasant things, ever (in fact, this will be stated to you as an introductory apology for bringing anything unpleasant up!). Do not inquire about a person's occupation or income in casual conversation, although it may be inquired of you (if so, this is just a way of getting to know more about your country, and not a personal investigation: answer specifically, but fully, with an explanation as to what things cost at home, why you do what you do, etc.). Do not inquire about your colleague's spouse, but you may inquire about his family life: Turks are very proud of their children. Do not give your opinions about Greeks, Cyprus (Turks and Greeks have been historic enemies, and Cyprus is currently an island divided into hostile Greek and Turkish sections), Kurds (Kurds are an ethnic minority struggling for independence within Turkey—and elsewhere in the region), human rights, Arabs, and Islam. Do not talk about sex, or tell dirty jokes: it is in very bad taste. Never discuss religion, and be very careful to eliminate all casual reference to God or religious figures from your vocabulary ("God, it's a hot day!" is *not* good).

Tone, Volume, and Speed

Turks generally speak in soft, quiet, and restrained tones, although they can get louder as they get interested in your conversation. The pace is generally similar to, or slightly faster than, Western speech.

Use of Silence

Passive silence—allowing time to pass simply without words—can be a form of proactive communication, and is used as a nonverbal way of avoiding confrontation, disagreement, or an unpleasant subject. If confronted with unexplainable silence, gently coax the conversation in a different direction, one that is more mutually harmonious.

Physical Gestures and Facial Expressions

Turks employ a great deal of nonverbal communication. You are advised to reduce the amount of body language you use, since you may inadvertently gesture in a way that is offensive. Closed-fist gestures of any kind are rude. Winking, whistling, and similar displays are considered very vulgar. Public displays of familiarity and affection with the opposite sex are rarely if ever expressed, except perhaps among teenagers. Never touch anyone on his or her head, even a child: this is considered the holiest part of the body. Do not point with or show the sole of your shoe to anyone: this is vulgar, as the bottom of the shoe touches the ground, and is therefore the dirtiest part of the body. Standing with your hands on your hips is very aggressive and should always be avoided. Also, sitting with your arms crossed is rude.

For any action or gesture that would naturally be done only with one hand, do not use your left hand, as this is considered the unclean hand (the hand used for personal hygiene). Pass all documents, food, and money only with your right hand (if you're a southpaw, you will have to practice this). You must remove your shoes before entering a mosque or a home, and you will need to wash your feet and hands before entering as well. Women may be restricted to specific areas and times when visiting mosques. Women entering mosques need to have their heads covered, their legs covered below the knees, and their arms covered below the elbows. Western women do not need to have their faces covered.

Finally, like most cultures in the eastern Mediterranean, tilting the head upward, as if nodding up and down, is actually a negative sign, especially if accompanied with slightly closed eyes, raised eyebrows, and/or a "tsk" or clicking sound (really bad!). The shaking of the head from left to right does not mean "no": it more likely means "I don't understand" (a question).

Waving and Counting

The pinkie represents the number 1, the thumb represents the number 5, with everything in between ordered from the pinkie down; however, instead of raising the fingers when counting, the whole hand is exposed, and each finger is depressed as the counting is done. It is very insulting to motion to someone with the forefinger (instead, turn your hand so that the palm is facing down and motion inward with all four fingers at once). If you need to gesture for a waiter, very subtly raise your hand. Waving or beckoning is done with the palm down and the fingers moving forward and backward in a kind of scratching motion. It may seem as if the person making this gesture is saying good-bye to you, when in fact you are being summoned over. If you need to point to something or someone, close your fingers, open your palm and face it upward, and pass your hand in the direction you want to indicate.

Physicality and Physical Space

Turks stand closer than most North Americans do, by about a hand's-length; resist the urge at first to move back. Never speak with your hands in your pockets: always keep them firmly at your side when standing. If men and women must cross their legs when they sit, it must never be ankle over knee, (for women, the preferred style is to cross ankle over ankle, and the bottoms of the shoes must not show to the other person). Remember, in public, formal is always better than informal: no gum chewing, *ever;* don't slouch; and don't lean against things.

Eye Contact

Eye contact can be very direct between same sexes, even between strangers; direct eye contact between the sexes, however, indicates flirting. The eyes are used extensively to convey sincerity and interest.

Emotive Orientation

Turks can be very emotive and outgoing. They rarely withhold their feelings physically, but are careful about what they say verbally.

Protocol in Public

Walking Styles and Waiting in Lines

On the street, in stores, and in most public facilities, little attention is paid to maintaining orderly lines. Due to the volume of passengers on public transportation, there can be much pushing and jostling. This is not primarily to get into a train or bus ahead of someone else, though; it is merely to get in!

Behavior in Public Places: Airports, Terminals, and the Market

Customer service for strangers is not a well-developed practice in Turkey; once you establish a personal relationship with a shopkeeper, however, you can expect much gracious assistance. Service is perfunctory, at best, in most stores and restaurants. Stores in the cities are open in the evenings and on weekends, as well as during the day, and most stay open on Friday (the Muslim Sabbath); legally, Sunday is the day of rest. A personal thank-you to store owners, waiters, chefs, and hotel managers for their services is important, as it will help establish the relationship you need to get good service. In food markets, do not touch the produce unless you are buying it; in goods stores, if you buy a product and have problems with it, returning the item may be difficult. Smoking is endemic, and you may have difficulty finding a no-smoking area, on public transportation, in restaurants, and in other public places (be sure not to smoke during Ramadan—Ramazan in Turkish—in front of devout Muslims, when they abstain; this is true for eating and drinking during the day during Ramadan when in the presence of observant Muslims, as well). Bathroom facilities can range from Western-style toilets to Asian-style toilets (holes in the floor, with buckets of water or hoses attached to a water line for cleanup instead of paper); be prepared.

When answering a telephone, say "Hello" or just your given name. Cell phones are ubiquitous, as the wire networks may be unreliable.

Bus / Metro / Taxi / Car

Driving is on the right, and whether in the country or city, being in a car can be hazardous to your health. The roads are not necessarily in good repair, marked, or where the maps say they are; and obtaining fuel when and where you need it can be a problem. There are dangerous areas in the major cities, and in the interior countryside, where guerrillas may be active. Driving in the interior country puts you at risk for being stopped, ambushed, or mugged. City traffic is maddening and chaotic.

Buses stop running usually after 11 P.M. or midnight. The best way to catch a cab is at designated taxi stands (hotels are good places, but often charge more for the same ride: a hotel surcharge is added to the meter fare, in some cases). When a taxi has been hailed, negotiate the price, as the meter may or may not be working (even if it is, you still need to negotiate the price). Whenever possible, have the address you need to get to written down on a piece of paper (or use the business card of the person you are going to see, if you can) before you hail the cab. A small map outlining the route is great, if you can have one prepared before you go.

Tipping

Tipping is universally required, everywhere you can imagine—and then some. Restaurant tips run about 10 percent, and are typically included in the bill (but double-check to be sure); a separate tip is not necessary if you have negotiated the fare for the taxi ahead of time, and figured in the tip. For everything else, a few coins are all that are needed, but you should always have a lot of spare change handy to see you through the day.

Punctuality

Punctuality is valued, but not required. For business meetings, be on time if you can, but don't worry if you are ten or fifteen minutes late; for social occasions, being up to a half hour late is fine. Making a general comment about the weather or the traffic is all you need to do to get off the hook for being late.

Dress

The standard in Turkey is more or less Western, but the main concern is the climate: Turkey can be uncomfortably hot in summer, and cold for a couple of months in winter. Therefore, many businessmen take their jackets and ties off in summer, but take your cues from the oldest person you are with first. Business dress is conservative, not dressy. A dark business suit is required for formal events. Businesswomen wear blouses and lightweight skirts or long pants. Women need to be especially careful not to wear skirts that are too short; they need to go clearly below the knees. Wear dress slacks, not jeans or khakis. Sneakers are only for the street or gym; shorts are never okay, on the street or elsewhere. Muslim traditions dictate that women dress so that their legs are covered below the knee, their arms are covered below the elbow, and their torsos are covered from their necks to their waists. Some Muslim women cover their faces, most do not; nonpracticing Western women need not cover their faces.

Remember, if you visit mosques, you will need to remove your shoes and walk barefoot while inside, or rent the slippers offered at the entrance.

Seasonal Variations

Turkey is warm and comfortable for most of the year in the west except for January and February, when it can be raw and chilly; the mountainous east can be cold in winter.

Colors

Neutral, dark, and conservative clothes are best for businesspeople of both sexes, whenever possible.

Styles

For the most part, clothing is simple, adapted to climate, and meant to keep one looking good and cool. Consider, however, that some places may be air-conditioned to arctic levels, so you might always want to have a lightweight covering available.

Accessories / Jewelry / Makeup

Makeup, hairstyle, and accessories are important for women, but only if used modestly. Perfume and cologne are popular, but usually are not made with alcohol (alcohol is prohibited in Islam).

Personal Hygiene

In Turkey, cleanliness is associated with purity. Do not blow your nose in public: it is considered very rude. Spitting does occur on the street, but is also regarded as rude. Muslim men may sport facial hair, usually in the form of a mustache. At the end of a meal, if you use toothpicks, you must cover the "working" hand with the other hand, so that others cannot see your mouth. Remember that Muslims consider dogs very unclean, and are usually very uncomfortable around them; therefore, do not refer to them or bring them along with you.

Dining and Drinking

Mealtimes and Typical Foods

Turkish food is one of the world's great cuisines, for it has developed at the crossroads of Asian and European cooking. It uses the ingredients of the region in exciting ways. The typical diet is based on breads, grains, rice, meats (goat, lamb, chicken), fish and other seafood along the coast, lentils, stewed vegetables, nuts, fruits, yogurts, and wonderful sauces. Sweet desserts and treats abound. Turks are familiar with Western food, but if you are hosting Turkish visitors in your home country, take them to the finest Turkish or Middle Eastern restaurant around: they will appreciate it. The foods are not necessarily hot and spicy, just spicy and flavorful.

Breakfast is served from about 7 to 9 A.M., and usually consists of fresh fruits, tea, and cakes or rice mixed with sweet dairy products, such as yogurt, and milk. Tea is usually drunk plain, but if you ask for milk or sugar, you will generally get some. But be careful not to request them in remote locations where they may be difficult to obtain: in this case, you run the risk of insulting your host's hospitality, and that is not a good thing. Yogurt and fruit drinks are sometimes served for breakfast.

Lunch is traditionally a one-hour meal, and consists of a main dish, or bread and meats, with a salad. It is not necessarily the main meal of the day; that is usually reserved for dinner. Lunch is served from about noon to 1 P.M. Typically, the drinks served with lunch and dinner are soft drinks, fruit juices, and/or tea, although wine can be served, along with beer and other alcoholic beverages.

Dinner is served from 6 P.M. on, with 8 P.M. the customary late time. The dinner menu is often similar to that of the more formal lunch, but with many varied and different dishes. Dinner drinks are similar to those served for lunch. When you come to a Turkish home, even for a brief visit, you will be served some sweet delicacy plus tea or coffee. The sweet is not a dessert; you will get that at the end of the meal as well. Sweets include the wonderful baklava and Turkish delight.

Regional Differences

As you move away from the western coast, the food becomes less wheat-based and less fish-based. The interior cuisine is basic and hearty, with large breads and spreads, and more Middle Eastern in style. Try the stuffed grape leaves, the sesame spreads, the wonderful and varied breads, and dips.

Typical Drinks and Toasting

Tea is usually served in little curved glasses that you hold not by the stem (too hot to handle that way), but by the lip: you never add milk, but you can add water as you drink it to dilute the tea, which is sometimes still steeping when you get it. The tea can come presweetened, so be sure to check first before adding sugar. Coffee is equally available, usually as a separate after-dinner drink. The coffee is drunk carefully (there are grounds on the bottom); it is also thick and black, and each cup is individually brewed, often with the sugar already in it (again, be sure to check before adding sugar), and milk is usually not to be added. Since it is offered all the time and everywhere, it is a gesture of hospitality, and you must always take the coffee or tea, even if you only put it to your lips or just take a few sips. Your cup will always be refilled if it is less than half full. Because you must never pour your own drink (be it juice or tea), you must always be alert throughout the meal as to whether your neighbor's cup or glass needs refilling. If it is less than half full, it needs refilling; alternately, if yours is less than half full, your neighbor is obliged to refill it. If he or she does not, do not refill it yourself, for this will cause him or her to lose face; instead, diplomatically indicate your need by pouring a little more drink into your neighbor's glass, even if it doesn't really need it.

If you are the honored guest, you will be expected to make a toast, usually soon after the host does or at the end of the meal, just before everyone departs. An appropriate toast is to the health of the host and all those present, and to the prosperity of the business under discussion.

Avoid drinking tap water anywhere in Turkey (this means you should brush your teeth with bottled water and not take ice in any of your drinks; drink only bottled water, or brewed tea or coffee or soft drinks, and avoid getting water from the morning shower into your mouth; never eat fresh fruits or vegetables that cannot be peeled first, and ideally cooked later before eating). This is a serious matter: there are some nasty bugs going around in developing countries. Also, avoid all dairy products except in the finest hotels, as the required refrigeration may be questionable.

Table Manners and the Use of Utensils

Dining is done with forks and spoons and knives, Western style. The knife is held in the right hand, and the fork in the left. Do not switch hands for knives and forks.

A word about smoking: it is ubiquitous throughout Asia, especially so in Turkey. People often light up between courses during dinner, as well.

Seating Plans

The host sits at the head of the table, with the honored guest seated next to the host. (Spouses are usually not invited to business meals in restaurants. Do not ask if your spouse can join you; it will embarrass your Turkish colleague. However, your spouse might be invited to a meal at home, especially if the spouse of the host will be there, which will probably be the case.) In addition, the honored guest sits on the side of the table farthest from the door. (At business meetings, the key people sit in the middle, flanked on either side in descending order by their aides, with the least important people sitting at the ends of the table farthest from the middle, and closest to the door; the arrangement is mirrored on the other side.) Men and women eating at someone's home might dine in separate areas (and spend the entire evening separated) or at separate times, with the men dining first.

Refills and Seconds

You will always be offered more food. Leave a bit on your plate if you do not want more food. You will be implored to take more two or three times, in the form of a little ritual. The game is as follows: first you refuse, then the host insists, then you refuse again, then the host insists again, and then you finally give in and take a little more. This is known as the *uzooma* (the seesaw dialogue of imploring, rejecting, and finally submitting). If you really don't want more, take very little and leave it on your plate. You may always have additional beverages; drink enough to cause your cup or glass to be less than half full, and it will generally be refilled. A reminder: never refill your own glass; always refill your neighbor's glass, and he or she will refill yours.

At Home, in a Restaurant, or at Work

The honored guest is served first, then the oldest man, then the rest of the men, then children, and finally women. Do not begin to eat or drink until the oldest man at the table has been served and has begun. You may want to ask your host when it is appropriate to begin. At the end of the meal, it is appropriate to thank the host or hostess for a wonderful meal. In restaurants, you often order each dish as you want it, so that they are not ordered all at once at the beginning of the meal. In informal restaurants, you may be required to share a table. If so, do not force conversation: act as if you are seated at a private table. Waitstaff may be summoned by making eye contact; waving or calling their names is very impolite. The business breakfast is unknown in Turkey, and most business meals are in fact lunches. Business meals are generally not good times to discuss business or make business decisions; they are intended to build the more important personal relationship. Take your cue from your Turkish associates: if they bring up business, then it's okay to discuss it, but wait to take your lead from their conversation. Water, and other drinks, may not be served until after the meal is over, as some believe that drinking while eating is not healthy.

When you are at a colleague's home for a formal meal, you will be invited to sit anywhere you like at the table; resist the impulse to sit down, and wait until your host gives you further instructions. These will generally come after the host or oldest man is seated, and often you will be placed at his side. It is a great honor to be invited into a Turkish home. Once inside, you may need to remove your shoes (this is not the custom in restaurants, however). You will know when you approach the home and see a row of shoes at the door (keep your socks in good shape, and wear comfortable but well-made slip-ons for such occasions). Once inside the home, do not wander around: much of the house is really off-limits to guests. If you move from room to room in a Turkish home, be sure to always allow the more senior members of your party to enter the room ahead of you. It is customary to say "Afiyet olsun" ("May what you eat bring well-being") before eating, and to say "Elinize saglik" (it is a compliment to the hostess, meaning "Bless your hand") after the meal.

Being a Good Guest or Host

Paying the Bill

Usually the one who does the inviting pays the bill, although the guest is expected to make an effort to pay. It will virtually be impossible to pay the bill, or even part of it, unless you are the host, but an effort should be made in that direction to show your willingness to do so. Western businesswomen will probably have a problem paying the bill at a restaurant if men are present at the table, so if you want to, make payment arrangements ahead of time, and don't wait for the check to arrive at the table.

Transportation

It's a very nice idea, when acting as the host, to inquire ahead of time as to whether your guests will require transportation. If necessary, you should arrange for taxi service at the end of the meal. When seeing your guests off, you must remain at the entrance of the house or the restaurant, or at the site where you deposited your guests into the car, until the car is out of sight: it is very important not to leave until your guests can no longer see you, should they look back. Guests are seated in cars (and taxis) by rank, with the honored guest being placed in the back directly behind the front passenger seat; the next honored position is in the back behind the driver, and the least honored position is up front with the driver.

When to Arrive / Chores to Do

If invited to dinner at a private home, do not offer to help with the chores: you are a guest. You should not expect or ask to visit the kitchen. Do not leave the table unless invited to do so. When in the home, be careful not to admire something too effusively: Turks may feel obligated to give it to you, and you in turn will be required to present them with a gift of equal value. Instead of saying things like "I love that vase," say something like "Vases that beautiful in my country are only found in museums." Your compliments will most likely be dismissed.

Gift Giving

In general, gift giving is common in many social situations in Turkey, but not as common in business settings. When going to Turkey on business, bringing a personalized gift for the key decision maker is enough. Your gift does not have to be elaborate or expensive. You present your gift when you arrive in the country; before you leave to return home, you will receive a farewell gift at the last meeting. When Turks visit your country, they will bring you a gift, and before they leave, you should give them gifts. Holiday cards are traditional and expected.

The most appropriate gift for a personal visit to a home, or as a thank-you for dinner, would be a box of fruits, pastries, cakes, cookies, or other sweets. Flowers are typically acceptable, but avoid chrysanthemums, as they are used at funerals. Carnations and roses (even red ones) are appreciated, but always give your hostess an odd number of flowers. It is not necessary to send a handwritten thank-you note the day after the dinner party. If you are staying with a family, an appropriate thank-you gift would be a high-quality item that represents your country and is difficult or expensive to get in Turkey; this is also a good idea for a key business associate. Avoid gifts from or about the United States that carry political messages, as relations between the United States and Turkey have been strained from time to time. An ornamental object, or something representative of native crafts, will be most appreciated. Be sure the gift you give does not have a tag or sticker on it that says it was made in the region. Avoid handkerchiefs, as they symbolize sadness, and cutlery, which symbolizes the severing of a relationship. A fine gift for a devout Muslim would be a silver compass, so that he will always know which direction to face when he says his daily prayers (Muslims must face Mecca no matter where they are when they say their prayers). Be sure not to give pork as food gifts to Muslims; also generally avoid alcohol, and any products that contain alcohol, including perfumes and colognes. Remember, any gift given by a man to a woman must come with the caveat that it is from both him and his wife/sister/mother, or else it is far too personal. For both giving and receiving gifts, two hands are used always. Gifts are typically not opened by the receiver in front of the giver; they are usually received after much imploring by you, graciously acknowledged, and placed aside to be opened once the giver is no longer present.

Gifts should be wrapped well. Typically, gifts are wrapped in ordinary paper first then wrapped again in bright, attractive colors; black and white both should be avoided because they are funeral colors.

Special Holidays and Celebrations

Major Holidays

Avoid going to Turkey for business during the entire month of Ramadan (*Ramazan*), which may fall in warm-weather months in Turkey, depending upon the lunar calendar. Many regions also have different local holidays, as well, so double-check with your associates in Turkey before making final travel plans.

Ramazan begins with people beating drums in the morning to awaken everyone to their morning meal, and ends with a cannon shot at dusk. It is a monthlong celebration, with both moderate and devout Muslims celebrating the event. At the end of *Ramazan,* during the Sugar Festival, children go door to door collecting sweets.

The Feast of the Sacrifice is celebrated a month and ten days after the beginning of *Ramazan;* it recalls the sacrifice to God that Abraham was willing to make of his son.

January 1	*Yilbasi* (New Year's Day)
February/March	*Ramazan* (Ramadan)
February/March	*Seker Bayrami* (Sugar Festival)
April 23	*Nisan Cocuk Bayrami* (National Independence Day and Children's Day)
April/May	*Kurban Bayrami* (Feast of the Sacrifice)
May 19	*Genclik ve Spor Bayrami* (Youth and Sports Day)
August 30	*Zafer Bayrami* (Victory Day)
October 29	*Cimhuriyet Bayrami* (Republic Day)
November 10	Anniversary of Kemal Ataturk's Death (at exactly 9:05 A.M., there is a standing moment of silence throughout the entire nation)

Business Culture

Daily Office Protocols

The traditional Turkish office may look like a traditional Western office in its design. With the exception of those holding higher positions, people work mainly in individual or shared cubicles. Doors, if they exist, are usually closed. In the Turkish business organization, hierarchy is strictly observed. Executives usually have their offices on other floors. You probably will not be invited onto the working floors until the proposed project has been set in motion. Because faithful Muslims pray five times a day, you will need to adjust your schedules to accommodate their needs. Usually, prayers are given upon awakening, and at noontime, midday, dusk, and before retiring; this means that twice during the workday, there will be time out for prayers. The prayer usually takes a short ten or fifteen minutes or so, and any quiet area will do. If you accidentally interrupt a Muslim during his prayers, just walk quietly away; there's no need for complicated explanations or apologies. Many organizations have prayer rooms set aside, with carpets. In addition, devout Muslims will not work on Friday (the Muslim Sabbath), and in fact begin to end work early on Thursday, before sundown. The official workweek is Monday through Friday.

Management Styles

Because of the rigid rank and hierarchy orientation, titles are very important; the highest ones (e.g., vice president) are usually reserved for very senior, executive-level positions, and should not be used as casually as they are in the United

States. Complimenting, rewarding, or criticizing employees publicly is not done. Any criticism must be done very carefully, in private. Deference is shown by subordinates to their seniors; paternalistic concern is often shown by executives to their juniors, although care is taken by all involved to preserve the face of others and to be considerate of the efforts that others are doing in their jobs on behalf of one's goals. Negotiations or projects can move very slowly at some times, and rapidly at others.

Boss-Subordinate Relations

The decision-making system usually works from the top on down, with key decisions often coming from individuals in high positions of authority. Bosses do solicit input from trusted subordinates, and there is an effort to be sure that all involved feel good about the project and know what to do, but they have the ultimate decision, and all know this. Superiors are expected to provide clear and fully informed instructions: that is their responsibility, and it is the responsibility of subordinates to carry out those instructions. Consequently, "management-by-objective" and other egalitarian and individually empowered management styles often may not work in this environment: without clear instruction from above, subordinates will either do nothing, or fill up the vacuum with their own ideas. They also lose respect for the manager for not making the decisions he or she should be making.

Conducting a Meeting or Presentation

At your first meeting in Turkey, you will probably be received in a very comfortable waiting area, which may or may not be where most of the meeting is conducted between yourself and your Turkish colleague. If this is the case, you are merely being sized up, and your colleague is probably a gatekeeper. When serving any refreshments in the office, be sure they are served in porcelain tea sets: the use of paper or Styrofoam shows disrespect and is in very bad form. There may be several people in the room with you and your Turkish contact whom you may or may not be introduced to. These "ghost people" are probably trusted friends or relations of your Turkish colleague, and he will no doubt want their input after the meeting. If you are not introduced to them, do not ask to be: acknowledge them with a smile and a nod, and proceed with your meeting. If you are meeting with a decision maker, the discussions may move to business more quickly, but taking the time to chitchat is very important; do not be put off by irrelevant, nonbusiness discussions: they are essential to building the all-important trust between you. Business is personal in Turkey: decision makers have got to know your face. Patience and third-party connections are key. This also means that you should always start as high up in the organization as you possibly can.

Negotiation Styles

At first, expect few decisions from your Turkish colleagues at the table and be willing to provide copious amounts of information, to the degree that you can, in response to their questions, and in anticipation of their needs. Presentations should be well prepared and simply propounded. Details are best left to questions and backup material, which should be in Turkish, if possible, and left behind. Ideally, you should present your material to your colleagues for study, along with a proposed agenda, prior to the meeting. Have extra copies available, as you might meet more people than you will expect (but you may not need them, as you will probably meet no more than a handful of Turkish businesspeople at any one time). Should you come with other team members, make sure that your roles are well coordinated. Never disagree with team members in front of your Turkish colleagues, or appear uncertain, unsure, not authorized to make a decision, or out of control in any way.

Turks love to bargain, and see this process as a way of getting to know you: it does not imply insincerity to offer one price, and then change one's mind later (as it often does with Pacific Rim cultures). In fact, to avoid this process will generate suspicion. Turks negotiate on a win/lose basis, at first. Contracts and contract law are well known and understood; expect and insist on well-executed documents to finalize an agreement. The state is often involved, either explicitly or implicitly, in many business arrangements, and the associated bureaucratic red tape can slow things down significantly, despite what you and your Turkish colleague have agreed to. Remember, the deal should be finalized with a celebratory meal. Keep communications open, especially when at a distance, and stay in touch often with your Turkish associates: share more information than you normally would, not less; and, because business is so intimately connected with the government bureaucracy and because the political situation can be fluid, try to have a contact on the ground in Turkey who can always keep you informed of what is really going on, if you can.

Written Correspondence

Your business letters should be very formal and respectful of rank and hierarchy. Surnames usually are written in uppercase; dates are given in the day/month/year format (with periods in between, not slashes); and an honorific plus the title is as common as the honorific plus the last name. You should write your e-mails, letters, and faxes in a formal, precise way; use a brief but warm introduction, then get down to business. Keep it simple, however, and outline all important matters. In Turkey, you may use the Asian or Western format for addresses.

ARMENIA, AZERBAIJAN, AND GEORGIA

These three countries span the rugged Caucasus Mountains, which separate Russia from both Turkey and Iran. Culturally, they both bridge and defend against the east and west; more specifically, depending on their national identities, they identify with or defend against Eastern Orthodox Christianity and Sunni and Shiite Islam.

Azerbaijan is a Turkic culture (natives of Azerbaijan, the Azeris, are a Turkic people), but with some Iranian influences. Azerbaijanis must struggle with managing the Western influences that bear down on this most eastern of the three cultures due to vast oil and gas supplies. The people practice Islam, so all the forms associated with that religion are present there, but in extremely modified forms; for example, there is much drinking of alcoholic beverages—in fact, toasting is an art in Azerbaijan. Toasts can last ten to fifteen minutes, and often go on throughout an entire meal and involve all people at the table. The toastmaster (the *tamada*) is someone who is known for his good humor, and rarely leaves anyone out of the toast. Vodka and wines are the common drinks. Azerbaijanis are extremely outgoing, emotive, and warm, as is the case with all Transcaucasus peoples. There can be much physicality (between same genders), and an introduction is usually an open door to a deep relationship (for example, never hesitate to borrow from a neighbor; but return it with something else, as well).

Armenia is a Christian country, with the Armenian Orthodox Church playing a significant role in most people's lives. Georgia had been the most profoundly Russified of the three countries during the Soviet era. All three countries have existed mainly as agrarian developing nations in a very challenging climate and topography. The region is essentially unstable as Azerbaijanis and Armenians sometimes clash over ethnic enclaves of their people in each other's countries, and as other indigenous Caucasian groups, such as the Chechens and the Ossetians, fight for independence and autonomy from Russia.

PART THREE

Southwest Asia and the Asian Arab World

Holiness and Humility

An Introduction to the Region

What is commonly known as the Middle East is "middle" only in the sense that it stands between the "Far" East and the "West." In reality, of course, it is its own world, and a very complex one at that. The "Middle Eastern" perspective, of course, is from the European vantage point. One could also refer to this area as the Arab World, as most Arabs live here, but so do many other ethnic groups, and the Arab world extends beyond the "Middle East." One could refer to this area as Islamic, as the majority of the population is, but many people are Jewish, Christian, Druze, Zoroastrian, Baha'i, and so on. One could call the area southwest Asia, but then we would be ignoring the similarities that unite many of the peoples in this region to peoples in North Africa and other regions beyond southwest Asia. Complicating the picture is the fact that combinations of many of the above are rampant: there are Christian Arabs, Arab Israelis, Jewish Syrians, and Christian Palestinians. Historically, the region is the crucible of the three great religious traditions of the West; it remains, despite massive wealth from oil and natural gas reserves, an intractably poor and politically unstable region. And it is the region that along with China will provide the century with one of its most compelling concerns: the coexistence of the West and Islam.

Getting Oriented

Southwest Asia and the Asian Arab World for our purposes consists of the following macrocultural groups:

- The Gulf Arab cultures: Saudi Arabia, Yemen, Oman, Kuwait, Qatar, Bahrain, the United Arab Emirates (UAE, including Abu Dhabi, Dubai, and five others)
- The Levantine cultures: Jordan, Syria, Lebanon, and Israel

As all of these countries are highly identified with Islam culturally, with the exception of Israel, we will begin our exploration with Saudi Arabia, the country most closely associated with Islam, and make some comments about country-specific variations as required. We will treat Israel separately.

(Please note: in the Arab world, the body of water that lies to the east of Saudi Arabia is generally called the "Arabian Gulf," not the "Persian Gulf.")

The Gulf Arab Cultures: Saudi Arabia

CHAPTER FIFTEEN

Some Introductory Background on Saudi Arabia and the Gulf Arabs

Arabs and Westerners often bring out the worst in each other, for each is sometimes quick to misunderstand the other, and to lay the blame for the misunderstanding on the other, as well. The stereotypes by each group of the other abound, and exist primarily due to the often willful refusal on both sides to understand and accept the culture of the other. Arabs, extremely proud of the power of their culture, which once ruled the world, are very defensive about their current position, having been reduced by several hundred years of Western exploitation to the status of a developing people in their own lands. The countries themselves are often artificially imposed political boundaries created by conquering (and then retreating) Europeans, and do not accurately reflect the cultural groupings of the Arab peoples themselves. Arabs are also extremely proud of Islam, and have defended its growth and development against what they sometimes see as the aggression and incursions of the West. Today, many Arabs see their struggle as the inevitable result of hundreds of years of Western exploitation, and find it increasingly difficult to adopt Western customs, institutions, and beliefs as a road out from poverty and underdevelopment; instead, they increasingly turn to their own Islam, and rediscover their pride, their power, and what is, for some, a God-given mission, to renew the world on their terms. Saudi Arabia today is the country responsible for the holiest of Islam's holy sites, Mecca and Medina, where Muhammad was respectively born and received his revelations from God, and as such, is the "center" and the most fundamentalist of all Islamic nations. If we understand the Saudi culture, and associated Saudi behaviors, we will be able to modify our behaviors when dealing with others in the region.

Some Historical Context

Saudi Arabia as a nation is a recent development: only in the late 1920s did the tribes in the region consolidate under the Saud family (al-Saud) to create a sovereign nation. Abdul Aziz al-Saud united the tribes through conquest and marriage, and strengthened his hold on the country through the application of strict Islamic law (justified in part as a way of developing Arab strength against the Westernized and impure Islam of the decaying Ottoman Empire, which governed much of the rest of southwest Asia up to the end of World War I).

An Area Briefing

Politics and Government

Today, the country is an Islamic monarchy: the king is the absolute ruler of the nation, although he is informed by a Council of Ministers (whom he selects). There is no representative government, and the only restriction on the king's powers is Islamic law, which is the law of the land. The oldest male descendant of the king would technically be in line to become the next king.

Schools and Education

All schooling is free and mandatory for all elementary, middle, and high school children, and free universities are available for those who qualify. Girls and boys are educated (although separately), and literacy is growing rapidly. Most Saudis, with the exception of nomadic tribespeople, are fairly well-off, and send their university-bound children abroad for their graduate education. There is, therefore, a knowledge and awareness of the West and its ways among the younger Saudis, and many speak English. Educated girls usually enter teaching and medicine, but women play almost a nonexistent role in business.

Religion and Demographics

Saudi Arabia is a fundamentalist Islamic state, ruled ultimately by the laws of Islam, which are rigorously applied. The majority of the people are Sunni Muslim, and there is fear and concern among the Sunni majority regarding the small Shiite minority that exists in the country. In addition, "guest workers" from other parts of the Arab and Islamic Asian world (particularly Pakistan, the Levant, Yemen, and parts of Africa) are sometimes perceived as a threat to the more puritanical nature of Islam in Saudi Arabia. (These guest workers can never become citizens, as no visitor to Saudi Arabia ever can, but they constitute the bulk of the workforce in the country, with Saudis holding the positions of authority in business, government, and the social world.)

One of the ways that the Saud family unified the nation was by appealing to and adopting the very strict Wahhabi sect of Islam: this group represented a return to a very fundamentalist interpretation of Islam and the Koran. Saudi Arabia, which is an ally of the United States in the region, curiously enough, is the most Islamic fundamentalist Arab nation (a challenge to the misguided popular belief that all radical Muslims are anti-American). There are no non-Muslim Saudi Arabians, and non-Muslim visitors, in fact, are legally prohibited from visiting the holy cities of Mecca and Medina. Mecca is the site of the annual hajj, during which devout Muslims from around the world converge to pray and become purified in the presence of the site of Muhammad's birth. In the center of the Great Mosque is a draped black cube around which Muslims pray and circle; inside of this cube lie the remains of the stone that Abraham was prepared to use for the sacrifice of his son.

Islam is the youngest of the West's three great religious traditions, beginning with Judaism and Christianity. As a Western religion, it is linked to the Judeo-Christian belief system and rejects Hinduism and Buddhism as "pagan," and not "of the book," or codified. Incorporating both Judaism and Christianity into its system of beliefs, Islam claims that it is the final revelation of a mono-theistic God, as revealed to the world through the prophet Muhammad, and that previous "messiahs," such as Jesus and Moses, were merely prophets, along with Muhammad, proclaiming the word of God. Muslims do not follow Muhammad (therefore, they are not Muhammadans, a very derogatory term created by West-erners who did not understand Islam); they believe in Allah, which is the Arabic name for the same God worshiped by Christians and Jews. Muhammad and his followers wrote down the law of God as revealed to them into the Koran (or Qu'ran), the Islamic holy book. It does not negate the Old or New Tes-taments: it merely provides, in the eyes of the Muslim faithful, the final re-quired text. Muhammad received his revelations from God in Medina; prior to Islam, the nomadic tribes of the region believed in a variety of pagan ideas, but with the notion of one God, and the laws under which people were to behave, Muhammad was able to unify the peoples of the Gulf Arab peninsula into the beginnings of a single Arab culture. This is one of the reasons why Gulf Arabs are singularly Muslim (this is not necessarily the case elsewhere in the Arab world). Islam spread rapidly throughout the Middle East, into Europe, and east-ward across Asia. While Islam underwent a serious split almost immediately following Muhammad's death (two major camps emerged, the Shia and the Sunni, in an effort to decide how to continue the faith), it nevertheless rapidly gathered huge followings. Sunni Muslims believe that the caliphs, or religious leaders, subsequent to Muhammad are legitimate; Shiite Muslims believe that the caliphs subsequent to Muhammad are usurpers, and therefore do not believe in Sunni authority. All Muslims must abide by five basic tenets, or Pillars of Faith:

- Proclaim the supremacy of the one true God, Allah, above all others
- Pray to Allah five times daily
- Observe Ramadan, the holy month, the ninth month of the Islamic calendar, which is essentially a celebration of the first time when God revealed his word to Muhammad
- Give alms to the poor and needy
- Perform the hajj, or spiritual (and physical) journey to Mecca, at least once in their lifetime if they are capable of doing so

Specific codes of conduct have developed over time, and have been codified into Islamic law, known as the Shari'a. The degree to which one follows these scriptures often determines how devoutly one applies the Islamic ethical code in day-to-day life; in Saudi Arabia, the Shari'a is enforced by the "religious police," or *mataween:* they are fully empowered to arrest, publicly whip, and otherwise ensure the complete compliance of the entire populace with the rigid fundamentalist Islamic laws.

Women and men play completely different roles in this society, with women primarily handling private life, and men handling public life. This means that women do the nurturing and educating, and men do the business and civic rul-ing. This does not mean that these roles—and subsequently men and women—are unequal, for both roles cannot be performed by or without the other. It will be very difficult for Western businesswomen who do not establish acceptance of their authority ahead of time to be effective in this male-dominated business environment; they can be, but only if their expertise is required, and only if they behave in their role as subject-matter expert according to all the strict require-ments of the Islamic code.

Fundamental Cultural Orientations

1. What's the Best Way for People to Relate to One Another?

OTHER-INDEPENDENT OR OTHER-DEPENDENT? There is a combination of deep concern for family, clan, and other membership groups that defines an individual (such as work and religion), and individual expression. Saudis, like all Arabs, are deeply connected first to their clan and their families: this is an intensely private life (and therefore, one needs to be very careful about inquiring about the family, among other things). However, individual pride, and how one is seen by others, is perhaps the most important aspect of Arab culture that non-Arabs need to be sensitive to. It is not a heightened sense of individualism separate from others; in fact, it is the opposite. Because of one's intricate relationships with others (there is an old saying that an Arab has one thousand close relatives), one is always keenly aware of how one is being perceived and of one's obligations to others. It is very important that you always show great respect for your Arab colleague. Arab pride must be supported and respected.

HIERARCHY-ORIENTED OR EGALITY-ORIENTED? As Muslims, all people are technically equal in their submission to Allah and his will; however, Arabs structure the secular world with clearly assigned roles, so that Allah's will can be fulfilled effectively. It is critical that everyone show respect for elders and devout Muslims, and men for women, sons for fathers, older brothers for younger brothers. All individuals have a role to play in this hierarchy, and are responsible to others and the greater Arab community to fulfill their role. Those above absolutely make the decisions for those below, and those ultimately in charge, the Islamic rulers and their *mataween,* have ultimate authority. There is a saying in Arabic, "The eye cannot rise above the eyebrow": it means that people must know their station and position in life, and make the best of it. Women and men are different and perform different roles: in Saudi Arabia a woman typically may not go out in public alone, or in the company of a man who is not a near relative (husband, father, son, or brother); if she does, both she and the man risk punishment, including jail.

RULE-ORIENTED OR RELATIONSHIP-ORIENTED? While many Saudis have had experience with the West, Islamic law, not Western rules, are the rules that are followed, and these are applied universally if they are universal, and subject to interpretation and uneven application if nonuniversal. This leads to a high dependence on power, authority, and subjective decision making based on the situation and the relationships between the individuals involved. Ultimately, face-to-face knowledge of the individuals involved in any interaction is the basis upon which final decisions are often made.

2. What's the Best Way to View Time?

MONOCHRONIC OR POLYCHRONIC? Saudi Arabia is essentially very polychronic, due to the influence of both agrarian and religious traditions. The clock is definitely not the determinant of action; it plays a role, most certainly, particularly in the larger more modern urban areas, and there is an acceptance of

Western organizational ideas (Westerners should not be late, for example). Nevertheless, there is forgiveness for the inevitable delays, and understanding when things don't go as planned or scheduled; people may or may not show up at invited events, things may or may not happen as planned. Things take the time they take, that's all (the concept of *buqrah*). Muslim laws even view planning too far into the future—or planning at all in some cases—as heretical, for it presumes that individuals can control events that are essentially in the hands of Allah. Even today, schedules tend to be loose and flexible; the workday begins around 9 A.M. and ends around 4 P.M. Most workers take an hour break after lunch. Because who (relationships) is more important than what (tasks) or when (time), there can be many interruptions during a meeting, and people's obligations to other people, who may come and go, are more important than doing things according to schedules. If you are being kept waiting, or are ignored because of someone else's needs, it is an indication of your importance relative to the other person.

RISK-TAKING OR RISK-AVERSE? Saudis, and most Arabs, are prone to taking risks when in positions of authority, but avoiding them when they are not. Within organizations, the decision makers can be bold, even reckless, but subordinates generally are not, and take action only when instructed to do so. Therefore, comfort with uncertainty, in general, is low, and much information may need to be exchanged with different people before decisions can be made. Even when decisions are made at the top, the concern for others in the group requires decision makers to consult with subordinates before making decisions. There will be much discussion with trusted others about what you, as a foreigner, bring to the table, *after* you leave the meeting.

PAST-ORIENTED OR FUTURE-ORIENTED? There is a distinct and inherent fatalism in regard to the effect of human action, fundamentally because only Allah determines what and when things will happen. Nevertheless, those empowered by virtue of their position are expected to make the decisions that keep the world running. Therefore, future benefits often do not motivate Saudis; doing nothing, or doing things for the here and now, is sometimes more important, and if things do not work out, that is to be expected—no mortal controls the universe, and all is ultimately determined. There is a deep belief that things will take the time they need to take, and that only Allah knows what that is (this has often been summarized as the "IBM" of the Arab world: *inshallah*—as and only if Allah wills it; *buqrah*—things will take the time they take; and *ma'alesh*—loosely translated as "don't worry," "don't sweat it," "it'll turn out okay, you may not see it now, but it's all for the best").

3. What's the Best Way for Society to Work with the World at Large?

LOW-CONTEXT DIRECT OR HIGH-CONTEXT INDIRECT COMMUNICATORS? Arabs are very context-driven communicators. They will speak in metaphors, and use stories or codified phrases; they will employ analogies, Islamic precedent, and much nonverbal behavior to convey true meaning. They generally avoid confrontation, and are honor-bound to do everything possible to make strangers like and honor them (they are lavish hosts). They will avoid unpleasant discussions as long as possible, and it is precisely because they shun unpleasantness in discussions that anger can blow fast and hard when disagreements can no longer be avoided.

PROCESS-ORIENTED OR RESULT-ORIENTED? Islamic law, and the complex study of Islam that developed in the Muslim world into its own field of scholastic inquiry, is fundamentally different from Western Greco-Roman philosophies of knowing. In Islam, interpretation and truth is dependent upon analogous reasoning, while in the West, such inquiry is based more on "argument" (proving and disproving). Decisions and actions therefore may be the result of reasoning that is not directed at a determination of truth, but rather context-based "correctness" based on similar experiences, often with the strict Islamic code as the only context. Combine this with a tendency to rely also on subjective experience, and the Arab mind is processing information, for the most part, in a different way than the Western mind.

FORMAL OR INFORMAL? Arab society is formal and ritualized, and each group has its own way of honoring the hierarchies, establishing respect and deference, and following (or not following) through on their responsibilities. They are even more formal when one is an outsider, which is always the case with non-Muslims.

Greetings and Introductions

Language and Basic Vocabulary

Arabic is the language of the Koran, and therefore, by extension, is the language of God. There are many forms of Arabic throughout the region, some more formal and some informal, but Arabic is the primary language. As a Semitic language, it is very different from other Asian and European languages, and is written from right to left in a flowing script. Written vowel sounds are assigned to consonant letters with diacritical marks, with words changing tense, agreement, and meaning based on the addition of suffixes and prefixes to the root or stem words.

Words and language have a power all their own in the Arab world; in fact, it has been said that the expression of a feeling or action can sometimes replace the feeling or the action itself. Therefore, the expression of anger, which may involve statements of violence, in fact may be a way of precluding the act of violence. Be extremely sensitive to the meaning of words, the emotion behind them, how they are used, and how you use them. Speech can be flowery, overblown, hyperbolic, and rich in texture; this is meant to honor both the speaker and the person to whom one is speaking. Many religious phrases are added onto everyday statements (e.g., "———, *Inshallah*"—"if God wills"; or "———, *mash'allah*"—"what God wills," usually said after speaking about someone's health; or "———, *alhamdu lillah*"—"Thanks be to God," spoken as a way of giving thanks for something that has happened, or which you hope will happen). Never use religious references casually or disrespectfully—it is assumed all people are religious in some way, even if not a Muslim—and be very careful never to use "God" in any way other than in the most respectful sense. There is a Classical Arabic, which Saudis claim to speak, with essentially three other basic dialects of Arabic spoken in the region: Egyptian/Sudanese, Levantine, and Gulf Arabic. All three are mutually intelligible to one another.

It is important to recognize that other non-Arabic languages are spoken throughout the region, including indigenous languages such as Berber in North Africa, Coptic in Egypt, Hebrew and Aramaic in the Levant, and Farsi (Persian) and south Arabian nomadic languages in the Gulf states.

Here are some basic Arabic phrases and their meanings in English:

marhaba, or *marhaba alan*	hello
marhabtayn, or *marhabtayn alan*	hello (response)
ahlan wasahlan	welcome
ahlan beek	thanks (response)
sabah alkayr	good morning
sabah annoor	good morning (response)
assalamu 'alaykum	peace be with you (general greeting)
wa'alaykum assalam	and upon you, peace (response)
min fadleek	please
aesef	sorry, excuse me
ma'a ssalama (go with safety)	good-bye
allah yisallimak (may God make you safe)	good-bye (response)
shukran	thank you
'afwan	you're welcome

English is taught in schools, so young people often speak and understand some English; businesspeople from the upper classes (most Saudis) speak English, since they were educated, in most cases, abroad. Most people on the street in most Arabic-speaking countries, however, speak little English.

Honorifics for Men, Women, and Children

Names will be Arabic in content in the region, but structured according to fairly complex and sometimes differing traditions.

Most people have several names, but the order of the names is similar to that of the West, with the given name first, and the family name last. Other names used may refer to one's role in the family (such as son) or an honorary association with an important or meaningful person (often a reference to an important person in Islamic history). It is important to address Arabs by their given (or first) names, because that is really their only true name (the other names being indications of genealogy or relationship). Several common relationship forms found in names are:

- *Bin* or *ould* (North African and Levantine), or *ibn* (Gulf Arab), meaning ". . . son of": for example, Abdel Azziz ibn Saud (Abdel, son of Saud); or Muhammad ould Haidalla (Muhammad, son of Haidalla)
- *Bint* or *binte,* meaning ". . . daughter of": for example, Fatima bint Saud (Fatima, daughter of Saud)
- *Bou* (North African mainly), meaning ". . . father of": for example, Habib bou Guiba (Habib, father of Guiba)

The honorifics Mr., Mrs., and Miss, are placed before the surname; and you should always use titles, if they are known (doctor, professor, etc.) before the surname, as well: for example, Dr. Habib, Professor Muhammad, Princess Asma, Sheikh Abdullah (sheikh is an indication of importance; it does not represent a specific title or position, nor does it represent the leadership of any one particular clan, tribe, or group).

Ma'ali is an honorific often used for government officials (it means "Your excellency"); high officials are given the honorific *sa'ada* before their names.

- *Al-* + family name: usually indicates "house of" as the family (final) name: for example, Muhammad ibn Abdallah al-Ahmar (Muhammad, son of Abdallah, house of Ahmar).
- Sometimes grandfathers, and male forebears even further back, are acknowledged in the string of names, so that there may be several *ibn* + name groupings within the name: for example, Muhammad ibn Abdallah ibn Muhammad al-Ahmar (Muhammad, son of Abdallah, son of Muhammad, of the house of Ahmar). Usually, after several generations, the most distant names are dropped. Arabs usually do not give their sons the same first name as the father, but commonly use the grandfather's name, so the first and third names are more often the same.
- A woman does not typically take her husband's family name when she marries: she keeps her family name, and is addressed as "Mrs. + her first name."
- Hyphenated names usually represent an attribute plus the name: for example, Abdel-Allah Muhammad ibn Kamal ibn Muhammad al-Tawil (Servant of God Muhammad, son of Kamal, son of Muhammad, of the house of Tawil).
- Muslim males who have made the hajj often use the honorific *hajji* as a title before the surname, and any other honorifics: for example, Hajji Dr. Abdel-Allah Muhammad ibn Kamal ibn Muhammad al-Tawil. Muslim females who have made the hajj often use the honorific *hajja* as a title before the surname, and any other honorifics.
- Women retain all male references to genealogy in their name after their given female surname: for example, Hajja Dr. Asmah bint Muhammad ibn Kamal ibn Muhammad al-Tawil (a devout, educated sister of the above-mentioned Abdel-Allah Muhammad who has made the hajj).

Single women traveling in the region may want to consider wearing a wedding band; it can help avoid a myriad of difficult questions and problems.

Finally, sometimes (especially in the Levant and Egypt) the honorifics *um* (mother) and *abu* (father) may be used in front of the given name, or replace a name completely. This is an affectionate way of referring to someone you may know.

The What, When, and How of Introducing People

Saudis may, upon greeting you, call you by your last or first name, with or without your title. Always wait to be introduced to strangers; never take that responsibility upon yourself, as doing so is considered inappropriate most of the time. Saudis, and Arabs in general, are most comfortable with third-party introductions, and because business is very personal, you will need an individual to introduce you to the required businesspeople. Never presume to seat yourself at a gathering: if possible, wait to be told where to sit. The seating arrangements have usually been carefully worked out in advance, and in most cases reflect the status of the individuals in the group, and the honor that is being accorded the guests. When departing, it is important to say farewell to every individual present: the American group wave is not appreciated. Once you greet someone you will encounter later that day in the same circumstances (e.g., at the office), you do not need to greet them when you see them again. Seniors, or those who are obviously the oldest in a group, are greeted first, seated first, and allowed to enter a room first (usually at the center of a group, however, and in most cases preceded by their younger aides).

Physical Greeting Styles

Close associates and businessmen (the operative part of the word is *men,* as this is only between men, and never between men and women) who have developed intimate working relationships often greet each other warmly, with hugs and kisses. Wait until your Saudi host initiates this behavior before initiating it yourself. Typically, the greeting here is the salaam, which involves a soft handshake with the right hand, after which, for extra sincerity, you may put your hand back to your heart and touch it. In addition, Saudis and other Gulf Arabs also reach out and touch the shoulder of the other person with their left hand. Traditionally, the salaam was performed by quickly touching your forehead first, then your heart, then the front of your abdomen with your right hand as you bowed slightly; this is still done on very formal occasions. Muslim women and men do not touch or shake hands (unless the woman is very Westernized). The handshake may be soft, almost limp sometimes. This does not signify insincerity; rather, it is an accommodation to the Western fashion while remaining humble and considerate.

The traditional business introduction also includes the exchange of business cards. Always take a large supply of business cards with you: you should give one to every new person you are introduced to (there is no need to provide another business card when you are meeting someone again unless information about you has changed, such as a new address, contact number, or position). Be sure your business cards are in fine shape: they are an extension of you as a person, and must look as good as possible. Embossed cards are extremely impressive, especially with logos in green (the color of Islam). Never hand out a dirty, soiled, bent, or written-on card. You should translate your business card into Arabic on the reverse side.

When presenting a business card, you give it to your colleague so that it is readable for him as you hold it (he will, in turn, present his card so that it is readable for you); you should hold the card with two hands in the upper corners as you present it. Do not worry too much about who receives and gives his business card first: the exchange is very quick, and because you would probably not be introduced to that person in the first place if you were not already seen as having an equivalent rank, there is no need to show deference. There is also no need for bowing.

Smiling and other nonverbal forms of communication may accompany the card exchange. Information about each other's status is the most important information to be exchanged, and this is provided directly on the business card, as well as indirectly through a number of high-context indicators, such as gender, age, and the number of people surrounding and assisting the other person. Should you meet more than one individual at a reception, you will have a handful of cards when the greetings are over.

As the business card exchange usually precedes a sit-down meeting, it is important to arrange the cards you have received in a little seating plan in front of you along the top of the desk or the table at your seat, reflecting the order in which people are seated. This will help you connect the correct names with the correct individuals throughout the meeting. Do this even if you are just meeting one person; it is expected. During the meeting, it is important never to play with the business cards (do not write on them—ever!); and when the meeting is over, never put them in your back pants pockets: pick them up carefully and respectfully, and place them neatly in your cardholder (a nice-looking brass card case would be perfect), then place the cardholder in the left inside jacket pocket of your suit (nearest your heart).

Do not photograph people without asking their permission, ever, and do not videotape freely. In some of the countries in the Arab world, videotaping is generally illegal.

Communication Styles

Okay Topics / Not Okay Topics

Okay: anything that reflects your personal interests and hobbies, religion, and your sincere appreciation of and curiosity about things native to the Arab world. Most Saudis whom foreigners meet are relatively wealthy and influential. They love horses and sports; camel racing and horse racing are popular (but there is no betting allowed). *Not okay:* Politics, current events, or any subject that might in any way be controversial needs to be avoided at first. Do not inquire about a person's occupation or income in casual conversation, although it may be inquired of you (if so, this is just a way of getting to know more about your country, and not a personal investigation: answer specifically, but fully, with an explanation as to what things cost at home, why you do what you do, etc.). Other personal questions may be asked of you ("Why are you not married?" or "Do you have any sons?"); the best responses are those that fit the Saudi context ("Allah has not blessed me yet, I wait patiently."). Do not inquire about family life, especially spouses, or the role of servants and household help. Do not give your opinions about Israel, Jews, foreign workers, Islamic fundamentalism, or women's rights. Do not talk about sex, or tell dirty jokes: it is in very bad taste. Discussions about your company and its work are very much appreciated, as they give Saudis a chance to learn more about you and your firm. The goal of all conversation, at least at the beginning, is to create and maintain a harmonious atmosphere, despite the difficult or confrontational nature of the topic being discussed. At first, speak about things that you believe you have in common, so that you can build a personal connection that will go far toward maintaining a harmonious bridge between you. This is appropriate for both individuals and organizations.

Tone, Volume, and Speed

The people of this region generally speak in soft, quiet, and restrained tones. Saudis, and most Arabs, raise their voices only when it is necessary to display anger—and at that point, it is usually too late in the relationship. They may speak rapidly, but if you, in turn, speak rather slowly, they may get the hint and slow down.

Use of Silence

Passive silence—allowing time to pass simply without words—can be a form of proactive communication and is used as a nonverbal way of avoiding confrontation, disagreement, or an unpleasant subject. If confronted with unexplainable silence, gently coax the conversation in a different direction, one that is more mutually harmonious.

Physical Gestures and Facial Expressions

You are advised to reduce the amount of body language you use, although Saudis and most Arabs are very comfortable with nonverbal behavior (you just do not want to inadvertently offend). Winking, whistling, and other similar displays are considered very vulgar. Public displays of familiarity and affection with the opposite sex are never expressed. Never touch anyone on his or her head, even a child; this is considered the holiest part of the body. Do not point with or show the sole of your shoe to anyone: this is considered vulgar, as the bottom of the shoe touches the ground, and is therefore the dirtiest part of the body. Any gesture involving a closed fist or made with the "thumbs-up" sign is considered quite vulgar. Standing with your hands on your hips is considered very aggressive and should always be avoided. Yawning is considered impolite; you must cover your mouth when you yawn.

For any action or gesture that would naturally be done only with one hand, do not use your left hand, as this is considered the unclean hand (the hand used for personal hygiene). Pass all documents, food, and money with your right hand (if you're a southpaw, you will have to practice this). You must remove your shoes before entering a mosque (and some buildings, as well as homes), and you may need to wash your feet and hands at the entrance fountain provided before entering a mosque as well. Women may be restricted to specific areas and times when visiting mosques. Women entering mosques need to have their heads covered, their legs covered below the knee, and their arms covered below the elbow; Western women do not necessarily need to have their faces covered. Smile whenever possible: it smoothes the way with strangers quickly and easily.

Waving and Counting

The thumb represents the number 1, the pinkie represents the number 5, with everything in between ordered from the thumb down; however, instead of raising the fingers when counting, the whole hand is exposed, and each finger is depressed as the counting is done. It is very insulting to motion to someone with the forefinger (instead, turn your hand so that the palm is facing down and motion inward with all four fingers at once). If you need to gesture for a waiter, very subtly raise your hand. Waving or beckoning is done with the palm down and the fingers moving forward and backward in a kind of scratching motion. It may seem as if the person making the gesture is saying good-bye to you, when in fact you are being summoned over. If you need to point to something or someone, close your fingers, open your palm and face it upward, and pass your hand in the direction you want to indicate.

Physicality and Physical Space

Saudis and most Arabs stand closer than most North Americans are accustomed to; resist the urge to move back. Many Arabs are comfortable at a distance where they can feel the warmth of the breath of the other person. Never speak with your hands in your pockets: always keep them firmly at your side when standing. If men and women must cross their legs when they sit, it must never be ankle over knee (for women, the preferred style is to cross ankle over ankle; but the bottoms of the shoes must not show to the other person). Remember, even in public, formal is always better than informal: no gum chewing, *ever;* don't slouch; and don't lean against things. Arabs are most comfortable when they are next to other people: in a nearly empty bus, movie theater, or restaurant, in most cases, Arabs will tend to sit next to or near the other people present, instead of far away from them.

Eye Contact

Eye contact can be very direct between strangers and once relationships are established. As a Westerner, you may be the object of other people's stares: this is not meant to be impolite; it is mere curiosity. However, rank changes eye contact patterns; interest in what one's supervisor says is often best shown by averting the eyes, not by making eye contact. The eyes are used extensively to convey true feelings in formal situations where it is difficult to express things verbally. Tune up your nonverbal antennae.

Emotive Orientation

Arabs are emotive and demonstrative. There can be much touching (at least between members of the same sex) during even the most casual conversation. Two men or two women often walk hand in hand or arm in arm down the street. Verbal communication often employs effusiveness, exaggeration, and flowery phrases: this is meant to show sincerity, not duplicity.

Protocol in Public

Walking Styles and Waiting in Lines

On the street, in stores, and in most public facilities, people pay little attention to maintaining orderly lines. Due to the volume of passengers on public transportation, there can be much pushing and jostling. This is not to get into a bus ahead of someone else, though; it is merely to get in! This is not meant to be disrespectful; if it is bothersome, just say so politely, and you will be treated well. If you ask an Arab for directions, he or she will make every effort to show you the way (even if he or she is not that certain!).

Behavior in Public Places: Airports, Terminals, and the Market

Pride will always demand that Arabs provide you with assistance; even if they do not have an answer, they will give you one. If you feel like you are on the outside, or being treated as a stranger, strike up a polite and respectful conversation: you will be treated honorably.

Establish a personal relationship with a shopkeeper, and you can expect much assistance as a newcomer; once this is done, you are treated royally. Stores in the cities are open in the evenings and on weekends, as well as during the day, but close during the Muslim Sabbath (Friday) and in preparation for it (Thursday nights), and on all Muslim holidays. A personal verbal thank-you to store owners, waiters, chefs, and hotel managers for their services is important, as it will help establish the relationship you need to get continuing good service. In food markets, do not touch the produce unless you are buying it; in goods stores, if you buy a product and have problems with it, returning the item is usually difficult. Smoking is endemic, and you may have difficulty finding a no-smoking area on public transportation, in restaurants, and in other public places (be sure not to smoke during Ramadan, when Muslims abstain; this is true for eating and drinking during the day during Ramadan when in the presence of observant Muslims, as well). When and if you do smoke, it is critical that you offer a cigarette first to everyone else at the table before you light up, and then offer to light their cigarettes for them. Bathroom facilities can range from Western-style toilets to Asian-style toilets (holes in the floor, with buckets of water or hoses attached to a water line for cleanup instead of paper); be prepared.

Unless they are in the company of other women or close male relatives, women generally do not go out in public, especially at night. Western women traveling alone in Saudi Arabia will place an unusual burden of consideration on the behavior of others toward them: many people won't know what to do, or how to act toward them; some other women will want to assist them, and certain men, no doubt, will try to take advantage of them. Traveling alone is not a good idea in any part of the Arab world for women.

Never bring anything into the countries of the Arab world that can be construed as pornographic or challenging to Islam in even the slightest way: videotapes, books, and magazines will be inspected and confiscated at most borders if so judged.

When answering a telephone, say "Hello" or just your given name. Cell phones are ubiquitous.

Bus / Metro / Taxi / Car

Driving is on the right, and whether in the country or city, being in a car can be hazardous to your health. The roads are not necessarily in good repair in the developing Arab world (but they are generally in very good shape in Gulf Arabia), marked, or where maps say they are; obtaining fuel, however, is usually not a problem. Driving on the good roads in Gulf Arabia, however, poses its own set of problems, since people drive like they own the road: at any speed, in any direction, at any time. It is very dangerous. Traveling alone is not done in

Saudi Arabia, and in other parts of the Arab world it may be dangerous in towns where you are not known. Driving simply puts you at risk of being stopped by police. Non-Muslims will be prohibited from entering Medina and Mecca.

The best way to catch a cab is at designated taxi stands (hotels are good places, but often charge more for the same ride: a hotel surcharge is added to the meter fare, in some cases). When a taxi has been hailed, negotiate the price. Whenever possible, have the address you need to get to written down on a piece of paper (or use the business card of the person you are going to see, if you can) before you hail the cab.

Tipping

Tipping is universally required throughout the Arab world, and then some. It is traditional to always give a little something to someone who has helped you out (in Saudi Arabia, these will often be guest workers from abroad). The offer may be refused in some cases, but if you insist, it will be graciously accepted and appreciated. Tips in restaurants run about 10 percent, and are typically not included in the bill (but double-check to be sure); a tip is not necessary if you have negotiated the fare for the taxi ahead of time, and already figured in the tip. For everything else, a few coins is all that is needed, but you should always have a lot of spare change handy to see you through the day.

Punctuality

Punctuality is valued, but not required. You should be on time, but you may be kept waiting for quite awhile: patience and good humor is required. Never get upset over time. If you are late, making a general comment about the traffic is all you need to do to get off the hook for being late. It will be understood.

Dress

Saudi men traditionally wear the *ghotra* (head covering) and *thobe* (white robe covering); Saudi women usually wear the black robe (*abaya*), plus a veil. It is *not* appropriate for non-Saudis to dress in traditional Saudi clothes; Westerners should dress in conservative business clothes, but may find it more comfortable to wear items that are as loose fitting as possible (the weather is hot, and you may be required to sit cross-legged from time to time on cushions). In all cases, for men and women, most of the body needs to be covered, including arms down to the wrists, torso up to the neck, and legs down to the ankles. (Men must not wear neck jewelry, even if it is not visible underneath clothing.) Clothes must not be tight-fitting or revealing in any way, either for men or women. If you're dressing casually, your shirt must be buttoned up to the neck. Women should not wear pants suits, as they reveal too much of the shape of the legs. Any clothing that is different from the prescribed norm will engender stares, and perhaps *mataween* intervention. Women whose legs are clearly showing above their ankles risk having their legs whipped in the street. Sneakers and T-shirts are only for the gym; shorts are never okay, on the street or elsewhere.

Seasonal Variations

In Saudi Arabia, it is always dry and hot: the air-conditioning, however, can be frigid, so be prepared with a shawl or another type of cover-up.

Colors

Neutral and muted, whenever possible.

Styles

For visitors, wear conservative Western clothes. Period.

Accessories / Jewelry / Makeup

Makeup, hairstyle, and accessories are important for women, but only if done modestly. In any event, they often can't be seen underneath the veil. Western women should avoid risking too much makeup. Curiously, the Saudis appreciate men and women who smell good. There is liberal use of cologne among men at work during the day; and if you visit a Saudi's home, a tray of perfume is often at the entrance, for women to use as they come and go (feel free). Arabs have a keenly developed sense of smell and taste. Colognes and perfumes are typically not made with alcohol (alcohol is prohibited in Islam).

Personal Hygiene

In Saudi Arabia, cleanliness is associated with purity. Washing both hands and feet more than once a day is very common. Do not blow your nose in public: it is considered very rude. Spitting does occur on the street, but is also regarded as rude. Muslim men may sport facial hair, usually in the form of a mustache. At the end of a meal, if you use a toothpick, you must cover the "working" hand with the other hand, so that others cannot see your mouth. Remember that Muslims consider dogs very unclean; therefore, do not refer to them or bring them along with you.

Dining and Drinking

Mealtimes and Typical Foods

The typical Saudi diet is rich in grains, breads, fresh vegetables, and fruits. Meats will include lamb, goat, and chicken. Gulf Arab cuisine includes dips made of eggplant (*babaghanoush*), hummus (a chickpea and sesame paste), and other ingredients. Olive products are varied, and there is liberal use of fruits (fresh and dried, especially figs, dates, raisins, and pomegranates) and nuts. Breads can be the pocket-type pitas and leavened or unleavened breads. Foods can be spicy, but are not necessarily hot. Although they are becoming increasingly familiar with Western food, Saudis and Arabs in general love their food, and most enjoy a fine local meal (if you are hosting them in your country, unless they directly express an interest in trying a local cuisine, take them to the best local Middle Eastern restaurant you can find, and tell the restaurant manager that you are hosting Arab guests: the restaurant management will usually go out of their way to make the meal very fine for you).

If you are serving a meal at home, be sure you do not use alcohol or pork in any of the dishes; and if you do, labeling the dish and serving it separately will still make your Arab guest uncomfortable—simply don't do it. You, as a guest in the region, may be rewarded with favored parts of the animal, such as the goat's eye or head: this is an honor that needs to be acknowledged before the food is consumed or rejected (if you cannot bring yourself to partake, acknowledge the honor, and suggest that while you will always hold the honor in your heart, you in turn will bestow it on someone who can also appreciate it in their belly: then pass the honored dish on to an Arab colleague). In fact, in the Gulf area, if you are invited to someone's home and see a sheep's carcass in front of or on the grounds of the house, this is an honor: it means the animal has been slaughtered in your honor, and you can be sure you will have the meat for dinner.

Most meals begin with tasty appetizers of dips and vegetables and breads, and are served buffet or family style, so there is much for everyone. The amount of food at a meal at which you are a guest in the region can be overwhelming; guests must be treated with great respect and honor. It is far better to return for more than to load up your plate at once and not be able to eat any more later.

Breakfast is served from about 7 to 8 A.M., and usually consists of tea and coffee, breads, jams, cheese, and olives. Tea is usually drunk with milk or sugar. Yogurt and fruit drinks are sometimes served for breakfast. The coffee is rich, dark, and served in small cups, usually without milk. It is often flavored with sweet spices, such as cardamom or cinnamon.

Lunch is traditionally the main meal of the day, and even today in busy cities, it can still be an elaborate affair with several courses—or it can be a simple snack prepared and eaten in a matter of minutes. Lunch is served from about noon to 2 P.M. Lunch consists of meat, fish, and/or vegetables, with rice or yogurt, and can be in a stewlike vegetable sauce. Typically, the drinks served with lunch and dinner are usually soft drinks, fruit juices, and/or tea, with Arabic coffee after the meal.

Dinner is served from 8 P.M. on, with nine o'clock the customary late time. Even if the main meal of the day was lunch, dinner is only slightly lighter—this is often the case with families at home. The dinner menu is often similar to that of the more formal lunch, with *felaffel,* lamb shish kebabs, and other more elaborate dishes. Dinner drinks are similar to those served at lunch. When you come to a Saudi home, even for a brief visit, you will be served some sweet delicacy plus a cool drink (usually iced water, lemonade, or fruit juice) and/or tea and coffee. The sweet is not a dessert; you will get that at the end of the meal as well. Desserts can be very sweet, such as honeyed pastries, not unlike baklava, with puddings made of sweetened yogurts, nuts, rosewater, and eggs.

Regional Differences

Chicken cooked with herbs, tomatoes, and spices is a favorite. Another favorite dish is *foul,* or fava beans prepared with olive oil and lemon. Stuffed grape leaves are popular appetizers, as well as *f'teer,* a kind of pizza filled with meat and vegetables. Cheese is popular, either as a feta-like soft cheese, or as a hard, cheddar-like white cheese. Remember, Islam prohibits the use of pork, and most meats of any kind for Muslims need to be prepared *halal* (meat slaughtered according to Islamic prescriptions). A staple grain is couscous, cooked in a thousand different ways with many different ingredients. Do not eat in front of your Muslim colleagues, or invite them to join you for a meal, during the day during Ramadan, as Muslims typically fast (and restrain from drinking and smoking) during the day, and feast with family and friends at night. Ramadan lasts for a lunar month: this is simply not a good time to do business or go out entertaining in the Arab Middle East.

Typical Drinks and Toasting

Tea and coffee are served everywhere, all the time. Sometimes tea or coffee is boiling hot: sometimes it is lukewarm; most of the time tea is served with milk or sugar. Coffee is served in small cups, always without milk; it is strong, black, and sometimes spiced. Always accept the cup of tea and/or coffee, even if you only put it to your lips or just take a few sips. Your cup will always be refilled if it is less than half full. The ceremony of tea/coffee/tea can last hours, as you chat and converse, and do business, and it goes something like this: you will be offered tea; when you are finished, you will be offered coffee; when you are finished, you will be offered tea again, and the whole process can repeat itself. This is an important relationship-building event. Typically, beer and other alcoholic drinks are not served: fruit juices and lemonades, along with tea, may accompany most meals. Because you must never pour your own drink (be it juice or tea or coffee), you must always be alert throughout the meal as to whether your neighbor's cup or glass needs refilling. If it is less than half full, it needs refilling; alternately, if yours is less than half full, your neighbor is obliged to refill it. If he or she does not, do not refill it yourself, for this will cause your neighbor to lose face; instead, diplomatically indicate your need by pouring a little more drink into your neighbor's glass, even if it doesn't really need it.

If you are the honored guest, you will be expected to make a toast, usually soon after the host does or at the end of the meal, just before everyone departs. An appropriate toast is to the health of the host and all those present, and to the prosperity of the business under discussion. Make it as eloquent and flowery as you like, but always be very sincere.

Avoid drinking tap water anywhere in the region (this means you should brush your teeth with bottled water and not take ice in any of your drinks; drink only bottled water, or brewed tea or coffee or soft drinks, and avoid getting water from the morning shower into your mouth; never eat fresh fruits or vegetables that cannot be peeled first, and ideally cooked later before eating). This is a serious matter: there are some nasty bugs going around in developing countries. In addition, avoid all dairy products except in the finest hotels, as the required refrigeration may be questionable.

A word about water and its use in the region: consider that most of the region is desert, so despite the graciousness of your hosts, water use is a serious concern in this part of the world. Even if you won't drink tap water, use it judiciously when you do use it.

Table Manners and the Use of Utensils

Before meals, as the food is served, guests say, "*Sahtain*" (the equivalent of "bon appetit"), or "*Bismillah*" (In the name of God); when the meal is over, guests should also say, "*Daimah*" ("may there always be plenty at your table").

You will either be served Western utensils or not. Throughout the region, people use spoons, forks, and knives, if necessary, or no utensils at all. Since the spoon is more important than the fork, if you are right-handed, keep the spoon in the right hand, and put it down to switch to the fork if and when you need it. Never use your left hand for eating, especially if you are eating directly with your hands.

What do you do when no utensils are available? Why, eat with your fingers, of course! Many think it makes the experience more fun, maybe because you're adding an extra sense to an already very sensory experience: the sense of touch. A great variety of foods can be eaten with the hands, including wonderful vegetarian or meat curries, shish kebabs, and the like, served with rice and sauce. You reach into the rice, take some with your fingers, gently roll it between your index and middle fingers and thumb (not your palms) into a kind of self-sticking ball, dip it into the sauce, mix it with a vegetable or a piece of chicken, then pop the whole thing in your mouth.

Here are some other things to note before eating such foods:

• Wash your hands before you sit down to eat. Many restaurants have washrooms and sinks out in the open specifically for this purpose. (However, you may want to wash your hands with bottled water at the hotel first, since the water at the restaurant may be more hazardous to your health than the germs already on your hands!). You will also need to wash your hands again at the end of the meal, especially after eating the saucy dishes, since you've probably got some messy fingers by the end of the meal. Don't worry, it's to be expected.

• Use your right hand when picking up and eating food: never your left hand. Keep your left hand at your side. Do not place your left hand on the table, and do not pass food with your left hand.

• Pork will typically not be on the menu.

• Alcohol will usually not be served with the meal.

• Men and women, in some establishments, may be asked to dine separately.

• If you absolutely cannot eat without some kind of utensil, it's perfectly all right to ask for one. The proprietors, or your hosts, are usually more than pleased to accommodate Westerners.

It is especially important that if men and women are dining together (rare in Saudi Arabia, but more common elsewhere), that women not directly touch food that is being served to a Muslim male, other than those who are her immediate relatives: to do so makes it impure.

A word about smoking: it is ubiquitous throughout the region. Usually, you do not smoke until the meal is over. In addition, at the end of some meals, particularly in Saudi Arabia and the Gulf region, incense or cologne might be passed around as a final refreshment: you lean over and gently inhale the sweet smell. Fresh mints or caraway seeds may be offered as a special treat just before you go.

Most discussion occurs before the meal, not after, although dining at someone's home will last well into the night. Expect to be told that it is too early to leave the first time you try; stay a while longer, but if the hosts serve some ice water or another cool drink, you should leave soon thereafter.

Seating Plans

The most honored position is in the middle of the table, with the second most important person, or the honored guest, seated next to the head of the table. (Spouses are usually not invited to business meals in restaurants. Do not ask if your spouse can join you; it will embarrass your Arab colleague. However, your spouse might be invited to a meal at home, especially if the spouse of the host will be there, which will probably be the case. The invitation will then be phrased, "My spouse invites your spouse." By the way, invitations, business or social, will most always be verbal, not written.) Be prepared that in some more traditional homes, you might sit on carpets on the floor at very low tables. In addition, the honored guest sits on the side of the table farthest from the door. (This is the same at business meetings, with the key people sitting in the middle, flanked on either side in descending order by their aides, with the least important people sitting at the ends of the table farthest from the middle and closest to the door; the arrangement is mirrored on the other side.) Men and women eating at someone's home may dine in separate areas (and spend the entire evening separated) or at separate times, with the men dining first; this is especially the case in Saudi Arabia and the Gulf region.

Refills and Seconds

You will always be offered more food. Leave a bit on your plate if you do not want more food. You will be implored to take more two or three times, in the form of a little ritual. The game is as follows: first you refuse, then the host insists, then you refuse again, then the host insists again, and then you finally give in and take a little more. This is known as the *uzooma* (the seesaw dialogue of imploring, rejecting, and finally submitting). If you really don't want more, take very little and leave it on your plate. Your host will constantly ask you if you are enjoying yourself and will implore you to have more. You may always have additional beverages; drink enough to cause your cup or glass to be less than half full, and it will generally be refilled. A reminder: never refill your own glass; always refill your neighbor's glass, and he or she will refill yours.

At Home, in a Restaurant, or at Work

The honored guest is served first, then the oldest male, then the rest of the men, then children, and finally women. Do not begin to eat or drink until the oldest man at the table has been served and has begun. At the end of the meal, it is appropriate to thank the host or hostess for a wonderful meal.

In informal restaurants, you may be required to share a table. If so, do not force conversation: act as if you are seated at a private table. Women should be sensitive to the fact that they may be seated only with other women. Waitstaff may be summoned by making eye contact; waving or calling their names is very impolite. The business breakfast is unknown in the region, and most business meals are lunches. Business meals are generally not good times to discuss business or make business decisions. Take your cue from your Arab associates: if they bring up business, then it's okay to discuss it, but wait to take your lead from their conversation. It is safer to never host Arabs in a nightclub or any establishment where liquor is served (even if they ask about going to a nightclub, they may be so doing for your sake, and it will make them uncomfortable if you actually go). Music may accompany the meal in restaurants, with performance dancing as well.

When invited to a colleague's home for a formal meal, you will be invited to sit anywhere you like at the table; resist the impulse to sit down, and wait until your host gives you further instructions. These will generally come after the host or oldest man is seated, and often you will be placed at his side. It is an honor to be invited into an Arab home, but a great obligation as well. (You may, in fact, be invited into a private home sooner than you are taken to a restaurant, as Arabs want to get to know you.) The salon, where you will be entertained, is a symbol in Arab culture of the honor and responsibility the host has to the guest. Once invited inside, you may need to remove your shoes (this is not a custom in restaurants, however). You will know when you approach the home and see a row of shoes at the door (keep your socks in good shape, and wear comfortable but well-made slip-ons for such occasions). Once inside the home, do not wander around: much of the house is really off-limits to guests. If you move from room to room in a Saudi home, be sure to always allow the more senior members of your party to enter the room ahead of you. Servants and household help are very common in middle- and upper-class homes; do not comment on them and do not offer to help: they are there to serve.

Being a Good Guest or Host

Paying the Bill

Usually the one who does the inviting pays the bill, although the guest is expected to make an effort to pay. Sometimes other circumstances determine the payee (such as rank). Making payment arrangements ahead of time so that no exchange occurs at the table is a very classy way to host, and is very common. Western businesswomen will have a problem paying the bill at a restaurant, as they will most always be with men at the table; make payment arrangements ahead of time, and don't wait for the check to arrive at the table. It may be easiest to do this at one of the international hotel dining rooms (they are rarely as much fun, but they are very convenient, and they do avoid a lot of problems!).

Transportation

It's a very nice idea, when acting as a host, to inquire ahead of time as to whether your guests will require transportation. If necessary, you should arrange for taxi service at the end of the meal. When seeing your guests off, you must remain at the entrance of the house or the restaurant, or at the site where you deposited your guests into the car, until the car is out of sight: it is very important not to leave until your guests can no longer see you, should they look back. Guests are seated in cars (and taxis) by rank, with the honored guest being placed in the back directly behind the front passenger seat; the next honored position is in the back behind the driver, and the least honored position is up front with the driver.

When to Arrive / Chores to Do

If invited to dinner at a private home, do not offer to help with the chores: you are a guest, and the servant or household staff performs such tasks. You should not expect or ask to visit the kitchen. Do not leave the table unless invited to do so. When in the home, be careful not to admire something too effusively: Arabs may feel obligated to give it to you, and you, in turn, will be required to present them with a gift of equal value. Instead of saying things like "I love that vase," say something like "Vases that beautiful in my country are only found in museums." Your compliments will most likely be dismissed. Remember also that Arabs consider it very bad luck to have their children praised: it can bring ill-fortune to them (comment on the children indirectly, but comment on them positively).

Gift Giving

In general, gift giving is not that common for social occasions, but is common in business situations between trusted colleagues. It is not only done as a gesture of thanks, but as a way of helping to ensure good business relations in the future (be careful not to go overboard here, as a gift that looks like an obvious bribe is not appreciated, and may land you in quite a bit of trouble . . . with the authorities in your home country, more than likely). In business settings, this usually takes the form of a personal gift that symbolically says the correct thing about the nature of the relationship. When going to the region on business, bringing a gift for the key decision maker is usually enough. Your gift does not have to be elaborate or expensive. You present your gift when you arrive in the country; before you leave to return home, you will receive a farewell gift usually at the last meeting. When Arabs visit your country, they will also bring you a gift, and before they leave, you should give them gifts. Holiday cards are much appreciated.

The most appropriate gift for a personal visit to a home, or as a thank-you for dinner, would be a box of fruits, pastries, cakes, cookies, or other sweets. Flowers are good to give as gifts, but avoid roses, as they are too personal. A man typically only gives a gift to a man, a woman to a woman; remember, any gift given by a man to a woman must come with the caveat that it is from his wife/sister/mother, or else it is far too personal. Sending a handwritten thank-you note the day after the dinner party is a very good idea. If you are staying with a family, an appropriate thank-you gift would be a high-quality product that represents your country and is difficult or expensive to get in Saudi Arabia; this is also a good idea for a key business associate. Avoid gifts from or about the United States with political implications (although relations between the United States and some Arab states are good, the politics of the United States in the region are questioned by many Arabs). In Saudi Arabia and the Gulf, gifts need to be a bit luxurious (these are essentially wealthy countries). Do not give alcohol (and this includes perfumes or colognes made with alcohol), pork, art or photographs that depict natural scenes or people (this runs counter to Islamic beliefs that man must not attempt to reproduce what God has made), or cutlery (which symbolizes the severing of a relationship). A fine gift for a Muslim would be a silver compass, so that he will always know which direction to face when he says his daily prayers (Muslims must face Mecca no matter where they are when they say their prayers).

For both giving and receiving gifts, two hands are used always. Gifts are typically not opened by the receiver in front of the giver; they are usually received after much imploring by you, graciously acknowledged, and placed aside to be opened once the giver is no longer present.

Gifts should be wrapped well. Typically, gifts are wrapped in ordinary paper first then wrapped again in green or other bright colors; white wrapping is perfectly fine.

By the way, if you have a copy of the Koran (received as a gift or not), never place it on the floor or below any object: it must be the highest book on the shelf. Do not give a copy of the Koran as a gift: it is far too significant for a business or social acknowledgment.

Special Holidays and Celebrations

Major Holidays

Avoid doing business during the entire month of Ramadan. Many cities have different local holidays as well, so double-check with your Arab associates before making final travel plans.

Islamic holidays are the most important holidays throughout the region (additionally, in Saudi Arabia, September 23 is celebrated as National Day). Islamic holidays are on the lunar calendar, so the dates change each year, and all holidays begin at sundown the day before.

The most important Islamic holidays are (in order of their usual occurrence):

Ramadan
Eid al Fitr: It is a multi-day (usually two or three) celebration of the end of
    the fast at the end of Ramadan
Eid al Adha: The Feast of the Sacrifice, celebrating Abraham's willingness to
    sacrifice his son
Hajj: The first day of the annual pilgrimage to Mecca
Birth of the Prophet Muhammad
Islamic New Year

Business Culture

Daily Office Protocols

The traditional Saudi office can be closed or open, but no matter how the architecture is designed, you can be sure many people will be coming and going. This is not so much a statement about your unimportance as much as it is a statement on the importance of your host: that he is needed by many, and that in the polychronic Arab culture, things are handled in order of their importance and not according to the clock. Be patient. In the Arab business organization, hierarchy is strictly observed. Executives are usually placed on different floors than the rank and file. You probably will not be invited onto the working floors until the proposed project has been set in motion. Because faithful Muslims pray five times a day, you will need to adjust your schedules to accommodate their needs. Usually, prayers are given upon awakening and at noontime, midday, dusk, and before retiring; this means that twice during the workday there will be time out for prayers. The prayer usually takes a short ten or fifteen minutes or so, and any quiet area will do. If you accidentally interrupt a Muslim during his prayers, just walk quietly away; there's no need for complicated explanations or apologies. Most organizations have prayer rooms set aside, with carpets. In addition, devout Muslims will not work on Friday (the Muslim Sabbath), and in fact begin to end work early on Thursday, before sundown. The official workweek is Saturday though Thursday, 9 A.M. to 4 P.M. Oftentimes, because of the heat, many businesspeople work into the night (with a break for lunch—sometimes at home—in the afternoon); do not be surprised if an early evening office meeting is scheduled.

Management Styles

Because of the rigid rank and hierarchy orientation, titles are very important; the highest ones (e.g., vice president) are usually reserved for very senior, executive-level positions and should not be used as casually as they are in the United States. Any criticism of Arab workers must be done very carefully, even privately. Deference is shown by subordinates to their seniors; paternalistic concern is often shown by executives to their subordinates. Superiors are very sensitive to inquiring about their subordinate's opinions; once a decision is made by superiors, the superiors are followed, often unquestioningly. If you are doing business with the correct person, things will probably move quickly; it is essential, therefore, to have a good and trustworthy contact in the Arab world (this "sponsor," in fact, is legally required in Saudi Arabia and other Gulf states) who can make the necessary contacts for you. Let this person take the time he needs to take to do this for you, for if you pressure him into making contacts sooner, he may connect you to someone who is not as useful as the one he was originally waiting for: this will not serve you. Again, be patient. Never use time as a means of pressure.

Boss-Subordinate Relations

The decision-making system usually works from the top on down, with key decisions often coming from individuals in high positions of authority. Superiors are expected to provide clear and fully informed sets of instructions: that is their responsibility, and it is the responsibility of subordinates to carry out those instructions. Consequently, "management-by-objective" and other egalitarian and individually empowered management styles often may not work in this environment: without clear instruction from above, subordinates usually will do nothing. They also lose respect for the manager for not making the decisions he should be making.

Conducting a Meeting or Presentation

At your first meeting in Saudi Arabia, you will probably be received in a very comfortable waiting area, which may or may not be where most of the meeting is conducted between you and your Saudi colleague. If this is the case, you are merely being sized up, and your colleague is a gatekeeper. There will be much hosting by your Saudi contacts with tea/coffee/tea. When serving any refreshments in the office, be sure they are served in porcelain, glass, or silver tea sets: the use of paper or Styrofoam shows disrespect and is very bad form. There may be several people in the room with you and your Arab contact whom you may or may not be introduced to. These "ghost people" are probably trusted friends or relations of your Arab colleague, and he will no doubt want their input after the meeting. If you are not introduced to them, do not ask to be: acknowledge them with a smile and a nod, and proceed with your meeting. If you are meeting with a decision maker, the discussions will probably be direct, forthright, and businesslike. If this is just the beginning of a business relationship, expect to spend most of the time sharing information about your organization with different individuals, or repeating the same things to the same individual. This is okay; it means your plans are advancing to the right people in the organization, that those you have previously met with have approved of you and moved you on, and that you are building a personal trust with the key decision maker. Business is personal throughout the region: decision makers have got to know your face. Patience and third-party connections are key.

Negotiation Styles

At first, expect no decisions from your Arab colleagues at the table, and be willing to provide copious amounts of information, to the degree that you can, in response to their questions and in anticipation of their needs. Presentations should be well prepared and simply propounded. Details are best left to questions and backup material, which should be available in both English and Arabic, and left behind. Ideally, you should present your material to your Arab colleagues for study, along with a proposed agenda, prior to the meeting. Have extra copies available, as you might meet more people than you expect. Should you come with other team members, make sure that your roles are well coordinated. Never disagree with each other in front of Arabs or appear uncertain, unsure, not authorized to make a decision, or out of control in any way.

Most Arabs love to bargain and see this process as a way of getting to know you: it does not imply insincerity to offer one price and then change your mind later (as it often does with Pacific Rim cultures). In fact, avoiding this process will generate suspicion. Final terms must be fair to all (win/win). Contracts and contract law are well known and understood; expect and insist on well-executed documents to finalize an agreement. Remember, the deal should be sealed with a celebratory meal. Keep communications open, especially when at a distance, and stay in touch often with your Saudi associates: share more information than you normally would, not less; and be prepared to make many trips, as needed. Nothing much will happen without you or someone from your group on site (therefore, try to have a contact on the ground in the region who can always keep you informed of what is really going on, if you can).

Written Correspondence

Your business letters should be very formal and respectful of rank and hierarchy. Given names usually are written in uppercase; dates are given using the day/month/year format (with periods in between, not slashes) if using the Western calendar, or year/month/day if using the Islamic calendar (subtract 622 years from the Western date, and add A.H. to the date ("after the hajj"); and an honorific plus the title is as common as the honorific plus the last name. You should write your e-mails, letters, and faxes in a formal, precise way: use a brief but warm personal introduction, then get down to business. Keep it simple, however, and bulletpoint and outline all important matters. You may use either the Western or the Asian format for the addresses.

CHAPTER SIXTEEN

The Gulf Arab Cultures: The Gulf Coastal States of Kuwait, Oman, Qatar, Bahrain, United Arab Emirates, and Yemen

KUWAIT

Kuwait in many ways is similar to Saudi Arabia, in that it is essentially very wealthy, due to oil, and has rigid class lines that define its society. Until oil was discovered, however, Kuwait's economy was derived mainly from pearls, and historically, Kuwait struggled to define itself independently of Saudi Arabia and Iraq. Today, the wealthy classes (constituting the bulk of national Kuwaitis) run all aspects of the country, with Palestinians and Pakistanis as foreign workers doing much of the employed labor (almost 50 percent of the entire population). Subsequently, many Westerners have presumed a perceived arrogance on the part of native Kuwaitis. While they are intensely Islamic, life is not as fundamentalist as in Saudi Arabia, and foreigners are tolerated. Women and men, unlike in Saudi Arabia and the rest of the Gulf region, work together in Kuwait, although women do not hold significant decision-making roles. Unlike in Saudi Arabia, a business meeting will probably be a little more austere, and coffee will be served only at the beginning and the end of the meeting. As a way of bringing the discussions to a peaceful close, the Kuwaitis may light some incense and talk about incidental things. Kuwaitis call the man's long flowing robe the *dishdasha,* and the woman's the *thoub* (their design makes them more or less formal). Kuwait's National Day is February 25.

OMAN

Oman is probably the most "liberal" of the Gulf States: women, in fact, often join men at social occasions, and alcohol is actually consumed in public in some circles (it is still not common, however). Instead of the Saudi headdress, Omanis wear a scarf, plus the *dishdasha*. National Day in Oman is November 18, and the sultan's birthday is November 19. The sultan is a Western-educated leader. As is the case with all the Gulf States, status and rank are highly regarded. Put all your educational degrees on your business cards, as you would in Kuwait and Saudi Arabia.

QATAR

Like Saudi Arabia, Qatar is a very fundamentalist country. However, it is run by a small royal family that has complete control over all aspects of life. While there is no drinking of alcoholic beverages, there is much coffee, and it is traditionally drunk from the same cup by a group of people. Be sure to finish all the coffee in the cup when it is handed to you as soon as you can, so it can be refilled and passed to the next person. Qatar's national holiday is Independence Day (September 3); another holiday occurs on the anniversary of the Accession of the Sheik Khalifa (February 22).

BAHRAIN

As residents of an island nation, Bahrainis have always traded with foreigners, so they understand non-Islamic ways, although they generally do not subscribe to them. There is a liberalism in people's attitude toward Westerners and Bahraini women that makes Bahrain a more comfortable place for Western businesspeople, including women. If you are entertained, by the way, at someone's "garden," you will be taken to the family's weekend "retreat"; it may not be elaborate, but the picnic lunch you will be served surely will be. Bahrain's national day is Ruler's Ascension Day (December 16).

UNITED ARAB EMIRATES

Each of the seven emirates that make up this federation has its own way of doing things, but there is nonetheless significant cooperation between them. They currently thrive on world trade, and are more liberal, at least in dealing with Westerners and adapting to Western ways, than some of their more fundamentalist Arab neighbors; for example, in Abu Dhabi, alcoholic consumption is allowed for Westerners.

YEMEN

Yemen is a time warp: it is "Old Arabia." It still operates according to family agrarian models based on traditional Islamic law and Arab customs. Greet people with the honorific *qadi* (judge), or, for more formality, *faqih* (religious scholar); they are both used before the given name. Do not use the family (last) name in addressing people. Women, after greeting other women, may stroke each other's cheek, as an extra sign of sincerity. Often women have their hands and feet decorated with henna artwork by female artisans. The designs are quite beautiful, and a definite mark of Gulf Arab women.

Qat, a mildly stimulating narcotic, is unique to the Yemeni diet. You may be invited to "a chew": you buy your *qat* at the market, take it with you to the gathering, and chew away. The proper technique is to take just a little from the purchased wad at a time, ball it in your hand, and put some in your mouth by your cheek. After a few minutes, the bitter juice should be spit out (follow the lead of one of your Yemeni colleagues). There is a sense of heightened awareness and then euphoria; finally, there is a "crash," during which the chewer becomes very tired. Yemenis do most of their business over *qat* chews. Join in if you want to do business in Yemen. Accompanying the *qat* is usually a water pipe and water for drinking (you won't want to eat, but you will become thirsty—don't worry, *qat* is not physiologically addictive, but people can develop a psychological need for it). You usually sit on cushions when you have a *qat* chew.

Curiously, bargaining is not a way of life in Yemen as it is elsewhere in almost all the rest of the Arab world. Yemeni men usually wear a small dagger as part of their daily dress (it is symbolic of their membership in tribes that made their living keeping pirates away from the Yemeni coast).

Dining in Yemen is a little different as well, as meals do not constitute the formal hosting events they usually are elsewhere in the Arab world. They typically occur between prayer times, and as is the case elsewhere in the Arab world, most conversation occurs before the meal, not during and certainly not after it (when it is time to go home). Typically, after you finish your meal, you get up to wash your hands (remember, you've probably eaten with your fingers), and then go into the salon for coffee. If you are in a restaurant, you can summon the waiter by clapping your hands together once or twice.

Yemen dress codes require that women wear pants underneath their dresses; and men, for modesty's sake, if dressed in Western clothes, often carry a scarf they can put in their laps when they sit down. In Yemen, you must treat everyone as an equal, especially in business. The people tend to get right down to business. There were once a great many Jews in Yemen, but today it is mainly a Muslim nation. Holidays in Yemen include Labor Day (May 1), Correction Movement Day (September 26), National Day (October 14), and Independence Day (November 30).

The Arab Levantine Cultures: Lebanon, Syria, and Jordan

LEBANON

This is a very fractured country, having only recently emerged from decades of civil war. Over 70 percent of the population is Muslim, about evenly split between Sunnis and Shiites, while the remaining 30 percent is mainly (though not only) Christian (Maronite Christian, or deviations of the Maronite order, who established themselves in Lebanon), who traditionally held the wealth and power in the country. This is the source of much of the country's difficulties. Its diversity, in good times, made Lebanon a fairly Westernized place, something that more fundamental Muslims often objected to. Today, Lebanon is returning somewhat to its role as a diverse secular nation, but the people's loyalties are to clans and membership groups, and not to the nation. Appropriate behaviors are dependent upon, therefore, the membership group that your individual colleague is associated with; the difficulty here will be identifying this and keeping different behaviors separate and appropriate. Westernized women, of which there are many, do play a role in government and business; these women are generally unveiled. The second language after Arabic is French.

SYRIA

Syria is a study in opposites: it is a modern authoritarian state superimposed upon an ancient religious and cultural crossroads. About 90 percent of the population is Muslim; however, the group that rules is the *Alawite* sect, which represents only about 15 percent of the population. Therein is the reason for the oppressive clamp the government has on all aspects of Syrian life. The remaining 10 percent of Syrians are a mixture of Christians, Druze, Jews, and other groups. Syrians are, compared to their Levant Arab cousins (Palestinians, Jordanians, and Iraqis), generally well educated and worldly, although very suspicious of the outside world, particularly the West. Although they identify with pan-Arabism, the closed Alawite nature of life in Syria prevents Syrians from full cooperation with their neighbors. Be aware that because of the government, many Syrians may be hesitant to express their views fully, but are, in fact, quite knowledgeable and friendly. Women can play some roles in the workforce, but mainly as teachers and medical personnel. Women are generally not veiled. The second language after Arabic is French.

JORDAN

Jordan is a monarchy, but a progressive one, in which the king has traditionally had a paternalistic concern for his people, who are primarily Bedouin (a nomadic tribe) and Palestinian. Because of the British rule over the Transjordan area prior to the nation receiving its independent status in 1946, English is the second language after Arabic. The Jordanian people still have strong connections with their roots, usually Saudi, Bedouin, or Palestinian. The country has a peace agreement, as does Egypt, with Israel, and there is a trend toward modernization. The challenge is to accomplish this without sacrificing its Islamic traditions while modernizing, while at the same time resisting the rising tide of fundamentalism. Remember that the queen of Jordan is an American: there is much between the two countries that links them, and this is a good point of conversation between Jordanians and Americans.

Before a meal (or sometimes as a simple between-meals snack), many small appetizers may be offered: these are called *mezzes,* and can include grape leaves, hummus and bread, and other treats. If you have been invited to someone's house for dinner, don't fill up on the *mezzes*: this is just the beginning. The *mensaf,* a traditional Bedouin feast, usually features a freshly slaughtered sheep, and many side dishes, served with rice. The *mensaf* is usually done in honor of an important event (your arrival, a wedding, etc.).

Jordanian secular holidays include Tree Day (January 15), Labor Day (May 1), Independence Day (May 25), Arab Army Day (June 10), King Hussein's Accession to the Throne Day (August 11), and King Hussein's Birthday (November 14).

| CHAPTER | The Judaic Levantine |
| EIGHTEEN | Cultures: Israel |

Note: As Israeli culture incorporates many Levantine cultural attributes, this chapter will identify only those cultural behaviors that may be different from general Levantine culture; specific emphasis is placed on Jewish customs and traditions, many of which have their roots in the Middle East and Europe.

Some Introductory Background on Israel, the Israelis, and the Jews

Israel, as is much the case for all countries in the region, is a new country in an ancient land. Originally the home of the Jews in biblical times, the country suffered through numerous historic invasions, and its original inhabitants were forced to leave and live in exile (the Diaspora) over several millennia. It wasn't until after World War II that the State of Israel was born. European Zionists—those who were philosophically and politically bent on establishing a Jewish homeland in the area that had been the Land of Israel—propelled this idea forward in the twentieth century. Of course, given the Arab experience with the West to that point, a Westernized state among Arabs on what Arabs believed to be Palestinian soil (appropriated without their consent) was cause for an immediate war, and Israeli-Arab tensions have been great ever since.

Today, the secular state of Israel is caught in a constant debate about what its future should be: should it remain a secular state, or should it become a Jewish religious state, an Orthodox Jewish state, a secular Jewish state? On these issues the numerous and powerful Orthodox Jews (Hasidim) clash not only with non-Jewish Israelis (of which there are many) and their Arab neighbors, but also with many secular Israeli Jews (there are more secular Jews in Israel than Orthodox). Jews make up about 80 percent of the population of Israel, many having immigrated just before and after the Holocaust. Most Jews in the Zionist movement were from eastern and central Europe. Jews from these areas (including the new wave of immigrants from Russia and the former Soviet Union) are referred to as Ashkenazi. The other great group were Oriental Jews, mainly from other parts of the Middle East and southern Europe (Spain and Portugal primarily), referred to as Sephardim. There is tension between these two groups, and other Jews who have sought identity and new lives in Israel (the Ethiopian, or African, Jews, for example, who are treated poorly by both Ashkenazi and Sephardim). Arab Israelis are primarily Palestinians, and there are Christian

Palestinians as well; there are also myriad other groups, representing just about every possible expression of religious faith, including Eastern Orthodox, Buddhism, and Hinduism. Native-born Jewish Israelis are referred to as *sabras,* the word for a cactus fruit (it's hard and prickly on the outside, but, if you can get it to open up, soft and tasty on the inside). As the Jews are a people besieged throughout history, and as Israelis in particular are still under constant pressure and threat, this defensiveness and "no-time-for-fooling-around-or-make-believe" attitude of the Israelis is understandable. The Israelis are an informal, no-nonsense, defiant, sometimes challenging people who will tell you just what they think about you or what you are talking about, or anything else that is on their mind . . . if they decide you are worth the discussion.

The two halves of the Israeli psyche find expression in the country's two great cities. Jerusalem is the conservative and religious-oriented city—as well as the capital of Israel—while Tel Aviv is the modern, secular, business-oriented, and Westernized side of Israel, and the two cities appear to be drifting further and further apart.

An Area Briefing

Politics and Government

Today, the country is a secular republic with a government built on the British parliamentary model, with a unicameral legislature, the Knesset, and a president and a prime minister. There are many political parties in Israel, but Labor and Likud are the two major parties. Palestinians pose the greatest moral and political dilemma for all Israelis, as Israelis struggle to provide them with sovereign land in exchange for security and peace. In addition, neighboring Arab lands, such as Syria and Iraq and Islamic fundamentalist splinter groups in Lebanon, still do not recognize the State of Israel, and guerrilla violence, in the form of Hezbollah and other radical Islamic fundamentalists, threatens to destabilize daily life through terrorism.

Fundamental Cultural Orientations

Israeli Jews are extremely individualistic: they each have their own ideas, opinions, and beliefs, and are difficult to organize into a cohesive team. The value orientation is, within and among other similar Jews, to be extremely individualistic; but when faced with members of other groups, Israeli Jews can act with unquestioning unity. This means that secular Jews, for example, are generally individualistic among themselves, but when faced with Orthodox Jews or other groups further outside, such as Muslim Palestinians, they will act with unity. Arab Israelis, on the other hand, are fairly group conscious, and generally harmony oriented, but have difficulty remaining unified, and can become fractious and individualistic when faced with the challenge of others from outside their group. For Jewish Israelis, hierarchy, status, rank, and the symbols of such are usually of secondary importance: it is an extremely egalitarian oriented society (second only to Australia, in fact), and people act accordingly. Relationships usually determine action, however, so whom you know is important, and the situation, which is always debated, is what ultimately determines decisions, often over existing rules or processes. In this society, rules and processes, while valued as part of the heritage from the West, may only be momentarily useful, and therefore are often of secondary importance at the moment when decisions need to be made.

Things change very fast in Israel, and one must be ready to seize opportunities quickly when and where they arise. In this sense, Jewish Israelis, while having a monochronic preference, can also be markedly polychronic. Things happen, unexpected events occur, more important people suddenly show up: this is normal, and people and schedules need to adjust. It is a very risk-taking culture: Jewish Israelis do not shy away from possibilities, nor do they shy away from conflict and confrontation: they seem, in fact, to thrive on it. They can be very direct, and will demand that you prove yourself and your product as better than the competition before they will feel comfortable. At the same time, while they may seem to haggle and disagree endlessly, when they have developed a comfort level with you, they may just as suddenly change tack and finalize an agreement: it is as if they have decided that enough is enough, and it is time to cooperate.

While Israelis are proud of their ancient traditions, they are always looking forward to a possibly finer tomorrow, and for ways to get there. Israelis, particularly those from European Jewish backgrounds, understand Western traditions and can think very conceptually and linearly; but such thoughts must never conflict with national ideals, Jewish goals, or sometimes even personal efforts. It is an extremely informal culture, where there simply is no time to waste on appearances, formalities, or niceties: who knows, you may not be here tomorrow. This is what can make Israelis so frustrating to outsiders, but also what makes them, like the inside of the prickly pear, such good friends and devoted colleagues, once a deep relationship is established.

Greetings and Introductions

Language and Basic Vocabulary

The main language is Hebrew, which is the ancient language of the Israelites, and which virtually died out as a spoken language with the Diaspora, although it continued to be used as a liturgical and literary language. Hebrew was resurrected as a spoken language by the Zionists at the time of Israel's rebirth, and is a source of immense pride among Jewish Israelis. It is related to Arabic, and many Israeli Arabs also understand Hebrew. Most Israeli businesspeople also speak English (certainly the Ashkenazi, but not necessarily African or Oriental or Russian Jews who immigrated recently), and English is the learned second language of Israeli Jews and Arabs (but not each other's language). There are not as many words in Hebrew as one needs to survive in the modern world, so new ones are always being created. Remember, both Arabic and Hebrew are written right to left (so translated materials should be designed to begin "at the back"). Yiddish is also spoken by older Eastern European Jews, as well as other languages from other immigrant groups.

Here are some basic Hebrew phrases and their English meanings:

shalom	hello / peace / good-bye
boker tov	good morning
erev tov	good evening
layla tov	good night

lehitraot	see you later
Ma shlomkha?	How are you?
slikha	pardon me
bevakasha	please / you're welcome
todah	thank you
ken	yes
lo	no

Plurals are created by adding the suffix *-im* in Hebrew: for example, Sephard becomes Sephardim.

Honorifics for Men, Women, and Children

Most Hebrew speakers will use the first name very quickly, sometimes with the honorific Mr. or Mrs. If the last (family) name is used, as in the West, it will most certainly be accompanied with the appropriate honorific, because it is unusually formal (most Israelis will probably switch to the first name very soon). The honorifics are *mar* (Mr.) and *gveret* (Mrs./Miss/Ms.).

As in the West, most modern married women take their husband's family name, or hyphenate their family name with their husband's.

The What, When, and How of Introducing People

If you are not introduced quickly to others in a group, it is perfectly all right to introduce yourself; in fact, if you don't, you may never get to know anyone else. While Israelis appreciate that you notice seniors first and show respect for the elderly, such attention is not codified in Israeli introductions. In fact, most greetings occur quickly and informally. Please note that this is not the case with Arabs.

Physical Greeting Styles

As is the case with Arabs, Israeli Jews can be extremely demonstrative, and greet each other with hugs and kisses—between the same sex and the opposite sex, as well. Please be advised, however, that Orthodox Jews do not follow this pattern. The custom for Orthodox Jews is for men and women never to touch a member of the opposite sex other than their spouse and close female relatives, and this means that women are rarely introduced to men. If they are, they will not extend their hand, and you should not take their hand, in this case. Handshakes are the common greeting between all Israeli Jews, and it is often a firm grasp.

Communication Styles

Okay Topics / Not Okay Topics

Okay: anything that reflects your personal interest in Israel—its food, people, history, Jewish traditions, and so on. *Not okay:* your opinions about the Muslim-Jewish or the Palestinian-Israeli conflict. If you are American, do not talk about U.S.-Israeli relations: you will be disappointed at the negative image Israelis have of Americans and their policies and behaviors toward Israel. There is much misunderstanding between American and Israeli Jews (if you are Jewish, you will immediately be asked why you haven't made the aliyah, or emigration to Israel). The goal of conversation between Israeli Jews is not necessarily to establish harmony (as it is with the Arabs), but to establish trust: a trust built not necessarily on agreement and similarities, but on respect for fundamental individualism and an ability to rely on you.

Protocol in Public

Israelis can be very animated and loud at a business meeting, on the street, or in a restaurant. However, as a foreigner, you should not respond in kind. There is little use of silence as a communication device. There can be much nonverbal behavior and gesturing. While Arabs do not appreciate being touched on the head, this holds no special meaning for Jews, except for the fact that observant Jewish men wear a *kipa* or *yarmulke,* which is a skullcap on the top of their heads, and observant women usually wear a shawl or head covering of some sort (Orthodox women shave their hair, and wear a wig in public). The bottom of the shoe holds no special meaning either for Jews, but many do avoid using the left hand. Synagogues may be visited, but head coverings are usually required, and modest dress is essential. In more Orthodox synagogues, men and women worship in separate areas. The Jewish Sabbath begins on Friday night and lasts until sundown on Saturday, and most stores, restaurants, and public services shut down. Elevators may be set to stop automatically on all floors during the Sabbath, since observant Jews are not permitted to work on the day of rest, and therefore do not operate elevators. The "thumbs-up" sign is considered to be obscene throughout the Middle East, for both Arabs and Jews, while holding the fingers together with the palm facing up and shaking the hand up and down is a sign for "patience, please." There are more and more no-smoking areas in Israel, but they are still not as common as in the West. Jewish women (with the exception of Orthodox women) are free to travel on their own, and can conduct business; Western businesswomen should have no problems with their authority being accepted in Israel.

Dress

Secular Jews in Israel dress just like Western Europeans and Americans: they are style conscious, and business suits and jeans are everywhere, and worn at the same appropriate times. However, when Israeli businessmen dress, they often leave the collar open, without a tie, and sometimes take their jackets off. Short-sleeved shirts, due to the hot weather, are also common in business settings. Orthodox Jews, however, dress much more modestly; women must have their arms covered to below the elbow and their torsos covered up to the neckline, and their dresses must go below the knee (they do not wear pants). Many Orthodox men (the Hasidim in particular) wear the old dress of the European shtetl (village), which is a fur-rimmed, black dress hat, a black business suit, a white shirt, and a subdued, dark tie. These men often wear a ritual undergarment that has long fringes, which are allowed to extend outside the outer garments. Orthodox men typically sport beards and mustaches that they do not cut, and Orthodox boys may follow the Orthodox tradition of wearing long sideburns with shaved heads.

Dining and Drinking

Mealtimes and Typical Foods

The Jewish diet may or may not be kosher, depending on whether the home or restaurant is observant. Kosher laws can be quite complex. Some basics involve the absolute prohibition against pork and pork products, shellfish, and the mixing of dairy products and meat at the same meal. In addition, all meats need to be slaughtered according to specific rabbinical requirements in order to be kosher. Additional special laws exist for Passover, during which no leavened food products can be served, or even be present in the house, in any form (typically, the house is scrubbed to remove any crumb of bread from the premises). Observant homes usually have four sets of dishes and cutlery—one for meat and one for dairy for daily use, and another two sets specifically for Passover—and they must *never* be mixed up. Although there is no prohibition against alcohol, curiously, most Israelis do not drink much alcohol. Beer may or may not accompany a meal; wine is more often used ceremonially at religious celebrations.

Table Manners / Use of Utensils / Toasting

The traditional toast is "l'chayim" ("to life"). Western utensils are used throughout Israel, and dining is done the Continental way, with fork in the left hand and knife in the right. The host sits at the head of the table, with the honored guest seated next to the host. In Orthodox homes, men and women may dine in separate areas, or at different times. If you are invited into an Israeli's home, you may or may not need to remove your shoes (check to see if shoes are lined up at the door: that's your cue to remove your shoes, if they are). As for the food, although it is generally similar to the food in the entire region, there is considerable influence of the cuisines of the immigrants, so be ready to sample foods from eastern Europe, Russia, Africa, and India, as well.

Gift Giving

In general, gift giving is not that common for social occasions or business situations, but when visiting a close friend, or staying at someone's home, you are expected to bring something useful and nice from abroad. This can be a household item—a vase, a tray, some personal bath accessories. Flowers are fine for social visits, and chocolates are much appreciated (make sure that they and any other foodstuffs, such as gourmet nuts and dried fruits, you bring as a gift are kosher).

Special Holidays and Celebrations

Major Holidays

In addition to the Islamic holidays mentioned in previous chapters for the Arabs, Christians also celebrate Christmas and Easter (Orthodox and Roman). However, the majority of the religious holidays are Jewish, and are based on the lunar calendar, which changes their dates each year.

Secular

January 1   Bank holiday
May 10   Independence Day
August 10   Bank holiday

Religious

March

Purim: celebrates the rescue of Persian Jews through the shrewd-ness and wisdom of Queen Esther. Special *hamantashen,* or "Haman cakes," (usually three-sided, with a fruit filling), com-memorate her triumph over the Persian king's minister, Haman, who intended to execute the Jews.

April

Tu B'Shvat (Arbor Day): celebrates the planting of trees (especially in Israel)

April

Pesach (Passover): celebrates the Exodus of the Jews from Egypt: it is a celebration of freedom, and the special feast (seder) fea-tures symbolic foods that represent the struggles of the Jews against the Egyptians: bitter herbs dipped in salt water symbolize the tears shed by the people when they were slaves; a hard-boiled egg represents rebirth; parsley represents spring plantings and new birth and sustenance; and matzoth, the unleavened bread that the Jews, in their haste to escape, had to eat because they did not have time for the bread to rise. Four cups of wine are drunk throughout the meal as the story of the Exodus is recounted.

May/June

Shavuot (Feast of the Weeks): celebrates God's gift of the Torah to the Jewish people. The Torah is the compilation of laws, writings, and thoughts of the Jewish people; it comprises the first five books of the Old Testament.

July/August

Tishah-b'Ab: commemorates the fall of the Temple in Jerusalem.

September

Rosh Hashanah (Jewish New Year): celebrated for two days with prayers in the temple, and a special feast to welcome in a good and healthy New Year.

September

Yom Kippur (Day of Atonement): following Rosh Hashanah by one week, it is the holiest of Jewish holidays, wherein the obser-vant pray for forgiveness for past sins, and hope to be entered into the Book of Life for another year. Observant Jews fast for the twenty-four-hour period.

September/October

Sukkoth (Festival of the Booths): follows five days after Yom Kippur, and commemorates the harvest and God's generosity in providing sustenance and shelter to his people. A shelter made of reeds and other items is built in the backyard of most observant homes in remembrance of the nomadic lives lived by the Israelites after the Exodus; it is also a harvest celebration.

December

Hanukkah (Festival of Lights): celebrates the rededication of the Temple in 164 B.C. after its desecration by the Syrian king and the miracle of the oil that kept the Temple lamps burning for eight days. Children play with dreidels (toy tops) and get gifts of money (gelt); special foods fried in oil (try latkes, or potato pancakes) are eaten in celebration of the event.

Business Culture

The official workweek is 9 A.M. to 4 P.M., Sunday through Thursday (9 A.M. to noon, Friday). However, businesses really slow down after Thursday night. Consider that Christians (Roman Catholic and Orthodox, and others) maintain their Sabbath on Sunday, and Muslims on Friday. As Jerusalem is a holy center for all three religions, the city has observances throughout the week, depending upon the religious affiliation.

Management styles between bosses and subordinates can be extremely egalitarian and direct. As a foreigner, you will be treated with respect, and hosted well, but in business negotiations, you will be bargained with, questioned, prodded, and expected to prove why your product is better than the competition's. Israelis love to bargain, and will expect all sorts of concessions; they will also be surprised if you do not drive an equally hard bargain in return. They will demonstrate all sorts of emotions around these issues, but do not take the show too seriously, if you know the terms of the sale are fair and reasonable. In the end, and the end may suddenly appear sooner than you think, they will settle for what is reasonable and good for both parties most of the time. You are building a long-term relationship the Israeli way, and that is what is important.

Written Correspondence

Your business letters should be very matter of fact and informal. If you have a personal relationship with your Israeli colleague, be friendly and warm, and inquire about his personal health and his family's in general terms. Use the Western format for the addresses. The abbreviation C.E. after a year means "common era," and is the equivalent of the Gregorian Western calendar abbreviation A.D. (*anno Domini*).

Index